LIVE-WORK PLANNING and DESIGN

LIVE-WORK PLANNING and DESIGN

Zero-Commute Housing

Thomas Dolan

John Wiley & Sons, Inc.

All photographs and drawings are courtesy of Thomas Dolan unless otherwise noted.

Library of Congress Cataloging-in-Publication Data:

Dolan, Thomas, 1949-
    Live-work planning and design : zero-commute housing / Thomas Dolan.
        p. cm.
    Includes bibliographical references and index.
    ISBN 978-0-470-60480-9 (cloth); 978-1-118-13028-5 (ebk.); 978-1-118-13029-2 (ebk.);
978-1-118-14404-6 (ebk.); 978-1-118-14405-3 (ebk.); 978-1-118-14406-0 (ebk.)
    1. Multipurpose buildings.   2. City planning.   3. Housing.   4. Sociology,
Urban.   I. Title.   II. Title: Zero-commute housing.
    NA4177.D65 2012
    728—dc23
                                                                    2011018346

978-0-470-60480-9

Printed in the United States of America

10 9 8 7 6 5 4 3 2 1

Contents

For Henry and Emily:
May you live near where you work, may you always love the work you do,
and may you dwell forever in a strong community.

Preface

Live-work is truly a phenomenon of our times, and all indications are that it will grow increasingly prevalent. Statisticians confirm what we readily observe: More people are deciding to work at home every day. Technology allows us to do so, the present economy may force us to do so, and the great demographic bulges of aging baby boomers and millennials appear to be voting with their feet in embracing urban forms of living that were considered marginal twenty-five years ago.

I am fortunate to have spent almost three decades, my entire professional career, designing live-work projects. It is gratifying to see what was once the exception become a highly desired building type. At the same time, though, it is clear that even as live-work has become mainstream and in great demand, there is a marked lack of both common language and practices, both of which create confusion and unnecessary effort; many, interested in creating live-work are unaware that we now have a robust and instructive stock of existing precedents from which to learn.

My purpose in writing this book is to create an enduring set of definitions and standards through which live-work can be understood and discussed by a wide-ranging audience including professionals such as architects, planners, government officials, and community activists to those who it ultimately impacts the most: our community dwellers. In my twenty-seven years of designing live-work, observing live-work projects around the North America, and studying the subject, I have seen most of the existing variations on Zero Commute Living.

When I think of live-work as a broad concept, I often recall a man I met on Dal Lake, in the Vale of Kashmir in the north of India, many years ago. This man spent a day paddling me in his *shikara*, or paddle boat, while smoking his hubbly-bubbly pipe under his cloak—a sort of serape-like swath of woven wool with a slit for his head and a hood. That evening, this kind man took me home to meet his family, and his first act upon entering the house was to take off his cloak and spread it on his bed. It was clear that what he worked in and what he slept under were one and the same (see Figure P-1).

Figure P-1: Shikara on Dal Lake, in the Vale of Kashmir, in the north of India; what the boatman worked in and what he slept under were one and the same.

This was an "aha!" moment for me. It led me years later, as a designer, to ask fundamental questions about the nature of how we live and how we work: Why do we leave our houses empty all day and our offices empty all night? Can we afford this kind of duplicative waste? What if deciding not to devote two separate locations to the two most time-consuming activities of our lives—living and working—actually resulted in happier people, better communities, and significant environmental and social benefits? What if the elimination of waste creates opportunities to build community? Thus was born a vocation for me, which is to create communities where the many functions of life are brought back together, where face-to-face interaction occurs as a natural outgrowth of good design, and where we are saving the planet while healing the disconnectedness in our lives. Such communities are what the world needs, and in this book you will learn how to create them.

The implications of live-work—and by extension live-work's recognition of the importance of physical proximity in the lives of those who choose to pursue Zero Commute Living—are both *far reaching* and *focused*.

Far-reaching: Live-work is perhaps the most immediate expression of a view of settlement patterns that sees the need for automobile transportation to meet all of one's needs as a measure of profound dysfunction. Such a view runs counter to conventional sprawl development—the prevailing model since World War II—and embraces compact, walkable communities à la New Urbanism, Smart Growth, or enlightened urban infill.

Focused: Live-work is the natural result of an individual's decision not to commute and the collective effect of many people making that same choice. That simple decision means that individuals have chosen to "put their lives back together" (no, this is not a twelve-step program) by focusing the majority of their day-to-day lives in one place. In doing so, they are no longer merely "sleeping at home" and "working at the office," each while the other sits vacant. Being in one place most of the time engenders an attachment to and pride in that place, and a demand for a more well-considered environment.

The evidence is clear that—whether it is the addition of a living component to a nonresidential place such as the colonization of a SoHo by outlaw artists, the insertion of live-work as infill in an existing neighborhood, or the inclusion of live-work in a mixed-use greenfield town center—the integration of live-work into a place means that a stronger sense of community results, life on the street takes on Jane Jacobs' desired eighteen-hour-a-day presence, and the neighborhood becomes a more desirable place in which to spend time.

There is, however, downside to live-work's relatively newfound popularity and it is my hope that this book will help reverse the negative trend of the willy-nilly placement of so-called loft condominiums as infill in an existing, viable industrial neighborhood without regard to the presence of retail, other city services, and transportation. This unfortunate practice is a prescription for conflicts with preexisting neighbors, and a distorted real estate market that prices such neighbors out, and ultimately it results in very little chance for a real urban place to emerge as a neighborhood. It is in fact the industrial equivalent of what used to be called "blockbusting." The clear lesson is this: As with most planning decisions, where one locates live-work is as important as how it is designed, entitled, permitted, and marketed. Suc-cessful examples exist, and failed examples exist. Both will be discussed in this book.

Speaking personally, my training in landscape architecture and regional planning has undoubtedly led me in a direction that is attuned to making places defined by the space between buildings. My education within institutions was a valuable gift, but perhaps more important has been what I have learned from seeing the world around me—especially when traveling among other cultures, but also in one particular place where I lived and worked for seventeen years, a former Italian family compound in the Temescal neighborhood of Oakland, California. There I learned about the power of place to assist—if not make—community, a lesson that has informed a lifelong quest for community in my work and in my life. People often visited this place, were pleased with what they saw, and either exclaimed, "It's great! How can I live like this? or, "This reminds me of a Balinese Kampong, or a Chinese Hutong." The first response was one of amazement, the second one of recollection. Both, however, displayed an instinctive recognition of a way of living that is timeless, adaptable, and basically suited to the human temperament.

There are many case studies in this book; the majority come from the Bay Area, the West Coast, and the southeastern United States, in part because my practice is in Oakland, California, and I have extensive knowledge of regional examples of live-work. Additionally, my long association with and active participation in the Congress for the New Urbanism has contributed to my deep familiarity with live-work examples in many New Urbanist communities, which to this day are largely concentrated in the southeastern United States.

It is my hope that the information presented in these pages, this synthesis of my knowledge and experience in the field and my deep commitment to live-work, proves to be a rich resource that helps countless others to achieve what has been the ultimate goal of my career: the creation strong, harmonious communities in which to live and to work.

More information about live-work and the author's work can be found in Appendix C: Live-Work Resources, Resources and at www.live-work.com.

Acknowledgments

There have been many people and events in my life that directed me towards live-work and its potential to build community. I am fortunate to be the son of an artist mother and a scientist father, both of whom encouraged me to follow my interests and supported me as I did so.

I am indebted to numerous teachers and professors, beginning with my high school drafting teacher, John Carey, who is really the man who inspired me to become an architect. The renowned city planner Edmund Bacon was a family friend, and his advice, encouragement, and limitless energy and are qualities I have missed since his passing. Significant contact while at the University of Pennsylvania with Buckminster Fuller was a strong influence as I began my graduate studies. As a result of Bucky's disavowal of separate disciplines, I took all notes in graduate school in a single stream-of-consciousness blurt without distinction between design, engineering, or construction. The ideas of both Ian McHarg—my department head—and Louis Kahn were ever-present in my time at Penn and remain with me to this day.

William Coburn, the architect with whom I apprenticed in the early 1980s, came up with the idea for a new artists' live-work building, which he sketched and I attempted to sell. In the process, I met Bruce Beasley, and as is detailed in the book, together we invented a new building type and brought several successful projects into being. I am grateful for Bruce's support and encouragement over the years—together we have made history.

Working with the city of Oakland has been a constant for virtually my entire career. While working on the live-work building code and the city's *Live-Work in Plain English* Web site, the wisdom of Calvin Wong, the expert code writing of John Ewegleben, and ongoing assistance from the world's greatest plan checker, Kenny Lau, have been invaluable. Margot Lederer-Prado, as a city staff member in several departments, has been a tireless promoter of small businesses in Oakland and friend to true live-work as well. While the land-planning advances of the "McHarg Method" were important and valuable, there always seemed to be something missing that I couldn't put my finger on. The first time I

was exposed to New Urbanism, at CNU IV in Charleston in 1996, the other shoe dropped, as it were. Yes, I had learned twenty years earlier where to put development—mainly where nothing existed in the environment worth saving—but not how to make communities! By that time I had already discovered the live-work courtyard community, but it was a great relief to find a community of like-minded professionals, the Congress for the New Urbanism, including Andrés Duany, who first encouraged me to write this book.

In addition to Bruce Beasley, I have enjoyed working with many clients on live-work projects over the years. Francis Collins, owner of Dutch Boy Studios and numerous other projects, is an ornery Irishman with a great sense of humor who grew up in the slums of Pittsburgh. He is also a great client and a good guy. Francis has not only employed me over the years to work on his projects, but he also voluntarily underwrote my writing of *Live-Work in Plain English* when the city of Oakland didn't have enough money to complete it. Kathryn Porter has been a good client and friend over the years, and John Protopappis has been a fine colleague and client for almost as long as I—and he—have been building live-work.

Numerous people have been instrumental in getting this book contracted with a publisher and then getting me to write it. Andrea Gollin served informally as my editor and confidant for a number of years as we created a book proposal, and she introduced me to John Czarnecki, my original editor at Wiley. Andrea Gollin also contributed significant and superb content editing to the final manuscript, coordinated with the editor, Lauren Poplawski. Along the way, Andrea Solk helped me with the book proposal and provided much-needed encouragement. I'd also like to thank my agent, Neil Salkind, for invaluable advice, as well as John T. Scott, my uncle, who provided a second set of eyes as I entered into my book contract.

Maria Garcia-Alvarez has coordinated all of the graphic material for the book, a task that I gladly handed off to someone as competent and efficient as she has proven to be.

While writing this book, I have been a part-timer at Thomas Dolan Architecture. I am grateful to Sandy Weider,

Janey Pezmino, and Sarah Schmitz for holding the fort at TDA.

I have been fortunate to have as contributors a talented group of professionals. Laurie Volk, Todd Zimmerman, and Jackie Benson are New Urbanists whom I have known for a long time. Their perceptive writings on the market and marketing are a great addition to the book. Dan Parolek is a colleague with whom I have had the pleasure of working in the past, and being The Guy Who Wrote The Book, I naturally turned to him for a piece on form-based codes. Rod Stevens wrote the piece on the New Urban Workplace on very short notice, which I appreciate.

A number of professionals took a look at portions of the book for me, including Wade Walker (traffic and parking), David Walsh (acoustics), Rosemary Howley (energy calculations, regulation, and conservation), and Sandy Margolin and Mark Goodman (nuisance easements and disclosures). I am grateful to you all.

Pam Strayer, my "West Coast sister," both suggested and conducted the interview in Chapter Five: Live-Work and Community.

Several colleagues and friends have been instrumental in moving the ideas in this book forward: They include Margie O'Driscoll, founding director of ArtHouse San Francisco, Cheryl Kartes, author of *Creating Space*, Penny Gurstein, author of *Wired to the World, Chained to the Home*, and Chris Andrews, my colleague and teaching partner at the University of San Francisco.

I would like to thank my life mentors: Judy Melchert, Danny Goldstein, and John Prendergast. Likewise, deep thanks to my design inspirations: Chris Alexander, Jan Gehl, Jane Jacobs, and the countless artists whose homemade live-work spaces have inspired me over the years.

As is noted in the preface, much of what I know and do in the world of design was not learned at school, but by traveling the world, and—perhaps most of all—living and working at the Avon Street Compound for seventeen years, where I truly learned about the power of courtyards to facilitate community when the right people are there too: Alice Erb, Ernie McCormick, Gordy Slack, and Adriana Taranta.

But most of all, I am grateful to Jennifer Cooper, my partner in life, the love of my life, my toughest critic, and my most encouraging companion. Her wisdom, and love, and energy, and intelligence are present throughout this work as they are in my heart. Thank you, Jenn!

CHAPTER 1

Introduction:
A Brief History and
Description of Live-Work

What is the significance of live-work? What are its implications for our lives? Live-work is not merely about buildings, or units, or lofts, or lifestyles. Ultimately, the cessation of commuting—and the provision of a built environment that allows one to exercise that choice—is about rediscovering settlement patterns and urban designs that bring our lives back together, that shorten or eliminate the separation between the most important parts of our lives, and that result in more livable, life-affirming environments for all.

Since the time people began to farm land and employ laborers, "work" has often been seen as an activity that is a subset of "life." For thousands of years, cities and towns contained shophouses—the original live-work buildings—in which work and commerce were carried on at the street level and some or all of the workers lived above or behind the work area. The shophouse (see Figure 1-1), as it has traditionally been called, is referred to as the flexhouse by New Urbanists, and that is the term used in this book. The form is further defined as "live-near" in Chapter Two: Definitions.

The onset of the industrial revolution and associated advances in transportation technology meant that daily commuting over some distance to a centralized, organized place of employment became the rule rather than the exception in those parts of the world most dramatically impacted by the industrial revolution—primarily the United States and much of Western Europe. As larger workplaces became more

Figure 1-1 A shophouse in Grenada, Spain (called a flexhouse in this book) where living and/or work occurs at the street level and living occurs above, enlivening the public realm while providing flexibility over time.

common, a significant shift occurred: The distance workers were required to travel each day increased; thus began the activity we call commuting.

As early as the late nineteenth century, the effects of technology and intense urbanization gave rise to movements for social improvement, leading to separated-use zoning. Living near industry—and therefore close to one's place of employment—was seen as posing a risk to health, safety, and welfare. While well intentioned, and in many cases necessary, the effect of this separation added to commuting time. Zoning laws were enacted requiring that separate sectors of the city be set aside for industrial and residential uses, which, while challenged in the courts, were upheld in the famous 1926 *Euclid* decision (see Chapter Six: Planning).

By the middle of the twentieth century, our society had "progressed" to the point where separation between the various activities of our lives in both time and place had been sanctified by social structures—institutions, employment, neighborhood organization—and codified by laws, specifically zoning and planning regulations that told us that we must work *there*, live *here*, buy *there*.

Flexhouses and housing over retail were an important element of the fabric of cities and towns in the United States and were built until the beginning of the Great Depression, when virtually all privately financed building ground to a halt. When construction activity resumed after the Second World War, changes in transportation and settlement patterns led most development away from city centers, following a more decentralized, single-use pattern commonly known as suburban sprawl. The flexhouse was not a component of this new pattern. Almost all forms of combined living and working arrangements became illegal in the United States, except in a few large cities.

Meanwhile, lengthy automobile commutes—enabled by cheap gasoline and newly built interstate highways radiating out from city centers—became the unquestioned norm, reinforced by separated-use zoning. Starting in the 1960s, suburban workplaces grew increasingly prevalent in an environment characterized by three segregated components: residential subdivisions, shopping malls, and office parks, all laid out as cul-de-sacs whose only entrance was from crowded arterial roads. (See Figure 6-1 for a diagram of this suburban pattern contrasted with connected, walkable urbanism.) With suburbs accounting for around 60 percent of all office floor space in the United States, the predominant commute pattern became suburb to suburb.[1]

Building officials closed ranks along the way in order to enforce the separation between residence and work through codes that segregate uses—such as living and working—into "occupancies," which, when mixed within a building, require a fire wall separation and sometimes entirely different construction types. Therefore, most building codes require that, for safety reasons, we must separate with fire walls the various components of our lives and the structure of our days.

Commuting, once a short trip by foot or by trolley, has become an ordeal. As discussed, suburban sprawl and segregated uses require one to make lengthy automobile trips not only to and from work but also to perform each and every function of life, from minor to major, from mailing a package to shopping for food. As a result, approximately 36 percent of our population—children, the disabled, and the elderly, who cannot drive—are forced to rely on others for their daily transportation needs.[2] Long commutes and the constant need for auto travel conspire to make our lives ever more disconnected and fragmented.

According to an August 2007 Gallup poll, "the vast majority of American adults employed full or part-time, 85 percent, say they generally drive themselves to work. Six percent of workers say they usually ride with someone else to work, 4 percent take mass transportation, and 3 percent walk." The average round-trip commute time reported in this same Gallup survey is 48.1 minutes.[3] Multiply that by five days, four weeks, and twelve months, and the result is 4.81 work weeks—almost twenty-five days—spent commuting.

Live-work—especially when located in a mixed-use live-work neighborhood—brings life's disparate functions back together and gives us back those nearly five weeks a year spent commuting to spend at or near home with our families and friends, in the garden, taking walks, and generally enjoying life. This book is about the ways that live-work is helping to bring people's lives back together, and the nuts and bolts of how to design it and get it approved and built.

The Modem and the Shipping Container

Live-work as we know it today owes its existence to two technological advances that occurred in the second half of the twentieth century: the modem and the shipping container.

The widespread adoption of modular shipping containers (see Figure 1-2) beginning in the 1950s and '60s meant

Figure 1-2 A ship in the Port of Oakland (California) loaded with shipping containers. California, the technological advance that made downtown multi-story loft buildings redundant and kicked off the first generation of live-work.

that an entire building type—the downtown loft warehouse—became redundant and essentially surplus.

As ports from New York to San Francisco containerized, suddenly landlords from SoHo to SoMa couldn't give their loft space away. Thus the first postwar generation of live-work began with artists, who seized this opportunity and began to colonize loft districts in ports and railheads throughout the industrialized world. Our most effective futurists, teaching by action (and art) rather than words, artists have always preferred to live where they work; stepping into the breach created by containerization was a natural move for them. Most of these early artists' live-work spaces were illegal; the first efforts to regulate them involved rudimentary attempts to maintain a modicum of life safety while looking the other way as the artists occupied and revived derelict areas.

Once it became clear that a trend was emerging, first in New York in the 1970s and then in San Francisco about a decade later, the loft phenomenon began to attract the attention of real estate developers, which led to greater scrutiny from planning and building departments. Increasingly, non-artists saw the appeal of loft spaces, and many simply treated them as spacious open-plan apartments (see Figure 1-3) in great, if edgy, new mixed-use neighborhoods. Lofts became hip, they appeared in Hollywood movies, and trendy loft conversions began to pop up in cities throughout the industrialized world.

Some see live-work as the most important change-inducing agent to impact cities since the invention of the skyscraper, or at least since cities began to empty out after the Second World War. In the 1980s, a new class of consumer—the yuppie—began to inhabit so-called lifestyle lofts, spawning espresso bars, tapas joints, and boutiques in newly gentrified neighborhoods (see Figure 1-4) and attracting visitors from the suburbs and other parts of town.

By the 1990s, most cities in North America had converted loft districts, and the familiar successional pattern of artists pioneering, yuppies colonizing, and the establishment of predominantly (albeit gritty) residential mixed-use neighborhoods had become an accepted component of the urban real estate cycle. Depending on whom you ask, this phenomenon, sometimes called the SoHo Cycle, is either feared (by artists and small business owners) or relished (by developers and speculators). Planners find it a quandary, although most come down on the side of the latter, calling it revitalization. Neighborhood activists are more likely to call the SoHo Cycle gentrification, a term that implies dislocation of the underprivileged.

Figure 1-3 Mezzanine bedroom view of a lifestyle loft at Willow Court, Oakland, California. 2007. Designed by Thomas Dolan Architecture.

New York's once-pioneering SoHo arts district is now home to Pottery Barn and assorted bed and bath outlets. Tribeca, sparsely populated by SoHo refugees (including the

Figure 1-4 A French patisserie in Tribeca, Duane Park, New York City, a warehouse district that was home to artists' live-work some thirty years ago and is now an established, decidedly upscale neighborhood.

author) in the 1970s, now sports Michelin-rated restaurants, private schools, and pediatric clinics, while the artists have long since fled to Williamsburg, Bushwick, Long Island City, Jersey City, Hoboken, and the hinterlands beyond.

The second technological advance—leading to the second generation of postwar live-work—was the advent of the computer modem, which, when combined with a scanner, gave us the fax machine in the 1980s, quickly followed by e-mail and the Internet in the 1990s. Home-based business start-ups are enabled in part by affordable home office automation and the Internet, which significantly lowers the barrier to entry. Suddenly it was possible to run a small business while appearing to be an established concern, all from the comfort of one's home.

"Home office" constituted the mainstreaming of live-work and increasingly occurred in new buildings (as well as renovations), whether they were single-family houses or purpose-built live-work projects. As discussed in Chapter Four: The Market for Live-Work, the number of people who work at home is growing (see Chapter Four: Market). And that work takes many forms, including telecommuting, consulting for offsite clients, or incubating a business. Examples of occupations that are often the work component of a live-work space include: consultant, artist, therapist, hairstylist, architect, author, and graphic designer. Live-work frequently functions as a small business incubator, part of the Incubator Cycle that will be discussed later. A business born and nurtured in such a situation might or might not outgrow its live-work birthplace.

However, many new residents of urban live-work, often children of the suburbs, have never known an absence of commuting; they're not quite sure how to handle this new situation. Many soon realize that working at home is fundamentally different from going off to the office every day. They're not out on the rialto or mixing at the water cooler. They are in one place most of the time, and they are alone most of the time. Most soon find out that they feel isolated, which can lead to some level of dissatisfaction.

What second-generation live-workers often do not perceive consciously is that this new and fundamentally altered relationship among work, residence, and place calls for an entirely different view of settlement patterns and how they meet our needs for interaction, commerce, services, and convenience. For example, a single-use residential subdivision where half the households consist entirely of residents working at home is bound to be full of people who are suffering from feelings of isolation with very little opportunity to alleviate the problem. The issue in this situation is not one that can be solved by remodeling the house; to be happy as

a live-worker, a work-at-home resident of such a subdivision likely needs to move to a walkable urban location where opportunities for interaction are more readily available.

Zero-Commute Living™

Beginning in the late 1980s, several factors conspired to make commuting less attractive and live-work more desirable, to the point that new buildings began to be designed and built with this use in mind, such as Ocean View Lofts in Berkeley, California (see Figure C-1 in the color folio).

Other than the fact that, in many cities, most of the buildings well suited to live-work conversion were already occupied, some of the other factors contributing to the rise of newly constructed live-work included:

1. Live-work's inherent affordability (i.e., eliminating a rent payment by combining home and workplace)

2. The transportation cost savings realized by not commuting

3. The increasing number of two-income households, where one breadwinner would do best being at or near home

4. The tremendous savings in time realized by not commuting, leading to more opportunities to walk, garden, and socialize in one's neighborhood

5. The role of the Internet, social media, and teleconferencing in making face-to-face meetings and onsite work less necessary

6. The advantages of being able to work when the spirit moves you, at any hour (a benefit artists have known for years)

7. The tendency for new construction live-work to be located near urban services, amenities, and transit

8. New-construction live-work being encouraged by codes and other governmental inducements

Recently, many aging baby boomers have realized they no longer need a big house in the suburbs; the kids are gone, the big yard and suburban school systems are no longer necessary, and they want to be where they can walk to cultural events, cafes, and nightlife. As a result, new buildings are being designed and built with these users in mind. The conversion and new construction of urban live-work lofts for aging boomers has been a significant factor driving the reinhabitation of urban downtowns. Likewise, the millennials, now entering household-forming age and less interested in the suburbs than were their predecessors, are an important market for rental lofts.

Figure 1-5 Flexhouses in a new neighborhood, Glenwood Park, Atlanta, Georgia, Planned by Dover-Kohl, 2004, whose configuration allows the flexibility for their uses to change over time: "buildings that learn."

Meanwhile, greenfield New Urbanist communities have become a primary locus of second-generation live-work. Live-work units are being included in many such projects, typically in the form a townhouse with a separated work space on the first floor—the flexhouse. Live-work in such communities tends to be located in or near the town center, in close proximity to services and in some cases transit.

Housing over retail has historically been an important form of live-work and should not be overlooked—it is an important component of a live-work neighborhood. The flexhouse, mentioned earlier, is a promising type that has recently reemerged. A "building that learns," the flexhouse usually takes the form of a series of rowhouse bays (see Figure 1-5) intended—and preapproved—to evolve from townhouse/home office residences (albeit with a full separation between ground floor and upper levels) into loft housing over retail in response to shifting demand and the maturing of the retail market in a given location. In fact, many flexhouses are used from the outset as housing over retail by separate parties, as in Habersham, South Carolina, described in a case study in Chapter Four: Market.

Overview of Live-Work

Live-work is a building or buildings that provide both residential and work space on a single property, some of whose residents might work there, and which might also accommodate nonresident employees.

In the larger sense, live-work is a land use and building type that is a combination of commercial and residential, yet is at once neither and both. In the case of a live-work neighborhood, defined in Chapter Two: Definitions, most residents work within a one-quarter-mile walk of where they live, if not at home. Housing over retail is also an important component of a live-work neighborhood, where most if not all the functions of one's daily life can be accessed on foot within a five- to fifteen-minute walk. Such "complete neighborhoods" may contain few named live-work units, but they meet the basic criterion of proximity that is essential to live-work.

Live-work takes a variety of forms and appeals to a wide range of users, from starving artists sharing a single kitchen and sizable work spaces in an old warehouse to wealthy empty nesters paying seven (or eight!) figures for chic lofts. Live-work can be a townhouse in a New Urbanist community such as Kentlands in Maryland (see Figure 1-6), where the offices of *The Town Paper* are located on the first floor, and the developer says he wishes he'd built four times as many live-work units.[4] Live-work can include an alley-facing home office in a greenfield community, which might double as a granny flat, a spare room, or a teenager's clubhouse. It can be a home office, or housing over retail, or a flexhouse designed to accommodate street-fronting live-work and intended to evolve into housing over retail as the market matures.

All of these are forms of live-work. In fact, architect and planner Andrés Duany, cofounder of the Congress for the New Urbanism, has stated, "In the twenty-first century all residences will be live-work."[5] The New Urbanism and its regulatory policy synonym, Smart Growth, "promotes the creation and restoration of diverse, walkable, compact, vibrant, mixed-use communities composed of the same components as conventional development, but assembled in a more

Figure 1-6 Flexhouses in Kentlands, Maryland, an early traditional neighborhood development planned by Duany Plater-Zyberk & Company.

integrated fashion, in the form of complete communities. These contain housing, work places, shops, entertainment, schools, parks, and civic facilities essential to the daily lives of the residents, all within easy walking distance of each other."[6] These aims are fully expressed in many built New Urbanist communities. "Live-works," as the New Urbanists call these building types, are a component of the town center of virtually every traditional neighborhood development (TND). Live-work is arguably the signature building type of New Urbanism, of urban pioneering in the form of loft conversions, and of the postindustrial city in the form of new infill lofts in places like SoMa, LoDo, and the Pearl District of Portland, Oregon.

Live-work, then, is about flexibility, mixed use, and proximity. Live-work units can be for residents who may work there or for workers who rarely sleep there. In fact, the same unit might accommodate both modes within a few short years. Live-work residents are fiercely loyal to the type for just these reasons: When their lives change, that's fine; they are in a unit that can accommodate the multiple stages of life, *and* their commute will always be a very short walk.

More than any other building type, live-work is a combination of uses that is sure to change over time, so it is particularly appropriate in a mixed-use or flexible-use district, sometimes called "a neighborhood that learns" (with apologies to Stewart Brand). An important result of this flexibility is that, unlike the offerings present in our most common forms of housing, a live-work resident typically does not have to move every time he or she enters a new phase of life, such as the transition from parent to empty nester. This is one reason why a live-work neighborhood can be called a "lifelong neighborhood," as mentioned in Chapter Five: Community.

Live-Work Types and Terminology

As live-work has evolved over the last forty years into a recognized land use and building type and a marketable real estate "product," it has spawned almost as many ways of describing, regulating, financing, and selling it as there are cities in which it exists. Each city, operating in a relative vacuum, has elected to reinvent the wheel when it comes to planning and building regulations. Central to this book is an attempt to create a common language, starting with the definitions in Chapter Two: Definitions. That language and the terms the author has coined include several ways of parsing live-work units and projects into types, as follows:

- Dominance and intensity of work use versus living activity: *work/live*, *live/work*, and *home occupation*

- Proximity between living and working activities, reflected in the form of the unit: *live-with*, *live-near*, and *live-nearby*
- Project scale, ranging from single-family residential to high-density urban lofts
- Location and construction, from greenfield to grayfield, and from new construction infill to renovation of existing buildings

Choosing to work at home and thus to stop commuting has many consequences at the individual, regulatory, and societal levels. The rise of live-work has been a sizable challenge for real estate and lending communities due to laws and regulations that discourage mixed-use buildings and development. Our government institutions, banks, and investors are still—in many cases—stuck in a mode of encouraging and funding separated, single-use developments, which live-work is not. Nevertheless, the rise of mixed-use planning practices, New Urbanism, and the real estate community's acceptance of live-work have combined to allow a greater understanding of live-work as a component of mainstream settlement patterns. This is especially true in the places where it is most common, such as loft conversions in larger cities and flexhouse live-works in greenfield New Urbanist communities.

Live-Work Planning and Urban Design

Most jurisdictions today are governed by conventional zoning, which separates cities into single-use zones. Many forms of live-work run counter to this segregated-use model. For example, home occupation—that is, an individual choosing to work at home in a residential zone—is seen by many as anathema to the residential character of that place. Nevertheless, home occupation, often called home office, is an important type of live-work, and one that is carried on by millions of people. Many cities have enacted home occupation regulations; most are written to limit the impact of the work activity on surrounding properties.

Yet, as noted, there are forms of live-work that occur in commercial or industrial districts (see Figure 1-7), places that traditional zoning deems out-of-bounds to residences. Such places are often pioneered by artists in outlaw live-work. Mainstream live-work development in such areas can result in unintended consequences, including imported NIMBY-ism, a particularly damaging expression of land-use incompatibilities, as is detailed in Chapter Six: Planning.

The presence of live-work conversions of existing buildings, often without benefit of permits, is an important indicator

Figure 1-7 New live-work lofts in an industrial district of San Francisco, where the presence of new residents—"imported NIMBYs"—caused repeated conflicts, often forcing industrial operators to curtail their operations or move altogether.

of a district in transition to a neighborhood. Such a transformation can be successful or not, depending on multiple factors, not least being:

- The viability of the existing commercial district
- The availability of services, transit, and other amenities
- The availability of sufficient in-place infrastructure
- The enactment of carefully crafted regulations and incentives

These prerequisites for a successful live-work neighborhood are addressed in Chapter Six: Planning.

As noted in the history recounted earlier, the colonization of commercial/industrial districts for live-work, usually led by artists, often serves as the catalyst for the transformation into mixed-use neighborhoods. The SoHo Cycle occurs widely and has frequently resulted in the revitalization of large and small downtowns, helping them fight back against urban flight by creatively reusing their existing infrastructure, their gridded, connected streets, and their historic building stock. When managed successfully, such live-work–led revitalizations can help counter freeway-driven "leakage" of commercial and residential activity and bring it back downtown.

Live-work combines two widely held ideals: *being my own boss* and *owning my own home*. It is also the only building type that combines housing and employment under one roof. For these reasons, live-work is often encouraged by planning departments and economic development agencies. "Live-work-play environments"—urban neighborhoods that combine housing, employment, and entertainment—are extremely attractive to economic development directors.

The Role of Artists

While some of our most interesting urban places were pioneered by artists who spontaneously created live-work neighborhoods by illegally occupying and popularizing them, the SoHo Cycle has required artists to endure repeated, involuntary moves from one district to the next. Tribeca (see Figure 1-8), in fact, was where artists moved who were priced out of SoHo.

The seemingly inevitable sequence of events that comprise the SoHo Cycle raises raises many important questions:

- What is the role of artists living and working in our cities?
- Do we as a society value the presence of working artists?
- Do we value artists enough to take regulatory or fiscal steps to ensure that a certain number of artists are able to occupy and remain in long-term affordable space?
- What do we as a society owe artists, if anything?
- Do pioneering artists, sometimes called the shock troops of gentrification, deserve better than an outlaw loft and eviction after a couple of years?

Such questions will be explored in Chapter 6: Planning. As the sculptor Bruce Beasley said as he began South Prescott Village—his pioneering artists' live-work project designed by the author: "You can't make art if you don't have a place in which to make it."

Building Codes

Building departments have often been reluctant to embrace live-work, particularly varieties that do not include a fire-rated

Figure 1-8 A storefront in Tribeca, lower Manhattan, located in the building where the author lived in 1975, a time when lofts were cheap and there were virtually no neighborhood or city services.

separation between living and working portions. It turns out that living and working in the same "common atmosphere" flies in the face of the basic tenets of life safety as laid out in model building codes. Until very recently, in the absence of locally calibrated code relief, a one-hour rated *occupancy separation* was often required between the living and working portions of a live-work unit, because they are viewed as separate occupancies.

The 2009 version of the International Building Code (IBC), the applicable model code throughout the United States—and, increasingly, the world—contains for the first time Section 419, devoted to live-work. While it addresses only one of the many types of live-work, one can infer from its basic principles—which include the omission of an occupancy separation between living and working portions—how one might write code for other live-work types.

Other building code issues in live-work depend on whether there is walk-in trade or employees. If the answer is yes, the work space is truly commercial and must be made fully accessible according to the Americans with Disabilities Act (ADA) or other local codes directed at disabled occupants. If walk-in trade and employees are not present, residential code is likely to apply throughout the unit.

Chapter Seven: Building Codes draws from the author's nearly thirty years of experience in the field, during which he has written a comprehensive live-work building code. Many significant building code issues are addressed in detail in that chapter; additionally, a model live-work building code system can be found in Appendix B: Model Live-Work Building Code System.

Common Mistakes in Live-Work

While some forms of live-work are well suited to almost any location, a project that either is built in the wrong location or designed without an adequate understanding of the unique needs of live-workers can lead to a situation that often fails to meet its full potential and, at worst, can result in a social and/or financial disaster. Some of the ways that a live-work project can go astray include:

- Failing to understand live-work's inherent potential for isolation
- Following on the above point, failing either to locate the project on a great street or to design opportunities for interaction within the project, or both

- Building unseparated live-work (live-with proximity type), which is permitted under IBC Section 419 (see Chapter Three: Design), and mistakenly assuming that the living and working portions of said units can be held or rented by separate parties
- Acting on a mistaken belief that live-work can thrive in isolated, single-use situations such as a cul-de-sac subdivision or an isolated industrial district (unless it's a pioneering artists-only project)
- Locating ownership or high-end rental live-work in an existing, viable commercial/industrial setting, where new residents are likely to immediately complain about the legal and long-standing commercial activities of their neighbors, who were—of course—there first
- Enacting planning and building codes ostensibly to encourage artists to occupy and improve existing commercial buildings in a potential "live-work-play" or "arts district" environment, then failing to enforce requirements that only artists will be permitted (an almost impossible combination of tasks)
- Developing an individual live-work project aimed at artists or small-business entrepreneurs, then allowing the project to devolve into strictly residential; the result will be a greatly diminished sense of community within the project once tenants or owners are "only sleeping there"

Retrofitting Suburbia

As noted earlier, most live-work built or renovated in the past forty years has occurred as either renovation within or infill to existing urban centers or greenfield construction in New Urbanist town centers. However, retrofitting the suburbs (see Figure 1-9), one of the greatest challenges that North American planners and designers are likely to face until at least mid century, will be about reintroducing proximity, community, and a revived public realm to replace the separation, isolation, and excesses of the private realm enabled by seemingly endless cheap oil. Live-work will play an important role in the remaking of suburbia, as it has and will continue to do in our urban centers. As parts of suburbia—such as failed shopping malls—lead the way beyond suburbia as we know it, the flexibility of live-work in its many forms will enable the transition to new patterns of development, such as the acclaimed Mizner Park in Boca Raton, Florida.

Figure 1-9 Ahead of their time, these four flexhouse live-works near Milford, Delaware, were the beginning of a project that foundered in the crash of 2008; others have fared better (see Habersham Case Study, Chapter Four: Market).

Conventional sprawl development—characterized by separated land uses, voracious consumption of land resulting in highly dispersed, low-density settlement patterns, and a supply of cheap gasoline—without which it could not exist—is, in the long run and perhaps the middle-to-short run, entirely unsustainable and contributes significantly to global warming. Enter live-work, the value of proximity, and the convenient choice: the reconstitution of our landscape into compact, walkable communities linked by efficient mass transit.

Forward-thinking planners have identified the need for automobile transportation as an important measure of dysfunction in a place; inevitably such a view will reach a tipping point and be more fully addressed in policy and planning regulations. California's pioneering global warming legislation, AB 32 and SB 375, which contains land use standards that guide its implementation, is an excellent example, although as of this writing it is largely untested.

The inherent principles of live-work—proximity, walkability, and community—will be important ingredients if we are to slow or halt human-caused global warming. In the face of the recent economic downturn and its effect on housing and real estate, one might ask: Can we afford the kind of waste inherent in letting office parks sit empty all night and residential subdivisions sit empty all day, and the wasteland that has resulted from it? This book argues that the elimination of waste—specifically, the excess amount of unused real estate when evaluated over the course of a twenty-four-hour day and a full week, and the time, fuel, and money wasted on an arrangement that requires excessive reliance on the automobile—presents an opportunity for the creation of community in the form of cities and towns whose basic unit is the compact, walkable, live-work neighborhood organized around a quarter-mile-radius pedestrian shed (pedshed).

CHAPTER 2

Defining Live-Work

Live-work is a combination of residential and commercial uses, yet it is at once neither and both (see Figure 2-1 for a typical building example). The term *live-work* means different things to different people, be they developer, designer, planner, regulator, or user. As a result, if one were to ask fifteen people what live-work is, it is likely there would be ten responses, and in a way all would be correct, because there are many types of live-work. However, this lack of consistency creates unnecessary confusion. The purpose of this chapter is to advance live-work terminology to the point of a usable, standardized lexicon, one that will be employed for the remainder of this book and universally adopted by professionals. Among the types of live-work defined in detail here are: the live-with loft (see Figure C-3 in the color folio), the flexhouse (see Figure 2-2), and the live-nearby accessory building serving as a work space (see Figure 2-3).

Figure 2-1 Union Street Studios, a typical live-work renovation in Oakland, California, was formerly a plumbing warehouse and was converted into eighteen live-work units in 2000. Designed by Thomas Dolan Architecture.

Figure 2-2 A dual entry—allowing one to turn and enter the retail space or proceed straight up to the residence—serves each of these two flexhouses at Serenbe, a traditional neighborhood development in Georgia.

Figure 2-3 A live-nearby accessory building in Oakland, where the owner sorted and selected some of the photographs that appear in this book. 2001. Designed by Thomas Dolan Architecture and Jennifer Cooper Designer.

The overarching definition of live-work is straightforward:

A building, unit, or compound in which residential and work activities are pursued on that same property by most, if not all, of the same people.

Live-work can also constitute part of a *live-work neighborhood* when (1) living and working space are within a five-minute walk of each other, and (2) the majority of the live-worker's needs can be met within a ten-minute walk of home or workplace.

The author, a practicing architect, has spent his entire career to date refining the many forms of live-work while tracking its evolution and studying its history and origins.

Trends in live-work design and development are somewhat of a moving target, which only intensifies the need for standardization of its terminology. Over the last twenty-five years, the author has created, refined, and put into use a set of definitions that have proven durable and have increasingly been adopted by those associated with live-work. The definitions spring from a division of live-work into types, parsed by: use, form, and scale characteristics.

The classification system in Table 2-1 provides a common language for those who contemplate, discuss, regulate, design, and build live-work. Only through the use of a common language will the discussions take place that lead to refinements to Zero-Commute Housing (a synonym for live-work) as an important element in the remaking of towns and cities to meet the needs of the twenty-first century.

Table 2-1 Live-Work Types

Use types	Determined by work-use intensity and dominance of residence versus work *activity*
Proximity types	Determined by the *form* of the unit, specifically how the work space and the residence activities are physically arranged in relation to each other
Project types	Determined by the *scale*, urban intensity, and transect location of the project

A word about terminology, punctuation, and distinctions: Live-work (hyphenated) is the name given to the overall subject of this book. The same combination of words using a forward slash (/), live/work, is one of three live-work use types.

Live-Work Use Types

The most basic means of differentiating live-work units is to divide them into types determined by work-use intensity, that is, dominance of work activity versus residence: home occupation, live/work, and work/live (see Table 2-2). These terms are in general use, although the distinctions between them as applied to specific circumstances vary widely, an ambiguity this book will alleviate.

Home Occupation

Basic Definition

Home occupation is a term used by many jurisdictions to grant residents the right to pursue small-scale work activities at home. This type of arrangement is what most people think of when they hear the term "working at home" or "home office." By definition, home occupation takes place in a residence, and it may or may not include a physically delineated work space, such as an office, studio, or workshop. Work-use intensity in a home occupation is categorized as Restricted (see Table A-2, Appendix A).

Table 2-2 Live-Work Use Types

home occupation	Work occurs within a residence
live/work	Work occurs within a unit; its dominance over residential activity will vary over time
work/live	Residence occurs within or adjacent to a commercial space; therefore, the work use is dominant

Physical Configuration and Use

Home occupation can be configured specifically to accommodate solitary work activity, client visits by appointment, and even a small number of employees. Dedicated work space in a home occupation (see Figure 2-4) may take the form of a home office, studio, or workshop, which might be located within the residential unit or building, or it might be located in an outbuilding, such as a converted garage, shed, or barn. A common form of home occupation in greenfield New Urbanist projects is a "granny flat" over an alley-facing garage, which can double as an office or studio when not used solely as a residence.

Location

Home occupation can occur in any residence or accessory building on the same property as that residence (see Figure 2-5); said activity will always be incidental and secondary to the primary use of the unit, building, or property, which is residence. Therefore, wherever a residence is permitted and located, it follows that home occupation can occur as well, enabled all the more by inexpensive small-office automation and online communication.

Use Evolution

In most situations, evolution of home occupation into commercial or work-only is not desirable, except in higher-density and/or mixed locations, due to the potential impact of higher-intensity work activities on residential neighborhoods. Most home occupation ordinances state that the work activity shall

Figure 2-4 This home occupation at Pinetree Studios in Oakland, California, is actually the middle floor of a live-near flexhouse. The worker here is a botanical illustrator; her drawing table is behind the drafting lamp in the center of the picture. 1990. Designed by Thomas Dolan Architecture.

Figure 2-5 An alley-facing outbuilding in Celebration, Florida, which could be used for home occupation or residence; this is another example of live-work's flexibility.

not impact parking or increase traffic in its neighborhood, and that its work activities shall not generate noises or odors perceivable beyond the home occupation's property line. It is possible that, over time, the evolution of a neighborhood around a residence may cause that unit or building to become more commercially oriented, in which case the home occupation might evolve into a live/work or work/live unit, or even a commercial-only space.

Live/Work

Basic Definition

Live/work is a term used to describe a unit in which the needs of the residential component and the quiet enjoyment expectations of the neighbors in the building or adjacent buildings take precedence over the work needs of the unit in question, meaning that those who pursue work activities must take into consideration the noise, odors, and other impacts they may generate. The predominant use of a live/work unit is residence; work activity is secondary or, if separated, of comparable importance. Employees and walk-in trade may be permitted, in which case accessibility measures are required in the work portion if public accommodation exists. In many cases, client visits are by appointment only, and employees are sometimes permitted but typically limited in number. Work-use intensity in live/work is categorized as Limited (see Table A-2, Appendix A).

Physical Configuration and Use

Flexibility is key in live/work. More than either home occupation or work/live, it is assumed that the dominance of

Figure 2-6 An artist's studio at South Prescott Village in Oakland, California. A movable partition allows the artist to vary the size of her work space to suit her needs at any given time. 1988. Designed by Thomas Dolan Architecture.

Figure 2-7 Office and white-collar activities are common in live/work units, such as this one in Oakland, California.

work versus residence in a live/work unit will ebb and flow over time (see Figure 2-6). For that reason, a live/work unit best embodies mixed use within the unit (or property) itself.

Live/work units can exist in townhouse configurations, with an important difference: Due to the lower-intensity work activities likely to occur there (see Figure 2-7), a separation is unlikely to be required between the shop below and the residence above, although it might be desired. Live/work units can be of any spatial configuration, and their work spaces might be anywhere: in the unit, in the building, or on the same property (see Figure C-4 in the color folio).

A common form of live/work is the urban loft (see Figure 2-8). It may be a single high-ceilinged space in a converted building or purpose-built from the ground up with multiple levels, sometimes in the form of a townhouse. Being the most flexible type of live-work, over time its use might be mostly residence, mostly work, or an even split between the two. Therefore, the work-to-residence balance might "flex" over a week, a month, or years. A dining area might double as a conference room; a work area might be given over to a party or reception; or former work space might become a child's sleeping area. Household size can change, and one's work situation can as well. Live-with spaces (defined below) and live-work in general adapt easily to such inevitable changes.

Location

Jurisdictions that have made the distinction between live/work and work/live have been inconsistent in ruling whether they consider live/work to be a commercial or residential type. A live/work unit is likely to be located anywhere in the

Figure 2-8 Union Street Studios, a typical loft in a converted warehouse, which was built under relaxed building codes and development standards in 2000. Designed by Thomas Dolan Architecture.

Figure 2-9 Flexhouses at Ruskin Square in Seaside, Florida, the first New Urbanist community built, in 1982 (see case study in Chapter 3). Seaside was designed by Duany Plater-Zyberk & Co., Town Planners and Architects.

middle range of urban intensity, meaning anywhere except the lowest-density residential areas and moderate- to high-intensity industrial districts.

Purpose-built live/work tends to take the form of a flex-house (see Figure 2-9), a courtyard live/work community, or an urban loft project. Renovated live/work tends to occur in former warehouses, factories, and commercial buildings, often located in commercial districts made redundant by the offshoring of industry and the adoption of shipping containers (see Figure C-5 in the color folio).

The locations of live/work units are often similar to those of work/live units. In fact, many urban locations that were once home to predominantly work/live units are now or will someday be home to live/work units. Notable U.S. examples are SoHo and Tribeca in New York, SoMa in San Francisco, LoDo in Denver, and the Pearl District in Portland.

Use Evolution

Live/work is made to flex. For that reason it is most suited to mixed-use neighborhoods and those in flux. In Stewart Brand's book *How Buildings Learn*, he states that we should design buildings from the outset with the understanding that they will learn and change over time, both in form and in use. Live/work units embody this truth as fully as any building type that exists today. The live/work use type is also a poster child for form-based coding (see Form-Based Codes sidebar, Chapter Six: Planning), a way of regulating development that emphasizes design and particularly the role buildings play in shaping the public realm, that is, "the space between buildings," and that places less emphasis on the use of the buildings. This deemphasis on use is in part because a building's function in shaping an urban place such as a street, plaza, or square is relatively static, but its use likely will evolve over time; use evolution will not affect the building's place-making function. A further expression of this anticipatory design idea is the flexhouse, defined and discussed later in this chapter.

Reversion to work-only in live/work may be acceptable, depending on surrounding users. In more commercial or industrial locations, reversion to residential only can often cause imported NIMBY (NIMBY: "not in my backyard") problems and is therefore discouraged.

Work/Live

Basic Definition

Work/live is a term used to describe a unit in which the needs of the work component take precedence over the quiet enjoyment expectations of residents (see Figure C-6 in the color folio). There may be noise, odors, or other impacts, as well as employees, walk-in trade, or sales. The predominant use of a work/live unit is commercial or industrial work activity; residence is a secondary, if not accessory, use. Employees and walk-in trade are usually permitted in such units, and therefore accessibility measures are typically required in the work portion, based on public accommodation standards for the disabled. Work-use intensity in a work/live is categorized as Open (see Table A-2, Appendix A).

Physical Configuration and Use

A work/live unit is always configured to specifically accommodate work activity and, as noted, is usually configured to accommodate walk-in trade and employees. The dedicated work space in a work/live unit is typically on the main or ground floor, and it is often separated from the residence by a wall or floor/ceiling (live-near, defined below). It may also occur in a separate space (see Figure 2-10) or building (live-nearby, also defined below). The residential portion of a work/live unit is typically smaller than the work space and can be on a different level or story within the unit or in a different building on the property.

True work/live units are not as common as home occupation (the mainstreaming of live-work) or live/work units. Units built as work/live often end up reverting to a form in which work is not the predominant activity, a phenomenon called "residential reversion" that will be treated later. The

Figure 2-10 An artist shows his work to a visiting gallery owner and collectors in a dedicated, separate work space at New Daylight Studios in Oakland, California.

Figure 2-11 A typical street in Tribeca, New York City, where many former loft warehouses were converted to live-work after the adoption of shipping containers rendered such buildings redundant.

prototype for a work/live unit is the artist's loft, in which the artist "lives for her work," needs lots of space with great light to make large artworks, and sleeps on a mattress in the corner. Following the line of this myth, she is also probably living in her unit illegally and is beleaguered by a predatory landlord and a heartless building department.

More recent work/live prototypes as of 2011 have included a purpose-built live/work planned in Sydney, Australia, with large ground-floor work spaces and residence above, and an "artists' guild" work/live project in Oakland, California, that anticipates woodworking and metal-sculpting activities, therefore projecting cavernous ground-floor work spaces alongside residential portions a mere three-hour fire-rated wall away.

A common form of work/live is the flexhouse, an ancient urban building type accommodating an activity sometimes known as living above the store. A ground-floor space, usually with a storefront, allows the public and employees to enter the space without passing through or impacting the residence, which is typically above or in an outbuilding behind (or both). While this form, essentially housing over retail, may be viewed by many as simply a mixed-use building, it is also an important form of live-work.

Location

Most jurisdictions that have made the distinction between work/live and other types classify work/live as a commercial activity due to the dominance of the work component. For that and other reasons, work/live units and buildings are more likely to be in locations that permit commercial, industrial, or mixed uses (see Figure 2-11).

Renovated work/live tends to occur in former warehouses, factories, and commercial buildings. Little newly constructed work/live has been built other than the proposed projects noted above. Illegal work/live in existing industrial and commercial buildings is, however, very common.

Use Evolution

Perhaps more than any other type defined in this chapter, space permitted as work/live, built as work/live, and sold or leased as work/live (sometimes with the wink of an eye) often ends up reverting to less work-intensive types. The most common occurrence is *residential reversion*, in which an occupant of a work/live unit discontinues (or never begins) working in the space, and simply treats it as an open-plan, spacious, trendy residential loft (see Figure 2-12).

Why is residential reversion such an important issue, and why should it matter?

It matters because residential reversion of work/live in industrial districts causes more problems than exist in any other aspect of the live-work world. Work/live is typically zoned by city planners as an attempt to rescue failing industrial districts by encouraging repurposing of underutilized buildings. The intent of most work/live legislation as it applies to existing urban districts is to allow the occupation of vacant warehouses by those who will both live and work there, who will coexist with their industrial neighbors, and who will put up with a relative lack of city services. When work/live spaces are occupied by working artists or small businesses renting the space, typically few problems arise.

Figure 2-12 A "staged" bedroom space in the Phoenix Lofts, the live-work conversion of a four-story concrete plumbing warehouse in Oakland, 2000. Designed by Thomas Dolan Architecture.

Such residents integrate well into existing industrial districts because their work activity is compatible with those around them (see Figure 2-13).

At the opposite end of the spectrum are those who purchase so-called live-work lofts constructed in industrial districts but have no intention of working in them, or their work is of a part-time, white-collar nature in a decidedly blue-collar context. As soon as the first delivery truck cranks up its diesel at 4:30 a.m., or a factory blows off its steam vents at 2 a.m., or a business operator washes meat-packing offal down the gutter, that buyer is going to get a lawyer (if he isn't one himself) and go after that business—one that might have been operating without harassment for decades

Figure 2-13 An artist's spacious and very industrial-scale workshop in a former jet engine repair and test facility at Alameda Naval Air Station, California, 1995. Designed by Thomas Dolan Architecture.

in that location, which is perhaps zoned for heavy industry. This phenomenon is called imported NIMBYism, and it can cause huge problems. Industrial districts are set aside for high-impact manufacturing; they are necessary to the function of cities and those businesses that locate there have nowhere else to go, short of relocating to another city or an exurban tilt-up district.

To summarize, residential reversion is common in work/live and is usually harmful when it occurs in existing industrial districts. Finding the means to head it off is perhaps the most daunting challenge in live-work regulation. This issue is discussed further in Chapter Six: Planning.

Neighborhoods and districts go though cycles, perhaps none on a more well-worn track than the so-called SoHo Cycle. As discussed in Chapter One: Introduction, it goes something like this: Artists discover a location and start moving into underutilized warehouses, renting from owners who are happy to look the other way while they are occupied illegally. The artists need places to show their work, so a few "experimental" galleries spring up. The press gets wind of it, and the district begins to get more attention. Cafés, galleries, and bars spring up. Until this point, most of the lofts are true work/live.

Meanwhile, the city begins to pay attention to the fact that many lofts are being lived in illegally, a fact easily verified via a nighttime windshield survey of lights on and curtains drawn. Building departments begin to lean on the landlords, who then point out to the tenant artists that their leases don't permit residence. Rents go up, many artists lose their spaces, and they are replaced by yuppies and trend-chasers. By this time, most of the lofts have reverted to live/work or simply residences. The galleries become more established, more services fill in at the ground-floor level, and an urban neighborhood is born. Depending on whom you ask, this is either a good thing (for planners and property owners) or a travesty (for displaced tenants). (See Figure 2-14 for an example of a venerable neighborhood restaurant displaced by rising rents in Tribeca.)

What about the artists? They move on, to repeat the cycle in another location, and then another.

Live-Work Proximity Types

There are three basic proximity types: live-with, live-near, and live-nearby (see Table 2-3). These terms refer to the form of the unit, specifically how the work space and residence are physically arranged in relation to each other.

Table 2-3 Live-Work Proximity Types

Live-with	Work and residence all occur in one "common atmosphere"
Live-near	Work and residence are separated by a wall or floor/ceiling
Live-nearby	Work occurs outside the residence but on the same property

Figure 2-14 Turnover in 2011 at the site of the former Delphi Restaurant in Tribeca, New York City, which was an affordable eating place for many residents and day workers alike before lofts in the neighborhood began to sell for exorbitant prices.

Live-With Proximity Type (Synonym: Loft)

A live-with unit is, shown in figure 2-15, entirely contained within the confines of one room or "common atmosphere."

It is the type of space that most people imagine when they picture a typical artists' loft. A live-with unit encompasses, within that single space: a kitchen/dining area, bathroom and sleeping space, and contiguous work space. This arrangement offers the greatest flexibility and the fewest interior partitions, allowing the user to adapt it to many different configurations. The amount of space devoted to the "live" area and the "work" area depends on the occupant's needs at the moment (see Figure 2-16) and as a result will likely vary over time (see Figure C-7 in the color folio).

The form of a live-with unit is typically either a single-level high-ceilinged space with few if any partitions or a two-level space with a full-height work space, a sleeping area and bathroom on a mezzanine level open to the work space below, and a kitchen/dining area below the mezzanine. Spatial delineation in such a unit is primarily determined by varied ceiling heights and outlook, a subject that will be treated in more detail in Chapter Three: Design.

Live-Near Proximity Type

A live-near unit, shown in figure 2-17, provides some separation between living and working spaces while still meeting the needs of those who feel that the proximity afforded by live/work is important. The form of a live-near unit can vary; it usually consists of a work space on a main floor (see Figure 2-18) and a living space above.

In the typical live-near configuration, depicted in figure 2-15, the separation is a floor/ceiling, which may or may not be fire-rated depending on the hazard level posed by the

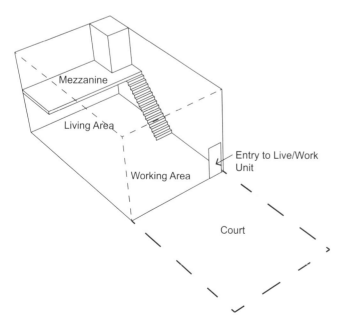

Figure 2-15 Diagram of a live-with proximity-type unit.

Figure 2-16 The loft/business owner holds a meeting in her live-with unit at Ocean View Lofts, Berkeley, California. 1993. Designed by Thomas Dolan Architecture.

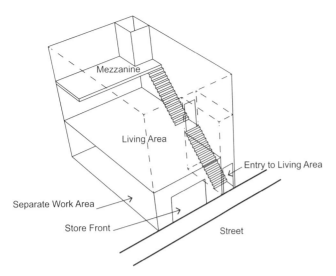

Figure 2-17 Diagram of a live-near proximity-type unit.

work activity. A work space in a different room from the living space is also a form of live-near; in that case the separation is a wall, which might be glazed (see Figure C-8 in the color folio), fire-rated, or neither. In some localities, building officials have required that all live-work units be live-near, with the separation a fire-rated assembly (see Chapter Seven: Building Codes). In a live-near unit, the living portion may more closely resemble an apartment or a townhouse.

The separation present in a live-near unit can serve to minimize exposure to hazardous materials or high-impact work activity, can allow work to go on without disturbance by family or a roommate, or can simply fill the need for that bit of distance created by a wall or floor. In a live-near unit, one's commute is a stairway or a door. Such a separation can make all the difference in one's work-life balance.

Live-near units are flexible in an entirely different way from live-with units. Their flexibility allows the owner or occupant users' ability to treat the live portion of a unit as separate from the work portion and to rent out or share the two spaces more easily.

Live-Nearby Proximity Type

In this configuration, shown in figure 2-19, a short walk separates the living portion and the work space—across a courtyard, to a converted garage or other accessory structure, or up and down an exterior or interior staircase, all on the same property. This term may also apply—although it is not so used in this book—to a work space that is not on the same property but is within a short walk. While live-nearby may initially appear to be simply mixed use, classification as live/work may permit its existence in locations where a residential or a commercial space alone might not be permitted. A live-nearby unit has many of the advantages of a live-near unit, only more so—except in inclement weather. One's commute requires a short walk; the work space feels more like a separate place than is the case with a live-near unit and is therefore somewhat more suited to client visits, employees, and walk-in trade.

The work space in a live-nearby unit is often located in an outbuilding, such as a disused granny flat over a garage or a converted garage (see Figure 2-20) or barn. In some multiunit buildings, there exists a "telework center" or common work space that is separate from the residences; this would also be a form of live-nearby.

As noted, housing over retail is essentially live-nearby and is most definitely a form of live-work if the

Figure 2-18 A downstairs work space in a live-near unit at Hannah Studios, newly constructed in a mixed industrial/residential neighborhood in Oakland, California. 1992. Designed by Thomas Dolan Architecture.

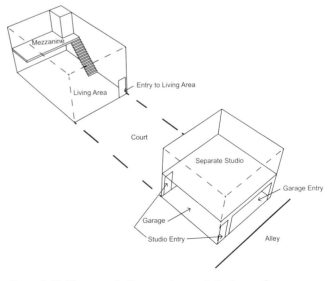

Figure 2-19 Diagram of a live-nearby proximity-type unit.

Figure 2-20 An artist's live-nearby studio behind her residence in Berkeley, built in 2007. Designed by Jennifer Cooper Designer.

occupant of the retail establishment lives in the same building, on the same property, or—although not defined as such in this book—in the case of a live-work neighborhood, within a five-minute walk.

Live-Work Project Types

Live-work project types vary widely (see Table 2-4) and have been built in countless forms. The most common project types are defined next; they are treated in greater detail in Chapter Three: Design.

Warehouse Conversion (District)

As was described in Chapter One: Introduction, most live-work warehouse conversions have occurred in port cities and railheads throughout the industrialized world. Most such cities experienced a tremendous decline in demand for downtown, multistory loft buildings as a result of the adoption of shipping containers. Notable U.S. examples are SoHo and Tribeca in New York (see Figure 2-21), SoMa in San Francisco, the Pearl District in Portland, and LoDo in Denver. Artists, who have always lived where they worked, seized upon the opportunities inherent in empty, cheap, high-ceilinged, well-lit space. Sometimes cynically referred to as "the shock troops of gentrification," artists have often pioneered neighborhoods, playing an important role in making them more attractive, and then being priced out as rents rise.

Most warehouse conversions are simple in concept although not always in finish or price, particularly as the loft district becomes a more upscale neighborhood. Depending on where one sits in the SoHo Cycle, a group of artists might sign a master lease and do the most minimal improvements to divide the building into multiple tenancies, or lofts (see Figure 2-22). Later in the cycle, the units often get smaller, but the finishes, services, and prices all move

Table 2-4 Live-Work Project Types

PROJECT TYPE	TRANSECT ZONE	DESCRIPTION
Warehouse Conversion	District	Conversion of an existing commercial building to multiple live-work units, often called lofts.
Home Office	T-2–T-5	Home occupation in or on the same property as a residence of any kind.
Townhouse (synonym: shophouse)	T-3–T-5	A stand-alone building, either attached or detached, that is physically set up to accommodate a variety of uses by a single user (i.e., there is no legal separation between residential and nonresidential uses).
Flexhouse	T-3–T-5	A building that learns: preapproved flexible use in a townhouse module, live-works, housing-over-retail live-near units. Separate entrances for live and work.
Courtyard Live-Work	T-3–T-5	A multiunit community of live-work units enering off of one or more courtyards.
Urban Loft Complex	T-4–T-6	"Lifestyle" lofts in a new building or a renovated commercial building.
High Density/Podium	T-5–T-6	Live-work units in a taller building with structured parking and liner retail, live-work, or flexhouses entering at street level.

Note: For the definition of the transect and a listing of the six transect zones, see page 28.

Figure 2-21 A typical building converted to live-work in Tribeca, New York City, with viable retail on the ground floor in this now-thriving, eminently walkable mixed-use neighborhood.

in an upward direction—toward what Vancouverites call "lawyer lofts."

Live/work units in warehouse conversions are almost invariably live-with spaces. Most are on a single level,

Figure 2-22 An artist's studio in a converted industrial building, heated with an industrial-grade ceiling-hung gas heater, lit mainly from skylights—an "internal" unit in a one-story building.

Figure 2-23 A typical loft at Union Street Studios in Oakland, a warehouse converted in 2000; the mezzanine is visible to the right of the picture. Designed by Thomas Dolan Architecture.

although if the ceilings are over fifteen feet, mezzanines are often added (see Figure 2-23).

The most common configuration of a warehouse conversion (see Figure 2-24) is a double-loaded corridor with units whose live portion is near (or even over) the corridor; the work space is usually near the large windows at the perimeter of the building (the missed opportunities for interaction that can occur in such a configuration is treated elsewhere in this book). Warehouse conversions are usually either work/live or live/work; as time passes, the former often evolves into the latter. Because warehouse conversions are often entitled and permitted as conversions of commercial space, they would virtually never be properly described as containing home occupation.

Home Office (T2–T5 Transect Zone)

Home office is a straightforward application of home occupation and is essentially congruent with it in the lexicon being established in this book. Home office generally occurs in an existing residence, making use of a former bedroom, study,

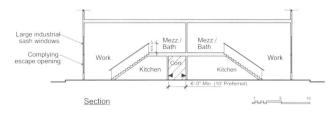

Figure 2-24 Section drawing of a typical double-loaded corridor design in a converted warehouse, in which the kitchen and bathrooms as well as mezzanines are concentrated at the core of the building and the taller, well-lit space is at the perimeter.

recreation room, garage, or other outbuilding, or it may be purpose-built into a new house or renovation.

Increasingly, home offices are being considered as an important element of new residential construction. A room or rooms located near the front door—or even accessed via a separate entrance—may be equipped with separate telephone/data lines and be adjacent to a bathroom that is accessible without entering the residence itself. Building to anticipate home office use allows client visits without disturbing the home environment and in effect creates a live-near unit whose work space is in the most public location in the residence.

Home office, like home occupation, is an *activity* as much as it is a project or building type. It represents the mainstreaming of live-work, and it has been made exponentially more common as a result of the rise of inexpensive small-office automation and the Internet, allowing anyone with a cordial phone manner, an attractive Web site, and a good business idea to compete with the most established brick-and-mortar business. Many who work at home for the first time (perhaps other than in college) are very self-conscious about the "professional" aspect of doing so. Most soon find that—on the contrary—they are the envy of their peers, clients, and vendors, who would rather be pursuing Zero-Commute Living themselves.

Isolation is a problem for anyone working at home alone, no matter what kind of live-work situation. This topic is treated in more detail in Chapter Five: Community. Beyond that, home office is the most likely project type to include families with children. However, nothing can render a home office intolerable like the presence of small children in one's work space (see Figure 2-25). For such an arrangement to work, a live-near arrangement is essential, and live-nearby is even better.

Townhouse Project Type, Synonym: Shophouse (T3–T5)

The attached townhouse is a form that has existed in cities for over five thousand years. It is a multilevel, single-household residence that is suited to home occupation and therefore only in rare circumstances to employees or walk-in trade. As such, it is arguably not required to be accessible to people with disabilities as of this writing because it is an independent single-family residence. It differs from the flexhouse, described below, in that there is no legal separation between residential and nonresidential uses. As is described in Chapter Seven: Building Codes, the latest model building code—

Figure 2-25 The author attempting to write this book at home while being tormented by his son Henry, age nine (with Nerf gun), and daughter Emily, age six.

the 2009 International Building Code—has for the first time recognized live-work as an occupancy that does not require a fire-rated separation between living and working portions. While this is an advantage to many, and benefits many types of live-with proximity types, the fact that the work space is not separated from the living portion in a shophouse means that, without significant alterations, it can be used only by one tenant or household; without a physical separation, there is little chance to rent out a portion, to split a unit with a partner, or to separate one's work à la live-near. Todd Zimmerman, who with his partner Laurie Volk contributed the Market portion of Chapter Four: Market, goes so far as to say: "This is a type that we have never recommended under any circumstances because it is utterly inflexible. Our objection (and stories of Certificates of Occupancy being rescinded when owners leased one or both shophouse spaces separately) was the genesis of the flexhouse concept."[1] An example of a shophouse, called in this case a "career home," can be seen in figure 2-26.

Tip
Wherever possible when constructing townhouse or street-facing live-work of any kind, build separated live-work (i.e., flexhouse live-near units with separate entrances for living and working spaces).

Flexhouse Project Type: A Building that Learns (T3–T5)

A flexhouse is a stand-alone building or unit, either attached or detached, that can accommodate a variety of uses, either as-built (through the use of fire doors) or through alteration,

Figure 2-26 "Career homes" in Richmond, California, which were built—with subsidies—to accommodate work activity on the ground floor without separation in the form of an enclosed stair or rated floor/ceiling from the living portion above. 2007.

such as removal of the first-floor platform that provides the privacy needed in a residential townhouse (see Chapter Three: Design, for urban design of townhouses and see Figure C-9 in the color folio for an example of a built flexhouse in Serenbe, Georgia).

Although not widely known by that name as yet, the flexhouse is one of the most common forms of live-work, particularly in the town centers of greenfield New Urbanist communities, where designers often refer to them as "live-works." The typical configuration is a downstairs work space with a retail-style storefront entry. To one side is typically an entry that leads immediately to the upstairs residence. There is also usually a door from the downstairs work space into the stairwell that leads up to the residence. Simply locking this door allows the upstairs resident—normally the owner—to rent out the downstairs work space. This project type is most akin to—in fact often is—living above the store.

A flexhouse may initially look like a storefront townhouse, or it may have residential fenestration and be raised a few feet above sidewalk level. Flexhouses are usually built with a bay width of twenty to twenty-five feet and a minimum of three bays (preferably between four and ten bays). Flexhouses are designed to be "buildings that learn"; that is, their use is expected to change and their configuration is flexible. Therefore, in the context of live-work, a flexhouse live-work unit might be a work/live or live/work use type in a live-near configuration, and it might be a dedicated retail space with a home occupation or a live/work configured as live-with

above. Flexhouses are ideally preapproved to change over time from all live-work to housing or live/work over retail, even to office over retail. The specifics of such preapproval will vary by location. See the Habersham Case Study in Chapter Four: Market, for a detailed treatment of flexhouses.

Flexhouses can be an excellent solution to the problem of an immature retail market in a new greenfield project, or in a neighborhood not yet "there." Stage One, full townhouses (see Figure 2-27), allows full occupancy even at street level, providing eyes on the street and revenue for the owner when retail might not be viable. Later, in Stage Two, as the retail market develops, flexhouses can be cut off at the knees, and the upstairs domain can be rented or sold separately while the downstairs becomes retail. This important project type is treated in detail in several later chapters, and is a subject of the sidebar on form-based coding in Chapter Six: Planning.

A unit type that has similar flexibility is a *maisonette*, a ground-floor multifamily unit with one or two levels, which, in addition to being accessed from common corridors, has an individual street entrance. Many of the great Manhattan apartment buildings feature maisonettes, some of which are now doctors' offices.[2]

Courtyard Live-Work (Transect Zones T-3–T-5)

Thomas Dolan Architecture was fortunate to be given the opportunity to introduce a new building type, the new construction live-work courtyard community. The first was South Prescott Village, begun in 1985 and completed in 1990. It constituted the first purpose-built multiunit live-work project built in the United States since before the Great Depression.

The idea for courtyard live-work is quite simple; however, it springs from needs that are not widely recognized. As previously noted, working at home alone can lead to a sense of isolation—just ask anyone who has done so for any length of time. Whether they are conscious of this fact or not, live-work residents need opportunities to interact—to step out of their units and cross paths with others (see Figure C-10 in the color folio).

The live-work courtyard community was conceived as a direct response to this need; the fact that Thomas Dolan Architecture was embarking on a project on a vacant lot gave the firm the freedom to design exactly what it felt was appropriate to serve the needs of artists, in this case, and more generally the needs of those who weren't going to commute and therefore were going to spend the vast majority of their time in this one place.

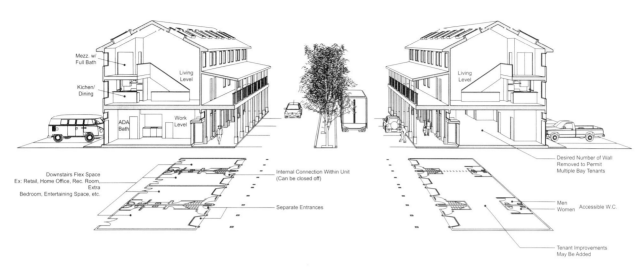

FLEXHOUSE
A BUILDING THAT LEARNS

STAGE ONE
Three-Level Townhouse
(Townhouse rented to one tenant, tenant
may sublet 1st floor with approval)

STAGE TWO
House Over Retail
(Upper-level housing rented or sold separately)

Mezz. w/
Full Bath

Kichen/
Dining

Living
Level

Living
Level

ADA
Bath

Work
Level

Downstairs Flex Space
Ex: Retail, Home Office, Rec. Room,
Extra
Bedroom, Entertaining Space, etc.

Internal Connection Within Unit
(Can be closed off)

Separate Entrances

Desired Number of Wall
Removed to Permit
Multiple Bay Tenants

Men
Women

Accessible W.C.

Tenant Improvements
May Be Added

Figure 2-27 Perspective drawing of a flexhouse, or "building that learns"; Stage One is rented as full townhouse tenancy; later, as the market matures to Stage Two, the downstairs bay(s) can be rented or sold to retail users and the upstairs units rented or sold as live-with or residential.
Thomas Dolan Architecture

Courtyard communities (see Figure 2-28), while often at a garden apartment or higher density, depart from the front yard/backyard paradigm of American settlement patterns. Instead, what prevails is a pattern of streets, courtyards, and gardens, all linked by passageways. Virtually all units open onto common courtyards in order to maximize opportunities for casual interaction as residents come and go. The design of courtyard communities is treated in greater detail as part of Chapter Three: Design, and Chapter Five: Community.

Urban Loft Complex (T4–T6)

In cities where the creative class is well represented, several factors converged in the mid- to late 1990s that resulted in the rise of urban loft construction as a developer-driven phenomenon (see Figure 2-29). In contrast, many early warehouse conversions were taken on by first-time, maverick

Figure 2-28 Filbert Court, a six-unit live-work courtyard community developed and built by the author in 1993; all units enter off of the courtyard (see aerial view in Figure C-26 in the color folio). Designed by Thomas Dolan Architecture.

Figure 2-29 A newly constructed loft building in the Dupont Circle neighborhood of Washington, D.C.

developers, many trained as artists and most of whom were not part of the mainstream development community.

As urban lofts were becoming a popular urban real estate "product," the increasing availability of inexpensive home-office automation and the rise of the Internet unleashed a torrent of home-based entrepreneurship. At about the same time, while developers large and small were becoming extremely interested in live-work, the stock of existing buildings that could be easily converted to live-work was nearly exhausted. Thus was born the new construction loft complex.

Urban loft complexes are sometimes located in existing buildings and are sometimes purpose-built from the ground up. Most are high-end condominiums, such as those depicted in figure 2-30 and elsewhere in this book. Few are aimed at or are affordable to artists. Many are permitted and represented as live-work but are primarily used and financed as residences. However, they differ from straight residential development in several important ways:

- They typically do allow work activity with few restrictions, including employees and sometimes walk-in trade.

- They are sometimes located in places that are not well served by normal residential amenities.

- Many are designed as relatively simple, if large units, and when designed properly they allow buyers opportunities to add their own identity to the spaces (e.g., keeping finishes very simple allows for personalization by the buyer). These are sometimes called hard lofts.

- In contrast, some lofts built from the ground up and sold as condominiums are fitted with expensive finishes and,

while they often contain design elements similar to hard lofts, such as exposed spiral coil ductwork and stained concrete floors, they are essentially spacious apartments. These are sometimes called soft lofts, lifestyle lofts, or even lawyer lofts (in Vancouver).

Urban loft complexes were a creature of the sustained real estate boom that characterized the 1990s and the first years of the twenty-first century. Condominiums are at present extremely difficult to finance, sell, or purchase with a down payment of less than 25 percent of purchase price. Virtually no new condominiums are being built in the United States as of this writing. It is possible that when construction and lending resumes, live-work may not qualify for residential mortgage financing as readily as in the past, but financing mechanisms likely will arise to meet what is apt to be a resurgent interest in urban living.

High Density/Podium (T5–T6)

Urban multiunit housing and mixed-use projects at densities of sixty dwelling units per acre and higher are typically built on top of structured parking, on so-called podiums. Podium projects throughout North America contain some or all live-work units, such as The Sierra in Oakland, California, a mixed live-work and residential project depicted in an overall view in figure 2-31. Most were built for the luxury condominium buyer. By definition, such buildings are served by elevators, and their units achieve some level of accessibility (unless they are multilevel). Flexhouse units or mezzanine live-with units both work well as street-level "liner units"

Figure 2-30 Several newly constructed lifestyle loft projects from the 1990s in an industrial district of San Francisco; their aggressively "designed" appearance sets them apart from their older, more utilitarian neighbors.

Figure 2-31 The Sierra, an eight-story mixed-use building occupying an entire city block in Oakland, California, is most notable for its liner live-work units, which are used for a variety of purposes. 2003. Designed by Kava Massih Architects.

Figure 2-32 A thriving corner store in a liner unit at The Sierra in Oakland, California. Kava Massih Architects, 2003.

(see liner retail in Figure 2-32) in podium projects surrounding parking structures, thereby enlivening the streetscape defined by these large buildings and hiding the parking within the building.

Other Definitions Related to Live-Work

Lifestyle Loft (Synonym: Lawyer Loft)

The lifestyle loft is a unit designated for live-work, usually a live-with unit used primarily for residence, that is typically but not always a condominium. This type of live-work tends to feature more expensive finishes in the units, common areas, elevator, lobby, and so on. Lifestyle lofts tend to revert to residential-only, and should not be located in active industrial districts in order to avoid conflicts with preexisting commercial/industrial uses. Instead, locate lifestyle lofts in areas well served by transit, retail, and other urban services.

Telecommuting

Telecommuting is the substitution of telecommunications for transportation in a decentralized and flexible work arrangement that allows part- or full-time employees or contract workers to work at home via a computer connected to the employer's data network. Telecommuting is suitable for well-defined and well-structured routine jobs with clear and fixed goals, but not for complex jobs with fuzzy or fluid objectives requiring personal contact.[3] The term *telecommuting* was coined by the U.S. aerospace engineer Jack Nilles in

1973 and popularized by the author Francis Kinsman in his 1987 book *The Telecommuter*. It is called telework in Europe and the U.K.

Telework Center (Synonym: Coworking)

A telework center is a facility that (1) provides workstations and other office facilities/services that an employee or contract worker utilizes (typically on a fee-for-use/service basis) for purposes of telecommuting and (2) an employer uses as a geographically convenient alternative work site for its users.[4]

Coworking

Coworking is a style of work that involves a shared working environment, usually an office, yet work activity is carried on by independent individuals who are usually not employed by the same organization.[5] Typically it is attractive to work-at-home professionals, independent contractors, or people who travel frequently and tend to work in relative isolation. Coworking is the social gathering of a group of people who may share values and are interested in the synergy that can happen from working with talented people in the same space.[6] Coworking is redefining the way some people work. The idea is simple: Those with workplace flexibility work better together than they do alone in facilities where independent workers cluster together in search of coffee, colleagues, conversation, and sometimes collaboration.[7]

According to French social science researchers Dominique Cardon and Christoph Aguiton, a coworking space is "a third place: something which is neither a desk in a company nor the domicile of the person; it is a kind of public place you can join when you want, with the guarantee of finding some social life and the chance of a useful exchange."[8]

Many coworking spaces are in urban locations or centers of communities, in part because independent workers who want contact with others gravitate to those settings. Coworking provides another means of bringing more people into places that can benefit from their presence and imagination.[9] A coworking center would be a natural combination with a live-work or residential use above or alongside it, thereby creating a live-work incubator.

Cohousing

Cohousing is a type of collaborative housing in which residents actively participate in the design and operation of their neighborhoods. Cohousing residents are consciously committed to living as a community, which is why the author refers to is as "capital C Community." The physical design of cohousing encourages both social contact and individual space. Private homes contain all the features of conventional homes, but residents also have access to extensive common facilities, such as open space, courtyards, a playground, and a common house.

Cohousing communities are usually designed as attached or single-family homes along one or more pedestrian streets or clustered around a courtyard. They range in size from seven to sixty-seven residences, with the majority of them housing twenty to forty households. Regardless of the size of the community, there are many opportunities for casual meetings between neighbors as well as for deliberate gatherings such as celebrations, clubs, and business meetings.

The common house is the social center of a community, with a large dining room and kitchen, lounge, recreational facilities, children's spaces, and frequently a guest room, workshop, and laundry room. Communities usually serve optional group meals in the common house at least two or three times a week.

The need for community members to take responsibility for common property builds a sense of working together, trust, and support. Because neighbors hold a commitment to a relationship with one another, almost all cohousing communities use consensus as the basis for group decision making.[10]

Cohousing is particularly well suited for live-work because its structure meets the need for interaction engendered by working at home; for that reason, many cohousing communities include residents who work at home.

Cohort Housing

While cohousing has become established in North America and parts of Europe over the past few decades, another form of housing has as its basic premise the idea that preexisting relationships, including extended families, faith-based groups, civic and cultural associations, and friendships, are the natural departure point when making housing and live-work choices, rather than the underlying organizational structure, as in cohousing. This fundamentally different "vernacular" approach is a concept defined by Jeremy Liu as cohort housing[11] and consists of families expressing their community and sense of belonging in the way they live. According to Liu, cohort housing, then, is facilitative rather than prescriptive, in that it allows relationships that already exist to be expressed in housing and live-work choices.

Many extended families, often from immigrant and low-income communities, have pooled resources to buy homes in close proximity to one another. Older members of the family often look after children, enabling both parents to work without child care expenses. In Liu's idea of cohort housing, family, friendship and organic ties support the sustainability of the community. Physical proximity enables cohort members to rely on one another for day-to-day needs, such as cooking meals, running errands, or property maintenance—and, in the case of live-work, for work-related collaboration and mutual assistance

The author has lived and worked in cohort housing for the majority of the past 28 years, first in the former Italian family compound he occupied with a cohort of friends and more recently the James Avenue Compound described in the case study in Chapter Six: Planning. There he has certainly learned that social cohesion and natural community are powerful assets and that the interactions that occur so easily in cohort housing are a natural match for the life of a live-worker.

Tip

Cohort live-work is a natural fit due to its preexisting community and the inherent need of live-workers for interaction, which will no doubt occur if the opportunities to do so are designed according to the principles laid out in this book.

Zero-Commute Living™

Zero-Commute Living[12] is a view of human settlements that sees the need for transportation as a measure of dysfunction in planning and therefore advocates the creation of urban places that minimize reliance on the automobile. Zero-Commute Housing is the ultimate expression of Zero-Commute Living.

Zero-Commute Housing™

Zero-Commute Housing[13] is a synonym for live-work.

District

A district is a bounded portion of a city whose land use is usually a monoculture set aside for a specific use (e.g., a commercial/industrial district, warehouse district, railyard, airport, etc).

Neighborhood

A neighborhood is a compact, walkable mixed-use place served by retail, transit, parks, and other urban services. Live-work has frequently been instrumental in transforming districts into neighborhoods. The catalyst for this process has often been districts' initial colonization by artists.

Live-Work Neighborhood

A live-work neighborhood is neighborhood in which many of the people who live there also work within five minutes of where they live and can meet most of their daily needs within a ten-minute walk of home, workplace, or live-work unit. Synonyms: complete neighborhood, lifelong neighborhood, naturally occurring retirement community (NORC— because when you get old and lose your driver's license, you can walk to everything you need).

New Urbanism

A growing movement, New Urbanism recognizes compact, mixed-use, walkable, connected, pedestrian-scaled neighborhoods as the building blocks of sustainable communities and regions. The charter of New Urbanism articulates the movement's principles and defines the essential qualities of urban places from the scale of the region to the individual building.

Smart Growth

The term *Smart Growth* is a synonym—although more policy-oriented—for New Urbanism, focused growth, and sustainable development. According to Smart Growth America's Web site:

> We believe that the American people deserve healthy cities, towns and suburbs; homes that are both affordable and close to jobs and activities; fewer hours in traffic and more opportunities to enjoy recreation and natural areas; air and water of the highest quality; and a landscape our children can be proud to inherit. We believe that ordinary citizens deserve a much greater say, and better options, in choosing their communities' future. (www.smartgrowthamerica.org)

Form-based Coding

Form-based coding is a method of regulating development to achieve a specific urban form. Form-based codes create a predictable public realm primarily by controlling physical form, with a lesser focus on land use, through city or county regulations.[14]

Tip

Whenever planning for live-work, make use of form-based codes as described in the sidebar in Chapter 6: Planning.

The Transect

The Urban-to-Rural Transect (see Figure 2-33) is a tool for understanding and planning urban development devised by Duany Plater-Zyberk (DPZ), promulgated in the SmartCode and other form-based codes and widely adopted by New Urbanists and others. Its marvelous simplicity and intuitiveness make it an excellent framework for devising plans and codes. Figure 2-33 depicts the six transect zones, corresponding to increasingly intense urban development as they progress upward from T-1 (natural zone) to T-6 (urban core). Transect

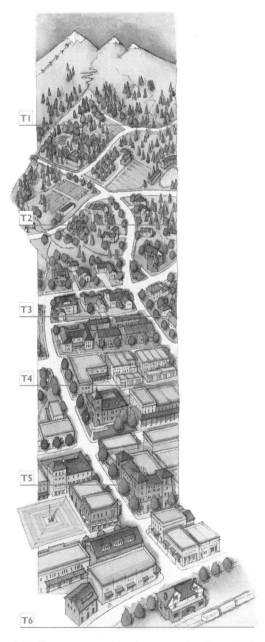

Figure 2-33 The transect and its six zones, T1 to T6, as depicted in a form-based code for Flagstaff, Arizona, by Opticos Design, Inc., 2009.

zones are used to label live-work types and their locations in numerous passages in this book.

> The six *transect zones* as defined in the SmartCode are:
>
> **T1 Natural Zone** consists of lands approximating or reverting to a wilderness condition, including lands unsuitable for settlement due to topography, hydrology, or vegetation.
>
> **T2 Rural Zone** consists of sparsely settled lands in open or cultivated states. These include woodland, agricultural land, grassland, and irrigable desert. Typical buildings are farmhouses, agricultural buildings, cabins, and villas.
>
> **T3 Sub-Urban Zone** consists of low-density residential areas, walkable to higher T-zones that have some mixed use. Home occupations and outbuildings are permitted. Planting is naturalistic and setbacks are relatively deep. Blocks may be large and the roads irregular to accommodate natural conditions.
>
> **T4 General Urban Zone** consists of a mixed-use but primarily residential urban fabric. It may have a wide range of building types: single, sideyard, and rowhouses. Setbacks and landscaping are variable. Streets with curbs and sidewalks define medium-size blocks.
>
> **T5 Urban Center Zone** consists of higher-density mixed-use buildings that accommodate retail, offices, live-works, and apartments. It has a tight network of streets, with wide sidewalks, continuous street tree planting, and buildings set close to the sidewalks.
>
> **T6 Urban Core Zone** consists of the highest density and height, with the greatest variety of uses, and civic buildings of regional importance. It may have larger blocks; streets have continuous street tree planting, and buildings are set close to wide sidewalks. Typically only large towns and cities have an Urban Core Zone.
>
> A *district* is an area of land that is used for a single purpose, such as a college campus, an airport, or an industrial park. Warehouse districts often transition into live-work neighborhoods, usually T4 or T5.

"T-zones have implications for architectural and urban form not so different from the old maxim for clothes, "Don't wear brown in town." A tower appropriate for "the city" doesn't fit on a market square in the Cotswolds. A thatched-roof cottage doesn't work

in Piccadilly Circus. A garden wall is different in the Cotswolds than in Mayfair; so are the pavements (sidewalks), the streetlamps on the pavement and the width of the pavement. And none of them are appropriate in the wildest reaches of the Scottish Highlands.[15]

Work-Use Intensities in Live-Work

The next categories, Open, Limited, and Restricted, refer to the different types of work-use intensities that can occur in live-work units.

Open *commercial*

Open work-use intensity activities are those permitted most often in work/live, as the most commercially oriented form of live-work. In an Open work environment, employees and walk-in trade are usually permitted (along with compliance with the Americans with Disabilities Act [ADA]); noise is relatively unregulated; heavy machinery, large work products, and hazardous materials may be present; and the work space may be served by a freight elevator and robust utility services.

Limited

Limited work-use intensity activities are those permitted most often in live/work, a more residentially oriented form of live-work. In a Limited work environment, employees and walk-in trade may be permitted (along with ADA compliance); noise is regulated; heavy machinery and objects are unlikely to be present; and hazardous materials may be present in lesser quantities than in an Open work environment, more likely when the unit's work space is separated from the residential portion, as in a live-near or live-nearby. Utilities and other services depend on the specific nature of the anticipated work but are more likely to resemble those that serve commercial establishments.

Restricted *residential*

Work activities permitted in home occupation are Restricted work-use intensity, and they are intended to be entirely compatible with and accessory to a residential environment. In a Restricted work environment, employees and walk-in trade are rarely permitted; noise generation is discouraged if allowed at all; and heavy machinery, objects, and hazardous materials are not typically present. Utilities and other services are of a residential nature.

CHAPTER 3

Designing Live-Work Meeting Its Unique Needs

An understanding of what makes live-work unique—that it is a combination of residential and commercial and is different from either single-use type—is essential for a designer of live-work. Living and working in the same place—or designing a building in which this proximity of activities is likely to occur—necessitates shifts in a designer's approach. Live-work units have varying relationships of proximity between living and working, as expressed in their form. Units can be designed to accommodate work activities that dominate the unit (work/live) or to host low-impact work activities in a residence (home occupation). This chapter draws from the author's quarter century of experience designing live-work and addresses the many possibilities in live-work design.

To design live-work, one needs to consider its role in context, even if one is designing a single live-work unit. Whether it is a loft renovation, infill, or greenfield, the site's relationship to the preexisting context and the effect that the introduction of live-work might have on the context are important to consider. Likewise, when undertaking strategic planning for a city, town, or other jurisdiction, live-work's unique place in the repertoire of building types must be well understood. In a live-work complex of many units or a series of live-work row houses or flexhouses, one must take into account their effect on the surrounding community.

The Genesis of Live-Work Design

When the author started designing live-work for artists in the mid-1980s, their resounding request was "light, space, and access." Artists wanted great natural light to paint or otherwise work by, meaning north light windows or translucent skylights that didn't create hot spots (see Figure 3-1). They wanted lots of space, meaning high ceilings and unobstructed large floor areas (see Figure 3-2). And they wanted easy access to move large art objects and art materials in and out of their units and the building, meaning large doors, wide corridors, and big freight elevators, or what are called straight stairs in New York loft terminology (see Figure 3-3).

Most early artists' lofts were live-with spaces—that is, early in the time of their evolution and often early in the life of an artist. When you're young and risk-oblivious, you don't mind having the turpentine at one end of your table and the olive oil at the other end. This is what some regulators call "dual-purpose space," as seen in Figure 3-4.

Being an artist has been called the most socially acceptable form of living outside the mainstream. It is also an occupation in which one's "life" and one's "work" are relatively indistinguishable; therefore, a single space where it's all mixed up—sometimes to the chagrin of planning and building officials—makes complete sense.

Figure 3-1 Great light. Ocean View Lofts, Berkeley, California, 1993. Designed by Thomas Dolan Architecture.

Figure 3-2 Space. South Prescott Village, Oakland, California, 1988. Designed by Thomas Dolan Architecture.

Even young artists get older, though, and begin to want a bit of separation from their work. The materials they use might be somewhat hazardous, such as oil paints or epoxy resins; there might be a partner or spouse who doesn't connect with the work; or the work might involve a studio assistant, client visits, or other circumstances where the privacy of the living portion becomes compromised. At this point, some separation becomes a good idea, giving rise to the live-near proximity type. The separation might be a wall—glazed, as in Figure 3-5—or a floor ceiling.

In the latter case, one's "commute" is a staircase, and it is really quite a different experience from having everything in one space, or "common atmosphere," as building officials label it.

In early live-work, and in some that is built today, the living portion's residential facilities tend to be minimal. The author's approach when designing live-with spaces is to enclose as little space as possible, to preserve an open plan whenever possible, and not to provide any enclosed storage space except a clothes closet. In New York and other big East Coast cities, it was important to provide cabinets for dishes and closets for clothes, because in the hot summer months

one opened all the big windows in one's loft and turned the whole place into a sort of sleeping porch. It could be bright and noisy at night, but one got used to that. However, a fine layer of soot covered everything (at least it did in the 1970s)—hence the need for cabinets and closets.

An important feature of many high-ceilinged lofts is a mezzanine (see Figure 3-6), or sleeping loft. It is an efficient way to use some of the volume of the space, and it provides a modicum of detachment from the main space. The city of Oakland, California—an example this book will return to often—has described and coded three types of mezzanines: regular, sleeping, and built-in sleeping bunk. (See Chapter Seven: Building Codes.)

In many live-work spaces, the primary delineator of space is not walls but variations in ceiling height. In a typical loft, there are three spatial experiences: (1) being in the double-height work space, (2) being in the more intimate space below the loft—often the place where the kitchen and eating area is, and (3) being in the loft, also intimate but with a view into and a sense of the spaciousness of the unit. These three types of experiences will be illustrated later in this chapter.

Figure 3-3 Straight stairs. Tribeca, New York City, allow large objects to be easily carried in and out.

Figure 3-4 Dual-purpose space (i.e., space that is used for multiple uses and frequently shifts uses) is common in artists' lofts and other live-with spaces.

User Needs and Live-Work Design

A list of qualities that are unique to live-work and who a typical live-work user is presented next.

1. You don't commute, which has implications for your daily life and choices. For example, a live-work user tends not to ever drive at rush hour and therefore does not add to the need for peak-hour road capacity. Furthermore, the time you are not spending on your commute is available to be used in other ways, be it time with family, with friends, or even working more and working when you choose to work (see Figure C-11 in the color folio).

2. You're in your unit or thereabouts most of the time and therefore care more about that place. Live-work is a way of "putting our lives back together," and choosing not to commute is often accompanied by an intimate connection with that one place where you both live and work. Being more place-centered tends to lead to a greater community awareness and involvement, allowing you to connect better to your community if opportunities for interaction on

Figure 3-5 Use of a glazed wall as a separation between living and work portions of a live-near unit. South Prescott Village, Oakland, California, 1988. Designed by Thomas Dolan Architecture.

Figure 3-6 A mezzanine as viewed from the main level of a live-with unit. South Prescott Village, Oakland, California, 1988. Designed by Thomas Dolan Architecture.

Figure 3-7 Isolation, one of the hazards of working alone at home, engenders a need for interaction. Ocean View Lofts, Berkeley, California, 1993. Designed by Thomas Dolan Architecture.

foot are nearby, such as in a compact, mixed-use, walkable neighborhood. You are no longer simply sleeping at home and working somewhere else.

3. Isolation is a potential problem (see Figure 3-7). Most of us derive social sustenance and stimulation from our workplaces. However, the majority of live-workers tend to work alone or with a very few employees. They are therefore not out on the rialto or mixing at the water cooler and thus risk feelings of isolation. Opportunities for casual interaction are important to counter this hazard, a subject treated more fully in Chapter Five: Community.

4. Your unit serves a dual purpose: it must include aspects and features of both a residence and a place of work. You might have employees, you might have walk-in trade, or you might have neither or both. Your work-life balance is likely to shift over time, and your unit should be flexible enough to allow such a shift. The flexhouse addresses this need through its ability to change uses easily; however, all

live-work units embody inherent flexibility as they accommodate both life and work.

5. You are likely self-employed, an entrepreneur starting or running a business. Self-employed people are initiators, living the American dream of being one's own boss. Live-work meets an important need to accommodate the incubation of small business in a way that is subsidized by its affordability and therefore reduced risk. The myriad types of live-work units and projects are well suited to different points along "the Incubator Cycle." For example, one might start with an idea in a home occupation setting (see Figure 3-8), then grow into a live-with loft that has more space, and then perhaps shift to a storefront in a live-near location.

At any point along the way, one might find oneself comfortable in a stable business at that scale and stay put (see figure 3-9); however, one might eventually grow to require an entirely separate work space at another location. In

Figure 3-8 Home occupation, the beginning of the incubator cycle in a converted garage, live-nearby space completed in 2003. Designed by Jennifer Cooper Designer.

any event, live-work plays an important role in incubating small businesses, and in many cases the flexibility of live-work design allows one to spend a longer duration of time in a given space, which means less frequent moves and fewer disruptions to one's business. While not attempted as of yet to this author's knowledge, a formal live-work incubator project would seem a timely and appropriate idea.

6. You match almost every demographic except (usually) families with kids. While there is no overarching reason why live-work could not accommodate families with children, the fact that some are located in gritty urban neighborhoods where schools and playgrounds are not necessarily of high quality, or are located in townhouse or multiunit configurations without much play space, means that most live-work users are either younger urban pioneers, childless and middle aged, or empty nesters. It is also a fact that trying to run a business or get any kind of work done is difficult when children, particularly small ones, are in the same space. At the very least, one needs a live-near unit if children are to be present in a live-work space.

7. You like to add your own identity to your space. While all occupants of a residence will furnish their homes to their own taste, the spaciousness of many live-work spaces and the nature of live-workers tends to result in far more alterations to spaces, such that if one is to come back and visit a project five years after its initial occupancy, even identical units will look and feel quite different. For this reason, the author has found it most workable to hold off on making or acting upon finish decisions, as users will prefer to do so themselves (see Figure 3-10).

Figure 3-10 A newly remodeled loft, ready for its occupants to add their own identity; the wood floor was preexisting. California Cotton Mills Studios, Oakland, 2005. Designed by Thomas Dolan Architecture.

Figure 3-9 A storefront live-work building that contains all three live-work proximity types, enabling great flexibility over time, 2003 (see James Avenue Live-Work Compound Case Study, Chapter Six). Designed by Thomas Dolan Architecture and Jennifer Cooper Designer.

Project Types

Renovation versus New Construction

Renovation for live-work involves several important design processes:

1. Determining whether the building is well suited for live-work. Factors to consider include:

   - Can ceiling heights accommodate mezzanines, which usually require a minimum of fifteen feet clear (see Figure 3.11)?
   - Is the structural grid of existing columns or trusses wide enough to coincide with unit demising walls? Sixteen feet should be considered a minimum and twenty feet or more is preferred (see Figure 3-12).
   - Is the building already sprinklered?
   - If in a seismic zone, has the building been retrofitted? If not, does your structural engineer see a huge expense?
   - Is the building arranged on its lot so that both exiting and bedroom emergency escape and rescue can be

Figure 3-12 A twenty-foot truss spacing adapts well to live-work at Willow Court in Oakland, California, , where each unit was defined by a truss bay (see case study in this chapter). 2007. Designed by Thomas Dolan Architecture.

accommodated? A building that faces onto more than one street makes this essential design task easier.

2. Assessing the design of the building in terms of any relaxed building codes that exist for renovating live-work:

   - Likely the building will be considered a "change of occupancy," which means that it will be required to conform in most respects to today's building code; a code analysis of the proposed project is a valuable exercise early in the process of site assessment and due diligence. (See Chapter Seven: Building Codes.)
   - The relaxed codes might make the project affordable enough to be less expensive than demolition and new construction, which may or may not be permitted.

Tip

Always perform a detailed code analysis of your proposed project early in the due diligence process and meet with local officials to determine your live-work code status and options.

Figure 3-11 Headroom is provided for mezzanines between the two trusses to the left. Willow Court, Oakland, California, 2007. Designed by Thomas Dolan Architecture.

3. Making use of the existing building's essential qualities while adapting it to a great live-work scheme. For example, the building may be well suited to cutting through the roof in one or more areas to create courtyards (see Figure 3-13) that can also serve as exit courts under the building code.

The farther a building's current configuration is from what the desired end product is, the more expensive the project will be. Conversely, if the building is easily demised and served by a relatively simple exit regime, it will be less expensive and easier to convert to live-work.

New construction, however, affords greater freedom (see Figure 3-14), is usually more expensive than renovation—although not always—and of course must conform to all of today's codes, including any live-work provisions that might exist in the applicable jurisdiction. Most new construction live-work does not "pencil" as rental, so it will likely be a for-sale project unless subsidized by other elements of a project in anticipation of, for example, its "flexing" into housing over retail.

Figure 3-14 South Prescott Village in Oakland, California, the first new construction live-work artists' studios built since the Great Depression, 1988. Designed by Thomas Dolan Architecture.

Rental versus For Sale

Building a rental live-work project may or may not differ greatly in overall design from a for-sale project, and in fact most savvy developers record a condominium map on their rental projects so that they can sell units at a later time if they so desire rather than having to undergo a cumbersome condominium conversion with sitting tenants—often a difficult process.

Rental projects tend to be built with fewer upscale finishes; durability is key. Most rentals do not include dishwashers. Most landlords, however, do provide refrigerators. A rental project is more likely to have a common laundry than a condominium project, which typically has washer/dryer hookups within each unit, although a common laundry—like mailboxes and other facilities—can be designed as a great opportunity to encourage interaction.

Tenants are more transient and therefore more tolerant of imperfections in a project, although they of course can and will call the landlord if there are problems. In contrast, buyers of condominiums in some states have outsized powers to make the developer's life miserable through construction-defect claims. Live-work buyers are literally invested in their units, and, if they do live and work there, they will demand a high-quality environment, because they will spend the vast majority of their time there.

Figure 3-13 A convivial courtyard carved out of the existing building form also serves as an exit court. Willow Court, Oakland, California, 2007. Designed by Thomas Dolan Architecture.

Tip
When building rental live-work, keep the finishes minimal and remember your tenants' desire to add their own identity; therefore, *the less you do, the more you give.*

Live-work buyers are more likely to need:

- Secure parking
- Nearby neighborhood services
- An attractive lobby, elevator, and corridors if the project is so designed
- Open space that encourages informal interaction and is pleasant to be in
- A well-finished unit, including kitchen and bath(s)

Therefore, design of a for-sale live-work project must evidence an awareness of these special needs and be drawn and detailed in a highly professional manner.

Artists' Lofts versus "Lifestyle Lofts"

Artists' lofts are usually rentals, are usually in renovations of existing buildings, and are more likely to accommodate true live-work. Artists and other similarly situated individuals are well served by spaces that are simple and minimally finished (see Figure 3-15), leaving much to the imagination and hard work of the tenant.

Figure 3-16 This lifestyle loft in a renovated warehouse has been staged for real estate showing purposes. Willow Court, Oakland, California, 2007. Designed by Thomas Dolan Architecture.

Figure 3-15 A simple artists' live-work space at Dutch Boy Studios, Oakland, California, renovated and legalized between 1979 and 2011. Designed by Thomas Dolan Architecture.

Such tenants do not need multiple bathrooms, expensive light fixtures, or hardwood floors (unless they exist). They are more interested in light, space, and access, as inexpensively as possible, and they are particularly receptive to common facilities and interactive open space.

In contrast, lifestyle lofts—sometimes called soft lofts—are usually for sale (see Figure 3-16) and often located in new buildings. Finishes are more expensive, appliances are more upscale, and living is emphasized in the space unless it is a flexhouse or other live-near configuration. Buyers of lifestyle lofts—typically, although not always—are less receptive to common facilities; many have most recently lived in a suburban residence or other more private situation.

Work/Live and Home Occupation

True work/live is—as of this writing—almost exclusively located in renovated warehouses being rented to artists and other similarly situated individuals. If there is to be walk-in trade or employees, either will require accessibility, including a level-in entrance, accessible water closet on the main level, and possibly accessible parking spaces.

Home occupation, when located in a residence, has unique needs. A quiet place to work, often separated from the remainder of the house, is desirable. Any residence or live-work space is subject to an "intimacy gradient,"[1] whereby the most public part is at the entrance and the farther into the unit that one penetrates, the more private the spaces become. An understanding of intimacy gradient can inform the design of a home occupation in this way: Locate the work space near the main entrance to the residence, accompany it with waiting space nearby, and locate a bathroom immediately adjacent to the work space. The result is a situation where a client or other work-related visitor does not go any farther into the house than is necessary, and the intimacy and privacy of the residence is preserved while serving the more public needs of the work activity. A variation on this design strategy is to provide a dedicated entry for the work space and again create a "public zone" just inside this entrance.

It is also possible to give a bathroom its own intimacy gradient, a handy trick when there is only one in a given unit. As shown in Figure 3-17, the more public part of the room is essentially a water closet, containing a lavatory and toilet. Behind a pocket door are a second sink and the tub or shower where the dirty towels and scattered toothbrushes can remain.

Tip
Design home occupation so the work portion either includes a separate entrance or is configured so that any client or other work-related visitor only goes as far into the unit as necessary, preserving the privacy and sanctity of the home.

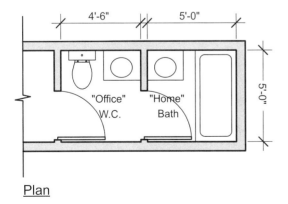

Plan

Figure 3-17 Drawing of a two-part bathroom that allows its front portion to serve the work function of the unit, while behind the pocket door is the bath—the more domestic function. Design originated by David Baker + Partners Architects.

Design Elements in Live-Work

Residential and Work Space Facilities

The needs of a live-work resident are relatively consistent throughout the range of units, tempered only by quality and level of finish and expense. In order to reside in a live-work unit, one needs:

- Heat (and air-conditioning in some places), at least in the living portion. A good inexpensive heat source in a moderate climate is a direct-vent gas-fired wall heater. Such units are approved for use in bedrooms—and by extension open loft spaces—because they derive their combustion air from outside. Radiant heaters—often ceiling-hung—are a good choice for large work spaces (see Figure 7-20).

- Hot and cold water. A water heater will need to be located somewhere in the unit, or—in larger projects—hot water can be supplied by a central boiler with a pump that circulates it through all the units.

- A toilet and lavatory sink.

- A shower or bathtub.

Tip
An inexpensive shower that can also be accessible for the disabled can be constructed on any area with a concrete floor: Simply slope the floor to a drain and provide proper clearances and a bench, and of course a shower head. Be sure your building department will allow such a shower without a curb.

- A kitchen including a sink, a refrigerator (supplied or not), and a range (supplied or not), plus some cabinets and small appliance electrical outlets.

- A dishwasher if it is an ownership unit.

- A garbage disposal (if no active composting program is available).

- A ducted range hood. This is a very good idea although not always required, especially if the kitchen is in the same common atmosphere as the sleeping area, where the absence of an exhaust fan can result in moisture problems and discomfort.

- Simple industrial-style ceiling fans in all high-ceilinged spaces.

Tip
Ceiling fans are an inexpensive and effective way to destratify the air in a tall space. Most have a switch that reverses the rotation, allowing warm air to be conducted upward in summer and downward in winter.

- A sleeping area: usually a minimum of seven by ten feet, with direct visual access to an emergency escape and rescue opening.
- Laundry hookups (either within each unit or a common laundry).

Building and Housing Codes Issues (see Chapter Seven: Building Codes, for more detail)

- Emergency escape and rescue (EER) opening(s) that serve every sleeping area (see Figure 3-18). The building code specifies the size and location of such openings. Most live-work codes have relaxed this requirement to allow EER openings to be some distance from the sleeping area as long as the sleeping area is visible from the outside of the opening.
- One or more exit doors out of the unit (depending on its size), leading to an exit path and in turn to a public way.
- Accessibility for people with disabilities if code so requires.
- Natural light via windows or glazing in doors or skylights (usually 8 percent of the floor area of each room).
- Natural ventilation via operable doors, windows, or skylights (usually 4 percent of the floor area of each room).
- Demising walls and floor/ceilings shared with other units that are one-hour rated and meet minimum noise attenuation standards (i.e., STC 50 and IIC 50; see Chapter Seven: Building Codes).
- A living portion that is not less than 265 square feet, or as specified by local housing code; space shared with the work portion can reduce this number in live-with units.

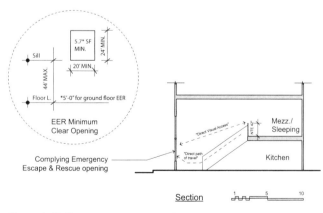

Figure 3-18 Emergency escape and rescue in a live-work unit, which permits the escape opening to be outside the sleeping area as long as the sleeping area is visible from the escape opening.

Work Area Needs, Which Will Vary Depending on Work Activity

- A "unit identity" sign holder mounted outside each unit in a multiunit building, capable of being customized by a live-worker while providing some design unity to the project.
- A cleanup sink, often a fiberglass laundry type with hot and cold hose-bibb type faucets to allow a hose connection.

Tip

A cleanup sink together with a washer/dryer hookup (with gas for a dryer) allow flexibility for a new unit (with kitchen) to be created later.

- A 220-volt receptacle, varying from thirty to seventy watts depending on expected uses (e.g., kilns, furnaces, or even arc welding).
- Robust electrical service size, one hundred to two hundred amps per unit.
- Enhanced floor-loading capacity beyond the forty or fifty pounds per square foot typical in more residentially oriented live-work, usually accommodated most easily on ground-floor or dock-high concrete slabs. Design for heavy uses should be slab-on-grade in a new building. Work with the building you've got. It will be a strong determinant of what type of units you will end up with.
- When your target market is artists, art access openings (see South Prescott Village case study) able to accommodate an eight-foot by eight-foot stretched canvas, and continuing that dimension along the exit path out to the street.
- Plentiful natural light admitted by windows and skylights.
- Mechanized hoists or simple pulleys for lowering large objects down from exterior art access openings, if such are present.
- Separately metered work space (gas and electric, usually not water); good for tax returns (think: home office) and useful if one wants to rent out a part of one's live-near or live-nearby unit; flexibility is greatly enhanced by separate meters.
- Exhaust fans that exceed what would normally be required by code.
- Oversized mail boxes and a large package drop box; possibly space for proprietary boxes, such as FedEx and UPS (see Clocktower Lofts case study).

- Office amenities: dual phone/data jacks, server location where all cables "home run," capability to separate upstairs living portion and downstairs work space networks and phone lines (in live-near or otherwise separated units), multiple fourplex receptacles on surge-protected circuits.

Level of Finishes in a Live-Work Unit

As was discussed earlier, deciding where to spend money and where not to spend it in live-work is best informed by the saying: "The less you do, the more you give." Unless what is desired are turnkey, move-in lifestyle lofts, allowing the eventual occupant as many choices as possible works well for all concerned. The end user wants to add his or her own identity to that unit and will feel deprived if the developer makes those decisions by installing, for example, a hardwood floor or expensive light fixtures. Some developers have even gone so far as to set up design centers that allow buyers to make finish choices for themselves, often in the form of upgrades (developers call them profit centers).

Why the need to add one's identity is especially true for live-work has something to do with the entrepreneurial, do-it-myself attitude of many live-workers. Flexibility is key: leave the choices to the buyer or tenant. Some examples of doing less include:

- Painted plywood (see Figure 3-19) and concrete floors or structural wood with a clear finish, such as two-by-six tongue-and-groove mezzanine floors.
- Porcelain keyless light fixtures, which cost less than two dollars (plus mirror-back bulb, a simple but effective choice) with rheostats where appropriate.
- Basic kitchen cabinets (see Figure 3-20) and bathroom lavatories.

Tip

Provide switched fourplex electrical receptacles spaced throughout the work space ceiling, thereby giving the tenant the opportunity to choose and supply his or her own lighting.

- Spiral stairs to unit mezzanines (see Figure 3-21). They are sculptural and evocative but small children, the elderly, and dogs hate them and they are difficult to carry things on. Always provide an open loft/hoisting option if spiral stairs are used, for move-in/move-out.
- Durable, simple finishes, such as varnished windowsills.

Figure 3-19 Giving more choice by doing less: painted plywood floors in new construction in a live-with unit at Ocean View Lofts, Berkeley, California, 1993. Designed by Thomas Dolan Architecture.

- Smooth wall Sheetrock (don't do skip trowel or orange peel, especially in work spaces).
- The ultimate in no-frills is called *shell space* (see Figure 3-22), sometimes called a hard loft, which is allowed in some cities and is treated more fully in Chapter Seven, Building Codes: fire-taped walls; stubbed-out utilities; cover plates on electrical (trim out); doors in, all life safety features complete on the building that contains the units (sprinklers, exit path, etc.). Note: Obtaining a certificate of occupancy (C of O) is usually not possible in a shell space until the appliances and fixtures are installed.

Having said all of this, in order to make spaces both special and attractive to the market, design elements that might enhance some of their basic functional components include:

Figure 3-20 Basic, durable kitchen cabinets located below a sleeping mezzanine at Henry Street Studios, Oakland, California, 1987. Designed by Thomas Dolan Architecture.
Photo Credit: Larry Harrel.

- Exposed trusses (see Figure 3-23)
- Exposed roof structure (see Figure C-12 in the color folio) and mezzanine structure (see Figure 3-24), such as two-by-six tongue-and-groove decking on 4x or 6x joists
- Well-placed, high-quality skylights and windows, as seen in Figure 3-25

Accommodating and Relating to the Outside World

Employees

Nonresident employees are permitted in most live-work units or, if it is a live-near, in the work area. The work area will need to be accessible for disabled persons, including an accessible water closet (men's and women's if there are more than four employees). In some live-work buildings, the accessible bathrooms are in a common location that can be shared by all.

Figure 3-21 Think twice: Spiral stairs, while space-saving when viewed in plan, are not universally loved. California Cotton Mills Studios, Oakland, 2005. Designed by Thomas Dolan Architecture.

Walk-in Trade versus Client Visits by Appointment

The primary break point for doing business with others outside the unit is when the trade is walk-in, à la retail, or employees. It is then considered a commercial establishment. If all client visits are by appointment and there are few or no employees, most building officials rule that accessibility is not triggered, although other provisions of the Americans with Disabilities Act (ADA) might do so (see Chapter Seven: Building Codes).

Parking: Open Commercial Access versus Residential Privacy and Security

In live-work, as in many other types of development, form often follows parking. Parking requirements are treated in Chapter Six: Planning, but here we examine where the parking is located, and for whom. In townhouse live-work, it is often properly located to the rear of the lot, in either

Figure 3-22 A live-work shell space ready for finishing out by the future tenant at Dutch Boy Studios, Oakland, California, 2009. Designed by Thomas Dolan Architecture.

a detached garage—perhaps with granny flat above or as a part of the ground floor of the unit, again accessed from

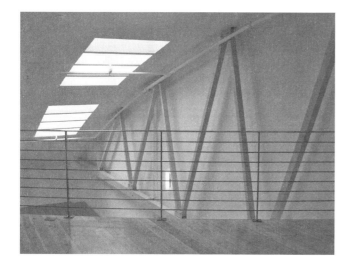

Figure 3-23 Exposed trusses can showcase a building's inherent nature; for aesthetic and functional reasons, it is usually not wise to bury them in the demising walls, which often contain plumbing vent stacks. Willow Court, Oakland, California, 2007.

Figure 3-24 The exposed underside of the mezzanine makes an excellent ceiling and honestly expresses its structure. California Cotton Mills Studios, Oakland, 2005. Designed by Thomas Dolan Architecture.

the rear. Good urban design practice dictates that locating a townhouse garage entrance on the street front of the building detracts from the quality of pedestrian life on the street. Most, but not all, live-work townhouses (twenty-two feet is a good working minimum) are wide enough to barely accommodate a two-car garage and a rear person-door or, in the case of a detached garage, a walkway alongside the garage.

In larger live-work buildings, parking is occasionally on surface lots, but typically it is in a parking structure, preferably hidden by liner flexhouse units or retail. An issue that is unique to live-work—although it applies also to housing over retail—is the dichotomy between the need for public access to parking for commercial uses and the need for residents

Figure 3-25 Well-placed skylights and windows are essential in live-work; if you need electric light before the sun goes down, something is not right. Filbert Court, Oakland, California, 1993. Designed by Thomas Dolan Architecture.

to have secure—usually gated or fenced—parking. In most situations, this problem is resolved by accommodating the residents in the building's garage and the customers with on-street parking.

Tip

Within a parking garage that serves residents and commercial users, provide surface, non-lift parking for the commercial users' cars and "puzzle system" Parklift® for residents, which provides gates and therefore security for their vehicles while allowing open access to the commercial parking.

Regular employees who drive to work pose a more lasting demand that must be handled. If the likely number of employees is anticipated correctly, extra parking can be included in the building, and the employees will have access to the same security controls as the residents. If large numbers of customers are anticipated, off-site parking—either surface or structured—must supplement on-street parking. Most larger projects that might generate significant employee or customer parking demand are subject to environmental review and include parking and traffic studies that recommend the number of parking stalls for each use. As is discussed in Chapter Six: Planning, examination of time-shared parking opportunities should be a part of any live-work or mixed-use parking and traffic study.

Design for Community

Making a Place That Is More Than the Sum of the Number of Units

As is noted elsewhere in this book, turning a warehouse for things into a warehouse for people is not this author's preferred design strategy. Likewise, when it comes to flexhouse live-work or townhouses, Andrés Duany said it best, as he often does: "Who wants to live in a townhouse that's not in a town?"[2]

While individual live-work units can be designed in many forms, sizes, and levels of finish, it is the way they address their surroundings, the presence or absence of opportunities for informal interaction, and the way that common facilities and public access are treated that make the difference between a great project, which will sell well or stay rented up, and a mediocre project, which will experience high vacancy rates in a down economy.

Place making is a term that is familiar to New Urbanists and most good designers. To paraphrase architect Louis Kahn, *space plus meaning equals place*. Due to its unique

qualities, live-work benefits tremendously from good place-making, and its contribution to making a larger place (i.e., enhancing its surroundings) can be significant.

Creating opportunities for informal interaction in live-work is discussed in more detail elsewhere in this book. Suffice it to say here that the two most important ways to encourage interaction and to allow a project to be more than merely a collection of units are:

1. Provide opportunities for interaction within a project by locating courtyards, gardens, and comfortable spaces (see Figure 3-26) along the entry path between the project entrance and unit entrances.

2. Locate the project on a great street (see Figure C-13 in the color folio), open the ground floor out onto that great street, and—if possible—use street-facing flexhouses, ground-floor retail, or liner units, and keep those ground-floor businesses open late into the night.

Skillfully accomplishing one or both of these two tasks at the outset of designing a live-work project is in many ways

Figure 3-26 An entry path—in this case a courtyard—designed to encourage interaction as people come and go. South Prescott Village, Oakland, California, 1988. Designed by Thomas Dolan Architecture.

the most important act its designer can perform. Doing so will go a long way toward assuring its success

For every individual, there is an appropriate point along the community/privacy continuum. At one end is being a hermit, and at the other end is living in a communal household where everything is shared. Most people's needs fall somewhere in between. It is this author's observation that if an individual finds a living and working situation that is at the right point along that continuum, it is more likely that he or she will live a fulfilled, socially connected life. Live-work provides options along that community-privacy continuum that aren't available in the standard housing market, a fact that—in part—explains its appeal.

Tip
Wherever possible, work diligently to provide places where interaction is easy, comfortable, and naturally occurring within your live-work project.

In addition to the two primary design elements just noted, certain facilities can be located within or adjacent to a live-work project that can—depending on the specifics of the project—enhance its functionality and sense of community by providing additional opportunities for interaction.

Common Residential Facilities

Any common facility in a larger live-work building will—if located and designed properly—create opportunities for casual interaction. Examples include common laundry, mailboxes (see Clocktower Lofts Case Study), hot tub/spa/sauna, and of course courtyards and gardens.

The best way to design such facilities to encourage interaction is to locate them near or along the normal path of travel of most residents and to provide benches or other sitting and gathering places nearby. Viewing live-work at the neighborhood scale, in most New Urbanist town centers there is a central mailbox location, which provides a way for residents to cross paths every day.

Coworking Space

"Coworking is a movement to create café-like community/ collaboration spaces [see Figure 3-27] for software developers, writers, and independents."[3] The inclusion of a coworking site in a live-work project can be a natural way to enhance interaction, collaboration, and a sense of community. Coworking as a named term originated in 2009, but it is predated by telework centers, some of which are a feature

Figure 3-27 A coworking space in Emeryville, California, that provides individual office stations and common facilities, such as conference rooms, large-format printers, and a café-like interactive space.

of cohousing projects where residents—because their work is some distance away or they are self-employed—share on-site office facilities in a space outside their individual units.

Tip
Combine upstairs live-work with a downstairs coworking space (and a café if possible) to make a de facto live-work incubator project.

Business Center

If a live-work project is intended primarily for white-collar workers, provision of a business center with facilities or equipment that would not be present in a typical home office can be helpful. Examples as of this writing include a high-speed photocopier with capability for large format and collating, a binding machine, and perhaps a drawing-size (D or E size) scanner, printer, or copier. What an individual can afford or fit into his or her unit changes as technology improves, so in live-work condominium projects a small part of the homeowners' dues should include a contribution to a revolving "technology upgrade" fund for the common office facilities.

Other Common Work Facilities

Common work facilities will depend on the orientation of the project and might include catering kitchen, fine-art press, or workshop (see Figure 3-28 for an example). In a project built for unknown users, setting aside unimproved space for an as-yet-unnamed common work use is a wise move.

Figure 3-28 A common work space with woodworking power tools that are available for use by occupants of a live-work project. Oakland, California.

Formal Community Types

Certain social arrangements and ownership structures that—due to their organized, "large C" community aspects—add cohesion and richness to a project. These include cohousing and cohort housing, both defined in Chapter Two. These strategies will be discussed in Chapter Five: Community, but a statistic worth citing here is that in the Santa Fe Cohousing, twenty-one out of thirty-three residents work at home, essentially making it a majority live-work community and likely not too far from the proportion who actually work in their units in a typical live-work project.

Other less formalized types include family grouping/compound (often a form of cohort housing), and congregate live-work, which capitalizes on:

1. The fact that kitchens and bathrooms are often the most expensive component of construction
2. The fact that there are people who would gladly share a kitchen and bathrooms and trade less privacy for a greater sense of community—and lower rent

Common Live-Work Unit Designs

As noted in Chapter Two: Definitions, there are three basic proximity types: live-with, live-near, and live-nearby. These terms refer to the form of the unit—specifically how the work space and the residence are physically arranged in relation to each other—and are an important way of defining live-work units' design (see Table 3-1).

Table 3-1 Live-Work Proximity Types

Live-with	Work and residence all occur in one "common atmosphere"
Live-near	Work and residence are separated by a wall or floor/ceiling
Live-nearby	Work occurs outside the residence but on the same property

Live-With Proximity Type

As described in Chapter Two, a live-with unit (see Figure 3-30) is entirely contained within the confines of one room or "common atmosphere." Within that single space, all of the activities of living and working proceed, without separation (see Figure 3-29), spatially and to some extent functionally: working, sleeping, bathing, entertaining, cooking, and eating.

A live-with unit's flexibility, in part facilitated by its lack of interior partitions, means that the unit's occupant has maximum freedom to use it as he or she sees fit at any time.

As noted, the amount of space devoted to the "live" area and the "work" area depends on the occupant's needs at the moment (see Figure 3-31). Live-with units are therefore best designed as simple enclosures with a minimum of features and partitions other than the basics of cooking and bathing. What is important is that they have great natural light via windows or skylights, lots of unencumbered space in which the occupant is free to do as he or she pleases, and—in the case of artists and businesspeople—easy ways to bring large objects in and out.

Figure 3-29 A typical live-with unit at South Prescott Village, Oakland, California, in which the work space is lit by clerestory windows set in the site-built truss above; sleeping and bathroom occur at the mezzanine level and the kitchen is below, 1988. Designed by Thomas Dolan Architecture.

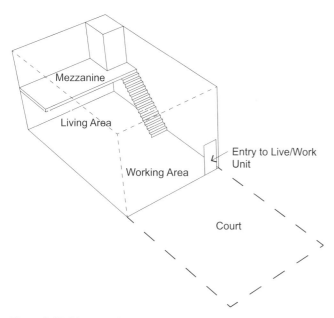

Figure 3-30 Diagram of a live-with proximity type unit.

There are two variations on the design of a live-with unit, the first being a single-level loft, usually with a higher ceiling than a typical apartment and—if in an unseparated townhouse configuration—wider bay spacing than a residential space. In a single-level live-with, or loft space, spatial delineation is minimal, but the arrangement of functions should conform to a pattern called "intimacy gradient," from *A Pattern Language* by Christopher Alexander et al.[4] The essence of the pattern, as noted above, is that the closer you are to the entrance of a house, or live-work unit, or garden, the more public the activities should be. As you move into the space from the entrance, there is a gradient of increasing

intimacy so that the farthest spaces from the entrance are the most intimate, such as the bedrooms.

While building codes prohibit fully enclosed bedrooms not located on an exterior wall, simple enclosure via furniture, such as bookshelves, can assist with the creation of a functioning intimacy gradient. The designer of a single-level loft space must be aware of this important pattern, but many of the elements that provide intimacy will be supplied by the occupant. In renovation live-work, kitchens and bathrooms are often clustered near the core of the building (see Figure 2-22); in the absence of a mezzanine, sleeping often needs to occur near windows. Therefore, entering at the building core creates a natural beginning for a unit's intimacy gradient.

The second live-with form is a two-level space with a full-height work space, a sleeping area and bathroom on a mezzanine level open to the work space below, and a kitchen/dining area below the mezzanine. This form creates a subtle but strongly felt difference between the three kinds of space within a two-level live-with unit:

1. The space under the mezzanine is the most intimate (see Figure 3-32) and, depending on fenestration, can be almost

Figure 3-31 Work space use shifting over time in a live-with unit, as seen in the moveable partitions built by this resident artist. South Prescott Village, Oakland, California, 1988. Designed by Thomas Dolan Architecture.

Figure 3-32 A sense of enclosure below the mezzanine created primarily by its floor/ceiling structure. South Prescott Village, Oakland, California, 1988. Designed by Thomas Dolan Architecture.

cavelike, but a cave with a view out into a taller—in fact, double-height—space. The kitchen and dining area are appropriately located in this intimate space, and living can of course spill out into the adjoining double-height space.

2. The space above the mezzanine is the two-level live-with unit's most private, being the farthest from the entrance via stairs. The experience of being in the mezzanine is one of safety, comfort (see Figure 3-33), and a view out to the larger double-height space. A principle in ethology, the study of animal behavior, called *prospect and refuge*, was first put forward in 1975 by English geographer Jay Appleton. The simplest way to visualize the principle is to imagine a deer standing at the edge of a forest, looking out over a large meadow. She feels protected by the forest; that is her refuge. She commands a view out across the meadow; that is her prospect. A person's natural desire to avoid the middle tables in a restaurant and sit with one's back to the wall comes from a primal desire for prospect and refuge, something that a mezzanine sleeping area that is open to below also provides. Once understood, the principle of prospect and refuge rarely leaves a designer's mind and frequently appears in built work.

3. The (usually) double-height space that is the two-thirds of the unit not covered by the mezzanine provides a tall, spacious feeling of openness. Equally important is the fact that the tall space in a two-level live-with unit provides the *prospect* for the two smaller spaces. Without it, they would simply be small rooms. Regardless of where one is in a two-level live-with space, one feels its height and

Figure 3-34 The view down from a mezzanine into a double-height space. Pinetree Studios, Oakland, California, 1990. Designed by Thomas Dolan Architecture.

its taller portion (see Figure 3-34) even when one's eyes are closed. Among other things, sound acts differently in such a space, and one is aware of that fact—consciously or unconsciously. Incidentally, adding height to a space in a new building typically does not add much cost: same floor area, same roof area, a little more wall, and maybe a few more windows.

Because of their flexibility and economy of space use, live-with units are the most commonly seen live-work configuration, especially in warehouse renovations. Their economy of space use is telling not only in the proximity of the two functions but also in the multifunctionality of the many portions of a live-with unit. A dining table will often be used for meetings, sketching, or computer work; a work space will often be used for parties, larger meetings, or to house the occasional guest. Such units are simple and inexpensive to build, and that simplicity allows occupants the most freedom to add their own identity through decoration, impromptu partitions, and inventive light-fixture adaptations.

Live-Near Proximity Type

As described in Chapter Two: Definitions, a live-near unit (see Figure 3-36) provides some separation between living and working spaces while still meeting the needs of those who feel that the proximity afforded by live-work is important.

The typical form of a live-near unit, while not the only one, is a flexhouse (see Figure 3-35), a variation of "living above the store." The form of a live-near unit can vary; however, it usually consists of a work space on one floor (usually

Figure 3-33 Intimacy of the mezzanine sleeping area in a live-with unit. South Prescott Village, Oakland, California, 1988. Designed by Thomas Dolan Architecture.

Figure 3-35 A live-near flexhouse in Serenbe, Georgia; the upstairs is accessed from a door to the right, and the retail space can operate independently; this is "living above the store"—or not.

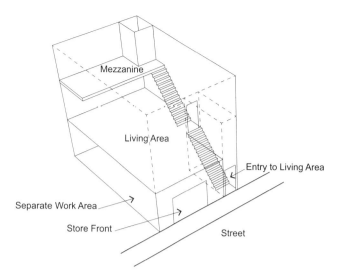

Figure 3-36 Diagram of a live-near proximity type unit.

ground) and a living space above. As illustrated in Figure 3-36, the separation is a floor/ceiling, which may or may not be fire-rated, depending on the hazard level posed by the work activity. As noted in Chapter Two, a work space in a different room from the living space is also a form of live-near. In that case, the separation is a wall, which might be glazed, might be fire-rated, or might be neither.

Live-near units are flexible in an entirely different way from live-with units. Their flexibility comes from being able to treat the live portion of a unit as separate from the work portion and to be able to rent out or share those two spaces more easily. This is a huge economic advantage for many, as evidenced by the multiple variations at Pinetree Studios, a project in Oakland, California, developed by the author in 1990. The project consists of four flexhouse live-near units that include a large open work space with washer/dryer hookups and a three-quarter bath on the first floor and a two-level living portion above, accessed via a separate front door. There is also a door between the living and working portions

at the bottom of the stairs to the loft above. These four essentially identical units were—and are—occupied in entirely different ways, all with no physical alteration to the original:

> **UNIT A:** Upstairs occupied by owners who work in a small portion of that space, essentially a home occupation; downstairs rented out.
> **UNIT B:** Entire unit occupied by owners; downstairs used as a recreation room and guest space as well as storage for water sports equipment.
> **UNIT C:** Entire unit bought as a partnership between two parties; the downstairs occupant lives there and drives a taxi in San Francisco; the upstairs is occupied by an artist who works there but lives in San Francisco.
> **UNIT D:** Entire unit occupied by an artist-owner who paints on the ground floor and lives and plays music above.

This variation in units' uses will be covered and illustrated in the Pinetree Studios case study. Other examples of live-near are shown in the "Flexhouse Project Type" section of this chapter.

Live-Nearby Proximity Type

In the case of a live-nearby (see Figure 3-37), in order to move from living space to work space, one must either leave the building one is in and traverse a courtyard or other space to the second building (see Figure 3-38), or one must leave

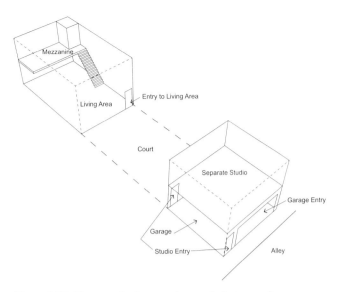

Figure 3-37 Diagram of a live-nearby proximity type unit.

one's unit and go downstairs or across the corridor. The work space in a live-nearby is essentially a separate place, such as a disused granny flat over a garage or a converted garage or barn, and is therefore—particularly if at grade level—suited to client visits, employees, and walk-in trade.

Live-nearby takes the definition of live-work into the realm of urban design and town planning. The creation a of live-work neighborhood (see Figure 3-39)—a place where one both lives and works within a five-minute walk and also can access most of the goods and services one needs within a ten-minute walk—is the ultimate goal of much of what is contained in this book. Some view a residence within a five-minute walk of one's workplace in a live-work neighborhood

Figure 3-38 A live-nearby accessory building accommodates an artist's studio behind the house in Berkeley, California, 2007. Jennifer Cooper Designer.

Figure 3-39 A live-work neighborhood where everything one could need for daily life—including residence and work—is available within walking distance. Nice, France.

as an extended form of live-nearby, although this extended definition is not adopted in this book.

Designers can create fabulous lofts, renovate warehouses reeking of industrial clank, and even build live-work townhouses on great streets, but if the buildings aren't well connected to a larger community and to the goods and services that their occupants need, what is built is often no better than conventional sprawl development. If a live-worker is required by location to get in her car and drive for fifteen minutes to perform every function in her life—as is often the case in either ill-conceived loft construction in industrial areas or artists' illegal housing in pioneering neighborhoods at the outset of the SoHo Cycle—then something is wrong that should be put right. Chapter Five: Community, discusses this subject further.

As noted, housing over retail is essentially live-nearby and is definitely a form of live-work. A few multiunit live-work projects contain a telework center or common work space that is separate from the residences; this would also be a form of live-nearby. For images of live-nearby, see the "Housing over Retail Project Type" section of this chapter.

Other Unit Configurations

Regardless of their relationship to grade level, most live-work units in multiunit buildings are configured as either a single level or a single level with mezzanine, or townhouse (i.e., multilevel). Almost all enter at the lowest level. In archetypal warehouse conversions with double-loaded corridors (not this author's favorite configuration, but it can be combined with courtyards), mezzanines and plumbing for kitchens below and bathrooms above are clustered along the core, near the corridor. The mezzanines look out over the double-height work space that is lit by full-height industrial sash windows. This is an efficient layout that concentrates the major plumbing and mezzanine structure, saving money by stacking the plumbing and the increased floor loads (see Figure 2-22).

In an arrangement that has worked well in a number of loft projects in San Francisco and Oakland, the sleeping loft is over the bathroom and walk-in closets and the kitchen is in part of the full-height space. An example of this type of unit can be seen in Figure 7-16.

Taking a cue from visits to open studios at some of Oakland's earliest live-work conversions—some legal, some not—Thomas Dolan Architecture designed a number of three-level spaces (see Figure 3-40 and Figure C-4 in the color folio) whose most appealing quality is that a portion is open from ground level all the way up to a roof some thirty feet above. This is shown in drawing form in Figure 3-41.

Figure 3-40 A three-level live-with unit open in some portions from first floor all the way to the roof. Filbert Court, Oakland, California, 1993. Designed by Thomas Dolan Architecture.

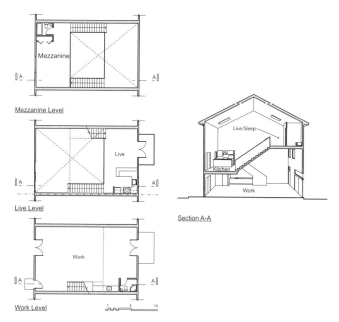

Figure 3-41 Three-level live-with unit; plan and section views.

Development Types

One can divide live-work—and in fact most urban development—into three categories of construction: renovation, infill, and greenfield. As it applies to live-work, the three categories typically play out as discussed next.

Live-Work Renovation Development

Renovation of existing buildings for live-work is still the dominant form within established cities. Warehouse conversions often cluster in former industrial districts, and their conversion to live-work is a powerful agent of change, often transforming the district into a vibrant, mixed-use neighborhood that attracts retail, demands previously absent city services, and sometimes provides employment. Thus unfolds the SoHo Cycle, which is discussed elsewhere in more detail. Renovation for live-work sometimes occurs in more dispersed locations, such as a disused school, armory, or other larger building (see Figure 3-42). It can also occur in smaller buildings, such as a former corner store, church, or commercial building. Such renovations almost always add diversity and therefore mixed use to monolithic, single-use locations.

Urban Infill Development

Infill is a term used to describe new construction on sites already served by urban infrastructure and typically surrounded by existing development. In a new building, the

Figure 3-42 The San Francisco Armory, once considered for renovation to live-work. Any large, vacant building is a good candidate for repurposing.

Figure 3-43 Flexhouses, Ruskin Place, an entire pedestrian-oriented public realm (all vehicular activity is behind) surrounded by live-works. Seaside, Florida, 1982. Designed by Duany Plater-Zyberk, Town Planners and Architects.

designer has greater freedom to work with the unique needs of live-work, as described in this chapter and elsewhere. In a manner similar to renovation, infill live-work can add diversity to a location whose character has become monolithic or simply neglected.

Infill is most successful when its design gives strong consideration to its context. In cases where vacant lots are surrounded by existing historic buildings (e.g., Tribeca in Lower Manhattan), the design of infill live-work should pay particular attention to its surroundings. Nevertheless, some attempts at infill make a deliberate attempt to set themselves apart from their context. While the aesthetic basis for such design is debatable, inserting live-work into a district that consists of preexisting active uses and development patterns, such as industrial or commercial use, will almost always cause conflicts if not handled properly.

Common Infill Live-Work Project Types

1. Flexhouse live-work, two- and three-story street-facing units with entrances at street level, or more rarely at a level above the street and accessed via common open space or an internal street. Such projects are best located in a medium-density context but are sometimes included as "liner" units in larger projects. In a flexhouse (see Figure 3-43), the work space is separated from the residence by a floor/ceiling.

2. Townhouse live-work, also called a shophouse in this book, where the ground floor work space is not separated from the floors above. This form is less common due to its impaired ability to flex without structural renovations,

despite its recent legitimization via the 2009 International Building Code.

3. Courtyard live-work, a multiunit project whose units open onto one or more common courtyards, gardens, and—sometimes to a lesser degree—the street. Such projects are best located in medium-density locations, possibly where the street is not as convivial or safe and where the all-important need for interaction among residents will initially be met in the courtyards.

4. New-construction urban lofts, a relatively recent invention that combines qualities of townhouses and apartment buildings. Many are in buildings with structured parking, making them expensive to construct and therefore to buy. Lofts can be similar to high-ceilinged apartments with large windows, often contain spatial volumes that extend up two or more stories within a unit, and tend to be wider than most townhouse bays, often twenty-two feet or wider (see Figure 3-44). While work activities are usually permitted in urban lofts, the real estate community and the buying public have generally viewed them as a residential "product."

Urban lofts are best located in areas relatively well served by transit, retail, and other services, not in isolated spots within viable industrial or commercial districts (see San Francisco Experience sidebar in Chapter Six: Planning). Alternatively, new loft projects and some other types of live-work can be well suited to areas that are on the edge (i.e., where residential, commercial, or industrial zones meet). Live-work lofts can serve as a buffer use between residential and commercial/industrial areas; buffer use needs to be considered in a locally calibrated

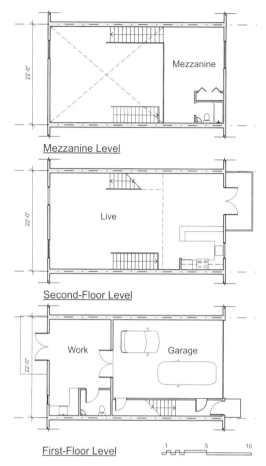

Mezzanine Level

Second-Floor Level

First-Floor Level

Figure 3-44 Twenty-two feet is a common bay width in new-construction live-work townhouses or flexhouses.

provides a flexible building type for which demand almost always outstrips supply as compared to units and houses that are not adaptable to the evolution of uses in a young town. A worthy goal for high-quality greenfield development and revitalization of existing neighborhoods alike is to create a "live-work neighborhood" in which all of one's basic needs—in addition to one's residence and workplace—are met within a ten-minute walk.

Common Greenfield Live-Work Types

1. Flexhouse live-work, the dominant form that contains a commercial space on the ground floor and living above that is separate and could be at times owned or leased separately. This is also called live-near, and it provides great flexibility, as its name implies. Andres Duany calls such units "move-up" live-works.

2. Townhouse, or unseparated shophouse live-work, now permitted under the International Building Code (IBC; Section 419) and distinguished by the fact that the ground-floor (or other) work space is open to the living space above (see Figure 3-45). This bears some similarity to a flexhouse,

Figure 3-45 The stair in this live-work townhouse is open to above, as permitted by IBC Section 419. Glenwood Park, Atlanta, Georgia.

way, their mixed-use, flexible nature has been shown to mediate conflicts between single-use zones in some cases.

5. Podium and high-rise live-work can take the form of townhouse liner units, or lofts located on upper levels of such buildings (see the Sierra case study in this chapter for illustrations of liners). Live-work is often combined with residential at this density, and where located above street level, such live-work would typically be best described as home occupation, meaning that working at home is an option but client visits are by appointment only, and employees or walk-in trade are not anticipated. This project type is typically located in the most intensely urban T5 or T6 Urban Core transect zones.

Greenfield Development

Greenfield live-work was pioneered in New Urbanist communities, where town planners and developers see it as an essential way to incubate the commercial centers of their "traditional neighborhoods" by providing life on the street where retail might not yet be viable. Flexhouse live-work with the important distinction that it is a form of live-with. Andres Duany calls such units "starter" live-work.

3. Detached work spaces or flexible use spaces combined with single-family houses or townhouses, often included in New Urbanist projects above or alongside alley-facing garages. A form of live-nearby, one form is a granny flat. Such spaces are well suited to home office or home occupation uses that usually don't accommodate walk-in trade or employees, as they are usually located behind the main building on a property (see Figure 2-5, Celebration, Florida).

Several of the infill types just mentioned are likely to occur in greenfield development as well and can be integrated with the other greenfield types described. Courtyard live-work certainly has a place in greenfield communities, as long as its street-facing units do activate the street and invite retail uses where appropriate. Housing over retail, which can also be called live-nearby, often is found in New Urbanist town centers alongside live-work townhouses. In larger greenfield settings, urban lofts and podium or high-rise live-work will occur, though more rarely.

Design of Project Types

Project Type: Warehouse Renovation

There have been hundreds of renovations of warehouse and industrial buildings throughout the industrialized world (see Figure C-14 in the color folio), some as relatively basic "hard lofts" and others as market-rate for-sale condominiums, sometimes called soft lofts or lifestyle lofts. Lofts can be intended for artists, but most are for those who want one or more of the following:

- An open plan living space
- A unit for both living and working purposes
- A single-purpose work space

Such lofts are popular for many reasons, not least for the flexibility that they provide, the quality and amount of space in them compared to a traditional apartment at a similar price, and—in many cases—their proximity to newly revitalizing downtowns.

The most important design task in live-work renovation is to create a project that not only has great units but also—through the design of the overall project—allows its occupants to identify with it as a special place and, therefore, to avoid a project organized around narrow double-loaded corridors that

lack opportunities for casual interaction. If the project is located on a great street or in a mixed-use, pedestrian-oriented neighborhood, its street front should be permeable, transparent, and oriented toward potential walk-in trade and the role it can play in revitalizing its neighborhood. If it is not located on such a street, one should plan for the fact that said street might be activated at a later time by providing flexibility to allow retail at the street-front side of the building if possible. If street activation is not possible but the project is a multiunit building, always consider the entry situation (i.e., what happens between the time when one enters the building and the time one when opens the door to one's unit). Where are the mailboxes? Are they situated so one can stop and chat while perusing mail? Is the lobby a congenial place? Are opportunities for interaction provided along the entry path?

While real estate bean counters will argue otherwise, the least desirable warehouse conversion building plan consists of a stair at either end and a long, straight, narrow corridor connecting the stairs and accessing all the units. Years of experience have shown that such a configuration is the least likely to result in a place with real meaning for its occupants; it is simply a collection of units. Warehouse or industrial live-work conversions—and new construction, for that matter—usually do best when their common spaces—really semipublic open space (indoors or outdoors)—are generous; are located along the entry path; and include places to sit (see Figure C-15 in the color folio), places to post notices or install art, and places that bring out what is unique about the building.

What *will* appeal to the bean counters is that making real places results in projects that stay full when the economy tanks, where friends tell friends when there is a vacancy, and where real community happens. One needs to remember that because live-workers don't commute, they are at home most of the time. They can become isolated if there are no opportunities for interaction, and they can become disenchanted and leave if the quality of their environment is that of a warehouse for people. Inexperienced developers will say, "I'm trying to provide the maximum amount of revenue-generating space! Each tenant will have to pay a higher common area maintenance fee if I provide all these amenities."

Good designers create experience; great live-work designers create community. A building might rent for one dollar per square foot per month for units located on a long, straight corridor with no common open space. Take 10 percent of that revenue space and design great interactive spaces along the entry paths, and the premium for a real community is likely to be 25 percent or greater, resulting in rents of $1.25 per square foot per month.[5]

There is often the temptation to make the flat roof of a building available and to smugly state that doing so provides lots of common open space. The fact is that such space is rarely used (except by smokers, if even that is allowed) and performs poorly as a builder of community. Again, it is the crossing paths as one comes and goes about one's daily life that builds, over time, "small c community" (as noted, large C is highly organized Community, such as cohousing). Any designer of live-work who ignores live-workers' unique needs for interaction with their neighbors and a higher quality of environment is missing opportunities and doing a disservice to his or her clients and end users.

Therefore, before getting to the job of designing units in any live-work project, it is important to design the entry situation and the common spaces so that they:

1. Create the structure of a "small c community"
2. Meet code requirements for access and egress

Once one has determined that every unit owner or tenant is provided with an opportunity for informal interaction as he or she comes and goes about daily life, the rest (i.e., individual unit design, covered earlier) is comparatively easy. This principle applies to all live-work project types, each in its own way. The case studies that follow illustrate design of live-work in actual built projects.

Project Examples: Market-Rate Condominium Renovation

As was noted in Chapter One: Introduction, artists and developers have been converting warehouses to live-work for at least forty years. Ownership units, usually condominiums, typically are created when the SoHo Cycle has run its course and most artists have moved on. The real test of market-rate lofts is their ability to create an internal sense of community and their relationship to the neighborhood in which they are located. The two examples that follow are located in very different kinds of neighborhoods.

Willow Court, located on an edge between a residential neighborhood and an industrial district—and not close to any services or mass transit—came to market in Fall 2007, a difficult time. After sales of all of the units failed to materialize, it was recast as a rental, and recently it was remarketed as condominiums at far lower prices.

The Clocktower Lofts project was built in 1990, and its pioneering aspect—meaning that it had little competition—enabled it to sell out in a lukewarm economy. It is situated in an ideal South of Market location in San Francisco, near services, open space, and transit; the project has since benefited greatly from San Francisco's powerful tech-driven economy.

CASE STUDY: WILLOW COURT

Type of Live-Work: Renovation lifestyle lofts in a courtyard configuration

Proximity Type: Live-with

Location: Oakland, California

Walk Score®: 63 (somewhat walkable)

Year Built: 2007

Architect: Thomas Dolan Architecture

Developer: XP Development

Willow Court (see Figure 3-46) is the renovation of a high, one-story, concrete block warehouse in an area of mixed housing and industrial uses in Oakland, California. Thomas Dolan Architecture, the author's firm, located two courtyards within the project, each with a fountain, onto which most of the twenty units open, thereby creating a courtyard live-work project

in a market-rate condominium renovation (see Figure 3-47).

The result is a community of live-workers who, while their project is not located adjacent to services or transit, are afforded ample opportunities for interaction within the project. Willow Court is located at an edge between a residential neighborhood and an area of warehouse structures. As such, it serves as a buffer between the two.

The building, fortuitously located on a corner, is one hundred feet deep. Its roof is supported by bowstring trusses that span that distance and whose bottoms sit at eighteen feet above the floor. This fortuitous dimension created an opportunity for mezzanines (see Figure C-16 in the color folio) and upper levels both below and in between the trusses, spaced at twenty-foot centers. The curving trusses,

(Continued)

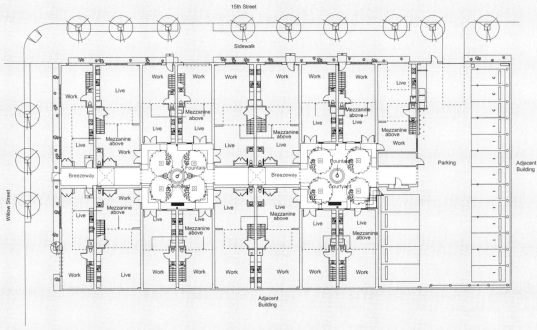

Figure 3-46 Site and floor plan of Willow Court in Oakland, California, showing the two courtyards carved out of the existing building, off which almost all units open, 2007. Designed by Thomas Dolan Architecture.

rather than being buried within the demising walls, remained exposed in the units, and the curved ceilings—while Sheetrocked—are nevertheless evocative of the building's industrial past. Secure parking is located at one end of the existing warehouse: One bay was sacrificed to accommodate it, and there is tuck-under parking below one upper-level-only unit, which is accessed via an exterior stair from the courtyard. All other units enter at grade from the courtyard, townhouse-style, and some units facing the street include storefronts, although retail is not currently permitted in that location.

Completed at the tail end of the last real estate boom, Willow Court experienced soft sales as interest in projects not located near urban services or retail declined sharply.

Lessons Learned

1. It is possible to transform such a sprawling warehouse into an environment conducive to interaction within the project, even if its surroundings are not very convivial.

2. While hindsight provides a wealth of knowledge that could not have been known in advance, there are clearly risks in developing market-rate live-work that is not located near services.

Figure 3-47 A courtyard at Willow Court, Oakland, California, where casual interaction occurs as residents come and go about their daily lives, 2007. Designed by Thomas Dolan Architecture.

Recent history has shown that projects built in close proximity to services have held their value better than isolated projects.

Type of Live-Work: Condominium warehouse conversion

Proximity Type: Live-with

Location: San Francisco, California

Year Built: 1990

Walk Score®: 92 (walker's paradise)

Architect: David Baker and Associates

Developer: Holliday Development

Description: 127 units, former home of Schmidt Lithograph, which printed labels for fruit crates

The Clocktower Lofts (see Figure C-17 in the color folio), developed by loft pioneer Rick Holliday and designed by David Baker and Associates, is a well-designed loft conversion that is located in San Francisco's South of Market (SoMa), the epicenter of the dot-com boom of the late 1990s.

There is some debate about why the most important start-ups of that era located in San Francisco rather than Silicon Valley, but most people agree that entrepreneurs and employees of the businesses sought interaction and collaboration, which were facilitated by the San Francisco scene. Thousands of live-work lofts were built during that time—many as new construction, which is treated elsewhere. People who wanted flexible, relatively affordable space were there to create the demand, and they bought the units as quickly as they were built. One might say that the San Francisco live-work boom coincided with the dot-com boom for good reason. The Clocktower is one of the earliest and is located near a multitude of city services and amenities.

The Clocktower is a renovation of a former printing press, and its artful renovation made good use of the entry situation in its location of mailboxes (see Figure 3-48) and a generous lobby.

There are beautiful courtyards in the building. They exist primarily as places to pass through or look out onto (see Figure 3-49). Few units open onto them, a missed opportunity in this author's opinion, but this fact makes the courtyards

Figure 3-48 The mailboxes in the Clocktower Lofts lobby are a natural place for casual encounters among live-workers. San Francisco, California, 1990. Designed by David Baker + Partners Architects.
Photo Credit: J.D. Petersen.

common to all residents without any particular sense of ownership by a few.

Lessons Learned

1. The Clocktower was a seminal project in a city that was ready for loft buildings and unit types. Its location in a walkable neighborhood, a short walk from the financial district and an even shorter one to South Park—a small and lively square surrounded by an interesting mix of building types and uses—greatly benefits the project. The continuing success of the Clocktower reinforces the basic planning truth that location does matter, a fact ignored by many subsequent loft projects in San Francisco.

(Continued)

2. The project's use of common courtyards and its designers' understanding of the importance of the "entry path"—locating mailboxes in a prominent place and creating relief from a double-loaded corridor scheme with well-designed courtyards—has been successful. In a building that takes up an entire block, such measures were needed to transform the building from a printing plant to a place of relatively small spaces (i.e., live-work units).

3. While not a lesson that is unique to live-work, Clocktower Lofts and many projects by Thomas Dolan Architecture have included fountains in their courtyards. It has been the author's experience that, while a fountain cannot replace all other ambient sounds, which in the case of Clocktower included traffic to and from the San Francisco–Oakland Bay Bridge passing within feet of the project, the sound of the water focuses one's attention and changes the "color" of the mix of sounds in very positive ways. At the Clocktower, the developer says that the freeway sounds are not audible at the courtyard-grade level—only the sounds of birds.[6]

Figure 3-49 This generous courtyard at the Clocktower Lofts in San Francisco, California, is a great place to cross paths; it is along the "entry path," although few units enter onto it directly, 1990. Designed by David Baker + Partners and Miller Company, Landscape Architects.
Photo Credit: J.D. Petersen.

Project Example: Artists' Work/Live Rental Renovation

CASE STUDY: CALIFORNIA COTTON MILLS STUDIOS

Type of Live-Work: Renovation work/live rental

Proximity Type: Live-with

Location: Oakland, California

Year Built: 2005

Architect: Thomas Dolan Architecture

Developer: Rush Property Group

California Cotton Mills Studios was built in 1917 and operated as the largest cotton mill west of the Mississippi. A city of Oakland landmark, it housed mini-storage for twenty years before it was converted to live-work in 2005 (see Figure 3-50).

The developer has a strong commitment to providing true work/live space, and as a result he included many features that allow the building to

(Continued)

Figure 3-50 A former cotton mill and ministorage warehouse, the building was clean and wide open when work began. California Cotton Mills Studios, Oakland, 2005. Designed by Thomas Dolan Architecture.

accommodate large work and a variety of users, including double doors into all units, wide corridors, heavy floor-loading capacity (inherent in the building), and a freight elevator adjacent to a loading dock.

Designed by Thomas Dolan Architecture, the seventy-four units are all live-with proximity types, and on the floors where there are ceiling heights of fifteen feet or higher (an important metric) there are full mezzanines containing the sleeping area, bathroom, and closet. On the floors where the existing ceiling heights are less than that, mezzanines are provided with reduced height storage below, and "sleeping mezzanines"—which under Oakland's live-work building code are only required to have a head height of five feet eight inches—are located above the unit bathrooms. Therefore, one can choose to sleep on the mezzanine or step up onto the sleeping mezzanine, in which case the mezzanine can serve as a dressing room, office, and so on (see Figures 7-16 and 7-17).

As is common in such projects, the plumbing stacks, mezzanines, and living areas are concentrated at the core of the building, on either side of the corridors. The work portions of the units are at the periphery of the building, are full height, and are lit by large industrial sash windows. Due to the historic nature of the building and its proximity to a major freeway (see Figure 3-51), the developer spent over a million dollars on reglazing two sides

Figure 3-51 Calcot is located alongside a major freeway, which posed noise and dust problems and—due to the necessity to keep west windows closed—precipitated an otherwise unnecessary addition of air conditioning. California Cotton Mills Studios, Oakland, 2005. Designed by Thomas Dolan Architecture.

of the building and replacing the other two sides' fenestration with sound-rated aluminum windows in a pattern that met with historic preservation officials' approval.

The building also received historic tax credits, which requires compliance with the U.S. Secretary of Interior's standards and the use of historic architectural consultants (in this case, Architectural Resources Group of San Francisco).

A 117,500-square-foot building, CalCot—as it is known to many—contains seventy-four units of work/live. The units range between 1,100 and 1,900 square feet and are rentals. While there are wide corridors and a generous lobby that serves as a small photographic museum devoted to the history of the California Cotton Mills (see Figure 3-52), due to structural constraints, the owner did not elect to dedicate any common space within the building. However, there is an outdoor common space that is extensively used by the tenants on the railroad side of the building, which is shielded from freeway noise. At Calcot, F3 (third Friday) open-studio events are held once a quarter. The last one (as of this writing) hosted 450 visitors. Tenants open their studios, while others hang art in the hallways.

(Continued)

Figure 3-52 Wide corridors and doors accommodate access for large objects, consistent with the true work/live nature of California Cotton Mills Studios. Oakland, 2005. Designed by Thomas Dolan Architecture.

There is a common laundry area on the ground floor at Calcot that contains seven washers and eight dryers operated by card readers. Due to the project's somewhat isolated location relative to services and transit, the city of Oakland required parking at a ratio of 1:1 for all units, which is primarily accommodated as surface parking around the building, although there is a small building attached to the main warehouse that contains twenty parking spaces.

Lesson Learned

The developer's strong commitment to true work/live, which is reflected in the design of the units and his choice of tenants, has helped the project to become a community. It is arguable that—most of all—the commitment of the tenants to their work, and the inherent need for interaction in such a large project that is so isolated, has overcome its lack of courtyards or common space along the project's entry paths. Therefore, if one is prevented from including such common spaces—as this developer was—creating a culture of work-oriented tenants can go a long way toward guaranteeing a strong community with which the tenants will identify. Were Calcot to become a primarily live-only building, it is likely that such a community would founder.

Project Type: Live-Work Courtyard Community

Courtyard live-work is an invention that is specific to this unique use type, although courtyard housing—defined as a project in which the units enter directly off shared courtyards and whose exterior spaces consist of courtyards and gardens joined by breezeways and passageways—has been built for thousands of years. To some extent, a courtyard configuration runs counter to the prevailing American model: little-used front yard, narrow side yards, and very private backyard, which of course has its applications when not excessively contorted to fit the needs of a drive-in culture. However, as stated, particularly in warm climates (although we now have skylights that don't leak and roofs that can retract), units that allow one to step out one's door and cross paths with someone else in the same boat (i.e., someone who has been working alone in front of a computer, a canvas, or a loom for the last few hours) are a natural fit for live-work.

Courtyard live-work is, most important, about making a community (see Figure 3-53), a subject that is treated in

Figure 3-53 Providing places where casual interaction will occur is a crucial ingredient in live-work design, here seen in the garden at South Prescott Village, Oakland, California, 1988. Designed by Thomas Dolan Architecture.

more detail in Chapter Five: Live-Work and Community. Suffice it to say here that the intent of the author and his first client, the artist Bruce Beasley, was to provide not only great units but places where live-workers could experience casual interaction, mostly in the courtyards and gardens of these projects.

It is possible to put numbers to the size and proportions of courtyards that work. They can't be so large that people crossing them never encounter each other, and they can't be so narrow that they make people uncomfortable. In general, they shouldn't be wider than thirty feet or longer than fifty feet. Multiple courtyards are preferable to one overly large plaza or quadrangle within a project. Christopher Alexander has, in A *Pattern Language* and other work, described "courtyards which live," "positive outdoor space," and "hierarchy of open space."[7] In *Life between Buildings*, Jan Gehl has described in detail the importance of creating an "edge zone" at the meeting between semipublic open space and the entrance to one's unit, stating that if the edge of a public space works, so in turn does the space.

Project Example: Live-Work Courtyard Community

CASE STUDY: SOUTH PRESCOTT VILLAGE

Name of Project: South Prescott Village

Type of Live-Work: New construction courtyard community

Proximity Type: Live-with (fourteen units) and live-near (two units)

Location: Oakland, California

Year Built: 1985–1990

Architect: Thomas Dolan Architecture and Santos and Urrutia, Structural Engineers

Developer: Bruce Beasley

South Prescott Village, designed by the author and begun in 1985 (see Figure 3-54), is the first multi-unit new construction live-work project built in North America since at least 1930. The "larger" project, including Henry Street Studios and Pinetree Studios, consists of twenty-five units on three sites linked by two streets, two courtyards, and a garden. Its courtyard orientation, specifically designed to meet the unique needs of live-work, constituted the invention of a new building type: the infill courtyard live-work community. In this project, the author originated many of the unit types and design ideas that are introduced in this book.

Working with a relatively blank slate, they were able to ask themselves, "What do artists want?" The first answers were **light** (see Figure 3-55), **space,** and **access** (to bring large works in and out; see Figure C-18 in the color folio). Understandably, the client, Bruce Beasley, didn't want to heat or maintain any nonrevenue space, so the units then became townhouses with direct access from grade. While first conceived by Bruce as a series of barracks-like buildings, Tom's experience living in a former Italian family compound led to a design that is a series of courtyards and gardens linked by passageways and streets. That "positive space" between the buildings became and continues to this day as one of the most important aspects of the design.

Bruce was interested in an income from the studios' rental, but he was also interested in:

1. showing the rest of Oakland that development was feasible in West Oakland;

2. showing that artists' live-work could be built and made to work economically as new construction, thereby demonstrating that artists could be reliable tenants; and

3. overcoming what seemed at times insurmountable obstacles thrown up by building codes, planning department, and lenders (no conventional financing was available).

The author was there with Bruce Beasley all the way, showing up at the construction site every day of every phase, the last one of which, Pinetree Studios, was developed by the author.

(Continued)

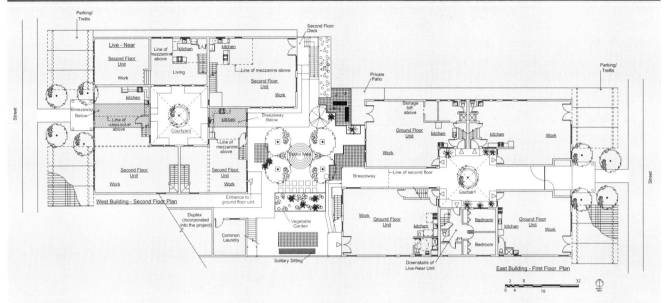

Figure 3-54 South Prescott Village site and first-floor plan; the first new construction artists' live-work project built in the United States since the (first) Great Depression. Areas in white are common open space. Oakland, California, 1988. Designed by Thomas Dolan Architecture.

Figure 3-55 Numerous site-built trusses were punched through with north-facing windows, thereby providing the natural light needed by the working artists. South Prescott Village, Oakland, California, 1988. Designed by Thomas Dolan Architecture.

Located in a residential neighborhood that is adjacent to mass transit (BART) but which was a rough place to live in 1985, South Prescott Village is built on six residential lots stretching from one street to another, and comprises two buildings, each surrounding a courtyard off which the majority of units enter.

Breezeways connect the street to the courtyards and continue on to a garden between the buildings. Pinetree Studios, across the street (see lower left of Figure 3-56), is essentially an extension of South Prescott Village.

The two most important design advances in live-work community design made at South Prescott Village were:

1. Realization of the importance of interactive open space

2. The differentiation of proximity types

The project contains sixteen units (eight each in two buildings). Of those, seven in each building are live-with units and one in each is a live-near unit. As noted, both buildings surround a twenty-five-foot-square courtyard onto which most of the units in that building open. It is in these courtyards and the

Figure 3-56 Aerial view of South Prescott Village, Oakland, California, showing the two twenty-five-foot–by–twenty-five-foot courtyards and the garden between the two buildings. Designed by Thomas Dolan Architecture, 1988.

garden that the important, casual interactions occur between tenants that—over time—lead to growing acquaintance and a sense of belonging to something larger than simply a collection of units.

The result is a community that has held together for twenty-five years. Regular barbeques are held in the garden. Many of the tenants there were invited to move in by existing tenants when they heard of upcoming vacancies. A growing cohort of professors at the local art college live and work there and even talk of a community of artists growing old together there. South Prescott Village has been visited by arts professionals and public officials from all over the world.

The author was visiting the project a few years after it was completed, at which time it was 100 percent artist-occupied. One of the residents came up to him and said, "You know, the most important work spaces for me are the courtyards and the garden." The author replied, "Oh, you must bring an easel out into the garden and paint, right?" "No," he said. "It's the exchanges that I have with other artists in the common spaces that so enrich my work that I consider these spaces to be so important." That interaction defines community in ways that this author could not have entirely anticipated (see Figure 3-53).

In addition to the invention of the two proximity types at South Prescott Village, the project was

designed with light, space, and access in mind. North-facing clerestory windows and skylights are plentiful (see Figure 3-57).

Ceilings are over ten feet high on the ground floor and up to twenty-two feet in the upstairs units, which all have full mezzanines. Every unit has an "art access opening," usually a pair of French doors (see Figure C-19 in the color folio) set three feet above floor level (this was the most affordable way to achieve this opening size) to allow an eight-foot–by–eight-foot stretched canvas to be moved through them. The ten-foot-wide breezeways at each street entrance have person-doors in their security gates, but they are also hinged to swing open and allow the entire ten-foot width to be utilized.

The buildings were designed to emulate early twentieth-century warehouses, to fit their residential context, and to meet these three main requirements: light, space, and access. No place in any unit is more than twenty-five feet from a window, skylight, or clerestory window—many of which are framed in site-built heavy timber trusses. Eschewing a high-tech aesthetic, the upstairs units and their mezzanines are topped by heavy timber roof structure; kitchens are simple but residential in feel. Due to the large amount of open space—like much live-work, these are essentially warehouses with kitchens—construction costs were kept

Figure 3-57 A live-with space: work space in foreground, kitchen below, and sleeping/bath above, and lots of light from windows and skylights. South Prescott Village, Oakland, California, 1988. Designed by Thomas Dolan Architecture.

(Continued)

very low, and the use of "cowboy contractors" accustomed to building suburban houses was an expedient and fortuitous choice. (Many said they'd like to live in one of the spaces.)

The inspiration for the site plan of South Prescott Village was, for the designer, family compounds and ancient cities whose outdoor spaces are defined by courtyards, gardens, and passageways rather than front yards and backyards. The owner, artist Bruce Beasley, refers to the feeling of the courtyards as akin to "meeting at the village well."

Lessons Learned

So many lessons were learned in this first project of its kind, which truly consisted of inventing a new building type: **the live-work courtyard community**. The lessons learned on these, the first projects of the author's career, continue to inform his work and that of the many arts professionals, government officials, and designers who have visited over the last twenty-five years.

1. The basic proximity types defined in Chapter Two, live-with and live-near, were first consciously built and articulated as part of the design of these buildings. This project initiated an understanding of the appropriate level of interior finishes, resulting in "the less you do, the more you give" as an important expression of the fact that live-workers want to add their own identity to their spaces. We learned about "art access" openings, most affordably achieved using prehung pairs of French doors. The contractors and inspectors didn't

understand why they were set three feet above the floor; the artists did.

2. Perhaps most important, an understanding of the unique nature of live-work and its potential for isolation gave rise to the courtyards and gardens placed purposely along the entry path, such that as one steps out of one's unit, the opportunity is there to cross paths with another resident who is taking a break from work to catch a breath of fresh air and, yes, encounter someone else in the same situation.

While the ideas put forth in a first project are initially somewhat conjectural, much seems to work well at South Prescott Village and its companion projects, Henry Street Studios and Pinetree Studios. (The latter was designed and developed as live-work condominiums by Thomas Dolan.)

As the architect, let me add a few personal reminiscences about this seminal project and encounters with tenants that have been both striking and rewarding. My favorite: One of the residents came up to me and said, "I never knew I could live like this. Now I never want to leave." Another said, "My friends ask me, 'Who do I have to kill to get a place here?'"

At times, in immodest moments, I have reflected on my experiences there and at similar projects and thought: These are the buildings the world needs, because they help make community, and they allow people to live locally and lightly on the land and work where they live.

Project Type: Flexhouse

The most common form of live-work in greenfield communities and some infill locations is the flexhouse version of an urban townhouse (see Figure 3-58). In it, retail or other work activity occurs on the ground floor and living happens upstairs. The variations in such buildings are in the work space and how it orients to the street, in the means of entry to the upstairs residence, and in the presence or absence of a fire-rated separation between the ground-floor work space and the living quarters above. In this book, a townhouse live-work

that does not have a separation between living and working levels is considered a shophouse, not a flexhouse.

"Living above the store" is a mode of existence that is as old as two-story buildings and towns themselves. It has only been over the last 150 years that commuting from a residence to a centralized work place began to be considered normal. Before that, one lived in the country and farmed or fished or hunted (or all three), or one lived in the town and engaged in commerce of some sort. Flexhouses—single-family residences with party walls, stoops, short front yards or dooryards, and small private backyards opening onto a carriage house and an

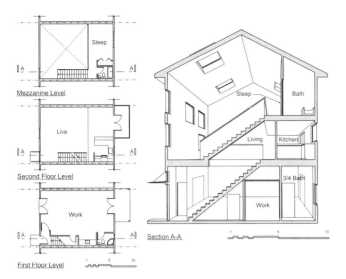

Figure 3-58 Plan and section of a typical flexhouse, using Pinetree Studios in Oakland, California, as an example, 1990. Designed by Thomas Dolan Architecture.

Figure 3-59 Flexhouse live-works fronting on a small park. Kentlands, Maryland, 1990. Designed by Duany Plater-Zyberk, Town Planners and Architects.

alley if it exists—are an important part of virtually all urban centers, and to this day one will find shopkeepers living above their business establishments all over the world.

Increasingly, flexhouse live-works—as New Urbanists call them—are being included in new town centers (see Figure 3-59), as infill in existing neighborhoods, and as liner units in larger buildings (see the Sierra case study at the end of this chapter). As has been discussed elsewhere in this book, the location of all types of live-work is crucial to its success and to the success of the neighborhood of which it is a part.

Flexhouses are intended to activate the street as soon as they are complete and occupied. As such, they must be designed to address the street, and they must avoid detracting from that street presence and therefore locate service access and garages at the rear and pedestrian entries at the street

front. A project example (The Waters) that deviated from that arrangement is included below.

Parking—for residents, employees, customers, or clients—is an important design issue. In flexhouses, parking is normally located in rear-facing garages or at the rear of the townhouse lots. Examples of different approaches to parking and unit entries are included in the next examples as well as in the Habersham case study in Chapter Four: Market.

Project Examples: A Brief Survey of New Urbanist (Mostly) Flexhouse Live-Works

The case studies that follow include observations the author made regarding live-work projects during short visits to each of the communities.

(see The Waters Case Study). The entry alcove is something that could be more difficult to pull off in a place where street crime is an issue. This is a very successful design and a valuable model.

Many of the flexhouse units are rented to retailers or business owners on the ground floor. The living portion (residential unit) above can (in many instances) be reached by a street-facing door (see Figure 3-60) and stairs to the second level. Ninety percent of these upstairs residential units are rented by the Serenbe Inn (across the street) for guests, particularly when the inn holds a corporate retreat or needs to accommodate wedding guests.

Lessons Learned

1. Great live-work fits well in a linear town center.
2. The adaptability of a flexhouse allows it to grow with the town.

Figure 3-60 Detail of a good, working flexhouse: dual entry to one side of the street facade; one's choice is to enter and turn left into the retail or continue through the door beyond and straight up to the residence (see Figure 2-32 for an overall view). Serenbe, Georgia.

CASE STUDY: THE WATERS

Type of Live-Work: Housing over retail, intended as flexhouse

Proximity Type: Live-nearby

Location: Near Montgomery, Alabama

Year Built: Ongoing

Founders: Ed Welch and Dale Walker

The live-work building at The Waters, near Montgomery, Alabama, presents a delightful retail front, and its covered corner sidewalk is a great place to gather (see Figure 3-61). The building is laid out in townhouse-width bays corresponding to the individual storefronts. Unfortunately the

designer—upon receiving input from a retail consultant that they should not dilute the retail front with residential entrances—elected to locate all of the residential entrances at the rear of the building (see also the Habersham Case Study in Chapter Four). The ground-floor entrances to the upstairs residential spaces are adjacent to the rear doors of the retail, and, alas, feel like service entrances (see Figure 3-62).

The second means of egress from the units is via an exterior exit balcony that runs the length of the rear. This in itself works well enough, but when combined with the rear entrances and their proximity to the carport and the units' tiny patios

Figure 3-61 The retail building at The Waters, near Montgomery, Alabama, including fine retail storefronts but no front entrances to the upstairs residences, an unfortunate decision in this case.

Figure 3-62 The only ground-floor entrances to the upstairs residential units are adjacent to the rear doors of the retail shops at the back of the building, and they truly feel like service entrances. The Waters, near Montgomery, Alabama.

(see Figure 3-63), the resulting entry experience feels like one is passing through leftover space to get to one's large, two-level unit.

The upstairs and downstairs of each of the buildings' bays were mapped separately, and they are structured to allow the insertion of a stair. However, no buyer elected to buy both upstairs and down, and now that they are sold this is unlikely to happen, defeating some of the purpose of building potential flexhouses. This author spoke to one enthusiastic resident of The Waters, who owns and runs the interior design shop in one of the storefronts. She lives a couple of blocks away and said that she would have bought above had it not been for the unfortunate rear-entry situation.

Figure 3-63 Rear entrance, small patio, and steps down to the adjacent carports; the upstairs exit balcony allows an alternate entrance to the residential portions of this mixed-use building. The Waters, near Montgomery, Alabama.

(Continued)

There are important lessons here, revealed by a visit to the back of the building. All the residential entries should have been in the front, either through a lobby served by an elevator or via individual or shared entries at the sides of the unit bays (see the Serenbe case study). Shared front stair/entries to serve pairs of units would have been a good solution, perhaps leaving the elevator at the back accessed via a breezeway from the front. The residential entries at the rear also negated one of live-work's most valuable contributions to the vitality of a town center, which is that due to its inherently mixed-use nature, it strengthens the eighteen-hour-a-day street. Unfortunately, the upstairs residents are not likely to use the front often enough to have a positive impact on the street, for they must make a special point to do so. The ideal: crossing paths and casual interaction occur naturally as one comes and goes. Such an outcome did not occur in this situation.

Lesson Learned

Locate the residential entries in the front, combined with a strong storefront character and a commercial quality to the overall building.

CASE STUDY: SEASIDE

Type of Live-Work: Flexhouse, verging on home occupation use at present

Proximity Type: Live-near

Location: Seaside, Florida

Year Built: 1980 onward

Town Planner: Duany Plater-Zyberk

Developer: Robert Davis

Ruskin Place in Seaside, Florida, the first New Urbanist community ever built, is home to a beautifully scaled series of live-work flexhouses (see Figure 3-64).

On the author's visit in 2010, Ruskin Place looks and feels quite different from how it did when he first visited eight years earlier, in part due to the maturing of the vegetation in Ruskin Place.

Additionally, the homeowners of Ruskin Place collectively decided to ban public events there, which has had the effect of rendering retail infeasible in the live-works' ground floors. The delightful café that was there eight years earlier is gone. The remaining businesses are art and antique galleries that—in Ruskin Place itself—appear to be open sporadically or by appointment only. The effect is essentially a down-zoning of Ruskin Place from live-work to home occupation. Based on two short visits to Seaside, eight years apart, it is the author's observation that

Figure 3-64 Spontaneous interaction in Ruskin Place, a public space, onto which front all live-work flexhouses, as seen in in 2002. Seaside, Florida, 1982. Designed by Duany Plater-Zyberk, Town Planners and Architects.

Ruskin Place has—through homeowners turned NIMBY and vegetation allowed to grow wild and dense—gone from an active place of interaction to a bit of a backwater, comparatively speaking. As stated elsewhere, live-work must provide flexibility to allow uses to change over time.

Lesson Learned

The intended work use in any live-work building needs to be calibrated to the desired nature of the public realm onto which it fronts, which may change over time, as it did here.

Type of Live-Work: Flexhouse

Proximity Type: Live-near

Location: Mount Laurel, Alabama

Year Built: Ongoing

Town Planner: Duany Plater-Zyberk

Developer: Elton B. Stephens Company (EBSCO)

The live-work units at Mount Laurel are minimally "retail" in appearance and composition (see Figure 3-65), there is some coordination of signage, and the awnings have a residential feel. However, what the live-works here got right were their alcove entries to both retail and residence. One enters the alcove, having seen something in the storefront, one hopes, and then either turns to enter the store or goes straight through a door to ascend into the residence. One could say that the retail here is not as aggressively commercial as it is in the live-works

Figure 3-66 This service alley in Mount Laurel, Alabama, live-works is intended only to meet the service needs of the retail and does not include entrances to the residential portions of the units.

in Rosemary Beach (see later case study), where—as a resort—recreational shopping is clearly de rigueur. People live in Mount Laurel, and the retail is reflective of that.

Two-story buildings facing each other across a street slightly off the center of the town center, the live-works at Mount Laurel are served by an alley (see Figure 3-66) shared with the back of an apartment building that was treeless, hard-edged, and dismal in feel. However, as distinct from The Waters, the rear entries appear to only serve the retail and can therefore be excused for their utilitarian feel.

Lessons Learned

1. Emphasize the **retail front to maximize flexibility of work uses.**

2. Loading and service areas to the rear can work well when they aren't mixed with residential entrances.

Figure 3-65 The live-work units at Mount Laurel, a traditional neighborhood development in the mountains of Alabama, are minimally "retail" in appearance and composition, and the awnings have a residential feel.

Type of Live-Work: Newly built greenfield project

Proximity Type: Live-with and live-near

Location: Near Montgomery, Alabama

Year Built: 2008 onward

Town Planner: Duany Plater-Zyberk

Developer: The Colonial Company

Duany Plater-Zyberk designed a row of live-work townhouses in Hampstead, near Montgomery, Alabama, that were based on typologies the planners had first built in Atlanta (see Figure 3-67) to coincide with the 2001 National Association of Home Builders' convention. To those three unit types, DPZ attached the names "live-within," "live-above," and "live-behind." (A fourth type, "live-in-front," was later added to the lexicon.[8])

Here the units built were what Duany described as "starter" and "move-up" units. The starters (see Figure 3-68) were small units without dedicated, separate work spaces—live-with units. The move-ups were what we call live-near, due to the fact that the ground-floor work space is separated from the upstairs living.

Lesson Learned

Live-with and live-near can coexist well side by side, even though they are aimed at different market segments.

Figure 3-67 The demonstration live-work building at the National Association of Home Builders' annual convention in 2001 in Atlanta, Georgia, likely the first time modern live-work was exposed to a mainstream audience. Designed by Duany Plater-Zyberk, Town Planners and Architects.

Figure 3-68 The Hampstead "starter" units are small and without dedicated, separate work spaces (i.e., live-with units). The move-up units are live-near; the ground-floor workspace is separated from the upstairs living portion. Hampstead, a traditional neighborhood development near Montgomery, Alabama, 2008. Designed by Duany Plater-Zyberk, Town Planners and Architects.

Type of Live-Work: Townhouse with dual entries

Proximity Type: Live-with

Location: Atlanta, Georgia

Year Built: 2003

Urban Designer: Dover, Kohl and Partners

Developer: Greenstreet Properties

The author visited a three-story live-work townhouse located facing a park in a newly developed neighborhood in Atlanta, Georgia. It is notable for the fact that it is level-in—and works as such—and furthermore does not include a separation between the first and second floors (see Figure 3-69 for an example of a similar open stair). Thus it does not meet the definition of a flexhouse. There are two

entries in the front (see Figure 5-27), suggesting that it can accommodate retail. Under the building code that was in effect at the time, to do so would require a fire-rated separation between the retail space and the stair/entry as well as a fire-rated floor/ceiling separating the two. However, the 2009 IBC now recognizes townhouse live-work that does not separate the residence, with several specific provisos: The building must be sprinklered, the total unit size is limited to three thousand square feet, employees are limited to five, and the work space must be on the ground floor (see Chapter Seven: Building Codes).

Whether the city of Atlanta would require this owner to install a sprinkler if he or she elected to carry on retail without installing a separation is an open question, but it is clear that the new IBC code provision would require it. The preferred solution would be to provide the separation, and the lesson for the rest of us is to build that separation to make the building easily adaptable to evolving uses. Such a separation would result in a flexhouse, a far more marketable configuration, as is detailed in Chapter 4: Market.

Figure 3-69 An example of an open stairway in an unseparated townhouse live-work, which would be permitted under IBC Section 419. Glenwood Park, Atlanta, Georgia. 2003.

Lesson Learned

A level-in, unseparated townhouse can be live-work; such a change requires an understanding of live-work building code, specifically IBC Section 419.

We now turn to a project in California, designed and built by the author in 1990.

CASE STUDY: PINETREE STUDIOS

Type of Live-Work: Flexhouse in a nonretail setting

Proximity Type: Live-near

Location: Oakland, California

Year Built: 1990

Architect: Thomas Dolan Architecture

Developer: Pinetree Associates; managing partner: Thomas Dolan

Pinetree Studios is the first new-construction condominium live-work project built in the United States (it was permitted as home occupation in Oakland), and it sits across the street from South Prescott Village in Oakland, California. Also designed—and this time

developed—by the author, it consists of four live-near flexhouses (see Figure 3-70). These are remarkable in that, while they are virtually identical in form, each was occupied—and even owned in one case—in different ways, beginning in 1990 when the project was completed and the units were sold.

Unit A was originally bought by a botanical illustrator and her partner. She lived and worked in the upper portion (see Figure 3-71). The downstairs portion of the unit—locked off at the connection between the upstairs and down in the entry at the bottom of the stairs—was rented out to someone who lives and works there and who enters the unit through its double (although not storefront) doors.

(Continued)

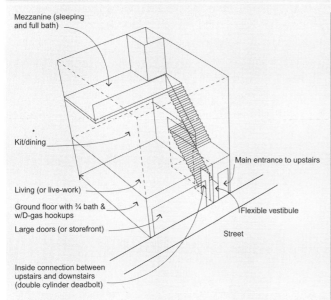

Figure 3-70 Axonometric of a typical flexhouse unit at Pinetree Studios, Oakland, California, 1990. Designed by Thomas Dolan Architecture.

Unit B was bought by a couple who occupied the entire space. She is a part-time painter who painted in the downstairs work space, which she shared with storage of her husband's extensive wind-surfing gear. When their grown kids visited, there was also a bed set up downstairs.

Unit C was bought in partnership by two friends. The downstairs is occupied as a residence by a man

Figure 3-71 Main-floor double-height living portion of a unit at Pinetree Studios, Oakland, California, which is also used as a work space, 1990. Designed by Thomas Dolan Architecture.

who drives a taxi in San Francisco. The upstairs is occupied by a *plein air* painter who holds classes and frequent open studios in his space. He does not live there and therefore uses his portion of the unit primarily as work space. However, the intent of live-work is preserved in the unit by the presence of the downstairs resident. Pinetree Studios was built as residences, and working is permitted there under Oakland's relatively unrestrictive home-occupation regulations.

Unit D was bought by one of the earliest practitioners of desktop publishing (i.e., producing print-quality content and design on a computer). Her computers were located on the middle level of the unit, and on the concrete-slab ground floor she worked on her large and very heavy letter presses, turning out printed material using the methods of an earlier century.

Therefore, Pinetree Studios is truly a building that learns: Four virtually identical units were used from the outset in four entirely different ways—none of them including retail due to the flexhouse's location in a residential neighborhood. Since 1990, most of the units have turned over, and their use configurations continue to "learn." Pinetree Studios is perhaps the first named flexhouse on the West Coast, although the form is ancient and the term was used by others prior to 1990.

Lessons Learned

Several specific design elements enable Pinetree Studios to be so flexible:

1. Separate entrances to the upstairs and downstairs portions, with an interconnection between the two at the bottom of the stairs that is equipped with a double-cylinder dead bolt keyed to the master. Thus the upstairs owner can lock off the downstairs space if it is rented out or vice versa.

2. The configuration of the downstairs work space includes a three-quarter bath and washer/dryer hookups including a gas dryer and a laundry/cleanup sink. These elements, while part of a single unit including the upstairs, allow an easy conversion of the downstairs to an independent live-work unit.

Urban Design of Townhouses and Flexhouses

It is a basic urban design tenet that the first floor of a residential townhouse should be set two or three feet above street level, so that a resident sitting in his front parlor does not find himself eyeball to eyeball with passersby. The elevation of the first floor alleviates this problem, affording a passerby a view mainly of the first-floor ceiling (see Figure 3-72). But what about a flexhouse that starts out as a residential townhouse but might eventually be retail and therefore required to be accessible and therefore level-in? One design solution that has been suggested is to build at grade, with a relatively high first-floor ceiling—twelve feet minimum—and then initially—in part or all of the first level—to build a floor at townhouse height that could easily be removed later (see Figure 3-73). The

Figure 3-72 Townhouses on a well-designed urban street, with their ground floors raised two to three feet above the sidewalk to provide the appropriate level of privacy in this building type.

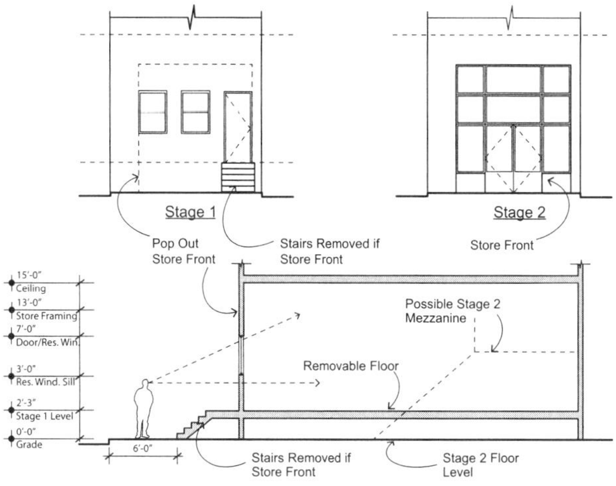

Figure 3-73 Townhouse/flexhouse conversion drawing, showing a removable first floor and a pop-out panel to allow the Stage 2 insertion of a storefront.

later transformation (Stage 2) would of course necessitate adjustments to the facade and to such details as the height of light switches. This "convertible ground floor" has not been attempted, to this author's knowledge, but it has been considered by at least one urban designer and will likely come to pass, perhaps after the Great Recession.

Another idea that has been contemplated by some is the pop-out front window, meaning that while the townhouse is originally designed with residential fenestration, a storefront opening is framed such that it could be easily retrofitted as part of Stage 2. This idea has also not yet been implemented in a built project. As an alternative to a raised floor, one can also create a dooryard in a grade-level flexhouse that moderates the intrusion of passersby but would be more easily adapted to a retail conversion.

Project Types: Housing over Retail and Live-Nearby

There is a long tradition of housing over retail throughout the world's towns and cities. It fits into a book on live-work for this reason: If you live on the same property as where you work, and your commute takes you out of your residence and down a hallway and an elevator or a set of stairs, this is the proximity type called live-nearby. It has the advantage of proximity afforded by live-work, combined with the greatest level of separation that still meets the definition of live-work.

A building can be designed and constructed as housing over retail, with or without potential direct connections between upstairs residential and downstairs commercial units. Its construction will be the same no matter whether the people who live upstairs work downstairs or not. Housing over retail may also be the ultimate configuration (stage 2) of flexhouse units that were originally sliced vertically. Also, housing over retail coexists very well with flexhouse or even townhouse live-work. They are often seen side by side in new town centers (see Figure 3-74).

CASE STUDY: ROSEMARY BEACH

Type of Live-Work: Housing over retail

Proximity Type: Live-nearby

Location: Rosemary Beach, Florida

Year Built: 1996 onward

Town Planner: Duany Plater-Zyberk

Developer: Leucadia

Rosemary Beach is a New Urbanist community whose size exploded to fully built-out within the first decade of the millennium (see Figure 3-74). The live-works on its main street, curving down toward the beach, appear to function well. Here, as elsewhere, it was important to see the backs of these buildings to get the full picture of how they worked. One building, as it turns out, is not a deftly connected live-work but five units of housing over retail, four of which are accessed through a lobby facing the rear with one stair and an elevator (see Figure 3-75).

The fifth upstairs unit is accessed via an exterior stair that skirts a charming street-facing courtyard (see Figure 3-76). This configuration functions as a live-nearby, although the upstairs tenants may or may not work downstairs.

Lessons Learned

In a mixed-use downtown, live-works can coexist well with housing over retail, which—as live-nearby—is essentially a live-work proximity type.

Figure 3-74 Housing over retail, a form of live-work (i.e., live-nearby). Rosemary Beach, Florida.

Figure 3-75 Rear view of the live-nearby building depicted in Figure 3-74, which has a rear entry to a common lobby served by elevator. Rosemary Beach, Florida.

Figure 3-76 A live-nearby unit within a larger housing-over-retail building. Rosemary Beach, Florida.

Name of Project: Celebration Live-Works

Type of Live-Work: Flexhouse and accessory buildings

Proximity Type: Live-nearby

Location: Celebration, Florida

Walk Score: 75 (very walkable)

Year Built: 1996 onward

Town Planners: Cooper Robertson and Partners and Robert A. M. Stern

Developer: Disney Corporation

In Celebration, a large New Urbanist community developed by Disney whose commercial center was built out very early in the project, live-work townhouses and flexhouses abound.

Some were rented as ground-floor apartments to enliven the street when Celebration first opened (see Figure 3-77). There are also, behind many of the single-family houses, granny flats above and beside alley-facing garages. Such spaces are ideal live-nearby work spaces. See Figure 2-5 for an example of an alley-facing outbuilding in Celebration.

Figure 3-77 Live-works in Celebration, Florida, whose downstairs were an important contributor to the project's early success and whose upstairs provided important rental housing; these are therefore live-near units.

Lesson Learned

Live-works of all kinds can help to immediately enliven a community's center from the time they are completed, and their flexibility can be a great asset as the community grows and changes.

Project Type: Infill Lofts

As has been noted, new construction infill lofts have arisen (see Figure 3-78) in many cities in response to changing conditions on the ground.

1. In some areas there are no longer buildings available to renovate easily for live-work; infill intermixed with already-renovated buildings can result in a more complete neighborhood.

2. In some cities, relaxed code provisions for renovation live-work have been applied to new construction.

3. As a simpler form of construction than traditional residential types, new live-work can be competitively priced.

In starting with a vacant lot, new-construction live-work lofts benefit from a relative paucity of constraints. Courtyard live-work has been discussed already, as has the need to create opportunities for interaction either within the project or by locating it on a great street. However, some lots are too narrow to accommodate courtyards or other common spaces, and some

Figure 3-78 New-construction lofts in San Francisco, California, constructed in a decidedly blue-collar neighborhood.

developers build at densities that they feel require them to maximize unit area and omit dedicated interactive open space (a strategy the author does not endorse). In such cases, providing the all-important opportunities for interaction is more challenging unless the project is located on a great street.

Therefore, for example, the urban loft building that was typically built in San Francisco in the 1990s was constructed over a ground-floor parking garage, is entered from a lobby at the street front, and contains multilevel units with large windows, multistory spaces, and sometimes multiple bedrooms. While urban lofts are often coded as live-work, many are simply called residential, sold as residential, and serve primarily as a place of residence for people who may work at home some of the time. Most lifestyle lofts are condominiums, and they suit the lives of those who do not want a conventional residence whose many rooms militate against a flexible life and evolving use of the unit.

Some design elements of many infill loft projects can be seen as having unintended consequences. Even though some loft buildings are located in relatively isolated locations—an issue addressed in Chapter Six: Planning—most will someday be part of a neighborhood and should be designed to address the street via transparency and multiple pedestrian entrances versus a relatively blank front with a small lobby entrance and a two-way garage entrance. It was common for such buildings from the 1990s to locate utility rooms, transformer rooms, and trash rooms at the street front (see Figure 6-41) rather than retail frontage or flexhouse liners that could serve to activate the street when it later becomes part of a real neighborhood.

The next case study of Yerba Buena Lofts describes an aggressively modernist project whose location is as convenient and central as Clocktower Lofts. It engages the street and relegates parking and services to the alley behind.

CASE STUDY: YERBA BUENA LOFTS

Name of Project: Yerba Buena Lofts

Type of Live-Work: New-construction infill residential lofts

Proximity Type: Live-with

Location: San Francisco, California

Walk Score: 92 (walker's paradise)

Year Built: 2001

Architect: Stanley Saitowitz/Natoma Architects, Inc.

Developer: Ed Tansev

Yerba Buena Lofts in San Francisco, by Stanley Saitowitz Architects (see Figure 3-79), is a decidedly urban, modernist project on an important street in the city. The building is entirely constructed of concrete and contains two hundred luxury "loft-style residences" that wrap around a four-story parking garage. Built at the height of the dot-com era, YBL, as it is often called, represents the ultimate translation of live-work entitlements into what is likely an entirely residential podium project. From the architect's Web site:

> The actual materials of construction are the final object. The patterned facade dissolves the figure of the building, creating the texture of street grain and expressing the mass.

Clearly, high design has come to live-work—or to loft-style living in any event. Yerba Buena Lofts has

Figure 3-79 Yerba Buena Lofts. San Francisco, California, 2001. Designed by Stanley Saitowitz/Natoma Architects.
Photo Credit:

been successful and sits well in the context of a very architecturally adventurous part of San Francisco. It is located adjacent to the Yerba Buena Gardens and just blocks from the Museum of Modern Art and the new Mexican and Jewish museums. It is therefore firmly ensconced in a walkable neighborhood well served by urban amenities.

Lesson Learned

From the architect, Stanley Saitowitz: "If you build better-quality buildings people know and are willing to pay more." This author's translation: High-art design has its place in the continuum of live-work design and development.

Project Type: Podium/High-Rise Liners, Flexhouses, and Lofts

Vancouver, BC, and the San Francisco Bay Area are two places that have seen larger, sometimes high-rise, projects that include live work or at least loft-style construction. The greatest opportunity for live-work in such projects are at the ground-floor level where "liner" units can surround the parking garage, can serve to activate the street immediately upon the project's completion, and can flex over time between residentially oriented lofts to live-with or live-near to entirely commercial. The goal in many such liners is that there will be a continuous facade of retail, an accomplishment that often takes years to realize; thus flexibility of use in the interim is essential.

CASE STUDY: LINER UNITS AT THE SIERRA

Name of Project: The Sierra

Type of Live-Work: Liner mezzanine live-work units

Proximity Type: Live-with

Location: Oakland, California

Walk Score: 91 (walker's paradise)

Year Built: 2003

Architect: Kava Massih

Developer: Crescent Heights

The Sierra is a large project that occupies an entire block of the Jack London Square district of Oakland. A double-podium project (i.e., one that includes a two-story parking garage embedded in the building), The Sierra includes five stories of residential units above the podium. Of note in the context of live-work are the liner units that surround the parking and do an excellent job of animating the four streets that surround the project while hiding the parking (see Figure 2-32). The liner units are configured as two-level townhouses, generally with the upper level being a mezzanine, although some have been built out to almost full plan.

What is remarkable about the liners at The Sierra is that they are truly functioning in a flexible way. They are not true flexhouses, because there is not a separation between work space and living space; in fact, many are not being lived in. At one corner is a thriving delicatessen, a favorite lunch spot in the neighborhood; a few doors down is an exercise salon, where one can look up at people riding exercise bicycles on that unit's upper level. Around the corner is a hair salon, open for business, whose owners sleep in the mezzanine of the unit (see Figures 3-80 and 3-81).

Some units are simply curtained, suggesting that they are strictly residential. While the entitlements

Figure 3-80 Hair salon liner unit. The Sierra, Oakland, California, 2003. Designed by Kava Massih Architects.

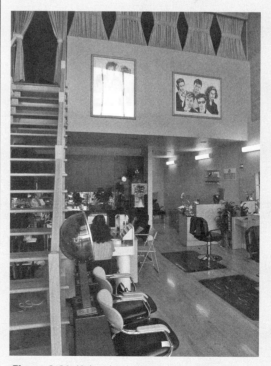

Figure 3-81 Hair salon in liner unit interior. The Sierra, Oakland, California, 2003. Designed by Kava Massih Architects.

(Continued)

for the liner portion of the project may not have permitted every use going on there at present or in the future, the units are all full and clearly a success, in part because of the flexibility that has been seized upon by their buyers.

Clearly the design of live-work requires an understanding of its unique qualities, of the fact that its uses will likely shift over time, and that therefore it must be designed with flexibility in mind. The next chapter discusses how to identify the market for live-work and how to actually sell or rent live-work units.

CHAPTER 4

The Market for Live-Work

Examining the Market for Live-Work

by Laurie Volk and Todd Zimmerman

Laurie Volk and Todd Zimmerman are co-managing directors of Zimmerman/Volk Associates, which has a national reputation for innovative market analysis based on its proprietary target market methodology. Specializing in the analysis of urban and new urban development and redevelopment, ZVA is recognized by the leading practitioners of the New Urbanism as the national expert on urban residential market feasibility.

The market for live-work has often been romanticized as the shopkeeper living above his store or the sculptor sleeping on a platform bed in the corner of her studio. While there are certainly many instances to validate these stereotypes, those people who live where they work can just as easily be a taxidermist working out of his garage or an accountant running her practice from a converted bedroom. In fact, it is that latter case—the home office user, ranging from the executive who works one day a week from home to the sole-practitioner professional—that comprises the bulk of the live-work market.

In the twenty-first-century knowledge economy, a certain class of worker is always at work, connected at home or away from home through a growing array and variety of wired and mobile devices. For these workers, the distinction of workplace has become greatly diminished and, for some, has vanished completely. Although there continue to be myriad surveys and a host of assertions about the market potential for dwellings that can accommodate an efficient and practical working environment, attempts to quantify that market—even on the gross national level—yield ambiguous results. (See Figure 4-1 for an example of purpose-built live-works located on a traditional neighborhood development's main street.)

Figure 4-1 The Marketplace at Habersham, near Beaufort, South Carolina, a series of flexhouses fronting on the main street of this New Urbanist traditional neighborhood development (see case study in this chapter), 2002–2006. Designer: Rick Black (conceptual), Ben Miehe (final design).
Photo Credit: Jonathan Herron

It is useful, we believe, to examine the live-work market from the perspective of both the user and the producer. Live-work is only one of many housing types for which the market has been unmeasured and, as a result, possibly underserved. Residential real estate—because it is rooted in place and requires a consumer to move in order to "consume" it—is unique in that it does not yield neatly to supply-demand analysis. From the supply-demand perspective, a market can look balanced, with no excess inventory, when, in fact, households are living in dwellings unsuited to their needs or desires because the appropriate dwelling units are not available or are not available in the neighborhood in which they want to live. This is why we refer to market "potential" rather than market "demand." The potential market for live-work consists not only of people who currently work at home full-time, or even those who work at home part of the time, but also those who would work at home if only their home could accommodate work.

The End-User Market for Live-Work

The evolution in workplace location since the nation's founding has been toward increased distinction between the workplace and home, from the typical eighteenth-century pattern of farmers living on their farmstead and shopkeepers living above their store to nearly total jobs/housing separation in the finale decades of the twentieth century. Patterns had changed so greatly that most laborers could no longer walk to their manufacturing jobs and white-collar employment was no longer concentrated in urban centers connected to close-in neighborhoods by efficient hub-and-spoke transit. Many transit systems languished or were abandoned as jobs scattered across the landscape. The stagnation in real wages beginning in the early 1970s and the concomitant growth of two-income families complicated workers' ability to live near their jobs.

However, it is possible that, enabled by the reurbanization of the United States likely in the first half of the twenty-first century, the distance between work and home will begin to contract.

Working where one lives is, of course, the ultimate measure of jobs/housing balance, and over the past half century, the prevalence of workers who usually work at home has seen both dramatic decline and remarkable recovery. The decennial census of population shows that the trough occurred in 1980, when only 2.2 million workers—2.3 percent of all workers—worked at home (see Table 4-1). According to the Census Bureau, this steep decline from twenty years earlier, when 7.2 percent, or 4.7 million, workers worked at home, was the result not only of the continued reduction in the number of family farms but also of the increased tendency of medical, legal, and other professionals to leave sole-practitioner home offices in favor of larger firms.

The decline reversed in 1990, when the number of workers who worked at home most of the time increased to 3.4 million, or 3.0 percent of the workforce. In 2000, the number had increased again to 4.2 million, or 3.3 percent of the workforce. The decennial census numbers end in 2000 since, for the first time in many decades, the 2010 census

Table 4-1 All Workers, and Workers Who Worked at Home in the United States, *1960–2000*

	Number of Workers			Percent Change		
Census date	Total	Worked at home	Percent worked at home	Ten-year period	All workers	Worked at home
1960*	64,655,805	4,662,750	7.2			
1970*	76,852,389	2,685,144	3.5	1960 to 1970	18.9	−42.4
1980†	96,617,296	2,179,863	2.3	1970 to 1980	25.7	−18.8
1990†	115,070,274	3,406,025	3.0	1980 to 1990	19.1	56.2
2000†	128,279,228	4,184,223	3.3	1990 to 2000	11.5	22.8

*Workers 14 years and older

†Workers 16 years and older

NOTE: People who regularly work at home one or two days a week but elsewhere during the other three days are not reflected in the work-at-home estimates from the decennial census, which means that estimates from the decennial censuses may differ from other sources that define working at home differently.

SOURCE: Census 2000 and 1960 to 1990 Censuses of Population, U.S. Census Bureau, Internet Release Date: October 20, 2004; Zimmerman/Volk Associates, Inc.

did not include a "long form" that would have queried travel time to work.

Data on working at home can be elusive and, at times, contradictory. The largest sample—from the decennial census—is measured by answers to the question "How did you usually get to work last week?" "Worked at home" is one of the options. The census defines "usually" as the most number of days during the week. Therefore, people who work at home fewer than three days a week are not included.

The real estate data uncertainty principle—that data can be accurate or data can be current, but they are rarely both—applies to working at home. While there are more recent sources of data than the 2000 census of population, those data use different definitions. The most recent work-at-home data come from the Census Bureau's 2005 Survey of Income and Program Participation (SIPP). Work-at-home data from SIPP classifies home workers in two categories: "mixed workers," those who work at home at least one full day a week but work elsewhere as well, and "home workers," those who work exclusively at home. The second of these is very roughly equivalent to the dece_____ _nsus data, although more broadly inclusive, so di_____ _ is not possible.

Data from SIPP _____ _line of workers who work at home _____ _rkers in 1995 to 7.8 percent in 20__ _____ _owever, there was an increase ove_ _____ _rom a significant dip in both numb__ _____ _1995 to 1997. In 2005, 11.3 million worke__ _____ _e (see Table 4-2).

The SIPP data provide the best detailed information on Americans who work at home, both full-time home workers and "mixed workers" who work most of the time out of the home but work at least one day a week at home (see Tables 4-3 and 4-4).

According to the SIPP data on home-based workers, people who worked exclusively at home were older, earned more, and were better educated than people who worked away from the home.

People who worked exclusively at home in 2005 had a median family income 12 percent higher than people who worked away from the home—$63,650 compared with $56,775 (see Table 4-4). The spread has increased since 1999, when the $52,625 median family income of home-based workers was only 9 percent higher than the $48,475 median for people who worked away from the home.

Home workers have significantly higher educational attainment. In 2005, 46 percent of workers who worked exclusively at home had a bachelor's or advanced degree, 20 percentage points higher than non-home workers.

Mixed workers—the dedicated home office market, those who spend at least one full day a week working at home but spend more time working away from home—are even more affluent and better educated than non-home workers, with a 42 percent higher income and 32 percent more likely to have a bachelor's or advanced degree.

Workers who work exclusively at home are more likely to be older than those who work outside the home. Home

Table 4-2 Work-at-Home Status of Employed People
Primary Job Only (Workers age 15 years and older, numbers in thousands), The United States, 1995–2005
(Workers age 15 years and older; numbers in thousands)

	Total Employed Number	Non-Home Workers[1] Number	Non-Home Workers[1] Percent	Work at Home Total Number	Work at Home Total Percent	Mixed Workers[2] Number	Mixed Workers[2] Percent	Home Workers[3] Number	Home Workers[3] Percent
1995	125,925	115,039	91.4	10,886	8.6	2,546	2.0	8,340	6.6
1997	132,692	123,432	93.0	9,260	7.0	2,875	2.2	6,385	4.8
1999	136,300	126,823	93.1	9,476	7.0	2,735	2.0	6,742	5.0
2002	138,355	127,935	92.5	10,420	7.5	3,126	2.3	7,293	5.3
2005	145,074	133,746	92.2	11,328	7.8	3,186	2.2	8,142	5.6

1. Non-home workers are defined as those who did not work a full workday at home as part of their work schedule.

2. Mixed workers are defined as those who worked at home at least one full day a week but also worked other days in a location outside of their home.

3. Home workers are defined as those who worked exclusively at home (i.e., every day they worked, they worked at home).

SOURCE: U.S. Census Bureau, Survey of Income and Program Participation, 1993 Panel, Wave 9; U.S. Census Bureau, Survey of Income and Program Participation, 1996 Panel, Wave 4; U.S. Census Bureau, Survey of Income and Program Participation, 1999 Panel, Wave 10; U.S. Census Bureau, Survey of Income and Program Participation, 2001 Panel, Wave 4; U.S. Census Bureau, Survey of Income and Program Participation, 2004 Panel, Wave 4; Zimmerman/Volk Associates, Inc.

Table 4-3 Class, Industry, and Occupation of Worker by Work-at-Home Status
(Workers age 15 years and older, numbers in thousands), the United States, 2005

Characteristic	Total Employed		Non-Home Workers[1]		Work at Home Total		Mixed Workers[2]		Home Workers[3]	
	Number	Percent	Number	Percent	Number	Percent	Number	Percent	Number	Percent
Total	145,074	100.0	133,746	100.0	11,328	100.0	3,186	100.0	8,142	100.0
Class										
Private for-profit	95,792	66.0	91,878	68.7	3,913	34.5	1,401	44.0	2,512	30.9
Private not-for-profit	10,297	7.1	9,701	7.3	596	5.3	252	7.9	344	4.2
Local government	10,728	7.4	10,305	7.7	423	3.7	127	4.0	296	3.6
State government	6,657	4.6	6,213	4.6	444	3.9	178	5.6	267	3.3
Federal government	4,286	3.0	4,136	3.1	150	1.3	73	2.3	77	0.9
Unpaid family	984	0.7	441	0.3	543	4.8	(S)	(S)	(S)	(S)
Self-employed, unclassified	15,496	10.7	10,354	7.7	5,142	45.4	1,078	33.9	4,063	49.9
Not otherwise classified	836	0.6	718	0.5	117	1.0	(S)	(S)	(S)	(S)
Industry										
Agriculture, forestry, and fishing	3,424	2.4	2,817	2.1	608	5.4	59	1.9	548	6.7
Mining	498	0.3	(S)	(S)	(S)	(S)	(S)	(S)	(S)	(S)
Construction	10,958	7.6	10,264	7.7	694	6.1	207	6.5	487	6.0
Manufacturing	17,134	11.8	16,251	12.2	884	7.8	301	9.5	582	7.2
Transportation, communications, and public utilities	9,532	6.6	9,048	6.8	483	4.3	128	4.0	356	4.4
Wholesale trade	5,004	3.4	4,391	3.3	613	5.4	190	6.0	423	5.2
Retail trade	25,114	17.3	24,057	18.0	1,057	9.3	245	7.7	812	10.0
Finance, insurance, and real estate	9,168	6.3	8,018	6.0	1,150	10.2	408	12.8	742	9.1
Business and repair services	9,188	6.3	7,860	5.9	1,328	11.7	368	11.6	960	11.8
Personal services	4,153	2.9	3,870	2.9	282	2.5	68	2.1	215	2.6
Entertainment and recreational services	2,660	1.8	2,341	1.8	319	2.8	34	1.1	285	3.5
Professional and related services	39,922	27.5	36,336	27.2	3,587	31.7	1,073	33.7	2,513	30.9
Public administration	7,758	5.3	7,471	5.6	287	2.5	98	3.1	189	2.3
Military	510	0.4	(S)	(S)	(S)	(S)	(S)	(S)	(S)	(S)
Occupation										
Executive, administrative, and managerial	18,414	12.7	15,885	11.9	2,529	22.3	908	28.5	1,620	19.9
Professional	24,029	16.6	21,209	15.9	2,820	24.9	930	29.2	1,890	23.2
Technician	4,452	3.1	(S)	(S)	(S)	(S)	(S)	(S)	(S)	(S)
Sales	16,645	11.5	14,661	11.0	1,984	17.5	602	18.9	1,382	17.0
Administrative support	20,275	14.0	19,174	14.3	1,101	9.7	271	8.5	830	10.2
Services	22,428	15.5	21,360	16.0	1,069	9.4	106	3.3	962	11.8
Farming, forestry, and fishing	3,827	2.6	3,209	2.4	617	5.5	53	1.7	564	6.9

Table 4-3 *(Continued)*

Characteristic	Total Employed		Non-Home Workers[1]		Work at Home Total		Mixed Workers[2]		Home Workers[3]	
	Number	Percent	Number	Percent	Number	Percent	Number	Percent	Number	Percent
Production, craft, and repair	13,610	9.4	13,072	9.8	538	4.7	148	4.6	390	4.8
Operators, fabricators, and laborers	20,824	14.4	20,430	15.3	394	3.5	82	2.6	312	3.8
Military	520	0.4	(S)	(S)	(S)	(S)	(S)	(S)	(S)	(S)

1. Non-home workers are defined as those who did not work a full workday at home as part of their work schedule.

2. Mixed workers are defined as those who worked at home at least one full day a week, but also worked other days

3. Home workers are defined as those who worked exclusively at home (i.e., every day they worked, they worked at home).

(S) Data suppressed in accordance with the Census Bureau's guidelines to protect respondent confidentiality.

Source: U.S. Census Bureau, Survey of Income and Program Participation, 2004 Panel, Wave 4; Zimmerman/Volk Associates, Inc.

Table 4-4 Selected Demographic Characteristics of Employed People by Work-at-Home Status (Workers age 15 years and older), the United States, 2005

Characteristic	Total Employed		Non-Home Workers[1]		Work at Home Total		Mixed Workers[2]		Home Workers[3]	
	Number	Percent	Number	Percent	Number	Percent	Number	Percent	Number	Percent
Total	145,074,000	100.0	133,746,000	100.0	11,327,900	100.0	3,185,620	100.0	8,142,310	100.0
Age										
15 to 24 years	20,303,400	14.0	19,875,300	14.9	428,067	3.8	75,941	2.4	352,126	4.3
25 to 34 years	31,625,400	21.8	29,641,800	22.2	1,983,610	17.5	637,424	20.0	1,346,180	16.5
35 to 44 years	35,115,800	24.2	32,163,200	24.0	2,952,550	26.1	951,778	29.9	2,000,770	24.6
45 to 54 years	33,830,500	23.3	30,893,500	23.1	2,937,000	25.9	844,613	26.5	2,092,380	25.7
55 to 64 years	18,602,800	12.8	16,568,300	12.4	2,034,550	18.0	503,522	15.8	1,531,030	18.8
65 years and over	5,596,480	3.9	4,604,330	3.4	992,159	8.8	172,345	5.4	819,814	10.1
Gender										
Male	77,404,200	53.4	71,640,300	53.6	5,763,910	50.9	1,766,520	55.5	3,997,380	49.1
Female	67,670,100	46.6	62,106,100	46.4	5,564,020	49.1	1,419,100	44.5	4,144,920	50.9
Race and Hispanic Origin										
White, alone	119,647,000	82.5	109,767,000	82.1	9,879,920	87.2	2,735,760	85.9	7,144,160	87.7
White, non-Hispanic, alone	102,576,000	70.7	93,345,800	69.8	9,229,830	81.5	2,577,790	80.9	6,652,040	81.7
Black, alone	15,981,300	11.0	15,286,300	11.4	695,031	6.1	201,472	6.3	493,559	6.1
Asian, alone	4,929,250	3.4	4,504,470	3.4	424,774	3.7	155,441	4.9	269,333	3.3
All other races, alone or in combination	4,516,690	3.1	4,188,480	3.1	328,205	2.9	92,948	2.9	235,256	2.9
Hispanic, of any race, alone or in combination	18,597,100	12.8	17,878,800	13.4	718,339	6.3	186,761	5.9	531,578	6.5
Nativity and Citizenship										
Native-born	125,418,000	86.5	115,279,000	86.2	10,138,800	89.5	2,823,450	88.6	7,315,330	89.8
Foreign-born	19,656,200	13.5	18,467,000	13.8	1,189,150	10.5	362,172	11.4	826,974	10.2
Citizen	8,519,790	5.9	7,900,740	5.9	619,052	5.5	207,956	6.5	411,096	5.0
Non-citizen	11,136,400	7.7	10,566,300	7.9	570,094	5.0	154,216	4.8	415,878	5.1

(Continued)

Table 4-4 *(Continued)*

Characteristic	Total Employed		Non-Home Workers[1]		Work at Home Total		Mixed Workers[2]		Home Workers[3]	
	Number	Percent	Number	Percent	Number	Percent	Number	Percent	Number	Percent
Marital Status										
Married	82,917,000	57.2	75,193,000	56.2	7,724,000	68.2	2,204,320	69.2	5,519,670	67.8
Spouse absent	1,761,780	1.2	1,682,000	1.3	79,779	0.7	(S)	(S)	(S)	(S)
Widowed	2,832,920	2.0	2,609,080	2.0	223,843	2.0	41,131	1.3	182,712	2.2
Separated	3,003,090	2.1	2,807,360	2.1	195,733	1.7	54,610	1.7	141,124	1.7
Divorced	16,477,800	11.4	15,186,100	11.4	1,291,660	11.4	366,597	11.5	925,065	11.4
Never married	39,843,600	27.5	37,950,900	28.4	1,892,690	16.7	518,960	16.3	1,373,730	16.9
Own Children Under 18										
Not present	85,607,900	59.0	78,788,900	58.9	6,819,020	60.2	1,873,340	58.8	4,945,680	60.7
Present	59,466,400	41.0	54,957,500	41.1	4,508,910	39.8	1,312,280	41.2	3,196,630	39.3
Family Income										
Under $25,000	24,317,000	16.8	22,238,400	16.6	2,078,560	18.3	352,607	11.1	1,725,950	21.2
$25,000 to $49,999	37,782,000	26.0	35,655,000	26.7	2,127,010	18.8	516,989	16.2	1,610,020	19.8
$50,000 to $74,999	31,978,200	22.0	30,057,100	22.5	1,921,160	17.0	582,653	18.3	1,338,500	16.4
$75,000 and over	50,997,200	35.2	45,796,000	34.2	5,201,200	45.9	1,733,370	54.4	3,467,830	42.6
Median family income	$57,456,000	—	$56,772	—	$68,004	—	$80,424	—	$63,648	—
Educational Attainment										
Less than high school diploma	13,198,600	9.1	12,751,600	9.5	446,942	3.9	40,599	1.3	406,343	5.0
High school graduate	38,642,000	26.6	36,990,000	27.7	1,652,050	14.6	267,961	8.4	1,384,080	17.0
Some college/ Associate's degree	52,280,600	36.0	48,685,200	36.4	3,595,400	31.7	1,030,620	32.4	2,564,780	31.5
Bachelor's degree or more	40,953,200	28.2	35,319,600	26.4	5,633,540	49.7	1,846,440	58.0	3,787,100	46.5
Metropolitan Status										
Nonmetropolitan	23,203,800	16.0	21,532,300	16.1	1,671,570	14.8	330,806	10.4	1,340,770	16.5
Metropolitan	121,871,000	84.0	112,214,000	83.9	9,656,360	85.2	2,854,820	89.6	6,801,540	83.5
Region of Residence										
Northeast	26,858,100	18.5	24,687,900	18.5	2,170,280	19.2	673,598	21.1	1,496,680	18.4
Midwest	33,510,000	23.1	30,993,100	23.2	2,516,910	22.2	648,806	20.4	1,868,110	22.9
South	51,224,800	35.3	47,968,600	35.9	3,256,160	28.7	939,411	29.5	2,316,750	28.5
West	33,481,400	23.1	30,096,800	22.5	3,384,580	29.9	923,807	29.0	2,460,770	30.2

1. Non-home workers are defined as those who did not work a full workday at home as part of their work schedule.

2. Mixed workers are defined as those who worked at home at least one full day a week, but also worked other days

3. Home workers are defined as those who worked exclusively at home

(S) Data suppressed in accordance with the Census Bureau's guidelines to protect respondent confidentiality.

Source: U.S. Census Bureau, Survey of Income and Program Participation, 2004 Panel, Wave 4; Zimmerman/Volk Associates, Inc.

workers under age 24 make up only 4.3 percent of total home workers, whereas workers under 24 make up 14.9 percent of non-home workers. Home workers aged 25 to 34 make up 16.5 percent of total home workers, whereas workers 25 to 34 are 22.2 percent of non-home workers.

Although there are no data on primary wage-earner characteristics, evidence suggests that a significant percentage of home workers are married women. The work-at-home category is the only one in which women form the majority, 50.9 percent compared to 46.4 percent of non-home workers. Nearly 68 percent of home workers are married, compared to 56.2 percent of non-home workers. It is likely, however, that caring for children at home is not a significant factor for home workers; children are present in 39.3 percent of home worker households, equivalent to 41.1 percent of non-home worker households with children under 18.

Just under half of people who worked exclusively at home are self-employed, compared to just 7.7 percent of people who worked away from the home (see Table 3-4). Home workers are more likely to be executives and managers than non-home workers, 19.9 percent to only 12.7 percent, and more likely to be professionals, 23.2 percent compared to 15.9 percent. An even greater disparity exists in these occupations for workers who work both at home and elsewhere—the natural home-office market—executive, administrative and managerial workers are 28.5 percent of these so-called mixed workers, and professionals are 29.2 percent. Professional services is the largest single industry category for both home workers and mixed workers.

Although home workers as a whole earn more than non-home workers, self-employed home workers earn significantly less than any other class of home worker, with a median monthly earnings in 2005 of $1,075 compared to $3,900 for home workers who work for a private company (see Tables 4-5 and 4-6). Median income data can be deceptive, since home workers in executive, administrative, and managerial occupations have median monthly earnings of $3,750 ($5,000 for "mixed workers") and those who are professionals have median earnings of $2,900 ($4,167 for mixed workers), compared to $4,000 for non-home workers.

Table 4-5 Median Monthly Personal Earnings by Class, Industry, Occupation, and Work-at-Home Status (Workers age 15 years and older), the United States, 2005

			Work at Home		
Characteristic	Total	Non-Home Workers[1]	Total	Mixed Workers[2]	Home Workers[3]
Class					
Private for-profit	$2,221	$2,167	$4,571	$5,250	$3,888
Private not-for-profit	$2,380	$2,361	$3,167	$4,108	$2,417
Local government	$2,850	$2,833	$3,326	$3,326	$3,333
State government	$2,751	$2,700	$3,750	$3,895	$3,637
Federal government	$3,750	$3,750	$5,417	$7,083	$5,000
Unpaid family	—	—	—	—	—
Self-employed, unclassified	$1,500	$1,732	$1,249	$1,666	$1,080
Not otherwise classified	$856	$1,000	$400	(S)	$399
Industry					
Agriculture, forestry, and fishing	$1,299	$1,496	$0	$80	$0
Mining	$3,159	$3,159	(S)	(S)	(S)
Construction	$2,395	$2,400	$1,999	$2,000	$1,999
Manufacturing	$2,833	$2,806	$4,667	$5,737	$3,618
Transportation, communications, and public utilities	$3,200	$3,200	$4,000	$5,708	$3,248
Wholesale trade	$2,808	$2,750	$3,750	$4,638	$3,000
Retail trade	$1,350	$1,351	$1,140	$2,708	$650
Finance, insurance, and real estate	$2,875	$2,833	$3,333	$4,417	$2,929
Business and repair services	$2,078	$2,045	$2,500	$4,800	$1,977
Personal services	$1,426	$1,462	$866	$866	$825

(Continued)

Table 4-5 *(Continued)*

Characteristic	Total	Non-Home Workers[1]	Work at Home		
			Total	Mixed Workers[2]	Home Workers[3]
Entertainment and recreational services	$1,423	$1,500	$1,000	$1,999	$836
Professional and related services	$2,403	$2,400	$2,566	$3,750	$2,000
Public administration	$3,333	$3,333	$3,893	$5,750	$3,000
Military	$3,500	$3,500	(S)	(S)	(S)
Occupation					
Executive, administrative, and managerial	$4,000	$4,000	$4,200	$5,000	$3,749
Professional	$3,500	$3,511	$3,333	$4,167	$2,900
Technician	$3,200	$3,167	$4,000	$5,375	$3,985
Sales	$1,786	$1,733	$2,500	$4,000	$1,999
Administrative support	$2,083	$2,084	$1,520	$2,250	$1,299
Services	$1,299	$1,300	$765	$1,800	$734
Farming, forestry, and fishing	$1,386	$1,516	$0	$137	$0
Production, craft, and repair	$2,600	$2,667	$1,500	$1,820	$1,500
Operators, fabricators, and laborers	$1,944	$1,949	$803	$708	$803
Military	$3,500	$3,500	(S)	(S)	(S)

1. Non-home workers are defined as those who did not work a full workday at home as part of their work schedule.

2. Mixed workers are defined as those who worked at home at least one full day a week but also worked other days.

3. Home workers are defined as those who worked exclusively at home (i.e., every day they worked, they worked at home).

(S) Data suppressed in accordance with the Census Bureau's guidelines to protect respondent confidentiality.

Source: U.S. Census Bureau, Survey of Income and Program, Participation, 2004 Panel, Wave 5; Zimmerman/Volk Associates, Inc.

Table 4-6 Class of Worker for Workers Who Worked at Home
The United States, 1980–2000

Class of Worker	2000		1990		1980	
	Number	Percent	Number	Percent	Number	Percent
Workers 16 years and over	4,184,223	100.0	3,406,025	100.0	2,179,863	100.0
Private wage and salary[1]	1,984,270	47.4	1,236,843	36.3	731,660	33.6
Federal government[2]	51,158	1.2	125,680	3.7	30,194	1.4
State and Local government	125,816	3.0	73,308	2.2	60,707	2.8
Self-employed[3]	1,910,919	45.7	1,828,470	53.7	1,230,106	56.4
Unpaid family workers	112,060	2.7	141,724	4.2	127,196	5.8

1. Includes Census 2000 categories of private for profit, self-employed in own incorporated business, and private not for profit.

2. Armed Forces personnel who were on ships at sea during the census were enumerated as working at home in 1990, but not in 1980 or 2000.

3. Census 2000 category entitled self-employed workers in own not incorporated business.

Source: Census 2000 and 1980 to 1990 Censuses of Population, U.S. Census Bureau, Internet Release Date: October 20, 2004; Zimmerman/Volk Associates, Inc.

These data would suggest that the more significant current market is for dedicated home offices, serving both the mixed workers and home workers. That does not mean, however, that there is not a potential market for more specialized live-work types, from the loft where artists and artisans can fabricate their works, to the flexhouse and shop house types that accommodate retail trade. That market is simply more challenging to quantify. Because that market is the aggregation of the individual circumstances of many artists and artisans and would-be retailers, it is most easily addressed at the local level, usually through survey research.

As the United States reurbanizes at every scale, the opportunity and attractiveness of specialized live-work buildings should increase significantly. Despite its advantages in efficiency and flexibility, working at home can also have its disadvantages, chief among these being isolation. However, working where one lives in a walkable, mixed-use neighborhood can offset the isolation of working alone at home; the option to socialize or brainstorm is a short walk away.

American neighborhoods, at every urban scale, are likely to become more walkable and include a greater mix of uses over the next several decades. The demographic foundation on which cities and towns alike can rebuild their downtowns and in-town neighborhoods is already in place. The two largest generations in the history of the United States—the baby boomers, born between 1946 and 1964, and the millennials, born from 1977 to 1996—are converging at life stages where there are no children in the household; baby boomers are becoming empty nesters while their millennial children are forming new households. As a result, one- and two-person households now comprise 59 percent of all American households.

The social and cultural amenities of urban life are highly attractive to these child-free households, both young and old. These demographics, combined with steadily increasing traffic congestion and rising gasoline prices, have led to significant changes in neighborhood and housing preferences, with major shifts from predominantly single-family detached houses in lower-density, auto-oriented suburbs to a diverse mix of detached houses, attached houses and higher-density apartments in downtowns and walkable, often transit-served, mixed-use traditional neighborhoods.

The impact on urban neighborhoods has already been documented. A study of building permit data (*Residential Construction Trends in America's Metropolitan Regions*, published by the U.S. Environmental Protection Agency in January, 2009) showed that from 1990 to 2007, "in roughly half of the metropolitan areas examined, urban core communities dramatically increased their share of new residential building permits." That "the increase has been particularly dramatic over the past five years"—that is 2003 to 2007—is clearly influenced by the demographic convergence.

By midcentury, it should be clear that the great demographic convergence will have had as profound an impact on American settlement patterns as the postwar baby boom did after the long hiatus of the Great Depression and World War II. Walkable, mixed-use neighborhoods at every urban scale can nurture a significant growth of the live-work market, providing a supportive context for a variety of home workers in a range of live-work unit types.

The Developer/Investor Market for Live-Work

Although the live-work market is significant and should grow, the production of appropriate units could be a challenge. Much of live-work development or redevelopment requires little or no specialized design and construction. The home office is hardly a specialized type; third bedrooms in model units have been merchandized as home offices for decades. Agricultural live-work—the farm as home to the farmer/owner and family, as well as, in larger operations, permanent or seasonal homes for farm workers—will never be a production housing type and will continue to be met on a case-by-case basis, ranging from prefabricated structures to custom construction.

Live-work spaces—usually lofts—for artists and artisans have long been a staple of urban redevelopment. New York City was home to live-work studios as early as 1857 with the Richard Morris Hunt–designed Studio Building in Greenwich Village. Just after the turn of the twentieth century, a number of buildings with high-ceilinged studios were constructed, culminating in 1916 with Manhattan's most famous studio building, the Hotel des Artistes on West 67th Street. Until recently, the only legacy of this early live-work construction has been the corruption of the term "studio" by real estate marketers into common usage for a one-room efficiency unit.

Although the loft is not a production housing type, by the early twenty-first century, it is the rare city that does not have one or more architectural firms that specialize in the adaptive reuse of nonresidential buildings. In some cities, where the stock of buildings appropriate for adaptive reuse has been depleted, new loft buildings—some even featuring design elements reminiscent of nineteenth-century warehouse structures—have been built; even in those buildings where work is a permitted use, most of the units typically are used exclusively as residences.

The live-work type that does not match the narrow range of housing types that American builders are comfortable producing is the flexhouse. While a range of variations on the shop house, including versions of the flexhouse, have been produced by small specialized builders—typically in greenfield traditional neighborhood developments—it is by far the least common live-work type (see Figure 4-2).

As the flexhouse becomes better understood, and as American neighborhoods evolve to be more accommodating of pedestrian-oriented building types, flexhouse production should increase. In addition to the specialized builders comfortable working in urban infill and new traditional neighborhoods, it is possible that America's legions of semiprofessional builder/investors will discover the potential of flexhouse development.

Figure 4-2 Flexhouses at Habersham, near Beaufort, South Carolina, called by the developer The Lofts at Habersham; most house separate tenants upstairs and down, are owned by investors. 2002–2006. Designers: Rick Black (conceptual), Ben Miehe (final design).
Photo Credit: Jonathan Herron

Despite significant housing industry consolidation over the past two decades, large housing producers still account for a minority of new unit production in the United States. In 2009, the top 100 house builders in the *Builder Magazine* survey accounted for less than 37 percent of all closings, down from a peak of approximately 44 percent in 2006. Likewise in commercial real estate, the aggregate annual production of commercial and industrial space by small producers outweighs the annual production of large developers. Most of the United States is built by conservative, semiprofessional entities, shunning innovation, building with as low a risk as possible, often with as-of-right zoning. Almost every marketplace has the usual array of strip centers, medical office buildings, and the rest of the United States' ubiquitous roadside real estate built by small limited partnerships; a typical example would be a real estate broker and a dentist.

In the appropriate locations, these small developer/investors, precisely because they are risk-averse, make an excellent market for flexhouse locations. With a group of flexhouses developed and owned by a variety of entities, the risk of reestablishing or creating a walkable mixed-use street, block, or neighborhood can be spread among many investors. Just as the risk is shared by all, so is the success; unlike auto-oriented locations, places where housing, workplaces, and retail are mixed within walking distance of each other can enhance the attractiveness and value of all uses and building types.

Although flexhouses have typically been used as an ingredient in establishing new mixed-use centers for new neighborhoods over the past few decades, the same approach can be used in existing neighborhoods. Provided that the basic retail dynamics are supportive, a row of flexhouses can reestablish a commercial core in a disenfranchised neighborhood or create a new retail center for a neighborhood making the transition from warehouse or industrial use to mixed use.

Despite its elusive nature, the market for live-work is certainly greater than the current inventory of live-work units would suggest and is likely to grow along with the development and reurbanization of U.S. neighborhoods. Working Americans who spend their workdays primarily at home are better educated and more affluent than those who commute to a conventional workplace every day. All that is lacking is widespread awareness of the market among producers of real estate for the live-work category to match its potential.

Type of Live-Work: Townhouse-style mixed-use development; 33 mixed-use buildings

Proximity Type: Live-near flexhouses

Location: Habersham, Beaufort, South Carolina, a large New Urbanist greenfield community

Year Built: 2002–2006

Architect: Rick Black (conceptual), Savannah, GA; Ben Miehe (final design), Charleston, SC

Town Planner: Duany Plater-Zyberk

Developer: Habersham Land Company Inc.

Habersham is a large New Urbanist community designed by Duany Plater-Zyberk and largely built out (see Figure C-21 in the color folio for the master plan). The developer jump-started the downtown by building flexhouses—mostly presold—that frame the town's main street very successfully (see Figure 4-3).

Figure 4-3 Street view of the Habersham Marketplace, Beaufort, South Carolina, during one of the frequent community events. 2002–2006. Designers: Rick Black (conceptual), Ben Miehe (final)
Photo Credit: Jonathan Herron

The Lofts—as the developer refers to them—consist of 33 mixed-use flexhouses in a site plan (see Figure C-22 in the color folio for the site plan) arranged on two sides of a street that includes a generous median in the style of the Ramblas in Barcelona or Mizner Park in Florida (although more down-transect than both examples).

A true mixed-use project that was designed for maximum flexibility. The flexhouses each contain a two-level residential unit above and a 710-square-foot commercial space on the ground floor. The total area of the ground-floor commercial space is approximately 24,000 square feet. Each flexhouse contains a total of 2,130 square feet on three levels (see Figure 4-4).

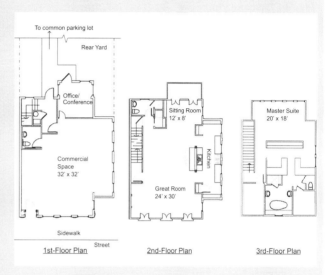

Figure 4-4 Floor plans of a typical flexhouse at The Lofts, showing ground floor retail and upstairs space accessible only from the rear, which can be residential or commercial use. 2002–2006. Designers: Rick Black (conceptual), Ben Miehe (final).
Photo Credit: Jonathan Herron

The first floor is set up to be commercial—usually retail—and is designed to house small mom-and-pop businesses. The developer points out that although 710 square feet seems small, there are currently three ground-floor spaces fitted with full restaurant kitchens that seat 30 inside and an additional 10 to 15 outside. Each first-floor space has an accessible unisex restroom and—depending on the use—the first floor may or may not have access to the backyard space behind. The developer has essentially secured preapprovals for any combination of uses for the building, such that any buyer or tenant only has to secure a business license from the town of Beaufort. While flexible entitlements are a stated goal of many who have built flexhouses, this is the only instance of which the author is aware of a project that has obtained such flexible entitlements.

(Continued)

The second floor is laid out as an open-plan loft (i.e., without interior walls). The living space is on the street side, which allows for balconies—a common Low Country design element—and provides "eyes on the street." The second floor also includes a dining and kitchen area. The structural separation between the first and second floor includes one layer of Sheetrock on the first-floor ceiling, supported steel bar joists capped with a metal deck. And then 4 inches of regular concrete, which achieves a fire rating of two hours. The second story features a stained concrete floor surface.

The floor/ceiling separating the second and third floors consists of laminated beams with three-inch tongue-and-groove wood planks. The stairs between the second and third level are open (see Figure 4-5).

The HVAC at the second-floor level is exposed spiral coil metal duct; all the plumbing is exposed cast iron. Exterior walls are concrete block, furred out to accommodate utilities and insulation. The structural separation between the flexhouses is rated at three hours.

An important and pioneering feature of The Lofts at Habersham is its robust construction, which was conceived and built to provide maximum flexibility. The buildings are designed to allow commercial on all three floors or residential on the second and third floors over commercial on the first floor. The commercial space is generally serviced from the street with access to the second floor only through a thirty-five- by eighteen-foot rear yard. Owners have the option of constructing an accessory building at the rear of the lot (see Figure 4-6).

Each lot and therefore live-work bay is eighteen feet wide by one hundred feet deep. There are assigned parking spaces in a common surface lot behind the rear yards—two for each upstairs residential

Figure 4-5 Open stairs between the second and third floors of a flexhouse at The Lofts at Habersham, near Beaufort, South Carolina. Also visible are the kitchen, stained concrete second floor, and exposed HVAC ducts. 2002–2006. Designers: Rick Black (conceptual), Ben Miehe (final)
Photo Credit: Jonathan Herron

Figure 4-6 Accessory buildings are permitted in the rear yards of The Lofts at Habersham, which also serve as the access route to the common parking area located to the back of the flexhouse lots. 2002–2006. Designers: Rick Black (conceptual), Ben Miehe (final)
Photo Credit: Jonathan Herron

unit. Street parking for The Lofts is provided in the front and serves the ground-floor commercial. The buildings are sprinklered under current commercial building codes (i.e., NFPA-13).

A typical buyer of a flexhouse is an investor or individual who plans to live above and rent the first floor out to a business or to rent both out separately. Some of the flexhouses are owned by businesses, whose owners sometimes rent the upstairs portion to employees. There is commercial activity in some of the upper levels, including the project sales office, a builder's office, and an architect's office; only the sales office is linked to the first floor.

The developer, Bob Turner, observes that in general, if a flexhouse is built in a commercial zone, then all of the above space use options could apply. Habersham's form-based code (by Duany Plater-Zyberk) specifically permitted flexhouses, accomplished by showing live-works as a use; the land on which The Lofts were built was designated as commercial. The real hurdle, he notes, is in the building itself, specifically the building's structure. The Lofts at Habersham—due to their being built to commercial standards, cost 8 to 10 percent more than a comparable wood-frame residential building with only one-hour separations (see Figure C-23 in the color folio). "Having at least a two-hour separation horizontally (party walls) and vertically (second floor) allows for mixed use in both directions. Typical 'live-works' only allow the resident to have first-floor commercial because they only have one hour separation in both directions; therefore upstairs use is essentially limited to home office types. We found that having increased fire separation in both directions gave us the most flexibility," Mr. Turner says.

Building a flexhouse that can accommodate commercial throughout raises disabled access questions. In general the intent was to locate business primarily on the ground floor. In order to permit independent commercial use on the second floor, The Lofts' stairs were designed to allow for a chair lift. Depending on interpretation of Americans with Disabilities Act (ADA), this might or might not be entirely compliant. ADA also requires two restrooms if there are more than four employees.

For that reason the developer roughed in plumbing to allow a second restroom to be added to the rear of the building.

Lessons Learned

1. It is worth it to buy the flexibility you need to weather an unpredictable economy by spending a little more on a building that can accommodate any possible mix of occupancies (users). If you obtain the entitlements up front to construct a set of buildings that can be housing over retail, office over retail, or even all office (although that option has street-activation issues), you have a better chance of keeping the buildings full or finding buyers who will appreciate their inherent flexibility and therefore risk-hedging investment value. However, with the adoption of the International Building Code's Section 419 and the requirement that all residences now be sprinklered, it is no longer necessary to provide more than a one-hour separation between any of the occupancies anticipated at Habersham or in most flexhouses.

2. In greenfield settings such as Habersham—a traditional neighborhood development—developers have struggled with finding the best way to create a vital town center. At Habersham, the developer's approach has been to compose the main street entirely of flexhouses, presold and built incrementally. In this way the developer was able to build out his main street without a huge outlay of capital and to maintain control of it by requiring that his management company manage the first-floor retail for five years after purchase. This is an innovative approach that—combined with the flexibility of the building type—has worked well at Habersham. Of the thirty-three flexhouses, almost all are sold; and all but six were bought by nonresident investors who rent out the upstairs mostly to millennials—who are attracted to the loft-like feel—and the downstairs to tenants chosen by the developer. Of those who owner-occupy, most both live upstairs and run a business downstairs—living above the store in the twenty-first century.

3. The author spoke with the developer about the fact that the upstairs portions of the units can

(Continued)

only be accessed from the ground floor (see floor plans, Figure 4-4), asking if the access had created any problems. In the author's survey of traditional neighborhoods in the southeastern United States (see case studies in Chapter Three: Design), he found at least one project where placing the entrances to the rear of live-works was problematic. The developer's response: "No, it has not been a problem. I agree that it is nice to come in off the street in some cases. But we would have to reduce the street frontage for the commercial by adding staircases. This idea may work better for condos where two buildings could share a common staircase, but it is difficult in a townhouse-type ownership—i.e., who heats and cools the corridor, cleans it, etc. In our case, the residents enjoy designated parking in the rear as part of their property/lot ownership. The residents above also have use of the rear courtyard, and they feel a part of the street through balconies/front windows. I also like rear access because it keeps the on-street parking for customers, not residents."

Marketing Live-Work

by Jackie Benson

Jackie Benson, president of J. Benson Marketing in Smyrna, Georgia, has been creating sales programs and selling live-works and other housing types in New Urbanist communities throughout the United States for thirty years.

In real estate, it is imperative for the builder/developer to plan for flexibility to meet market demands and fluctuations. Yet, while live purpose-built live-work's design for an evolving, changing market is an advantage in marketing, paradoxically it is also a challenge—its flexible design makes it slightly unconventional. Successful sales are based on the ability to observe, design, build, and communicate.

Extrapolating from Zimmerman/Volk Associates' definition of the potential market for live-work, the creative, independent live-work buyer is likely to make a purchase based on how much flexibility is offered by the design. To date, little definitive research exists regarding the percentage of live-work unit buyers who actually work at home. Some buyers lease out one or both of the spaces in their unit, essentially treating it as an investment in a young community that is likely to grow and appreciate in value. Sales data on live-work conversions, new lofts, or new greenfield town centers is anecdotal in the discussion that follows and is based on interviews with developers and owners of live-works.

Live-work housing types have been included in many of the master plans for greenfield and infill New Urbanist developments created over the last ten to fifteen years. Infill live-works are no longer a new phenomenon in many parts of the country, nor are retrofits, which include housing over retail in small towns and conversions of loft buildings and commercial buildings in larger cities.

Most homebuilders today recognize the need to include a work space in the floor plans they offer, something beyond a desk space in the kitchen. Additionally, companies that specialize in home office furniture and those that help clients convert closets into work space have arisen in the past few years to accommodate the growing demand for home offices.

Live-work is often included in master plans in a transitional location where single-family residences or townhouses give way to a block or more of live-works and then true town center retail, often combined with housing above, an arrangement that Thomas Dolan calls live-nearby. Live-work and its inherent flexibility have served to incubate many New Urbanist town centers, as is detailed in The Lofts at Habersham Case Study earlier in this chapter.

Tip

Build your community's initial main street as all flexhouse live-work, and build it early. Attract investors but retain the right to manage and choose ground-floor tenants for the first five years. When you control the tenant mix, you can steer your young community in the right direction.

Norton Commons

At Norton Commons, near Louisville, Kentucky, the street scene on Thursday evenings in the summer is of families patronizing the town's restaurants and other businesses while enjoying live music performed by local musicians. The number of people who attend this weekly event has exceeded four hundred at times and includes those from the neighborhood or nearby communities as well as followers of the band of the evening. Essentially, it took one restaurant/bar located in the first row of live-works created at Norton Commons to get the ball rolling. The sales team's office, located next door to the restaurant, stays open on Thursday evenings, and other businesses profit by staying open as well. The sales associates at Norton Commons regularly invite prospects to the event–that way, potential buyers get to experience what living in Norton Commons is like, and it has been an effective for those interested in the live-work units to get a sense of what "could be" from a retail/rental perspective. In other situations, the success of a particular restaurant might lead to the need for more space in the town center; in this way live-work attracts tenants for its commercial and residential buildings.

Hammond's Ferry

At Hammond's Ferry, near Augusta, Georgia, at a specific intersection, the master plan called for live-works and/or commercial buildings with residences above. Single-family residences and townhouses were built and sold before construction started on three corners of the intersection. Once a local restaurateur decided to locate on the lower floor of a corner building, a destination was created for neighbors and local residents. Above the restaurant are three (currently rental) apartments, accessed from the street. While the activity created by a restaurant poses some parking and noise issues (outside dining in a Southern climate), the neighbors have, for the most part, been grateful to have this restaurant next door. The location is now a very popular gathering place and is located within easy walking distance of the river park, a featured amenity at Hammond's Ferry. Across the street, the builder lives above the retail space he created, alongside another rental unit. The third corner has gallery space and some businesses, plus a few rental apartments above. This mixed-use intersection has created a vibrant live-work community where social interaction is ongoing for nearly eighteen hours a day.

The Basics of Marketing

Marketing "live-works" (as the New Urbanists call live-work) is not an exact science. Selling flexhouse live-work, the signature building type of New Urbanism, is all about the community in which it is located and to which it can contribute

much. If a buyer is sold on the community, he or she is likely more than halfway to the point of writing an offer. In other words, sell the community first and the "product" (or housing type) next.

In the case of developer/builders who are looking to sell live-work units to investors, the marketing message and the sales message must be more specific, whether through true media advertising or through targeted direct mail, e-blasts, social media, or signage. The flexibility of live-work, its ability to respond to market shifts (such as occurred abruptly in 2008), is a strong selling point for both investors and end users, and one that should be emphasized in any sales program. Again, the reader is referred to the Habersham Case Study in this chapter and the developer's extra efforts to make his units: (1) as flexible as possible under the building code; (2) pre-approved by planning for multiple use combinations; and (3) containing the right tenant mix as controlled by the developer.

If the live-work unit is built before contracting a buyer—that is, if it is not presold—their is usually a model unit for salespeople to show, which helps buyers visualize their use of the unit and how they might personalize the space—a particular need that live-work occupants have, and one that every agent should understand. Staging with furnishings can stimulate a user-buyer to see how living and working can exist simultaneously in the spaces provided. Most investors, however, do not need to see a model live-work unit.

At the 2001 Home Builders Show in Atlanta, three live-works designed by Duany Plater-Zyberk (DPZ) were available for tour to the sixty thousand builders who came to the conference. One was a large multistory version with two stories above the work area, what Thomas Dolan would call a live-near; the second was a smaller version with one story above the shop/work area, or what Dolan would call a live-with. There was also a single-floor unit with work area accessible from the street and residential attached behind the storefront. These units received significant attention and publicity and may have been the first time that live-work was widely recognized as a housing type and showcased to builders.

Selling Live-Work

Interviews with sales associates in communities with new live-works indicate that the majority of buyers arrive at the sales center knowing that this type of housing will fit their needs, whether as a user or as an investor. Nevertheless, sales associates must be armed with factual information as well as photos or models to demonstrate this product. It is important to help the buyer understand the nuances of owning and/or occupying this hybrid building type. Potential buyers will want to be informed about insuring the property and the tax implications of working at home or owning investment property. Community codes, covenants, and restrictions that affect use and maintenance must be thoroughly explained in the sales discussion prior to executing a contract. Sales associates should also be well versed in the mix of retail, commercial, or service company locations within the existing or planned town center or live-works and the type and size businesses that are already planning to open. It is important to be able to show the rental records and leasing trends from the neighborhood to investors so that they can determine the feasibility of investing in this live-work housing type. End users or investors should be informed as to: whether they can rent out the downstairs and upstairs separately; whether ADA will allow for renting the upstairs portion to a commercial operation (see Chapter Seven: Building Codes); and whether—if the retail market is soft—it is possible to rent the first floor to a residential or office tenant or use it as part of the residence. Knowing the answers to all of these questions and being ready with all of the facts that emphasize the "flex" in flexhouse are essential.

Another important item to consider in training sales associates in new communities or infill communities and conversions is the process of qualifying the prospective buyers, which of course presupposes that the sales associate has investigated financing options for live-work, a hybrid building type. Building trust is the most important element in any real estate sales transaction; unfortunately, some salespeople jump in and immediately start selling, neglecting to ask questions to learn more about the buyer and his or her situation. Instead, sales associates should listen more than they speak; then they will know what is most pertinent to the buyer.

To add to the delicate nature of the sales pitch approach, today's Gen X and millennial buyers are averse to "selling." They purchase, they are not sold! They trust the information they get from their friends and the Internet more than they trust a "salesman." Typically, these buyers come to the sales environment armed substantially more knowledge than most buyers in the past. They have done their homework and ask very specific questions, so sales associates must be well prepared.

Marketing Materials

Marketing materials used to acquaint a buyer with the live-work building type should show schematics of possible furniture arrangement and include photos of interiors of already completed and furnished residential or commercial spaces. When a buyer starts to imagine his or her own furniture in the space, a sale is certainly close. While it is difficult to convey the experience of owning a live-work unit through printed material, there are ways to use testimonials from owners and neighbors to convey the neighborhood's feel and promote the daily experiences enjoyed by residents. Technological advancements in virtual tours and panoramic viewing have expanded possibilities for marketers, enabling them to show what will be built if an actual model unit is not part of the sales environment. Widespread, almost universal use of e-mail and social media means that many forms of visual marketing are available to savvy salespeople today.

Marketing Communications

Purchase of live-work is a very considered decision and can take some time while the buyer considers the variables. There may be a period of weeks or months when the sales associate's task should be to stay in touch with the potential buyer and keep him or her informed of the progress, or sales, of this product or of sales in general in the neighborhood. For example, for a retail business, it is imperative to have a critical mass of potential customers if the business is to survive. Often the live-work in master-planned communities comes in the second or third phase; subsequent infill offers an important advantage due to its location and proximity to other businesses. For home occupation or professional services, such critical mass is not a factor since these live-work scenarios involve little, if any, foot traffic. However, pointing out to such potential buyers that their clients could walk to their appointments certainly can't hurt.

As with any real estate marketing, keeping in touch with the lead list created by calls, inquiries, and site visits is the first and foremost tool of marketing communications. Training the sales associates is imperative to a successful marketing plan. The next item in the marketing plan is the use of events and publicity to create interest and build traffic to the sales center. At Habersham in Beaufort, South Carolina, the developer studied the local area for a year to understand some of the retail needs that the town center (mostly live-works) could meet. Twelve new businesses are now located in the live-works, and a short list of others will be part of the mix. Their goal is to sponsor events that enliven the street, thereby positioning Habersham as a destination entertainment/ business/retail center, with both locals and vacationers as the target customers. A farmers' market is held weekly, and seasonal events abound. Habersham residents have gotten involved and help staff these events. Developer Bob Turner invested in a unique tent/awning, which can be raised easily to provide shelter from sun or South Carolina's rainy season. This is placed on the broad median of the main street—really a green—to animate the street and encourage attendance at weekly events (see Figure C-24 in the color folio).

Another unique marketing tool used at both Habersham and Serenbe, near Atlanta, Georgia, is to have interested renters ready to move into new live-works. In the case of Habersham, these tenants are retail businesses that want to be part of an active town center; others are lined up to lease the residential units. At Serenbe (see Figure 4-7), the Inn at Serenbe contracts with live-work owners to use furnished residential space as overflow accommodations offered by the Inn.

Figure 4-7 Flexhouses at Serenbe, Georgia, are often owned by investors who rent out the ground floor to retail tenants and make the upstairs units available to a local inn for overflow during large events such as weddings.
Photo Credit: Robert Raush

Many of the Inn's weddings and corporate events require more rooms than those at the Inn itself; with this arrangement, the residential portions of live-work units provide extra lodging for the Inn's guests. This arrangement works for the investors who have a retail business ready to lease, as it is a convenient rental pool for the upstairs residences in the live-work. According to interviews with sales associates at both Habersham and Serenbe, there are only a few shopkeeper live-works where the owner both lives and works in the unit.

When live-works were offered at Rosemary Beach, Florida, the buyers were, for the most part, already owners of property there. They were buying for investment at a time when this community was experiencing phenomenal sales. Marketing to current owners is one of the first steps a developer should take when offering live-works. In fact, at Rosemary Beach, current owners were advised of releases several weeks before the product was available to the open market. At the time, this strategy did not involve discounts, only first right of refusal.

Conclusion

Live-work real estate has evolved into a vital product for the future. Technology has drastically changed the workplace; the home can now be a place where our work life and family life coexist in some relationship of proximity or separation, as described in this book. As individuals and groups start new businesses, many are increasingly aware of the potential and advantages of live-work. Real estate development must constantly adapt to "the new normal"—today, and in the foreseeable future, live-work types are an essential ingredient in successful communities in which diversity of building type and breadth of market defines their unique positioning.

CHAPTER 5

Live-Work and Community: A Natural Marriage

Introduction

Most development that has occurred in the United States and Canada since the Second World War has been in suburban locations regulated by separated-use Euclidean zoning. An important, if unintended, effect of this massive dispersal of residences, office parks, and shopping centers across the landscape has been an increasing dominance of the private over the public realm, such that the average American has few opportunities for casual interactions outside of workplace, home, and school. One could argue that the sense of community that naturally arises out of a robust public realm has literally been bred out of us; many of us barely know what interaction in the public realm even is, unless we encounter it on vacation visits to other cultures, where we often experience a primal sense of recognition that there is a better way to live.

Modern society is organized around many standard practices that we have accepted for decades. Among them are: commuting to work, spending time at home on weekends, and assuming that one's life is centered in at least two places—home and work (or school)—each with its own set of social interactions.

For those who choose to work where they live, these fundamental practices and accompanying assumptions are challenged, with implications that are not always well understood.

An important distinction for live-workers is a more compact, less geographically dispersed way of living, one we are calling putting our lives back together.

When one spends less time commuting and more time in one place, the possibility for a stronger sense of community naturally arises. One sees one's neighbors at all times of the day. One walks to services and to secure needed goods on a daily basis, or, if they are not within walking distance, one considers moving to where that is possible.

In fact, live-work functions best in the context of compact, walkable communities, whether within individual multiunit projects or the neighborhoods of which they are a part. The author has observed that many who have chosen to put their lives back together have discovered that the interactions that arise out of that choice are nothing short of transformative. Thus, as one live-worker told the author, "I never knew I could live like this! Now I never want to leave!" The naturally occurring sense of community that is often an outgrowth of well-executed live-work is the subject of this chapter.

Live-work and community can be seen as symbiotic in two important ways:

1. The presence of live-work in a neighborhood helps build strong, convivial, safe communities that are able to "learn," or adapt, over time and remain vibrant.

2. Live-workers, due to the often-isolated nature of their workdays, crave opportunities for the types of casual interactions that—over time—build a sense of community. Such interactions can be provided either through the design of the individual live-work project or locating the project in a compact, walkable mixed-use neighborhood.

Live-work is inherently different from both a single-use residence and a dedicated separate workplace that requires a commute. The difference is physical, involving location and movement (the elimination of a commute), but its most important effects are social. The choice to consolidate the diurnal functions of a "normal" commute-driven life into a single location almost always results in significantly truncated work-related social contact. Gone are mixing at the water cooler along with regular lunches, breaks, and after-work drinks with one's workmates. As a result, he or she is likely to experience live-work's most common downside: a sense of isolation (see Figure 5-1). Humans are social beings; when isolated, most of us seek to correct this condition through contact with others.

The combination of working alone, at home, and the irregularity of a live-worker's ventures into the public and semipublic realm means that the design and location of live-work projects should maximize opportunities for informal, spontaneous interactions. In the author's experience, when one pays attention to this important need and shapes the semipublic or public realm properly, the response of live-workers is overwhelmingly positive.

Addressing live-work's inherent potential for isolation presents a unique opportunity. The author has repeatedly observed that it is a basic human need to step out one's door

Figure 5-2 A lively public realm is one of the two primary means of meeting live-workers' needs for interaction; locating a live-work project on or adjacent to such a street is ideal.

after several hours of concentrated work and encounter—in a comfortable setting—other people in the same boat, as it were (see Figure 5-2). Problems arise when designers and developers fail to understand the distinct qualities and unique needs of the inhabitants of live-work space, a condition that has resulted in essential needs going unmet in some built projects.

Therefore, more than any land use or building type of which this author is aware, the majority of residents, workers, and users of live-work space require interaction outside of their units to alleviate live-work's unique potential for isolation and to animate their lives through contact with others that is comfortable, spontaneous, and a normal part of daily life. Ultimately, the elimination of the waste inherent in a commute-driven lifestyle can present an excellent opportunity to create community.

Zero-Commute Living

Live-work is sometimes called Zero-Commute Housing. Due to the fact that live-work combines most of the activities of one's life in one place, the life experience of a person who works at home—the nature of social interactions and the rhythm of the day and the week—is fundamentally different from that of a typical commuter. This is why the term Zero-Commute Living applies: It really is a different way of life, characterized by:

- The bringing of one's previously dispersed life activities together in one place, and a correspondingly increased focus on that one place

Figure 5-1 A home office in a residential neighborhood, where opportunities for interaction are limited. James Avenue Live-work Compound (see case study in Chapter Six).

Building Live-Work, Building Community: An Interview with Architect Thomas Dolan

Note: This 1992 interview by Pam Strayer was conducted in response to the successful community building already evident in the first few years of occupation of South Prescott Village (1988, designed by Thomas Dolan Architecture), the first new-construction courtyard live-work community built in the United States since the Great Depression.

Q. Many multifamily and multiunit live-work buildings are designed with little attention to the possibility that they can facilitate community; what is your alternative to this?

A. Creating spaces in which casual, informal interaction between live-work residents occurs naturally is the most important element in encouraging a sense of community. The nature of those spaces can make the difference between an alienating structure and a fully functioning community. The entry situation—that transition between the moment one enters the complex and the time one closes one's own door—determines whether one feels a part of something larger, something greater than one's private, insular, often isolated life. This brief passage, however fleeting, offers the opportunity for interaction, the chance for communication with other residents. This, then, is the starting point of community.

Q. How does interaction occur in a multiunit live-work complex?

A. In designing and later observing the residents of several multiunit live-work communities I designed, I have discovered that three types of interaction take place between the residents:

(1) *Formal visiting* requires a definite intention on the part of the visitor, to which the response may be: "Come in," "Go away," or "Come back another time."

(2) *Meeting at a common destination* requires a definite, purposeful intention to go to that common destination (laundry room, garden, pool, spa, etc.) on the part of two (or more) individuals who meet there. The actual meetings are usually spontaneous and casual.

(3) *Crossing paths* are meetings that, though never planned, are the result of normal day-to-day comings and goings. Crossing paths leads to interactions that become more or less regular, thereby contributing to a sense of familiarity and even safety.

In my experience, the third kind of interaction works best at creating, at a comfortable pace, a sense of familiarity and the kinds of growing acquaintances that lead to a natural, voluntary sense of community.

Q. How can the desired interaction that creates community be encouraged?

A. Situations can be created that become comfortable settings for interaction as residents cross paths, specifically through the design of how and where people come and go through the common spaces. The architect's challenge is to shape common spaces that are neutral and non-threatening and that invoke a sense of well-being, of comfort in greeting a neighbor, enabling one to pause, chat, and move on.

The architect who takes up the challenge of building a community does so knowing that the building itself is half the equation; the residents are the other half. It is through the practice of architecture, what Louis Kahn called "The thoughtful making of spaces that evoke a feeling of appropriate use,"[1] that a feeling of communality among inhabitants can be encouraged. When the design succeeds, the result is a functioning community, a union of people and place.

Q. Why is the design of a live-work complex such a great opportunity to encourage community?

A. Live-work is simply a term meaning that most of one's life is centered in one place (much as farmers, housewives, and villagers have done forever) and that one's work is often a solitary activity pursued in an isolated space. As distinct from those who work outside of their homes, live-workers are not interacting with peers during their typical workday. They tend to spend their days working alone or perhaps in close proximity to a mate or family. This solitary isolation in both work and life eventually gives rise to a need for contact with others, a need that is often not perceived until after it has been met and embraced.

Q. So, design can facilitate community?

A: Absolutely. I have discovered that the special needs and constraints of live-work have created unique opportunities. Over the years, residents of the multiunit live-work complexes I have designed have remarked repeatedly on a new kind of richness and an unexpected openness in their lives. Ironically, many have told me they had no sense of what they were missing until they became part of a live-work courtyard community.

The artists of South Prescott Village regard its courtyards and gardens as a fundamental part of their work space—not that they actually use these areas for studio space, but rather their interaction with other artists has exerted a tangible influence on their work (see Figure 5-3). For some, the collaborations that have arisen from such contact with others have changed the course of their work and their lives.

Something seems to be working here, something new, and something old: a post industrial form of socialization, perhaps, or the simple pleasure of meeting at the village well.

Those who carry on the activities of both working and living in the same place do more fully inhabit that place: It will ever be thus. People fully inhabiting a place means a greater caring for that place and for the other people with whom they share it. This may be the great lesson of live-work communities: the rediscovery of the power of fully inhabiting a place, of the well-being that results from it, and of relating to the surrounding community *as* a community.

Figure 5-3 Interaction in the garden at South Prescott Village, Oakland, California, where two courtyards supplement the central garden as places where residents cross paths as they come and go about their daily lives. 1988. Designed by Thomas Dolan Architecture.

- Feelings of isolation, giving rise to the need for interaction with others and the strong desire for a sense of community that is particularly noteworthy among live-workers
- The gift of time and the saving of money not spent commuting
- The savings realized by dispensing with separate work quarters
- The reduction of significant duplication and waste that frees up time and resources for the things that matter in one's life—friendships, family, gardening, walking, civic activities
- In the words of a live-worker the author spoke with in 2010: "It's all here, right here in our community: friendships, casual interaction, basically my entire social life exists here, right outside of my door. I never knew I could live like this; now I know I'll never leave."—Angie

Bradsher, resident of The Waters, a traditional neighborhood development near Montgomery, Alabama.

To live and work in one place can be personally revolutionary: It means that one's attention is far more focused on that place. That focus naturally leads to an enhanced sense of investment in one location and often a greater desire on the part of live-workers to reach out to their neighbors, to be more involved in civic activities, and—as stated—to be more demanding of a livable physical environment, both in the common spaces within a project and in the public realm. When a critical mass is increasingly focused on a place, it leads to an enhanced emotional investment in that place. As the sense of community builds, residents require an environment in which its semipublic and public realms and "third places" (see discussion below) are important components of the community.

Figure 5-4 A great street and therefore a lively public realm, Aix-en-Provence, France.

The author has evolved and observed two effective ways to provide opportunities for interaction and community in and around live-work projects:

1. Wherever possible, no matter what size live-work project, be it multiunit, fee simple townhouse, or single-family residence, locate it on a great street (see Figure 5-4) and/or in a mixed-use, walkable neighborhood that provides opportunities for informal, casual interaction on the street, in cafés and restaurants, and throughout the neighborhood. Such streets are typically found in vibrant urban neighborhoods, be they existing, revitalized, or newly built.

2. Within a multiunit live-work project, provide opportunities for interaction as residents come and go about their daily lives, in the form of spaces in which it is comfortable to encounter others on a casual but often-repeated basis. Such spaces, ideally located along or near the "entry path" of the project, are typically in the form of courtyards, gardens, or simply widened portions of passageways, where it feels comfortable to stop and chat or perhaps sit and visit for a while. As noted in the interview on pages 96–97, when successfully designed and constructed to include such interactive spaces (see Figure 5-5), a live-work community will become more than the sum of the number of units, a real place that its residents identify as both home and workplace, and about which they care intensely.

These two methods of fostering interaction are united in that each provides opportunities for casual contact as the resident goes about his or her normal comings and goings—the kind of interaction that, over time, stregthens a sense of

Figure 5-5 One of the courtyards at South Prescott Village, Oakland, California, where the kinds of interactions that occur have created a strong a sense of community. 1988. Designed by Thomas Dolan Architecture.

community. The first method, of course, relies on a present or expected robust public realm *adjacent to or very near to* the live-work. The latter method, which is particularly appropriate when the public realm does not yet exist in the project's location, provides settings for that important interaction *within* a project.

It has been said that the most important amenity in successful New Urbanist greenfield and infill projects is their sense of community. Due to the increased need for interaction engendered by live-work, that "amenity" is not optional. Zero Commute Living means that when a large number of people live and work in one place, both within multiunit live-work projects and on streets that house large numbers of people who work at home, the opportunity exists for a significantly improved sense of community, itself a revolution in our excessively privatized society.

Thinking about live-work and community raises the question: What if being able to live near where you work was an established mode that through regulation is made a right and an entitlement encouraged by codes, policy, and best practices? Best practices already exist, and are illustrated throughout this book. Most forward-thinking jurisdictions have some reference to live-work in their general plans. However, integrating live-work into a compact, pedestrian-orientated neighborhood—one we are calling a live-work neighborhood—is not typically addressed in most codes, standards, policies, or financing mechanisms outside of New Urbanist neighborhoods and areas where form-based coding exists (see form-based codes sidebar in Chapter Six).

Community Building with Live-Work

Live-work differs significantly from the two single-purpose building types and land uses that it combines, residences and workplaces. While live-work certainly bears some resemblance to stand-alone residences and workplaces, it has *unique aspects and needs* that must be understood.

- Not commuting means you are not deriving stimulation from social interactions in your workplace. Isolation is a likely result, giving rise to a greater need for interaction.

- Gathering the primary activities of life—living and working—into one location means more focused attention paid to that one place and greater demands placed on its quality. Because one is neither "just sleeping" in one's residence nor "just working" in one's workplace, one's emotional investment in that one place is greater than is customary for someone who works and lives in different locations, and it is expressed in a more "rooted" sense of belonging to that place.

- Live-workers have a particular set of needs regarding the proximity between their living quarters and their work space, a subject treated in other chapters (proximity types: live-with, live-near, live-nearby).

- Live-workers have a desire for flexibility in terms of time spent working, space used for working or living, and the sense that such needs will change over time.

- Acceptance of mixed use as an ordinary condition of life is an integral part of live-work. Thus placement of live-work in mixed-use neighborhoods makes sense. In fact, any neighborhood where people work at home (and where don't they?) is, ipso facto, mixed use.

- Live-workers are inclined to walk to places where goods and services are available, if they exist within one-quarter mile.

- Live-work is not work unhitched from place. It is the opposite of that, although many people who work from home do adopt such a mode when they travel for work, as do all business travelers/peripatetics.

Neighborhood Scale

The following is a general treatment of live-work and community, describing how live-work scales from the neighborhood down to the building containing the individual units.

When considering urban places in general and live-work in particular, there is plenty of evidence that:

1. Designers and town planners acting on an understanding of the role of place-making in the design of neighborhoods can result—and has resulted—in places imbued with a tangible sense of community.

2. Many who were raised in the ultra-privatized realm of suburbia are almost oblivious to the possibilities inherent in point 1.

3. Nevertheless, many of these same people vacation in places that do have a strong sense of place, as seen in Figure 5-6.

4. These same people, once exposed to the power of community in a well-designed place, may be sufficiently attracted to consider living in such a place.

5. Some empty nesters and other newly, or already-shrunken, households will therefore gravitate toward walkable, compact mixed use communities (see Figure C-25 in the color folio). Likewise, studies have shown that millennials

Figure 5-6 Outdoor dining contributes to the strong sense of place in the Porquerolle Islands, located off the French Riviera.

Figure 5-7 A new flexhouse with ground-floor work space and living space above at Bluwater Crossing, Carlsbad, California. Designed by MVE & Partners, 2009.

are also attracted to such places, as was discussed in Chapter Four: Market.

6. Many such folks, even though they may not be employed full time, like the idea of having a work space available, especially one that is flexible and can double as a rental or as expansion space (see Figure 5-7).

A Live-Work Neighborhood

While live-work is typically seen as a set of building types, many—if not all—mixed-use neighborhoods are essentially live-work neighborhoods. Attributes of such neighborhoods fulfill many of the ideals of New Urbanism and of good mixed-use urban design.

While a live-work neighborhood need not—and generally will not—consist entirely of live-work buildings, the presence of such building types and their inherent mixed use and flexibility will make a tremendous contribution to the vitality of that neighborhood, allowing it to evolve. In addition to live-work building types, there can be stand-alone residences or apartment buildings, office buildings, general commercial buildings, housing over retail, and office over retail. All of these can be components of a live-work neighborhood if the recipe is right and the place feels right.

Live-work neighborhoods also go by several other emerging, perhaps competing, names, such as lifelong neighborhood, complete community, and live-work-play neighborhood. Regardless of their name, each typically shares these characteristics:

- It contains sufficient numbers of flexible buildings and spaces to enable it to be a "neighborhood that learns."

- Many of its residents do not need to commute by car or even train or bus. There are places in the neighborhood where one can work, interact with others working there, host or attend meetings, make copies or odd-sized prints, and occasionally have work transcribed, collated, mailed, and so on. Public transit is readily available and serves to connect the neighborhood with the city and region.

- There is a workable balance of residence, employment, retail, and entertainment. The neighborhood provides a setting for most residents' needs for socializing and serves as the place where they work, where their children go to school, where they shop for their daily needs, and where they go for regular entertainment. It is therefore possible for one's social life to consist primarily of spontaneous encounters in the public realm—on the street, in parks, cafés, restaurants, playgrounds, libraries, art galleries, and so on.

- The neighborhood is connected and gridded, usually with small block sizes. There are civic spaces and institutions present, such as parks, libraries, and art galleries.

- The design of the public realm is pedestrian-friendly without being hostile to the automobile. The market takes care of "third places," places that are neither work nor home yet are natural meeting places. An example is a favorite local café, and one of the reasons why Starbucks has been so successful is the existence of people who work at home and need a place to meet work contacts. There is arguably a correlation between the need for third places and the prevalence of home office, live-work, and work unhitched from place.

- Live-work neighborhoods are sometimes called Naturally Occurring Retirement Communities (NORCs). Aging in place or moving in with others is possible due to the walkability of the neighborhood (it won't matter when one's driver's license is taken away) and health care services that are within walking distance.

Locate space for and aggressively pursue a café or other third place on the ground-floor streetfront of your live-work project.

A Complete Neighborhood

It is arguable that live-work—whether it takes place primarily in live-work units per se or not—is the temporal glue that holds its neighborhood together, combining employment and housing and almost automatically creating an eighteen-hour-a-day community. Without such mixed use, that location is abandoned at night or empty by day—which means it is not really a neighborhood worth spending time in.

Building on the title of Stewart Brand's book *How Buildings Learn*, it is also true that neighborhoods learn, and the more flexible the uses in the individual buildings, the more able that neighborhood is to grow, adapt, and flex according to changing circumstances—in other words, to learn. A neighborhood that learns is one that remains viable over time and is less likely to end up with boarded-up storefronts, graffiti, and rising street crime as economic activity shifts to other more adaptable venues. Therefore, live-work is a building type that keeps on giving back to the neighborhood through its adaptability and therefore durability.

Therefore, the beauty of live-work as it is often coded and as it is perceived and used by its occupants is its flexibility. Over time, live-work units will see many sets of work uses and occupants, from live-work combinations to work-only to live-only. Therefore, if not coded in an overly restrictive manner, live-work can be a building that learns in ways that single-use buildings often cannot, within a neighborhood that learns.

Nature has taught us that monocultures are vulnerable to disease and other problems and that evolution favors diversity. The same is true in terms of uses and their flexibility. Flexhouses, or live-work buildings that learn, are one of the best ways to ensure an adaptable community and therefore one that stays viable. A viable, flexible neighborhood is one that has a fighting chance of being a lifelong community, which is described in the next section.

Within an individual live-work unit, one's workday social life is either within one's own household or is carried on electronically. However, as stated, eventually a solitary home-based worker will seek contact with others.

Nevertheless, there are live-work projects—often illegal—in converted warehouses that are scores of blocks from any city services, retail, or other residential users. The need for interaction and a sense of community in such a setting presents issues that must be addressed within each project, and were discussed earlier and in the live-work courtyard community section.

In order for a live-work project to be successful, one must understand the hand-in-glove fit between live-work and a compact, walkable neighborhood. Once one leaves one's live-work unit and ventures out onto the street, one encounters the public realm. If it is not lively and welcoming, the live-worker is living either a sort of pioneer existence or a very car-dependent life that has more in common with suburbia than a livable city. In such cases it is doubly important to provide opportunities for interaction within the project.

Why does the necessity for live-work need to be inserted into the discussion of community and neighborhood? Scratch the surface of any great neighborhood—or sit on a bench and watch—and you will discover human beings carrying on *our two most essential activities: living and working.* If you don't see both, it's likely you are not seeing a neighborhood. So live-work is—in the most important of ways—not just about unit types, such as live-with and work/live and lofts and garrets and complexes and compounds. It is the underlying spatial juxtaposition of these two activities that makes for a lively, livable place. So yes, a live-work neighborhood can, in fact, contain no live-work units per se. It can be apartments over retail or offices next to restaurants next to townhouses. Almost all of Manhattan is a live-work neighborhood of various shades. So is most of San Francisco, and Boston, and downtown Philadelphia, as are most older cities in Europe and Asia. Even in urban residential neighborhoods, the number of people who work at home (which is growing all the time) is part of what provides eyes on the street, part of what comprises the lunch trade at neighborhood restaurants, and part of what keeps the corner grocer alive.

Further examples of live-work as a component of a complete neighborhood can be found in the Glenwood Park case study in Chapter Three: Design, in Kentlands, Maryland (see Figure 1-6), Tribeca (see Figure 1-8), and throughout this book.

A Lifelong Community

A *lifelong community* is a place where one can go through all the stages of one's life within a one-mile radius, as opposed to being required to uproot oneself and move to an entirely different community each time one's life situation evolves. It is a place where one can meet all of one's daily needs: living, working, shopping, services, and schooling, as well as have access to religious and civic buildings (church/mosque/temple, post office, library, government). Lifelong community is also a synonym for live-work neighborhood. This type of neighborhood represents the climax state of a community, to borrow a term from the science of ecology. Any settlement that fails this test, which in North America north of the Rio Grande means the majority, has a poor chance of becoming a community. As long as the segmentation of the housing market into "markets" parsed by age and household size persists, and as long as housing providers—and the zoning laws they follow—require that each market occupy a distinct and disconnected location, complete communities will elude us.

Table 5-1 follows an individual's entire life cycle, showing how a person could remain rooted within the same community throughout his or her life. In the Conventional Housing column, the chart illustrates how one must constantly move and uproot oneself as life proceeds. In contrast, the Lifelong Community Accommodation column shows how one can stay rooted in a community that provides a diversity of housing types within a live-work neighborhood. Properly designed live-work projects and live-work units themselves aid this more sustainable picture by being adaptable and therefore requiring one to move less frequently.

Table 5-1 A Lifelong Community: Life Stage/Living Situation Chart

Life Stage	Work Activity	Life Situation	Live-Work Opportunities: Proximity Type	Conventional Housing in Segmented Markets	Lifelong Community Accommodation (Example: Stapleton, Colorado)
1. Baby/toddler/preschool	Eating, sleeping, learning, soaking it all in	Entirely dependent	Parents can possibly work at home but need separation: live-near or live-nearby	Single-family residence (SFR) or apartment	In-law apartment, small house, townhouse
2. Elementary to middle-school-age kid	Learning, socialized by age seven	Mostly dependent, decreasingly so	Parents can possibly work at home but need separation: live-near or live-nearby	SFR, big backyard, garage	Townhouse, house with small yard but nearby park
3. High school student	Learning, becoming mobile and independent	Relatively independent, especially when driving*	Studying at home is a form of live-work	SFR, big backyard, garage	Townhouse, house with small yard but nearby park
4. College student	Learning, exploring freedom	Possibly away from family, semi-independent	Studying at home or in one's dorm is a form of live-work	Dorm, student apartments	In-law apartment, small house, townhouse, shared house
5. Grad student, young professional	Employed or intensely involved with school	Independent and free, in search of suitable genetic material	Live-with a very workable solution for this group	Apartment, downtown loft, small house, townhouse	In-law apartment, small house, townhouse, shared house in walkable neighborhood with lots of action
6. Dual income/no kids	Both employed or self-employed	Paired off, kids may be on the way; still lots of free time	Live-with a very workable solution for this group	Apartment, small or larger house, townhouse	Apartment, small house, townhouse, loft
7. Parents of preschool-age kids	One or both employed	Fully nested, overwhelmed by new responsibilities	Good time for half of couple to work elsewhere; live-nearby a good option	Larger SFR in residential subdivision	Small house, townhouse, with playground nearby
8. Parents of school-age kids	One or both employed: often career prime time	Mainstream family preoccupation	Good time for half of couple to work elsewhere; live-nearby behind a SFR a good option	Larger SFR in residential subdivision	Small house, townhouse, with playground nearby
9. Empty-nester couple	Both likely employed and/or retired	More time for new interests; still paying for college?	Live-work of all types an excellent choice	Downsize to smaller house, townhouse, apartment (who wants a townhouse that's not in a town?)	Downsize to smaller house, townhouse, apartment in walkable neighborhood with lots of action

Table 5-1 *(Continued)*

Life Stage	Work Activity	Life Situation	Live-Work Opportunities: Proximity Type	Conventional Housing in Segmented Markets	Lifelong Community Accommodation (Example: Stapleton, Colorado)
10. E-tiree	Still working at a reduced pace	More time for new interests; good time for self-employment	Live-work of all types an excellent choice; more likely live-near if real work being done	Over-55 suburban community, retirement community	Smaller house, townhouse, apartment in walkable neighborhood with lots of action, good neighborhood support; "safe urbanism"
11. Aged and infirm	Not working	Needing care and attention	Most work not happening (writing one's memoirs? Looking after grandchildren?)	Continuing-care retirement community, nursing home, assisted living	Aging in place until necessary to move to a care facility, which is located in the same neighborhood

*Or able to get around by public transit

Table 5-1 describes the live-work and housing types that are appropriate to the different phases of one's life. By way of example, following (see Figures 5-8, 5-9, and 5-10) are several building types found in one community, Stapleton, Colorado, where a former international airport was transformed into a lifelong community. It is very possible to stay within Stapleton, not move far or often, and accommodate all the phases of one's life.

Live-Work Building Types and Community

Each live-work type and community has the potential to enhance a sense of community, either within the individual project or by relating and contributing to its neighborhood setting, or both. Table 5-2 describes the types of community-enhancing design strategies that are most appropriate for each live-work project type.

Table 5-2 describes forms of live-work projects. As noted, there are essentially two ways to meet live-workers' unique needs to encounter opportunities for interaction:

1. Locate the project on a great street in a live-work neighborhood, which has been discussed at length and is addressed most directly in numbers 4, 6, 7, 8, and 9 in Table 5-1.

2. If a great street is not yet at hand, design the building to encourage interaction as residents come and go about their daily lives.

Figure 5-8 A Stage 5 location (see Table 5-1) in Stapleton, Colorado: apartments on a walkable street where a graduate student or young professional might live and possibly work, likely at a home occupation work-use intensity (see Appendix A). 2009. Designed by Calthorpe Associates.

Figure 5-9 A Stage 8 location (see Table 5-1) in Stapleton, Colorado: single-family residences on a common court where a family with school-age kids might live and possibly work, although due to the presence of kids some separation would be needed, such as live-near. 2009. Designed by Calthorpe Associates.

Design for Community in Multiunit Live-Work Buildings

A multiunit live-work building or compound, an apartment building, or a mixed-use building or collection of buildings can be designed in two ways that have entirely different results for the experience of their users, which—after all—should be the ultimate measure of its success or failure as a project.

1. It can be a collection of units whose relationship is ill considered, whose potential for encouraging interaction and therefore community is ignored, and whose residents live entirely private lives without any meaningful relationship with their neighbors. This is "normal," and is depicted on the left side of Figure 5-11.

2. It can be a thoughtfully designed place whose semipublic realm is well considered, where interaction is encouraged and facilitated by the design of the entry situation, where the project's relationship to the public realm is one of permeability and reinforcement, and where a sense of community naturally arises as a result of spontaneous interactions in the semipublic and public realms. (This configuration, depicted on the right in Figure 5-11, is, alas, rare.)

Figure 5-10 A Stage 10 location (see Table 5-1) in Stapleton, Colorado: flexhouses on a walkable street where an e-tiree might live and possibly work, likely at a home occupation work-use intensity (see Appendix A). 2009. Designed by Calthorpe Associates.

Table 5-2 Live-Work Project Types and Opportunities for Community

Project Type/ CASE STUDY	Proximity Type/Form	Primary Work-Use Type	Community-Enabling Form/Location/ Opportunities	Transect Location	Comments: How Interactions Are Likely to Transpire
1. Warehouse conversion in established remote industrial district/CALCOT, Chap. 3	Live-with	Work/live	Minimally finished lofts with some common open space inside or outside	District	Not recommended except for artists' rental; community develops as a result of interactions in the common spaces, if they are designed properly
2. Warehouse conversion in close-in loft district/ CLOCKTOWER, Chap. 3	Live-with	Live/work	Well-finished lofts with designed common open space inside or outside	District becoming a neighborhood: T-5 or T-6	More likely condos; community develops as a result of interactions in the common spaces, if they are designed properly
3. Multiunit new construction live-work in an established, distinct industrial district	Live-with or live-near	Live/work	Usually podium configuration, often without open space; street activation often absent	District being forced to become something else by Imported NIMBYs	More likely condos; NOT RECOMMENDED
4. Multiunit new construction live-work in a higher-density mixed-use setting/Yerba Buena Lofts, Chap. 3	Live-with, usually	Live/work	Usually podium; well-finished lofts with designed interactive common open space inside or outside	T-5 or T-6	Liner flexhouse or townhouse units recommended; community develops as a result of interactions in the common spaces, if they are designed properly, or on the activated street

Table 5-2 *(Continued)*

Project Type/ CASE STUDY	Proximity Type/Form	Primary Work-Use Type	Community-Enabling Form/Location/ Opportunities	Transect Location	Comments: How Interactions Are Likely to Transpire
5. Multiunit new construction live work in a medium density residential or mixed-use location/SOUTH PRESCOTT VILLAGE, Chap. 3	Live-with or live-near, usually	Live/work	Best location for courtyard live-work	T-4	Likely tuck-under parking; community develops as a result of interactions in the common spaces, if they are designed properly; street activation moderately important
6. New-construction flexhouses in a greenfield town center, revitalizing infill location or as liners in a larger building/ HABERSHAM, Chap. 4; THE SIERRA, Chap. 3	Live-near	Live/work but separated occupancies	Locate on a great street: very important	T-4 or T-5	Parking in garages inside building, in separate alley-facing garage with granny flat, or behind the flexhouse; the interaction that leads to community happens on the street onto which building faces or nearby in the neighborhood
7. New-construction unseparated* live-work townhouses/GLENWOOD PARK, Chap. 3	Live-with	Live/work	Locate on a great street: very important	T-4 or T-5	Parking in garages inside building, in separate alley-facing garage with granny flat, or behind the townhouse: the interaction that leads to community happens on the street onto which building faces or nearby in the neighborhood
8. Housing over retail, new or renovated/ROSEMARY BEACH, Chap. 3	Live-nearby	Separate occupancies: home occupation or live/work over retail.	Locate on a great street: very important	T-4 or T-6	The interaction that leads to community happens on the street onto which building faces or nearby in the neighborhood
9. New or renovated home occupation in a single-family residence in a walkable neighborhood/JAMES AVENUE, Chap. 6	Live-with, live-near, or live-nearby		Important to locate within walking distance of services	T-3 or T-4	The interaction that leads to community happens on the street onto which building faces or nearby in the neighborhood and town center
10. New or renovated home occupation in a single-family residence in a CSD† subdivision	Live-with, live-near, or live-nearby	Home occupation within the house; live/work in the accessory building, if present	Extraordinary measures may be needed in such a monoculture	T-4	Isolation a major hazard; potentially an alienating situation

*Not detached, but live and work separated

†Conventional sprawl development

Spanning the history of live-work conversions over the last fifty years, advances have been made in design for community that evidence an understanding of how live-workers interact. For examples of this, please refer to the South Prescott Village case study in Chapter Three, the Habersham case study in Chapter Four, and the Ocean View Lofts case study in Chapter Five. However, one can often find less successful examples of live-work, a shortcoming in the design professions that this book is intended to address.

As in many apartment buildings, a double-loaded corridor design, which maximizes private unit area and minimizes common space, is still common in warehouse loft renovations. We have coined an expression to describe this approach in live-work: "turning warehouses for things into warehouses for people." Not only are people not meant to be warehoused, but live-work's unique needs for interactive open space render this accepted model for an apartment building inappropriate. Such an approach is not as detrimental

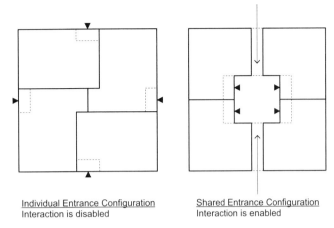

Individual Entrance Configuration
Interaction is disabled

Shared Entrance Configuration
Interaction is enabled

Figure 5-11 Two ways to design the entry situation in a multiunit building: The individual entrance configuration emphasizes privacy; the shared entrance configuration is far more likely to meet live-work's inherent need for interaction.

for apartment dwellers who typically work outside of their residences and derive social sustenance at work. When rental markets are strong, double-loaded corridor projects may stay rented. When markets soften, the places that are designed for community will stay full, tenants will tell their friends when units go vacant, and the continuity of the community will prevail.

Tip

Always design multiunit live-work projects with at least 10 percent of the gross area of the project (5 percent in multistory projects >20 units) devoted to interactive open space, located along the entry path and well-supplied with places to stop, sit, and chat.

While design for community is also treated in the Chapter Three : Design, it is worth emphasizing here the ways that a sense of "small c" community can be fostered and encouraged within in a multiunit live-work building.

First we look at the three primary modes through which live-workers physically interact (also discussed in the 1992 interview with the author earlier in this chapter):

1. The direct approach by an individual, such as knocking on a neighbor's door, perhaps calling first, perhaps not. This approach is the least spontaneous and mutual, and may be met with "come on in," "come back another time," or simply nobody home.

2. Meeting at a common destination, such as a common laundry, spa, pool, business services center, or mailboxes. Such meetings require the two people who interact to have chosen to go to that destination, and the more

plentiful such destinations there are, the greater the opportunities for interaction.

3. Crossing paths as one comes and goes about one's day-to-day life. This is the most spontaneous form of interaction, although it can also become regular depending on the intersecting daily routines of the live-workers.

As noted in the interview with the author earlier in this chapter, the third type of interaction is the most effective, over time, at leading to a sense of community. The designer's greatest challenge is providing places where this third type of interaction can occur. If executed successfully, the result will be a great project that the live-work residents will truly identify as a place that has meaning for them. Several courtyard live-work projects designed and built by the author in the 1980s and 1990s have demonstrated this principle, called "meeting at the village well" by artist Bruce Beasley (see South Prescott Village in Figure 3-53; Filbert Court in Figure C-26 in the color folio; and Ocean View Lofts, Figure 5-12); they all exist as strong communities to this day.

An Important Discovery: The Live-Work Courtyard Community

This author was fortunate to have the opportunity to design an entirely new building type: the first new-construction live-work since the Great Depression or perhaps the first ever in the United States, depending on who is doing the analysis. Presented with a flat site in a disinvested inner-city residential neighborhood and the task of designing live-work for artists, he was able to ask himself, "What do artists—who will live and work here—need that is different from those who will only live there or only work there?" Among the needs: The artists in the live-work unites would be there all the time and would want lots of space, great natural light, and a way to move large artworks in and out of the units. But also, they would want opportunities for interaction that can lead to "small c" community—not intentionally so at first, but over time.

Together with the client, an artist himself, the author looked at this relatively large site in Oakland, California. The client didn't want to have to heat or maintain any common indoor space, so he wanted all of the units to have exterior entrances, as in townhouses or (as we soon learned) courtyard housing. He proposed what he called "the dumb plan," consisting of barrackslike rows of buildings facing onto a common, double-loaded pathway. That struck the author—who lived at the time in a former Italian family compound organized around a delightful courtyard—as less than ideal (see Figure C-27 in the color folio).

At the client's dining room table, together they sketched a scheme in which breezeways linked courtyards—onto which almost all of the units open—and a central garden. Thus was born that day South Prescott Village, whose built form today reflects that early sketch, and it has been visited by designers and arts professionals from all over the world.

Twenty-five years after the first building was occupied, South Prescott Village and its companion projects—Henry Street Studios and Pinetree Studios—are a viable community whose residents hold regular barbeques and who tell their friends whenever a unit comes vacant (see Figure C-28 in the color folio). There is a growing cohort of professors at the local art college living and working there, and there is even talk of aging artists living out their golden years there. Chapter Three: Design, includes a case study of South Prescott Village, which goes into greater detail, as does the 1992 interview with the author earlier in this chapter.

The author has visited South Prescott Village on a regular basis since it was completed and occupied. One of the more common sentiments he has heard from tenants—other than their thanking him for having designed the place—is the following: "I didn't know what I was missing until I experienced it. I didn't know one could live like this. Now that I have, I don't ever want to leave." What they are referring to is a multiunit live-work community whose semipublic open spaces—the courtyards and gardens—contribute to a sense of community with which the residents identify strongly. In fact, they are the heart of the project, as has been true of subsequent, similar projects.

Since the completion of South Prescott Village, the author has designed numerous courtyard live-work communities, including Ocean View Lofts, Hannah Studios, Temescal Lofts, and Filbert Court, some photographs of which can be found in the color folio (see Figures C-29 and C-15).

One of the most important observations that the author has made over the years is that—while the strength of the communities that arise in these projects continues to amaze him, the surest way for a live-work courtyard community to become far less of a community is for a large percentage of the residents to stop working there. People treating a place as an apartment building and working elsewhere are then deriving social sustenance from their workplace and no longer have the need for interaction that live-workers do. Less need means less inclination to interact, and there goes the community. The author observed this cycle at one artist-only project he designed that fell on somewhat hard times due to the early 1990s recession. The owner was forced to open up the building to whoever answered his ads, and for a time there was a marked decrease in the sense of community there.

CASE STUDY: OCEAN VIEW LOFTS

Type of Live-Work: Originally artists' studios in a live-work courtyard community

Proximity Type: Designed as live-near, devolved to mostly live-with

Approval Status: Live/work (thirteen units) and work/live (one unit)

Location: Berkeley, California

Walk Score: 94 (Walker's Paradise)

Year Built: 1993

Architect: Thomas Dolan Architecture

Developer: Michael Feiner and Partners

The first new-construction live-work condominiums built and permitted as live-work (not housing),

Ocean View Lofts is a fourteen-unit live-work courtyard community located in what is now a very desirable part of Berkeley. Originally conceived as a thirty-unit project covering twice the amount of land it presently occupies, Ocean View Lofts encountered a severe version of Berkeley-style NIMBY responses when proposed. See Figure C-1 in the color folio for a street view of the project.

The project location is very walkable, being adjacent to bus transit, to the famed Fourth Street shopping district (recently crowned with an Apple Store), and to supermarkets and other services.

Organized around a central courtyard with a fountain also designed by the architect (see Figures C-15, 3-12, 5-12, and 6-35), all of Ocean View lofts' units except one give out onto that courtyard, encouraging interaction and a sense of community. The primary reason that interaction is not as great

(Continued)

Figure 5-12 The courtyard, onto which all but one unit open—with benches set into the fountain area at Ocean View Lofts, Berkeley, California. 1993. Designed by Thomas Dolan Architecture.

Photo: Dixi Carrillo

in the courtyard as at South Prescott Village is that—with notable exceptions— as of this writing many of the units at Ocean View seem to be used primarily for residence purposes. Nevertheless, there are three businesses in the building that are known to the author, each with its own character:

1. The one work/live unit (over 1,500 square feet), which faces the main street and contains two work spaces and two bedrooms is now occupied by a business that makes and trades sports memorabilia. It is not clear if anyone lives there, but as a work/live unit, it is acceptable for it to devolve into work-only. Berkeley is one of the few cities that actually

distinguished between live/work and work/live types, choosing to do so by applying an arbitrary break point based on size. At the time this project was approved in 1991, a unit under 1,500 square feet was considered live/work and therefore subject to primarily residential occupancy requirements under the building code; conversely, a unit over 1,500 square feet was considered work/live and therefore subject to primarily commercial occupancy requirements under the building code.

2. One of the upstairs units facing the courtyard has been occupied since the inception of the project by a computer consultant, whose work space is filled with computers. His use of the space is basically home occupation, in that he rarely has client visits and conducts his business electronically or at clients' locations (see Figure 3-7).

3. The third unit where work is going on at Ocean View belongs to a consultant who does at times have meetings in her beautiful space (see Figure 2-16), which seems well suited to such use even though it is a live-with unit.

As an early live-work project on the West Coast, Ocean View Lofts departs from New Urbanist live-works in that it has no retail component, only two units closest to the street on the ground floor that are fully accessible.

Lessons Learned

1. As noted, the project was originally conceived as over thirty units on more than an acre of land extending between two streets. Almost all of the units were to be live-near, with work space below and living space above. Two factors caused the project to shrink at both macro and micro scales:
   a. Intense NIMBY pressures forced the developer to abandon the western half of the project
   b. A sagging real estate market combined with the smaller size of the project forced the developer to split the remaining seven units around the courtyard in half, mapping the downstairs work spaces as decidedly inferior live-work units compared with

their airy and spacious upstairs neighbors. The year, 1993, was a poor time to hit the market in California, so economic expediency caused seven great live-near units to be split into unequal halves in order to be sold.

2. As a result of dividing the project during design into smaller units, many are not used for both living and working; as a consequence, the kinds of interactions that occur in a project where almost everyone works there are simply not present.

3. More than any project the architect has designed, the sense of surprise and wonder that occurs when one enters the courtyard is tangible and appreciated by residents and visitors alike. The author deliberately employed a different finish on the courtyard walls, the plantings and fountain complement each other, and the six-foot band of trellis and deck that surrounds the courtyard serves to mediate between the common courtyard and the unit entries, a design element inspired by Jan Gehl's work.

4. Ocean View Lofts is overparked by any observable measure. The author has visited the project scores of times over the last eighteen years at all hours of the day and night and at all times of the week. Never has he seen more than 60 percent of the twenty-two spaces occupied. At the time it was approved, Berkeley required one parking space for every 500 square feet of aggregate work space, which was calculated at that time as 80 percent of a unit.

5. While the parking is excessive, its location behind the facade was accomplished as part of the design review process in Berkeley (see Figure C-11 in the color folio)—a positive outcome for the project and an improvement over South Prescott Village, where the parking is located in front of the project, albeit under trellises.

CHAPTER 6

Live-Work Planning Issues and Regulatory Solutions

Introduction

Live-work is sometimes called Zero-Commute Housing. This chapter examines the many regulatory and planning policy implications of the cessation of a simple daily event—commuting—and the construction of buildings that allow live-work to occur, which is a challenge for many conventional planners. Live-workers choose to combine two significant parts of their lives that a planning official would define as different uses: living and working, or residential and commercial use. Planning policy and regulations that apply to either one as a single use often do not apply in the same way to the hybrid called live-work.

The prevailing form of land development regulation in the United States is Euclidean zoning, enabled by a 1926 Supreme Court decision, *Ambler v. Village of Euclid, Ohio,* that established the rights of government to enact land use regulations. Euclidean zoning establishes zones in which specific uses are permitted, conditionally permitted, or prohibited. Generally speaking, the zones segregate uses: a residential zone allows only housing, a commercial zone allows only retail and office, and an industrial zone allows only manufacturing and warehouse uses. Many cities have adopted mixed-use zoning or zoning overlays, generally in their downtowns; however, most conventional greenfield development conforms to strictly segregated zoning and tends

to consist of retail shopping centers, residential subdivisions, and office parks, each arranged as a "pod," connected by arterial highways as depicted in Figure 6-1.

Enter live-work, an inherently mixed use. At times, live-work has blindsided jurisdictions' planning staff, in part because it often springs up spontaneously and can be decidedly unplanned. While it makes functional, economic, and environmental sense, live-work presents a quandary to conventional planners. At first blush, live-work does not fit neatly into segregated use zones. It has elements that are pure residence, which is not difficult to zone by itself, but the work aspects might include walk-in trade, employees, and work activities and processes that might not be anticipated in a given zone. Conversely, live-work can accommodate elements of pure commercial/industrial use, but accompanied by residence.

Urban planners do more than enact and enforce zoning regulations. Proper application of planning practice and regulations focuses on the ways in which a building's presence and uses impact on the public realm and the social contract. Planners envision how a jurisdiction or region will develop; ideally they envision an intended physical form and character accommodating appropriate and compatible uses and human activities. Sometimes they respond to citizens' expressed needs; sometimes they discover development patterns and trends and attempt to find ways to accommodate them within their existing planning framework, which might

Figure 6-1 The contrast between conventional sprawl development (CSD) and traditional neighborhood development (TND): the latter is mixed use, connected and walkable; flexhouse live-works would typically be located in the area shown as "shop" in the upper (TND) portion of the drawing.
Drawing by Duany Plater-Zyberk & Company, Town Planners and Architects.

Figure 6-2 A warehouse renovated for live-work with an "arty" lobby. Tribeca, lower Manhattan, photographed in 2010.

be Euclidean zoning. The latter, reactive mode has most often been the case with live-work.

In what is often the first wave of live-work, artists colonize buildings orphaned by the adoption of shipping containers and the decline of manufacturing (see Figure 6-2). Most do so illegally, hiding from not only the building official but also city planners. Upon discovering this viable and vibrant activity in once-underutilized and disinvested warehouse districts, often near downtown, many planners have responded by making it legal to live where one works in at least some parts of their jurisdiction (see Figure 6-3). Such efforts have sometimes been successful, facilitating the evolution of mixed-use neighborhoods that add to the vitality of that city. Unfortunately, by then the artists are long gone, having been displaced by higher rents as the district changed into a neighborhood.

Artists and other similarly situated individuals, such as artisans, craftspeople, and small entrepreneurs incubating new businesses, have been important agents of change in urban districts throughout the industrialized world, and many of those places—SoHo, SoMa, and LoDo—have evolved into

highly desirable mixed-use neighborhoods inhabited by urbanites of all walks of life. As has been noted, while SoHo was first occupied by artists in the 1960s, by the mid-1970s most had moved on to Tribeca (see Figure 6-4) and thence to a series of other districts in Manhattan and beyond, priced out of each pioneering neighborhood in succession.

Planners responded to the initial artist-driven surge of live-work by striving to make it legal in multiple ways, either through legalizing outlaw spaces or creating regulations that allowed for the orderly renovation of commercial and industrial buildings to accommodate live-work. While it is true that planning regulations always have a strongly localized orientation, no single way to respond to the problem of fitting live-work into Euclidean zoning models has emerged. Nevertheless, there are common elements in some of the best live-work planning regulations, which will be discussed in this chapter and embodied in the suggestions for a model planning code found in Appendix A.

The second wave of live-work was, as described elsewhere in this book, triggered by the adoption of home office automation and the resulting ease with which one can establish a home office. At about the same time, developers in

Figure 6-3 A typical live-work unit in a renovated warehouse: a relatively "raw" space, ready for the tenant to move in and add his or her own identity. Dutch Boy Studios, Oakland, California. 1996–2011.

cities were finding that the supply of easily renovated commercial buildings was dwindling, leading them to turn to new-construction versions of live-work. New-construction infill live-work, essentially a new building type, has been in-

Figure 6-4 Duane Park, formerly the nexus of Manhattan's butter, eggs, and cheese district, now spruced up as a delightful park in the upscale mixed-use neighborhood that is Tribeca today.

troduced in a number of cities with varying degrees of success. As it turns out, the specific location where live-work is built is as important as what type is constructed, as will be seen in some of the examples below. Where it has been mislocated, existing commercial-industrial districts have often been disrupted by the presence of new live-work. In places where it is properly located and designed, live-work is a tremendous enhancement to the function of that place and often hastens its evolution into a mixed-use, walkable neighborhood. Sometimes these two locational phenomena occur simultaneously: that is, a district is essentially forced into becoming a neighborhood as artists and industry are pushed out.

Beginning in the early 1980s with Seaside, Florida (see Figure 6-5), designers and developers—the vanguard of New Urbanism—began to create greenfield town centers with housing over retail, often configured as live-work townhouses or flexhouses.

Figure 6-5 Ruskin Place in Florida is composed entirely of live-work flexhouses fronting onto it, and has undergone changes over the last ten years (see case study in Chapter Three). Seaside, Florida, the first New Urbanist town. 1980 onward. Designed by Duany Plater-Zyberk & Company, Town Planners and Architects.

A far cry from that which would be permitted under Euclidean zoning, such new town centers typically are built under form-based codes that emphasize the design of the buildings and their effect on urban form and "the space between buildings," especially streetscape and the public realm. Form-based coding deemphasizes the preeminence of use and anticipates uses changing over time. For that reason, flexhouses are sometimes called buildings that learn. An important and intentional result of creating flexhouses is a mixed-use street, where residents live upstairs and work downstairs, thereby providing eyes on the street and activating the neighborhood throughout the day. One might say that a typical New Urbanist town center is a live-work neighborhood.

An important distinction between live-work conversions of existing buildings and greenfield New Urbanist flexhouses is the attitude of their occupants toward work and a divergent set of mythical forebears:

- Loft living often embodies a view of life that seamlessly integrates work into life. Its myth: the artist.
- Flexhouses typically reinforce a physical separation between living and working, at best in close proximity. Its myth: the mom-and-pop store whose owners live upstairs.

This chapter—and this book as a whole—explores both modes and both myths.

New live-work functions best when it is built in the context of—and comprises an important element of—a mixed-use, compact, pedestrian-oriented community. Live-work conversions and urban infill live-work will, if concentrated in neighborhoods, typically attract or are composed of ground-floor shops and businesses that serve their neighbors.

Placemaking with Live-Work and Form-Based Codes
By Dan Parolek

Dan Parolek, coauthor of Form-Based Codes: A Guide for Planners, Urban Designers, Municipalities, and Developers *(Wiley, 2008), is principal of Opticos Design Inc., an award-winning multidisciplinary design firm in Berkeley, California, that specializes in creating great places by revitalizing old and creating new pedestrian-oriented neighborhoods and cities and designing well-crafted traditional and classical architecture.*

The concept of live-work embodies the same objectives as a form-based code (FBC) at a building and neighborhood scale; it reinforces and enables the organic evolution of places over time and therefore is a critical component of reinforcing, revitalizing, and creating walkable urban places. In addition, similar to the methodology used in creating an FBC, one can primarily think about live-work as a range of forms (proximity types) supported by a carefully considered and regulated set of compatible uses (use types based on work-use intensities) related to a particular context. In terms of regulating live-work, it should be reinforced that the relaxed development standards concept, mentioned in the development standards section of this chapter, does not mean "anything goes" in terms of regulation but rather conveys the need for a radical change in the way we approach zoning. We need to break down barriers for creating, protecting, and revitalizing a vibrant mix of uses—the form-based code is the right zoning tool to accomplish this.

Definition and Process

In an FBC, the organizing principle is the intended physical form or character of place rather than use. The urban-to-rural transect, as is defined in this book, is one example of a highly effective organizing principle based on intended character and form of a place. Creating an effective FBC is like following a proven recipe: There is a specific set of components (ingredients) and process (instructions) that have established a set of best practice standards and have shown successful results time after time in case studies. A more thorough overview of the definition and the process for creating an FBC can be found in the book *Form-Based Codes: A Guide for Planners, Urban Designers, Municipalities, and Developers* or on the Form-Based Codes Institute's Web site (www.formbasedcodes.org). This being said, the FBC is not the only solution or approach to zoning for vibrant mixed-use environments and integrating live-work, but it is a method that has

(Continued)

shown very successful results in a short period of time.

Why is Integrating Live-Work into FBCs Important?

The proven methodology behind the creation of FBCs and the concepts of live-work introduced in this book are necessary new tools and approaches that will enable code writers and planners in general to refine and broaden the application of mixed use within zoning codes. Integrating live-work into FBCs (zoning) is important for four reasons:

1. *Effectively refining the application of mixed-use within zoning codes:* Many of the most highly desired and visited areas within American cities were originally built as mixed use without any zoning (or predated its enactment); this informally provided live-near and live-nearby proximity types and live/work and work/live work-use types, as defined by this book. In many instances, long after they were created, these areas were zoned with use-based zoning that rendered much of the complexity and diversity that is inherent in them—from a form and use standpoint—non-conforming, thus hindering their ability to remain vibrant or to evolve.

   On several occasions, attempts to fix this problem have led to an overgeneralized application of mixed use in zoning which has failed in two different ways: (a) It has allowed noncompatible commercial uses to detrimentally spread into neighborhoods, thus compromising the quality of the neighborhood; (b) it has also allowed noncompatible residential uses to spread into industrial areas, thus compromising the viability of these uses. The first example has occurred in almost every downtown in American cities and towns; the latter example occurred in many industrial districts, including the SoMa district in San Francisco, as described in this book. To provide a more refined and appropriate application of mixed use within FBCs, a clearer differentiation of live-with, live-near, and live-nearby, along with the appropriate work-use intensity, will create the right regulatory framework to enable these existing places to evolve and thrive.

2. *Creating vibrant neighborhoods:* A single-use approach to zoning has created sterile, single-use environments that are highly automobile-dependent. Integrating live-work concepts into FBCs for these neighborhoods, whether new or existing, will enable and encourage them to become more diverse, walkable places. A simple example is allowing artists' studios or dance classes up to a certain maximum size in ancillary structures in primarily single-family neighborhoods. Home occupation should be encouraged, and former and new flexhouses should be permitted to function as intended, which is as a form of live-work.

3. *Reinforcing a diverse mix of "missing middle" building types:* "Missing middle" building types are those such as duplexes, fourplexes, townhouses, bungalow courts, and live-work (flexhouse) building types, which are at a medium level of intensity. Integrating live-work into an FBC can enable a community to provide more housing choices with missing-middle building types and thus meet the growing market demand for walkable urban living. These types had historically been integrated throughout a neighborhood but, for various reasons, including poor zoning, have rarely been built in the past fifty years. Live-work (flexhouses in particular) and other creative housing types that respond to the need for changing and flexible work environments, such as telecommuting, should be carefully integrated into any FBC planning effort.

4. *Incubating local businesses:* On struggling main streets, live-work regulations can, and oftentimes do, revitalize main streets and incubate small businesses. Live-with and live-near proximity types should be integrated into these situations at work/live or live/work-use intensities to allow greater flexibility in occupying buildings, thus encouraging the first stage of revitalization.

Ways to Integrate Live-Work into FBCs

There are two primary ways to integrate live-work into FBCs: within building-type standards and as a use type within the land use table.

◀ **Figure C-1.** Ocean View Lofts, a new live-work building in a mixed residential neighborhood context in Berkeley, California; the architect worked closely with the city's design review staff to make a building that fits its context well. Passersby often ask: "How long has that building been there? Fifty years? Eighty?" The project was completed in 1993 by Thomas Dolan Architecture. See the case study in Chapter Five. Photo credit: Dixi Carrillo.

Figure C-2 A typical renovated live-work building in Oakland, California, Union Street Studios was a former plumbing warehouse. The architect carved a courtyard out of the middle of this large volume and located a significant number of units so that they open directly onto it. As a zero-lot-line, sprinklered building, Union Street studios enjoyed certain code advantages not available under today's California Building Code. Thomas Dolan Architecture, 2000.

◀ **Figure C-3** South Prescott Village in Oakland, California, is the first new-construction live-work courtyard community built in the United States. Originally designed to exclusively accommodate artists, the project has been visited by arts professionals and government officials from all over the world. Thomas Dolan Architecture, 1986–1990.

▼ **Figure C-4** A three-level live/work unit, at Filbert Court, Oakland, California, which is open from first floor to roof in the work area. The photographer is standing on the stairs to "the boxcar," seen at the left-hand end of Figure C-26. A six-unit project designed and developed by the author, the project contains two such triple-height spaces, three live-near units, and one live-with unit. Thomas Dolan Architecture, 1993.

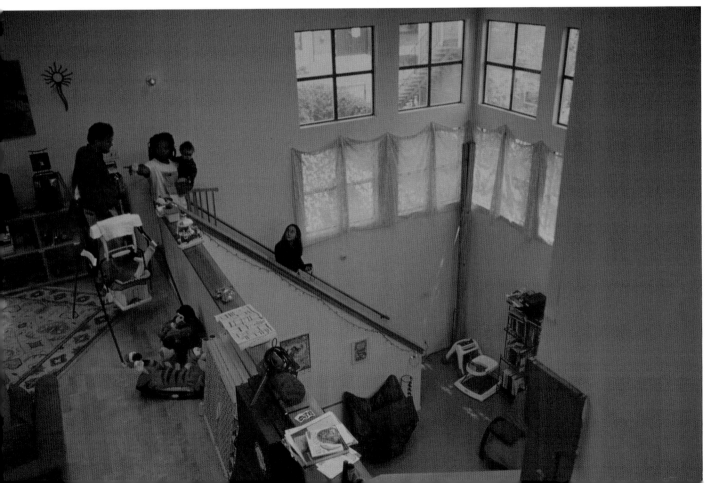

▶ **Figure C-5** A former warehouse in Tribeca, New York City, where the author lived in 1975 in a second-floor, 3,000 square foot corner loft; the rent was around $300. A former loft warehouse district made redundant by the adoption of shipping containers, at that time artists were pioneers in Tribeca, soon to move on, a result of the SoHo Cycle. Lofts in that area now regularly sell for $15 million.

◀ **Figure C-6** An artists' work/live space at South Prescott Village in Oakland, California. Originally occupied exclusively by artists—whose portfolios were viewed by the owner, artist Bruce Beasley—the project was designed to meet artists' needs for great light, large volumes of space, and access to bring large works of art in and out. Thomas Dolan Architecture, 1986–1990.

◀ **Figure C-7** A live-with unit, located where the term was coined by the author, at South Prescott Village in Oakland, California. This unit is spanned by a forty-foot-long site-built truss with simple north-facing windows installed in the wall panel behind it. The bottoms of the trusses sit twenty feet above the unit's floor, which is simple painted plywood; while the volumes are large, no point in any space in the project is more than twenty feet from a window or skylight. Thomas Dolan Architecture, 1986–1990.

▶ **Figure C-8** A glazed wall separates the live portion from the work space beyond in a live-near unit at South Prescott Village, Oakland, California. Each of the two buildings has one live-near unit, aimed at artists who want a bit more separation from their work. On the left is an "art access" opening, most affordably accomplished using a prehung pair of French doors. A baby was born in this unit in the 1990s. Thomas Dolan Architecture, 1986–1990.

▲ **Figure C-9** Flexhouse live-work, Serenbe, Georgia. This unit is distinguished by its exterior stair that ascends from a side yard. The upstairs residential portions of these flexhouses are often rented out to supplement the capacity of the Inn across the street when weddings and other functions are held. Serenbe's urban design is modeled on English village high streets, being one lot deep and backing up to farmland.

▼ **Figure C-10** Some friends gather in the courtyard of the James Avenue live-work compound, Oakland, California, which was designed and built by the author and his firm, Thomas Dolan Architecture, with Jennifer Cooper, Designer, and was built from 2000 to 2003. Set on a triple south-facing lot on a yield street, the corner storefront building and land was transformed into a series of indoor and outdoor rooms as shown in the case study in Chapter Six.

◄ **Figure C-11** Entrance to the courtyard from the parking lot at Ocean View Lofts, Berkeley, California, 1993. Despite the fact that the city of Berkeley required 22 parking spaces for 14 units, there are always numerous empty stalls, which could have accommodated a greater density than the 30 du/acre built. Due to Berkeley's difficult entitlement environment that halved the project's available land area, 6 live-near units were divided into 12 smaller live-with units, some of which had originally been intended as ground-floor work space connected to an upstairs living portion.

▼ **Figure C-12** At Hannah Studios, in Oakland, California, seven units of new construction surrounding a central courtyard, the underside of the tallest unit's roof is pictured here; it has since been made into a four-level unit. The project was built as new construction in a mixed residential/industrial area, something not normally permitted in Oakland but accomplished in a convoluted way: constructing a commercial building, then the next day applying to convert it to live-work. This code loophole has since been closed in Oakland. Thomas Dolan Architecture, 1992.

◀ **Figure C-13** Rosemary Beach, Florida, is a successful New Urbanist resort community down the road from Seaside, the first New Urbanist town. On its main street, whose deflected vistas direct one toward a common green and the beach beyond, are flexhouses and housing over retail, or live-nearby. Locating live-work on a great street is one of the two primary means of meeting live-workers' need for informal interaction. Duany Plater-Zyberk, Town Planners, 1996 onward.

▶ **Figure C-14** Dutch Boy Studios, on Oakland's famed Studio Row, has been called "the mother of all live-work conversions." A former paint factory, Dutch Boy was bought by a young artist, Francis Collins, who employed his fellow artists to work on building a great artists' studio complex that, after fifteen years of wrangling with the city, is about half-legalized and still a great community of artists. Legalized with the assistance of Thomas Dolan Architecture, 1996–present (ongoing).

◀ **Figure C-15** The courtyard really is the heart of the Ocean View Lofts live-work project, the place where residents and guests cross paths and become acquainted over time. Located in Berkeley, California, this new-construction community is built around a courtyard with a fountain designed by the author and inspired by Islamic gardens. Integrated into the fountain structure are places to sit and listen to the sounds of the courtyard—the fountain, birds, music coming from units. Thomas Dolan Architecture, 1993. Photo credit: Dixi Carrillo.

◀ **Figure C-16** Built as condominiums but caught by the economic downturn and forced to become rentals, Willow Court is located at the edge of a residential area of West Oakland, California, adjacent to an industrial district. A former warehouse, its 100-foot-span bowstring trusses spaced at twenty feet on center afforded the opportunity to build between them right up to the roof, as is seen in this picture. The author sketched the design for the project the first time he visited the building—including a pair of courtyards off of which almost all the units enter—and it was essentially built as sketched. See the case study in Chapter Three. Thomas Dolan Architecture, 2007.

Figure C-17 The Clocktower Lofts is an early loft project in San Francisco, designed by David Baker and Associates and his longtime client, developer Rick Holliday. Completed in 1990, the project stands out as well located in a walkable mixed use neighborhood, in strong contrast to many of the lofts built later in the decade, which are far from any services. A former printing company, the building covers an entire city block and is immediately adjacent to a major freeway, yet its courtyards provide a quiet respite. See case study in Chapter Three. Photo credit: J.D. Petersen.

▶ **Figure C-18** Windows and skylights are an essential element in live-work, particularly that designed for artists, as South Prescott Village in Oakland, California, was. All upstairs units include art access openings, generally prehung French doors, as they were the most affordable way to achieve such a large opening. In this unit, the railing beyond is removable to allow lowering of large objects to the ground. Thomas Dolan Architecture, 1989.

▲ **Figure C-19** Another variation on an art access opening at South Prescott Village, Oakland, California. Built for a very low per-square foot cost, the project used standard residential elements including aluminum windows (but true divided light), painted plywood and concrete floors, basic kitchen cabinets, and acrylic dome skylights. Some call live-work construction warehouses with kitchens, and there is a kernel of truth to that. Thomas Dolan Architecture, 1989.

▶ **Figure C-20** The main street at Habersham, South Carolina, is lined entirely with live-work flexhouses. Most are owned by investors who rent out the downstairs to retail tenants and the upstairs lofts to millennials. The developer has successfully incubated his downtown—and weathered the downturn—by building extremely flexible units and allowing them to adapt to market conditions. Photo credit: Jonathan Herron.

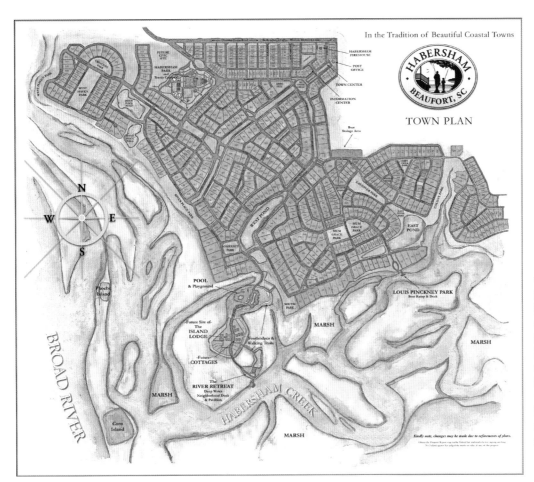

◀ **Figure C-21** The Habersham Master Plan includes the town center (to the left of the logo on the plan), comprised of The Lofts at the Marketplace, which are live-near flexhouses. The town, near Beaufort, South Carolina, is in classic Low Country terrain and is surrounded on two sides by wetlands. Photo credit: Jonathan Herron.

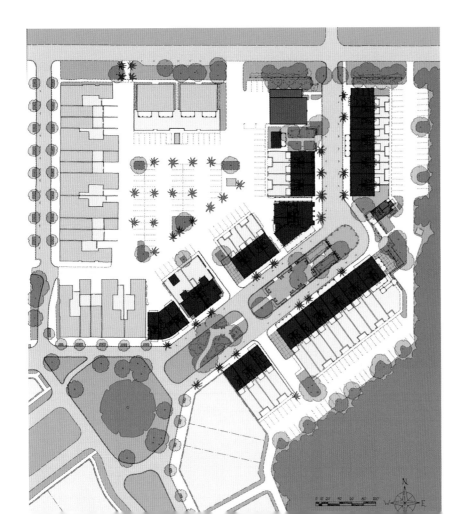

◀ **Figure C-22** The site plan of The Lofts at Habersham shows the main street's wide central median—really a green—where events are held regularly. Upstairs residents at The Lofts park in assigned spaces in common parking lots and enter through their rear yards. The retail facades of the flexhouses define the life on the street, and patrons who have driven park curbside. Photo credit: Jonathan Herron.

▶ **Figure C-23** Painted a color one might see on an Irish pub, this typical flexhouse exudes retail charm. The developer of Habersham manages many of the ground-floor portions of the flexhouses, thereby steering the tenant mix in ways that enhance the town center. The Lofts at Habersham define a great, convivial street where acquaintances are made and friendships grow, as residents of Habersham meet their daily needs on foot. Photo credit: Jonathan Herron.

Figure C-24 Regular events are held in the Habersham town center, whose main street is defined by The Lofts and enlivened by retail activity, restaurants, residents, and visitors. The pedestrian clearly has the upper hand at an event like this—always as good sign in a pedestrian-orienented town center. All of the pieces are here, and they are put together with great skill: flexhouses, colonnades, mature trees, a well-designed green, and the mix of uses inherent in live-work. Photo credit: Jonathan Herron.

▲ **Figure C-25** The Californian is a mixed-use podium project in the heart of Berkeley, California. The ground floor includes a Trader Joe's supermarket, and the podium courtyards are a welcome respite for residents, who appreciate a place to sit, as is seen in this picture. Kirk Peterson and Associates, Architects, 2010.

▲ **Figure C-27** Friends and family enjoying a meal under the lemon tree at Avon Street, a former Italian family compound in the Temescal neighborhood of Oakland, California, which was the author's home and workplace for seventeen years. Four houses around a courtyard, Avon Street is a strong community comprised of friends who have become like family to each other, without any formal structure except condominium documents. The courtyard makes the difference, and its power has informed the author's work ever since he moved there in 1983.

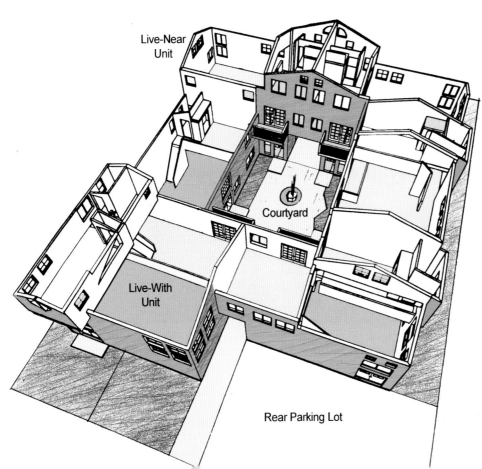

◀ **Figure C-26** Aerial perspective of Filbert Court in Oakland, California, a live-work community whose courtyard provides an entrance to all units and contains a fountain designed in collaboration with the author and brick paving salvaged from the 1989 earthquake. The courtyard defines this community, whose residents cross paths in it on a daily basis as they come and go. Thomas Dolan Architecture, 1993.

Live-Near Unit

Courtyard

Live-With Unit

Rear Parking Lot

◄ **Figure C-28** The owner, Bruce Beasley, lends a hand at a group sculpture-raising in the courtyard at South Prescott Village, Oakland, California. This sculpture was being erected for the opening celebration at this, the first building of its kind, in 1988. Since that time the courtyard onto which all of the units in the building open has played an important role in the success of this project. Sculpture by Gale Wagner. Building by Thomas Dolan Architecture.

Figure C-29 Temescal Lofts, Emeryville, California. The house forms superimposed within the commercial form serve to emphasize a dichotomy resolved: living and working. The four units' street front follows the diamond-shaped lot, wrapping around a common courtyard to the rear. Thomas Dolan Architecture, 1993.

◄ **Figure C-30** South Main Live-Work: This live-near flexhouse has a flex space on the ground floor with a separated two-story unit above. This building is incubating a new neighborhood main street in the South Main neighborhood in Buena Vista, Colorado. Architect: Opticos Design, Inc. Photo Credit, Dan Parolek.

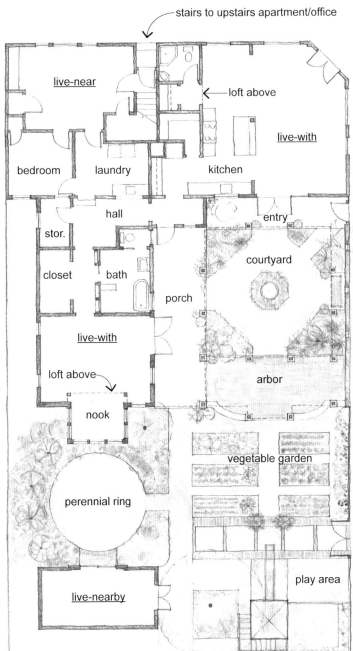

stairs to upstairs apartment/office

live-near

loft above

live-with

bedroom

laundry

kitchen

hall

entry

stor.

closet

bath

courtyard

porch

live-with

loft above

nook

arbor

perennial ring

vegetable garden

live-nearby

play area

▲ **Figure C-32** The loft above the desk in this picture is a built-in sleeping bunk under Oakland's live-work building code, and therefore the great room of the James Avenue Live-Work Compound qualifies as a stand-alone live-work unit. In Oakland, any structure "originally designed for commercial or industrial use" can be converted to live-work. As a former corner grocery store, this portion of the building qualified for conversion to live-work. Thomas Dolan Architecture and Jennifer Cooper, Designer, 2000–2003.

▲ **Figure C-31** The James Avenue Live-Work Compound makes use of its entire 5,700-square-foot lot, having started with a storefront apartment building and expanded to the south (toward the bottom of the picture), adding a bedroom/live-with wing, a live-nearby garden house, and various garden structures that help to define outdoor "rooms." Likewise, inside are three large ground-floor spaces at each extremity of the ell, any of which could be independent live-work units at some time. Thomas Dolan Architecture and Jennifer Cooper, Designer, 2000–2003 (the author's and Jennifer's residence and place of work).

▶ **Figure C-33** James Avenue Live-Work Compound. The garden house was built in 2001 and served as the place where the author edited some of the photographs for this book. It is a case of live-nearby, being a separate building. As an accessory building in Oakland, it cannot legally be used for residential or commercial purposes, a shortcoming in the code that needs to be changed. Thomas Dolan Architecture and Jennifer Cooper, Designer, 2000–2003.

◀ **Figure C-34** Outdoor rooms at the James Avenue Live-Work Compound. The indoor and outdoor spaces bleed into each other (see plan). Some of the outdoor rooms are fully roofed, as in this porch; others are partially roofed with an arbor, and some are enclosed only by buildings, walls, and an overhanging tree. The owners often take work out into these spaces, rendering them integral to the live-work function of the compound. Thomas Dolan Architecture and Jennifer Cooper, Designer, 2000–2003.

Figure C-35 Another outdoor room at the James Avenue Live-Work Compound, in this case centered around a fountain. Thomas Dolan Architecture and Jennifer Cooper, Designer, 2000–2003.

◀ **Figure C–36** The former storefront turned great room/live-work space at the James Avenue Live-Work Compound. While exposed to the street, the addition of insulated, translucent shades provides adequate privacy, allowing the storefront windows and corner doors to remain for a future restaurant or café. Thomas Dolan Architecture and Jennifer Cooper, Designer, 2000–2003.

▲ **Figure C-37** Ocean View Lofts courtyard entry. This is the place where the surprise happens as one is greeted by a bubbling fountain and entirely different exterior wall finishes—the point being that the courtyard is a special retreat, a semipublic space where live-workers can cross paths as they come and go about their daily lives, the most effective way to make a community. Pictured: Wendy Morris and the author. Thomas Dolan Architecture, 1993. Photo credit: Chip Kauffman.

▲ **Figure C-38** Flexhouses, Kentlands, Maryland. An early and successful New Urbanist greenfield project; the developer of Kentlands told Diane Dorney, the owner of the *Town Paper*—whose offices are shown in the photograph—that he wished he'd built four times as many live-works. At the time, Ms. Dorney lived upstairs in the residence above the *Town Paper's* offices. Town Planner: Duany Plater-Zyberk.

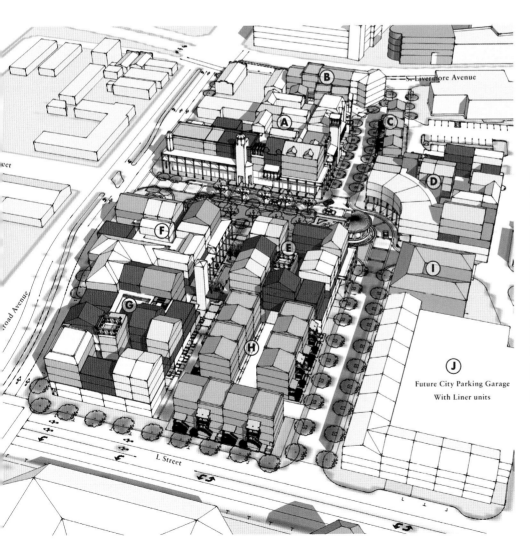

◀ **Figure C-39** Aerial perspective of Livermore Village, a grayfield makeover of a former supermarket site immediately adjacent to a revitalized main street in this prosperous midsize California city. The project includes 300 units of housing, including liner flexhouses surrounding a double parking podium topped by courtyard housing. A town green, mixed-use retail building, and mix of housing types for a diversity of incomes all add up to a mixed-use town center within a growing downtown. A joint project of Thomas Dolan Architecture and Opticos Design, Inc. Entitled 2006 (unbuilt).

Integrating Live-Work within Building Type Standards

Building-type standards are an FBC component often used to supplement the building form standards of an FBC. This component typically introduces a matrix of allowed building types with type-specific regulations that supplement the more zone-specific standards. A variety of building types typically is allowed within each zone. Most FBCs created to date use a generalized live-near proximity type (flexhouse) that is often called live-work as one of the named building-type categories. However, for each community, a range of live-work building types should be defined and expanded based on the context, the micro-scale analysis completed during the early stages of the process, and the vision plan. An example of this is in the Lower Arsenal Specific Plan in Benicia, California.

In this FBC (see Figure 6-7), the design team created and regulated a courtyard live-work type (see Figure 6-6) that would be applied within the sub-area of the plan that transitioned from the existing live-with (artists in renovated warehouses) to an area where live-near, live-nearby, and general commercial uses could coexist. The form regulations within the FBC regulated to allow live-with or live-near units

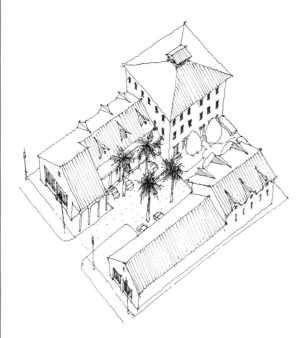

Figure 6-6 This live-with courtyard housing type internalizes potential impacts of more intense uses, such as sound and noise, within the courtyard.
Image Courtesy of Opticos Design, Inc.

oriented around a courtyard, which would internalize impacts (noise, odors, etc.) in open (higher-impact) use intensities.

Integrating Live-Work as a Use Type into the Use Tables

A second way of integrating live-work into FBCs is to insert them into the use tables. Contrary to the mistaken belief of many, carefully considered use tables do play an important role within effective FBCs. The best way to integrate live-work into the use table is to create a separate live-work use type (use category). This avoids the confusing question, "Which use does live-work fit under?" that often occurs when trying to integrate live-work within a use-based code. It is difficult, if not impossible, to categorize live-work forms and uses simply as residential, commercial, or industrial. Under the live-work use type one should integrate subcategories of work/live, live/work, and home occupation; the limited, restricted, and open work-use intensity classifications; or a similar system of classifying use intensity and the relationship of proximity (form) between the residential and work uses (i.e., live-with, live-near, and live-nearby). In addition, within each form-based or transect zone, each of these subcategories can have different levels of permitting required based on the size of the use. For example, a T-4 neighborhood may allow a music studio or artist studio and gallery in an ancillary building (live-nearby) under 500 square feet to be permitted by right but require a minor use permit (staff level approval) for the same use over 500 square feet. In that same context, it may be that any size of a more intense use (such as welding, etc.) require a use permit (public level of review). If employing this approach, one should be sure that the use definitions are very clear and ideally use the standards set forth by the author in this book (see Appendix A) for the type of work, employees, walk-in trade, noise, and so on.

Live-Work Considerations within the Typical Form-Based Code Process

There is a defined, effective three-step process (see Figure 6-8) for creating an FBC; live-work considerations should be carefully integrated into all three. These three steps are: documentation,

(Continued)

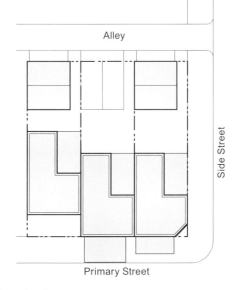

Alley

Side Street

Primary Street

Figure 6-7 A typical live-work building type spread within a form-based code.
Image Courtesy of Opticos Design, Inc.

visioning, and compiling the code. The next section gives a brief overview of how live-work should be considered within each of these phases.

Phase I: Documenting

The first step of creating an FBC is documentation and analysis, which is completed at the macro and micro scales. The intent of the macro scale

analysis is to look at a city or region holistically and determine the neighborhoods, districts, and corridor framework. This step ideally should be done within a comprehensive or regional planning process. During this step, existing live-work proximity types and use types within each neighborhood or district should be noted for further study in step two. Following that step, during the micro-scale analysis,

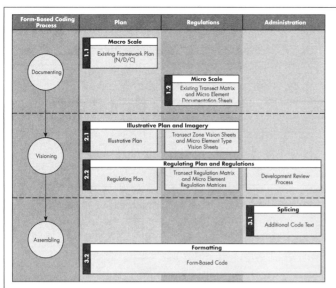

Figure 6-8 This diagram gives an overview of the typical three-phase process inherent in effective form-based code creation.
Image Courtesy of Opticos Design, Inc.

existing examples of live-work (both form/proximity and use type) should be carefully documented with photographs and sketches. This documentation will begin the assessment of which live-work forms exist and need to be reinforced within the FBC regulations: (1) those that are missing, and (2) those that should be introduced in the visioning process and ultimately included in the FBC to enable areas to revitalize and prosper.

Phase II: Visioning

A typical way to effectively utilize live-work proximity types combined with different work-use types within a visioning process is to locate them to provide appropriate transitions (see Figure 6-9). These transitions may be from a main street into a neighborhood that can be provided by live-with (a loft in existing shopfront building), live-near (flexhouse), or live-nearby (use in an ancillary structure) applications. Another type of transition would include repositioning from the primary commercial/retail node along a main street to edges that would likely

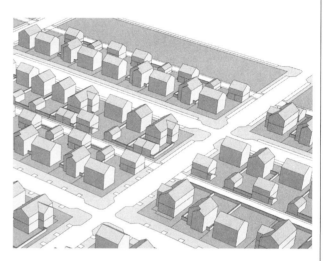

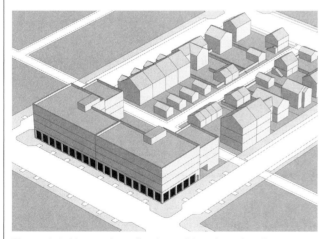

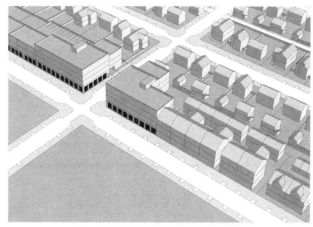

Figure 6-9 Live-work applications of form-based coding.
Top: Allowing and encouraging live-nearby applications in ancillary buildings within neighborhoods maximizes walkability and is the appropriate application of live-work and mixed use to a historic neighborhood.
Lower right: Live-work units with flexible ground-floor spaces are being used to transition around a corner from a main street into a neighborhood.
Lower left: Along a main street corridor, flexhouses, or simply buildings with flexible ground-floor spaces, provide good transitions into residential areas along the corridor and allow a main street to evolve as the market grows or shrinks.
Images Courtesy of Opticos Design, Inc.

want to allow more flexibility of use. In this case live-with or live-near applications would typically be appropriate in various forms, as well as housing over retail, really a form of live-nearby. These applications can provide incubator spaces for struggling or newly created main streets and for small businesses; they often help revitalize existing main streets.

There are many examples of flexhouse types providing incubators for new-neighborhood main streets in New Urbanist projects. One example can be seen in the flexhouse type built within the South Main Traditional Neighborhood Development project in Buena Vista, Colorado (see Figure C-30 in the color folio). This building provides a live-near condition with a separated, two-story living space above a ground-floor flex space, each of which has a separate entry from the street. In this instance, a two-hour fire separation was provided between the ground floor and upper spaces; it allows a live/work use intensity at a Limited level but not an Open level on the ground floor. The ground-floor space is occupied by the real estate branch of the project's development company.

Tip

a. Carefully consider frontage types for all live-work applications, based on the context and desired character.
b. During the review process, ensure that builders are providing the appropriate fire separation—if required—for live-work buildings that have residential and nonresidential uses. See Section 419 of the International Building Code (IBC) or International Residential Code (IRC), as applicable, and see Chapter Seven: Building Codes, and Appendix B.

Phase III: Compiling of the Code

In this last step, be sure that the details of the live-work application are fully fleshed out. This would include creating clear definitions of live-work and all of the proximity and work-use types, integrating live-work building types into the Building Type Standards as applicable, and clearly integrating live-work into the use tables.

Especially when writing a zoning code that has conventional and FBC components, one must take care to ensure that regulations throughout the document are consistent with one another. The "Specific to Use" regulations section is an area where inconsistencies are often found. To avoid such inconsistencies, be sure that all form-related standards are in the FBC, not the Specific to Use section of the code. One will likely need to step back once the entire code is drafted and perform a thorough review to make certain that there are no regulations in place that will prevent the community from effectively using live-work concepts. An example of this might be off-street parking standards, and how one deals with them as uses change within a live-work application over time.

Based on this brief overview, it should be clear that live-work and form-based code objectives are very complimentary to one another. In terms of place-making, FBC is a tool that can be used to create and reinforce vibrant, walkable urban places that will evolve over time. The FBC must thoughtfully integrate live-work, which is a critical component in these locales.

The Best Locations for Live-Work

The assumption often made is that planning regulations should designate certain areas as best for live-work and others as inappropriate. Such an assumption misses the essential point, which is that there are people actively living and working under the same roof in all kinds of urban situations, zones, and districts. A central premise of this book is that one should have every right to do so as long as one is not impacting neighbors or creating conflicts with longstanding neighbors, businesses, or activities. A more productive approach to the question of where to locate

requires stepping back to look at the many types of live-work. An artist crashing on a mattress in the corner of a work/live rental loft in a former commercial building in an active industrial district is likely to be doing so in an appropriate location, whether the space is currently legal for live-work or not. An upscale, newly constructed loft condominium project, however, is best located in an area well served by retail, transportation, and other city services and decidedly does not belong in an established industrial district.

These two examples touch on a number of attributes of individual live-work situations, including:

- Tenancy: rental versus ownership
- Building type: new construction versus renovation
- Work-use intensity: whether work or living activity dominates
- Services: the presence or absence of city services and nearby retail
- Context: neighboring land uses and their effects on live-work users, and live-work's effect on its neighbors
- Economics: the occupant's income and work circumstances

These and many other factors determine what types of live-work fit best in specific parts of a city, and are summarized in Table 6-1. There is a type of live-work that is appropriate for virtually every location in a city except the most intense industrial districts.

Table 6-1 Best Locations for Work-Use Types and Project Types Use Types

Use Type and Proximity Type	Description of Project or Unit Type	Residential Zone: Work-use intensity: Restricted**	Commercial Zone: Work-use intensity: Limited**	Industrial Zone: Work-use intensity: Open	Mixed-Use Zone: Work-use intensity depends on proximity type and environs	Comments
Work/live live-with	Loft renovation	No, except neighborhood storefront conversions	Yes	Yes: rental, artists only	Yes	Hazmats as allowed by building code and exceptions; good incubator space
Work/live live-near	Flexhouse or separated work space within unit	No	Yes	Yes	Yes	Employees and walk-in trade usually OK
Work/live live-nearby*	Work space outside of residential unit	Yes; work use as allowed per Table A-1, Appendix A	Yes	Yes	Yes	Employees and walk-in trade usually OK if at grade or elevator-accessed level
Live/work live-with	Loft or townhouse that is open floor-to-floor	Yes	Yes	Not usually***	Yes	Walk-in trade and employees permitted up to 3,000 SF, above which must be live-near w/fire separation (IBC 419)
Live/work live-near	Other type of separated work space within unit (not a flexhouse)	Yes, possible restrictions on walk-in trade and employees	Yes	Not usually***	Yes	Per building code, walk-in trade and employees permitted if at grade or elevator-accessed level
Live/work live-nearby	Work space in a separate building or unit	Based on specific work use (see Table A-1 Appendix A)	Yes	Yes	Yes	Per building code, walk-in trade and employees permitted if at grade or elevator-accessed level
Flexhouse *Live/work* live-near	Flexible townhouse bay or multilevel unit in a multi-unit building; upstairs formally separated from main level	Yes	Yes	Not usually***	Yes	Ground floor use may change and/or be held separately; per building code, walk-in trade and employees permitted if at grade or elevator-accessed level

(Continued)

Table 6-1 *(Continued)*

Use Type and Proximity Type	Description of Project or Unit Type	Residential Zone: Work-use intensity: Restricted**	Commercial Zone: Work-use intensity: Limited**	Industrial Zone: Work-use intensity: Open	Mixed-Use Zone: Work-use intensity depends on proximity type and environs	Comments
Home Occupation live-nearby*	Residence and work space in separate building or unit*	Yes	Yes	N/A***	Yes	Work activity in a separate building and work spaceuse intensity based on zone and Table A-1 (Appendix A); can be considered a mixed-use building (i.e., apartments over retail); possible restrictions on employees and walk-in trade
Artist or Artisan's *Work/live* Loft live-with	Artist or artisan's loft	Rarely, except neighborhood storefront conversions	Yes	Yes; artists and artisans rental only	Yes	Almost always a renovation of an existing commercial, industrial or civic building

*On the same property.
**Work use as permitted in underlying zone and per Table A-1 (Appendix A).
***Stand-alone residences not usually permitted in industrial districts.

Planning for Live-Work Types as Parsed by Work-Use Intensity

Permitted work-use intensities (Table 6-2) are classified by work activity as either Restricted, Limited, or Open in Appendix A, Table A-1, and their respective maximum allowable areas are detailed in Table A-2.

Home Occupation

Many jurisdictions affirm a resident's right to work in his or her residence under home occupation regulations. The number of people who do so is huge and growing all the time. As has been noted, a home occupation is just that—working in a residence; its permitted work-use intensity is Restricted (the lowest). Accordingly, most home occupation regulations place importance on preservation of the character of the residential neighborhood, seemingly assuming that commercial activity will somehow diminish its quality of life. Therefore, walk-in trade is typically prohibited, and the number of employees is either strictly limited or prohibited altogether. Commercial signage is also typically forbidden or limited to a smaller, inconspicuous sign. In addition to the obvious home occupation—that of home office activities whose only contact with the outside world is electronic—a therapist, a sole-practice architect, or a hairstylist are all viable home occupations. A home occupation activity is typically not permitted to generate noises or odors perceivable beyond that home occupation's property, and any interference with the residential neighborhood's traffic patterns or availability of on-street parking is discouraged. A home occupation usually allows client visits by appointment only and therefore no walk-in trade. Typically a very limited number of employees are permitted, or sometimes no employees are allowed, depending on locally calibrated regulations (see Table A-4, Appendix A).

Table 6-2 Work-Use Intensity Types in Live-Work

Home Occupation	Work occurs within a residence; work uses are Restricted
Live/work	Work occurs within a unit whose dominance over residential activity will vary over time; work uses are Limited
Work/live	Residence occurs within or adjacent to a commercial space, whose use is dominant; work uses are Open

Naturally, home occupation is most often found in residential neighborhoods, but there is no good reason why it can't occur in any legal residence, which usually means anywhere in a city except industrial districts. Typically, a home occupation unit can function as a residence when work activity ceases. Conversely, if living activity ceases in a home occupation unit and work continues, negative effects may transpire if it is not already in a mixed-use neighborhood.

It is arguable that if some percentage of residences in a given neighborhood are being used as home occupation, a mixed-use neighborhood has then emerged that will create demands for a different neighborhood structure than, say, a single-use suburban residential subdivision. One can only imagine what such a subdivision would be like if half of its residents stopped commuting. At some point in the evolution of gasoline prices, this is likely to occur, with not entirely predictable consequences.

Live/Work

Live/work (as opposed to live-work) is a type that describes a unit where neither working nor living activity is dominant (see Figure 6-10). It is well suited to commercial and mixed-use zones or greenfield town centers. Live/work— in any proximity type—can function particularly well as a buffer or transition between single-use zones, such as between residential and commercial zones (see the Willow Court case study in Chapter Three: Design), as can work/live. Work-use intensity in live/work is Limited, which places it in the middle range. See Tables A-1 and A-2 in Appendix A for more information regarding permitted uses and areas.

Depending on proximity type, a live/work unit that is a live-with (i.e., contained within a single common atmosphere) is appropriate in all locations except industrial zones, where its resemblance to a residence is likely to make it a target for residential reversion. Many cities require that in residential zones, a live/work unit, regardless of proximity type, must conform to home occupation regulations with respect to employees, walk-in trade, and so on. An example would be a leftover storefront building in the heart of a residential area, as in the James Avenue Compound case study later in the chapter.

To reiterate, live/work, a hybrid that can go either way, is best regulated with great care in industrial zones if it is permitted at all. Typically, a live/work unit, being the most flexible of types, does not adversely affect its environs and

Figure 6-10 A live/work unit where, as is common, the work portion (see temporary movable wall at left) and kitchen are on the main level and the sleeping and bathing accommodations are at the mezzanine level. South Prescott Village, Oakland, California, 1988. Designed by Thomas Dolan Architecture.

can function when work activity ceases or living activity ceases. However, if work activity ceases and the project is located in an existing commercial/industrial neighborhood, this residential reversion can wreak havoc if imported NIMBYs begin to complain about their established neighbors' heretofore accepted and permitted activities, with the result being that the established businesses are often driven out.

A live/work unit that is a live-near or live-nearby proximity type is usually a townhouse style unit or perhaps a liner unit in a larger building in a higher intensity urban context (transect zones T-5 and T-6). As noted in Table 6-9, such a building is most appropriate on a commercial street, where the ground floor might become retail one day, if not immediately. In this case, of course, walk-in trade and employees would be both permitted and expected.

Type of Live-Work: Mostly home occupation at present

Proximity Type: Live-with, live-near, and live-nearby

Approval Status: Home Occupation (no maximum square footage requirements in Oakland); storefront is a live-work unit, having been legally converted from a portion of a "building originally designed for commercial or industrial use" per city and state law.

Location: Rockridge Neighborhood of Oakland, California

Walkscore: 88 (very walkable)

Year Built: 1930, renovated 2000, new outbuilding (garden house live-nearby) 2001

Architects: Thomas Dolan Architecture/Jennifer Cooper Designer

Developer: Thomas Dolan and Jennifer Cooper

The James Avenue Live-Work Compound is the rehabilitation of a corner storefront in an otherwise entirely residential neighborhood with added live-nearby work space and multiple large indoor and outdoor rooms. When the owners bought it in 1999, the James Avenue Live-Work Compound was a derelict former corner store with three apartments (see Figure 6-11) located on a triple, south-facing, otherwise vacant lot save one large grapefruit tree.

As a zero lot line building on two streets, one of which is a secondary "yield" street, the project struck the author and his wife, also an architect, as a perfect place for a live-work compound (see Figure C-31, the site and ground floor plan, in the color folio). The original building consisted of a corner store, the apartment "behind" the store, actually extending along Clifton Street (see site/1st floor plan), and two apartments upstairs. The architects first rented out the upstairs, then set about gutting the downstairs and adding a master suite, a series of garden structures (see Figure 6-12), delineating outdoor rooms, and a garden house.

The compound (see Figure 6-13) now accommodates all three proximity types on a 57- by 100-foot corner lot with ample outdoor space including a grape arbor, vegetable gardens, and a play structure. The compound is located within a five-minute walk of ten restaurants, a library, a supermarket, and other neighborhood services including the author's present office. Within the compound are:

- Live-with space in two of the large rooms, one a loft in the bedroom (where part of this book was written) and the other in a corner of the great room, shown in Figure C-32 in the color folio

- Live-near space in one of the apartments upstairs (Jennifer Cooper Designer's office)

Figure 6-11 A rear view of the James Avenue Live-Work Compound in Oakland, California before the major renovation in 2000 and outbuilding addition in 2001. Designed by Thomas Dolan Architecture and Jennifer Cooper Designer.

Figure 6-12 Rear view of the James Avenue Live-Work Compound in Oakland, California after the major renovation and addition in 2000 and 2001. Designed by Thomas Dolan Architecture and Jennifer Cooper Designer.

- Live-nearby "shedworking" space in the garden house (where the slides for this book were edited), as seen in Figure C-33 in the color folio

Lessons Learned

1. It is possible to take a small-scale neighborhood building and convert it into a true live-work place. A vast industrial warehouse isn't necessary. Zero or nearly zero lot line building placement enabled use of the entire lot, which was essential. Well-defined indoor and outdoor rooms (see Figure

Figure 6-13 A street view of the James Avenue Live-Work Compound in Oakland, California, where part of this book was written, where the designer Jennifer Cooper (the author's life partner) works, and where life and work are fully integrated, employing all three of the proximity types defined in this book. 2000. Designed by Thomas Dolan Architecture and Jennifer Cooper Designer.

C-34 in the color folio) as well as easy indoor/outdoor flow help the compound to feel much larger than its 5,700-foot lot. Most of the spaces are relatively small, yet they easily accommodate their intended uses (see Figure C-35 in the color folio).

2. The compound is flexible, as live-near often is:
   - The 2,200-square-foot main floor residence is designed to devolve into two units should the owners elect to downsize.
   - The apartments upstairs can of course be rented out, or used as an expansion of the downstairs residence or student housing for one of the couple's offspring.
   - The living room of the apartment behind the store (presently a bedroom/craftsroom/passage) could again become an office (see Figure 5-1); it is located near the Clifton Street entrance, meaning that clients could enter without passing through the rest of the house.
   - It is even possible that the corner live-work (see Figure C-36 in the color folio) could become a café or bookstore at some later time, because Oakland has revised its zoning to allow former storefronts in residential neighborhoods—for the last thirty-five years relegated to residential use only—to return to commercial use.

Tip

Enact regulations to allow storefronts and other small commercial buildings to be converted to live-work, even though they may be marooned by other uses, such as single-use residential development.

Work/Live

The term work/live describes a unit type where the work activity and/or the space devoted to it is dominant and the work-use intensity is Open (the highest). Mixed-use zones and commercial zones are well suited to work/live, where employees and walk-in trade are encouraged. True work/live, particularly when the work use is similar to that in the underlying zone, is the most appropriate type in industrial zones, especially when regulatory provisions to prevent imported NIMBYism are in place. Work/live is typically not appropriate in residential zones unless the work space is separate, as in a live-nearby situation, and even these require work-use intensity to be scrutinized and carefully calibrated to local conditions.

New-construction work/live is rare. As housing recedes as the primary economic driver of construction and development, and job creation comes more to the fore, units aimed at work activity with the possibility that living can occur in them are one possible evolution of work/live. The city of Oakland, California, has attempted to regulate work/live in a new zone called Housing and Business Mix (HBX) by defining it in terms of three building forms intended to prevent pure residential use, or residential reversion (treated below) from occurring. These relatively inflexible new regulations require work/live units to be a live-near proximity type and specify that the work activity be carried on at the ground floor or entry level of the unit. Such regulations, while adopted, have not been put to the test as of this writing (2011) because the current recession has prevented new projects from being built.

The most common form of work/live is where the movement really began, with renovations of existing commercial buildings for rental work/live, often for artists, in districts not well served by city services, retail, or transportation. Regulation of renovation work/live has usually come in the form of zoning overlays and building code bulletins that allow it to occur when accompanied by the addition of some life safety elements. Once artists and others begin to occupy lofts as work/live, changes often occur in the applicable district, transforming it into a viable neighborhood. The SoHo Cycle is treated elsewhere in this book; suffice it to say that there is much for regulators to learn regarding how to anticipate and plan for this phenomenon.

Typically a work/live unit located in a commercial or industrial location does not adversely affect its environs and can function when residential activity ceases. Conversely, if work activity ceases or does not occur in a work/live unit, residential reversion is the result, which can create problems.

Planning for Live-Work Types as Parsed by Proximity Type

Proximity types (Table 6-3) describe the physical relationship between living and working portion of units. As, such they are the most tangible way of distinguishing unit types and therefore play an important tool in planning and regulating live-work.

Live-With Proximity Type

The live-with proximity type (synonym: loft) is the most flexible, perhaps the most common, and in some ways the most difficult live-work to regulate (see Figure 6-14). Such units are usually found in multiunit projects with a common lobby and circulation. Sometimes regulatory prob-

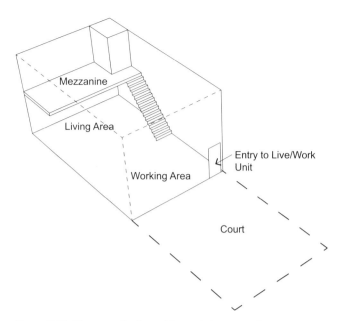

Figure 6-14 Diagram of a live-with proximity type unit.

lems arise in live-with when attempts are made to apply inappropriate paradigms, such as separated-use zoning; others arise from building code concerns. Whether it is an illegal artists' loft in an old warehouse, a legally converted loft in a rapidly gentrifying district, a newly constructed unit in a courtyard community, or a podium project, lofts are a well-recognized type whose design is treated fully in Chapter Three: Design.

A live-with unit is the most fully mixed use of the proximity types, and as such its work use, or the amount of space devoted to work versus residence, will not be static (see Figure 6-15) and is therefore difficult to regulate. Live-with occupants use their spaces differently at different times of the day and the week, as well as over longer periods. While there are reasons to designate certain portions of a unit for specific uses such as sleeping or work, experience has taught most planners and designers that imposing such regulations can be frustrating, meaningless, and, ultimately, unenforceable. People rent and buy lofts specifically because they are flexible; trying to prevent that through regulation presages a losing battle. Instead, the inherent flexibility of live-with should be embraced and facilitated.

As noted in Chapter Two: Definitions, live-with units have multifunctionality, meaning that some parts of the unit will be used for both living and working activities depending on the need at the time. While not strictly within the purview of planning regulations, it is certainly arguable that live-work occupants tend to blur the distinction between "life" and

Table 6-3 Live-Work Proximity Types

Live-with	Work and residence all occur in one "common atmosphere"
Live-near	Work and residence are separated by a wall or floor/ceiling
Live-nearby	Work occurs outside the residence but on the same property

Figure 6-15 A live-with unit at West Boulder Reserve, MacLoed, Montana; the work space, which doubles as a spare bedroom, is at the mezzanine level in this home occupation space. 1991. Designed by Thomas Dolan Architecture.

Figure 6-16 A live-with unit: blurring the distinction between life and work. Claremont, California. Photograph taken 2007.

"work" (see Figure 6-16). Nowhere is this more true than in a live-with unit.

A live-with unit is not the best choice for someone whose work is noisy, dangerous, or involves hazardous materials or processes. Nevertheless, a townhouse bay live-with that contains a main floor plus a mezzanine for sleeping and other living activities could accommodate a limited number of employees, and the 2009 IBC allows five employees in a live-with townhouse (see Chapter Seven: Building Codes). Depending on the work activity permitted in its location, such a unit might at times be home to residence-only or work-only activities.

Live-work entitlements always allow residence and some type of work to occur. Conversely, there typically are not zoning regulations that prohibit the cessation of living or working activity in a unit. The former—resulting in a single-use commercial unit in most cases—is not typically desirable in a residential neighborhood. The latter, known as residential reversion, is common and problematic in commercial and especially industrial locations; its implica-

tions are discussed elsewhere in this chapter. As a general observation, however, attempts to require live-workers to always live and always work in their units usually come to naught.

Lofts tend to be more difficult to regulate because—paradoxically—they are so simple, because they sometimes arise out of quasi-legal situations, and because their essence is to be adaptable to changing needs and therefore varied uses. Planners often become uncomfortable when uses are less than fully predictable. More so than perhaps any other urban building type, lofts represent freedom for occupants to do as they wish. There isn't a room on a floor plan that says "dining room," there isn't a front door with a two-tone chime, and there often aren't many finishes in the space beyond code minimums. Loft residents like the fact that they can move in and add their own identity to the space—this is an essential truth of live-work, nowhere more evident than in lofts. Lofts have been called "warehouses with kitchens," and while such a sobriquet undervalues many great live-work projects, there is a kernel of truth to it.

Live-Near Proximity Type

A live-near unit and its separate living and working space (see Figure 6-17) often takes the form of attached, rowhouse-like buildings whose facades define a street. This form, which has existed in cities for thousands of years, appears most commonly as the flexhouse (see Figure 6-18).

Flexhouse live-work is sometimes configured as courtyard communities (see Figure 6-19), which may or may not have a strong relationship to the street.

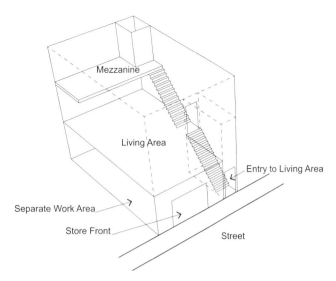

Figure 6-17 Diagram of a live-near proximity type unit.

As noted in the Chapter Two: Definitions, live-near units are flexible in an entirely different way from live-with units. The flexibility of live-near units derives from being able to treat the live portion of a unit as separate from the work portion, and being able to rent out or share the two spaces more easily.

Such flexibility can make planning officials uncomfortable, albeit in different ways from those that apply to a live-with unit. A flexhouse is ideally preapproved to flex in terms of use over time without subsequent planning approvals, as distinct from a townhouse that is open to below and therefore is only practical for a single user. The issue of approvals that allow a flexhouse to "learn" is quite separate from the physical form and varies significantly by jurisdiction.

Figure 6-18 Live-near flexhouse live-works facing Ruskin Place in Seaside, Florida. 1982. Seaside was designed by Duany Plater-Zyberk & Company, Town Planners and Architects.

Figure 6-19 The courtyard at Filbert Court, a six-unit live-work courtyard community developed by the author in Oakland; all of the units enter off of the courtyard, encouraging repeated informal interactions between the condominium owners. Three are flexhouses and three are live-with units. 1993. Designed by Thomas Dolan Architecture.

A flexhouse can be a residential or live-work townhouse, housing or live-work over retail, or even office over retail. Mixed-use town centers or walkable commercial nodes are ideal places for such a freely regulated flexhouse, whose design issues are treated in Chapter Three: Design, and the Habersham case study in Chapter Four: Market.

The clearly separated living and working spaces of a live-near unit provide a kind of certainty to regulators, in that the kitchen is in one part and the (usually) required accessible water closet is at the level-in entrance level. Building officials can apply different codes to each part, and planning officials can look up retail and residential in their zoning codes and rule accordingly, although for planners it is often not that simple. Form-based codes as described in the sidebar by Dan Parolek ("Placemaking with Live-Work and Form-Based Codes," p. 114) are often the best solution.

Coding questions that arise when planning for flexhouse live-near units include those that would apply to any retail or commercial establishment, such as parking, loading, signage, design review, and other development standards that are treated elsewhere in this chapter.

Sometimes a community envisions future retail in a given location where indications are that retail will prosper and will, in turn, enliven the street. Not all flexhouses will become retail, in part because not all locations are right for retail, whether at completion of construction or sometimes ever. Therefore, flexhouses are a hedge for a community that wants retail but isn't sure the market is ready for it in that location (see Figure 6-28).

Experience has shown that when a building is required to be constructed with retail spaces on the ground floor that have no connection to the housing above, the ground floor can sit empty for years unless the building is in a neighborhood with an active street life. Such vacancy does not do a city or its residents any good, and it harms the developer, who—had he or she been able to construct a flexhouse that connects the street-front portion to upstairs—would likely have been able to rent or sell such units far sooner as live-work and therefore achieve immediate activation of the street.

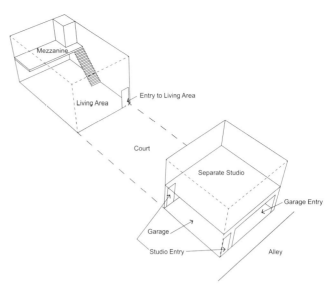

Figure 6-20 Diagram of a live-nearby proximity type unit.

Tip

A way of regulating a flexhouse configuration—either as townhouses or liner units, is to require that the developer hold the units as rentals for a set period of time—such as five years—before the decision to sell units or not is made. Such a period might be extended on a discretionary basis if deemed appropriate by planning officials.

As is shown more fully in Chapter Three: Design, once the decision is made to sell a vertically demised flexhouse, the option for ground-floor retail to occupy a width of more than one bay is virtually eliminated. Various means can be devised to determine when to give up on multibay retail; one trigger might be the retail vacancy rate nearby. For a jurisdiction that wants an occupied ground floor, an activated street, and the possibility of retail at some point, allowing pre-entitled live-work flexhouses is a wise move.

Flexhouses are further discussed in the "Project Types" section later in the chapter.

Live-Nearby Proximity Type

Live-nearby is more straightforward for conventional planners because the living and working portions are in separate units or buildings (see Figure 6-20). Nevertheless, as noted in the example in the sidebar by Dan Parolek, live-nearby

as a building form is well suited to such coding. As noted in Chapter Two: Definitions, in live-nearby, a short walk separates the living portion and the work space—for example, across a courtyard to a converted garage or other accessory structure. While this type may initially appear to be simply mixed use, classification as live-work may permit its existence in locations where a residential or a commercial space alone might not be permitted.

There is one fly in the ointment of many local municipal planning codes. The work space in a live-nearby unit is often located in an outbuilding, such as over a garage, or in a converted garage or barn. These are typically referred to as accessory buildings, and many planning codes prohibit their use for commercial or residential activity. Such regulations ignore the fact that commuting, while the norm for the last 150 years, is becoming unnecessary for increasing numbers of people, who prefer to incubate their new business idea at home or simply maintain a small business there. Most people are familiar with the stories of Apple, Google, and Hewlett Packard, all of which were started in garages (essentially a form of live-nearby) in Silicon Valley. While it can be argued that the conversion of a garage to a work space removes a required off-street parking space, it is sometimes true that the decision to work at home coincides with the resident's decision to give up one car.

Some jurisdictions require accessory buildings for home office use to be built to full commercial building standards, including sprinklers and independent means of egress from each level, a subject discussed in Chapter Seven: Building Codes. This is understandable in cases where walk-in trade and/or more than one or two employees are anticipated, but a line must be drawn that allows the pursuit of this vital economic option to be encouraged rather than penalized. There is no reasonable argument why an upstairs space in an accessory building that may flex from residential to live-work to work-only with few or no employees and no walk-in trade should conform to commercial building code occupancy requirements.

As noted, housing over retail is essentially live-nearby and is most definitely a form of live-work if the occupant of the retail lives in the same building, on the same property or—some would say—in the neighborhood.

Housing over retail is an important component of a live-work neighborhood. Considering it as a building type, it makes little difference whether the upstairs, downstairs, or accessory building are occupied by the same party. How this might be regulated differently than a mixed-use building in terms of parking standards, for example, would primarily involve recognizing that if some percentage of residents commute elsewhere, if some work in the building, and if some employees and customers require parking, there exist opportunities for time-shared parking to reduce the need for dedicated off-street parking spaces.

The author, who has lived where he worked for much of his thirty-year career, recently moved his office to a location two hundred yards from his residence in a walkable neighborhood. He now rarely drives, because virtually everything he needs is within walking distance. He refuels his car roughly once a month. As a result, he considered (but did not adopt in this book) expanding the definition of live-nearby to include—in the right setting—work space and residence separated by as much as a five-minute walk, if they are also located in a live-work neighborhood that provides the majority

of the live-workers, needs for goods and services within a ten-minute walk of both home and residence.

Tip
Allow and encourage the construction and conversion of accessory buildings as live-nearby work spaces at work-use intensities appropriate to the specific transect zone.

Planning for Live-Work Types as Parsed by Project Type

Additional planning issues that are specific to project types and how they might be best regulated are discussed here (see Table 6-4); project types are more fully discussed in Chapter Three: Design.

Artists' Work/Live Rental Renovation

As discussed, live-work often begins in a given locality with the colonizing of former warehouses by artists and other similarly situated individuals (see Figure 6-21). Once this phenomenon is identified, an orderly process of legalizing live-work is a wise step for a city to take, both to preserve life safety and to address issues of speculation and landlord exploitation.

Despite the apparent inevitability of the SoHo Cycle, some projects can remain artist-occupied for a long time. Unless there is a nonprofit developer involved who can leverage subsidies to assure long-term affordability, such projects are best maintained as rentals. Once lofts are converted to condominiums, it is unlikely that the artists will remain. Unlike the average condominium buyer, artists—who are working

Table 6-4 Live-Work Project Types and Planning Issues

Type	Issues
Artists' work/live rental renovation	Legalization of existing live-work; renovation standards; compatibility of work; industrial areas can be OK; rental only unless subsidized; artists' protection and their place in a city
Market-rate live-work condominium renovation	Locate where services exist; disclosures of neighboring commercial/industrial activity; work activities always permitted
New-construction lofts	Mostly condo; must locate in areas well served by amenities and transit; not in existing industrial areas; disclosures of neighboring commercial/industrial activity address imported NIMBYism
Live-work courtyard community	OK to locate in residential or commercial areas; can be rental or ownership; interactive open space design standards essential
Townhouse live-with	Permitted under new building code; inflexible as to tenancy and work activity without the addition of a separation, but suitable for small owner-occupied businesses
Flexhouse, or mixed-use live-near	A "building that learns"; flexible development standards; best located on a street with retail potential
Other types: cohousing, congregate live-work, cohort housing	Many shared facilities; congregate less likely to gentrify

Figure 6-21 An artist's work/live studio in a landlocked situation, where the only light and ventilation source is from skylights. The David Gray Building, Oakland, California, 2007. Designed by Thomas Dolan Architecture.

in their units—often feel a common purpose with their commercial and industrial neighbors. As a result, they tolerate the occasional noxious odors and noises that are permitted in an industrial zone—and in fact artists' work activities often contribute in this respect.

Preventing gentrification in artists' live-work is a difficult issue, and to the extent that a society—or the citizens of a locality—value its artists as the keepers of our culture, such an effort is worth undertaking. While it was thought at one time that planning and building codes to permit live-work would allow artists to flourish, such has not proven to be the case. Legalizing live-work has mostly benefited real estate developers and encouraged the SoHo Cycle, whose result is the displacement of low- and moderate-income artists. Retaining artists in a community is ultimately about money, not codes. As long as an artist or small businessperson has a long-term rent-controlled lease or ownership of his or her space, he or she can remain in place. Under free-market real estate conditions, those who deliberately place themselves outside the mainstream are likely to be forced to move along as neighborhoods change.

Some cities, such as Boston, Massachusetts, have dedicated staff time to the preservation of artists' live-work. Included in their kit of tools is an artist's certification process and a series of projects developed for artists only or with a certain percentage of units set aside for artists of moderate means. (More information on the program can be found at the Boston Redevelopment Agency's Web site on the Artist Certification Guidelines webpage: www.bostonredevelopmentauthority.org/econdev/ArtistCertificationGuidelines.asp.)

An entirely different approach, effective whether combined with subsidies or not, is to build units whose configuration almost guarantees that they will not become lifestyle lofts. In Providence, Rhode Island, a developer seeking to attract artists has renovated historic buildings into six-bedroom, six-workspace, two-bathroom, one-kitchen units, with generous hang-out space in the units. This form of congregate, or *cohort*, live-work is inexpensive to build—plumbing is where much of the money goes in individual units—and unlikely to ever be occupied by conventional households.

The regulation of live-work renovations aimed at the artists' rental market—which is large, especially combined with the market for young, adventurous entrepreneurs—must take into account artists' special needs, which are treated in Chapter Three: Design. Such projects must be designed, coded, and financed to discourage appropriation by more upscale occupants, and must take into account the importance of location. For example, not only will yuppies not move into congregate live-work; they are also less likely to move into thriving industrial areas that artists gladly tolerate in exchange for lower rents; if they do, it is often problematic.

Market Rate Live-Work Condominium Renovation

Most market rate warehouse renovations are a housing "product" where the resident is permitted to work (see Figure 6-22). There are occasions when projects are designed and built as work/live, where working can be the primary activity, but the majority are spacious residences with high ceilings and great natural light. If a project is to retain a measure of flexibility, it is important for all buyers to be aware that work activities can and will occur in adjacent units, although they may be of more limited impact than those in rental live-work in industrial districts. Jurisdictions are advised to enact regulations that prohibit live-work residents from revising their covenants to preclude work activity, a lesson the city of Vancouver, BC, learned when it happened there (see Work/Live in Vancouver below).

Location of renovated loft condominiums is important, but they are of necessity built where existing buildings are available. In many cases such buildings are in older warehouse districts. They can be very close to cities' downtowns if they have escaped the wrecking ball, as is true of the LoDo neighborhood in Denver, for example. Loft condominiums can be an ideal repurposing of such buildings, which are often historically significant. The block structure of such districts often lends itself well to revitalization as a mixed-use, pedestrian-oriented neighborhood, and in fact the

Figure 6-22 Renovated live-work condominium in a former plywood distribution warehouse with 100-foot-long bowstring trusses, between which the units were located. Willow Court, Oakland, California, 2007. Designed by Thomas Dolan Architecture. (See case study in Chapter Three.)

development of loft condominiums is arguably the most important contributor to such transformations.

However, many warehouses and industrial buildings are far from any city services, in entirely automobile-dependent districts that accommodate many longstanding commercial users. Locating loft condominiums in such districts is a prescription for disaster, as has been observed in cities such as San Francisco. Residential reversion, imported NIMBY-ism, and the acrimonious conflicts that ensue are a pattern to avoid. In cases where such development occurs, it is important to enact safeguards for the existing commercial and industrial owners such as nuisance easements (if possible) as well as covenants and disclosures. However, a far better solution is to limit live-work in such districts to rental renovation only, a ruling that is best revisited from time to time.

New-Construction Lofts

Increasingly, cities are permitting new-construction live-work. Perhaps the most extensive foray into the realm of allowing new loft construction in virtually all industrial districts was the case of San Francisco during the late 1990s dot-com boom. Due to the lack of a sufficient stock of older buildings and a strong demand for market-rate housing at prices lower than those in established neighborhoods, the city elected to translate its live-work zoning and building codes—including significant relaxations in development standards—to allow new loft buildings to be constructed.

The San Francisco Experience

In the late 1990s, San Francisco received national attention due to the controversy over the development of live-work units (see Figure 6-23). The issue became so heated that the city's board of supervisors declared a moratorium on this development type in 1999. Urban designers and planners around the country questioned why the San Francisco supervisors would make this decision. Professionals in the field, and New Urbanists in particular, usually support this building type as the embodiment of a mixed-use, pedestrian-friendly development. The problem in San Francisco was not live-work as a development type per se, but how and—most important—where it was being built (see Figure 6-24).

Much of the so-called live-work being built in San Francisco was what the author refers to as "substandard luxury housing": substandard

Figure 6-23 A purpose-built live-work building in SoMa (South of Market), San Francisco, California. Relaxed development standards encouraged a large number of such projects to be built in the 1990s.

Figure 6-24 A series of live-work buildings form a street wall along Third Street in a mostly industrial portion of San Francisco, California, which at the time was poorly served by urban infrastructure. A light rail line has since been installed, arguably in part as a result of the presence of live-work projects.

because it was built to lower standards than other types of housing; luxury because it arguably was expensive for what one got; and housing because it was generally residential, not live-work as it is usually defined (i.e., a place where most of the people living there also work there).

Live-work lofts were pioneered in the 1960s and 1970s. In San Francisco, as elsewhere, artists were often the first to discover that the high ceilings and big windows in abandoned warehouses were ideal for combined studio and residential space. Because they had few options, building owners often welcomed the artists and winked at quasi-legal loft conversions.

Building inspectors eventually became aware of the illegal dwellings and began to cite these illegal uses, but in San Francisco—as in many other cities—it was artists who initiated the movement to legitimize them, pushing for planning and building codes that required live-work units in the city to: (1) be specifically for artists, except in a portion of the neighborhood immediately south of Market Street (SoMa); (2) only be created through the conversion of existing industrial and commercial buildings; and (3) benefit from significantly relaxed building code requirements and development standards. Because they were seen as commercial spaces with residential as an accessory use, live-work units were exempt from school impact fees, inclusionary zoning, and other requirements, including on-site open space.

Almost immediately after passage of live-work planning regulations in 1988, the artist-only provision was flouted by developers and regulators alike and "overlooked" by the latter, who pleaded enforcement difficulties. A buyer was simply required to sign a form upon purchase of a loft declaring him- or herself an artist, which usually happened at close of escrow and meant very little. Additionally, the city's planning regulations were also changed to permit new construction of live-work in most nonresidential zones outside the city core. Spurred by the sustained high-tech dot-com boom, Mayor Willie Brown and his staunch pro-development allies encouraged live-work, portraying it as a solution to the city's housing shortage. Residential lenders began considering these "loft condominiums" as residences. By the late 1990s, the trickle had become a trend, culminating in a land rush. Between the legalization of live-work in San Francisco in 1988 and the 1999 moratorium, over 3,500 loft units were built or entitled, mostly new-construction for-sale condominiums selling for upward of $600/square foot until the recession hit. Some might say:

> Prices were high in San Francisco. So what else is new? If so many of these live-work units were being built and sold, they must have been meeting a genuine need. What's wrong with that?

The biggest problem with the new live-work in San Francisco was the effect the construction of these units had on their surroundings, which speaks to the inappropriateness of their locations. Lofts were being built in industrial or lower-income mixed-use areas, wherever vacant and cheap land was available. For example, in industrial areas, typically between ten and fifty units were built on a lot adjacent to an existing, often long-established use, such as a printing company, auto body shop, or meat packing plant. The units weren't cheap; consequently the new residents typically were well-heeled, SUV-driving BoHos (bourgeois bohemians, a term that does not seem to have survived the 1990s), flush with the sense of entitlement of first-time homeowners. Despite disclosures and disclaimers by developers and sellers about the nature of these existing districts, the first thing these new arrivals often did after they moved in

(Continued)

was to complain about the ongoing commercial activities of their neighbors.

A basic rule of real estate economics is that when a higher-value use—in this case essentially multifamily residential—is introduced into an area where it was not previously permitted, land prices will rise to meet the land values for that use. This is exactly what happened in San Francisco. In many cases, long-standing businesses were forced to move repeatedly until they finally left the city, driven out by complaining newcomers (imported NIMBYs) and rising land prices.

Lower-income neighborhoods were also adversely affected by loft development. While construction of loft buildings was primarily occurring as infill on vacant lots and therefore not displacing local residents, many affordable quarters for artists and small businesses were vacated and converted to pricey loft condominiums or, at the height of the dot-com boom, to offices. Rents and sales prices in traditionally affordable areas rose. This is a happy result for owners eager to sell, but for others it forced a sad ending to residence in stable, affordable neighborhoods. San Francisco, once a city with sizable working-class neighborhoods, has become largely a place for the well heeled.

The controversy, then, was about important elements of San Francisco being lost: industrial areas and affordable neighborhoods. A city needs back-office space; it needs the small businesses that serve the big downtown businesses; it needs places that fix cars, print business cards, and process fresh meat. A successful metropolis needs places to store and transfer the materials and goods required by an urban economy. It also needs affordable neighborhoods to house its schoolteachers, mail carriers, and nurses.

One might suggest that the high prices and dislocation that accompanied the San Francisco loft experience are simply signs of transition to a postindustrial urban economy. Certainly Zero-Commute housing and telecommuting are recent advances with tremendous implications for settlement patterns. However, the willy-nilly location of so-called live-work projects in San Francisco without regard to the proximity of services or impacts on adjacent uses amounts to no planning at all, a fact that has been acknowledged by some of the city planners who worked on this issue.

So, when the moratorium is lifted and demand for live-work returns, what should be the revised shape of live-work development in San Francisco, and what lessons were learned?

Lessons Learned

1. Recognize that most new live-work lofts are primarily examples of a housing type where people might work. Live-work, residential lofts, shop-houses, live-near, live-nearby: All of these types should be integrated into the city's overall housing strategy. Such projects need to be located near transit, schools, open space, shops, and employment.

2. Live-work residents' unique needs for social interaction need to be accommodated. Most people who work at home work alone. Feelings of isolation are normal, and are the most common complaint associated with live-work. Although we all have different needs for human contact, live-workers benefit especially from opportunities for informal interaction. Therefore, locate new projects in lively neighborhoods where opportunities for interaction are available nearby.

3. In the right locations, flexhouses (i.e., buildings that learn) should be allowed. Live-work lofts in San Francisco went through many iterations of displacement and repurposing during the 1990s. First, the artists who had pioneered live-work were supplanted by higher-income residents. Toward the mid-1990s, research showed that only 15 percent of live-work units in the SoMa area were occupied by people actually working in them. As the dot-com boom peaked, start-ups bought large blocks of live-work condos for office space.

The San Francisco loft boom telescoped much into ten years, which makes it a useful example to study today. Planning ahead for a hybrid building's multiple incarnations makes perfect sense in the right locations, and such flexhouses should be preapproved as live-work, all-work (i.e., commercial), or all-residential, and not require any further approvals to shift between any combination of these uses. In some cases retail might still be required on the first floor street front; in other cases the number of employees might be limited.

One can see from the example, "The San Francisco Experience," that just as economic cycles were not abolished by the "new economy" of the 1990s, basic planning principles cannot simply be ignored. New-construction lofts can be a great addition to a city's range of available housing and live-work options, but they should be designed and located in a way that respects their context, that fits well into existing city infrastructure and services, and that enables them to become a component of a viable neighborhood, be it new or existing.

Many of the issues discussed in Market-Rate Warehouse Conversions section above apply to new lofts. When they are located in existing industrial or commercial areas, all of the tools mentioned in this chapter and elsewhere in the book—nuisance easements (if possible), covenants, disclosures, and so on—must be deployed. Better yet, always locate ownership live-work where urban infrastructure—in the form of easy access to nearby goods and services–is already present.

Live-Work Courtyard Communities

As discussed, Thomas Dolan Architecture (TDA) began working in the field of live-work design in 1985 when approached by the artist Bruce Beasley to design such a project. South Prescott Village is new-construction live-work, and it has the distinction of being the first of this type to be built since before the Great Depression. On six assembled lots in a residential neighborhood, TDA designed sixteen units in two buildings, each surrounding a common central courtyard and together opening out onto a common garden space in the block interior (see Figure 3-54, South Prescott Village Site Plan).

In designing this and subsequent projects, TDA discovered a number of important planning and design principles, which the firm has applied and refined over nearly three decades of work in the field. Because one of the greatest downsides of live-work is the potential for isolation that comes with working at home, the provision of courtyards and other common spaces that provide opportunities for interaction as one comes and goes were an important advance in the evolution of live-work design. Providing semipublic open space specifically designed to facilitate interaction is a

Figure 6-25 Casual interaction in the courtyard, South Prescott Village, Oakland, California,1988. Designed by Thomas Dolan Architecture.

natural fit with the needs of those who do not commute (see Figure 6-25).

Live-work courtyard communities were indeed a valuable discovery, and others have been built since, including Ocean View Lofts in Berkeley, California (see Figure C-11 in the color folio) and Willow Court and Filbert Court in Oakland, California.

Courtyards and other similar common spaces located along the entry path of a project can be an essential design element: not just an amenity but in many ways the heart of a project.

Tip

When writing regulations for live-work, it is advisable to specify that the required open space be designed to encourage the casual interaction that enriches the lives of live-workers. The specifics of the design of such spaces are discussed in Chapter Three: Design. What makes courtyard live-work so compelling is that, when designed properly, it becomes a place that has real meaning for its residents. More than a collection of units, a live-work courtyard community is a setting for lives lived fully, and results, over time, in the creation of lasting communities whose residents are reluctant to leave and whose remaining residents often tell their friends about openings in this special place.

Live-work courtyard communities are often located as infill in residential neighborhoods or commercial districts. Opportunities for interaction that would typically arise on a lively, walkable street are not always present in such locations. For this reason, the importance of the courtyards (see Figure 6-26) and other interactive, semipublic spaces within the project are of paramount importance; their omission constitutes a missed opportunity of the highest magnitude.

The kinds of interactive spaces that particularly animate a live-work courtyard community can—and should—be included in other project types. Podium projects on large lots often benefit from courtyards located at upper levels, such as on the top of the parking garage, which is typically fronted by housing or live-work units. Again, the important element to keep in mind is how effective the space can be at providing opportunities for informal interaction that live-work residents need.

Townhouse Live-Work

Section 419 of the IBC—which is treated in detail in Chapter Seven: Building Codes, and in Appendix B—has made an ancient building type step up to the twenty-first century by permitting work activities, employees, and walk-in trade without requirements for separation (see Figure 6-27) of work space from the residential portion, which is usually located upstairs.

Figure 6-27 Townhouse live-work in Glenwood Park, Atlanta, Georgia, which has two entrances at the ground floor—suggesting both living and working activity—but no separation between the first and second floors, i.e., the stairway is open; see Appendix B for a full treatment of IBC 419, live-work units.

While far less adaptable than a flexhouse, townhouse live-work is an important component of many urban downtowns, residential districts, and greenfield New Urbanist projects.

Flexhouse

The flexhouse (see Figure 6-28), or live-near live-work, is the most common project type in New Urbanist town centers, is common in medium-density infill locations, and is also well-located in street-level liner units of larger podium projects that might include housing or other uses above A flexhouse differs from townhouse live-work in that it includes a physical separation between main floor work area and upstairs living space; each part has a separate entrance.

As stated in Chapter Two: Definitions, a flexhouse is a building that learns, meaning that its uses are purposely flexible, and the building can shift to serve different purposes in response to changing market conditions and other factors. See

Figure 6-26 The courtyard at Ocean View Lofts, Berkeley, California, 1993, a live-work courtyard community All but one of the units opens onto the courtyard, an ideal place for casual interactions (see case study, Chapter Five). 1993. Designed by Thomas Dolan Architecture.

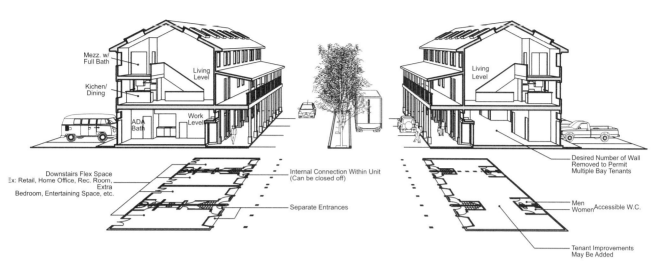

FLEX HOUSE
A BUILDING THAT LEARNS

STAGE ONE
Three-Level Townhouse
(Entire townhouse rented to one tenant;
tenant may sublet 1st floor with approval)

STAGE TWO
House over Retail
(Upper-level housing rented or sold separately)

Mezz. w/
Full Bath

Living
Level

Kichen/
Dining

ADA
Bath

Work
Level

Living
Level

Downstairs Flex Space
Ex: Retail, Home Office, Rec. Room,
Extra
Bedroom, Entertaining Space, etc.

Internal Connection Within Unit
(Can be closed off)

Separate Entrances

Desired Number of Wall
Removed to Permit
Multiple Bay Tenants

Men
Women Accessible W.C.

Tenant Improvements
May Be Added

Figure 6-28 A building that learns: perspective section and projected plan views of the two stages of a flexhouse block; Stage One is full townhouse tenancy; Stage Two accommodates multibay retail and upstairs residential or live-with units.

Figures 6-29 and 6-30 for a view of Ruskin Place in Seaside, Florida, showing the change that can occur in a flexhouse. The builder of a flexhouse is asking permission from the planning department to construct a building—usually a townhouse bay form—that may start out as all residential, then become a live-work containing a business below and its owner above, then at some point may host multi-bay ground-floor retail and housing or live-work—or even office—above. Many businesses incubate in such structures, starting in a bedroom, taking over the ground floor, then either occupying multiple ground-floor bays or the entire height of the townhouse bay.

As noted in the sidebar by Dan Parolek, regulations that govern the form of buildings and how they address and define the public realm—while deemphasizing use as the primary regulatory tool—are perhaps most appropriate for the flexhouse type. Nevertheless, development standards for a building form that can potentially vary so greatly in its number and type of users poses a difficult predictive task,

Figure 6-30 A 2010 view of the same flexhouse building shown in Figure 6-29 but without the café on the ground floor. The café's closure was likely the result of the Ruskin Place (Seaside, Florida) residents' collective decision to ban public events and to discourage walk-in trade. 1982. Designed by Duany Plater-Zyberk & Company, Town Planners and Architects.

Figure 6-29 A view of the Studio 210 café on the ground floor of a flexhouse in 2002. Ruskin Place, Seaside, Florida. 1982. Designed by Duany Plater-Zyberk& Company, Town Planners and Architects.

one that must be addressed with informed reason. Most flexhouses will see retail at some point in the life of the building. Virtually all will start with residents and likely continue to be inhabited. As is discussed in the "Development Standards" section of this chapter, opportunities for time-shared parking and a middle-ground approach to these and other standards make sense.

In some New Urbanist communities, flexhouse live-work was constructed very early in the project's life cycle in order to bring life to its center and to be ready for a time when retail will be viable, while immediately activating the street with ground-floor occupancies. Dubbed "live-works" by New Urbanists, flexhouses are the one building type that developers almost invariably regret not building in greater quantity; in short, they should be part of the mix in any new downtown or infill revitalization. The Habersham case study in Chapter Four: Market, illustrates the use of flexhouses as an effective method to jump-start the downtown of a greenfield New Urbanist community.

Affordability—that is, not maintaining and paying for separate work and living spaces—is one of the strongest motivating factors in deciding to live where one works. Some people who live in live-work do work there; some don't. Some work there but don't live there. By and large, the author's experience has been that such unpredictability can be recast as flexibility and embraced. Why flexibility relates to affordability is very straightforward: A building owner or even a long-term tenant wants to be able to adapt to economic and other forces as they arise. Whether I am living in a townhouse live-work, a work/live loft, or a flexhouse, I don't want to have to go back to the planning department and ask, "Mother, may I?" every time the economy hiccups.

What is the proper role of planning officials in the regulation of uses in live-work? If the uses are to be flexible—within the bounds of life safety considerations—then what is to be regulated? More naturally than for many other building and land use types, the answer may lie in form-based coding, treated in this chapter in the sidebar by Dan Parolek.

Development Standards

Live-work regulations have often been invented one city at a time. The purpose of this section is to raise commonly encountered issues and bring together the most effective regulatory solutions in practice today or as recommended by this author.

Relaxed Development Standards

One appeal of many cities' live-work ordinances—designed as they were to encourage redevelopment of existing vacant buildings and, in some cases, vacant land—is that many development standards are relaxed. As discussed in Chapter Seven: Building Codes, building codes are also often relaxed to make conversion of existing vacant warehouses less costly. For example, for those who built new live-work in San Francisco, paying industrial prices to build what was essentially substandard luxury housing was a good deal.

Relaxed development standards are normally enacted because doing so is good public policy in that it creates incentives for the achievement of a greater good that overrides the compromises involved in relaxing standards. The most common example—actually made a state law in California—involves relaxation of development standards in order to encourage the reuse of vacant industrial buildings made redundant by major technological shifts. Using (Oakland) California as an example of relaxed planning regulations: in renovations of existing buildings "originally designed and constructed for commercial or industrial use," no additional parking is required even though none may exist, open space is not required, and school tax is levied at the far lower commercial rate that assumes no children are present in commercial space—which is generally accurate in live-work, as noted in Chapter Four: Market.

For reasons of consistency with existing regulations—a commonly sought goal as regulators scratched their heads regarding this new animal called live-work—many cities have elected to view live-work as a continuing commercial use. The theory is that if a previously commercial building adds residential activity to 25 percent, 33 percent, or even 49 percent of an existing building, the majority remains commercial and therefore is not subject to normal residential standards. Of course, under building or housing codes, proper residential facilities must be provided.

Because many cities have sought to reinvent the live-work wheel, so to speak, its novelty has led to some significant disasters, most notably conflicts between residents of poorly located live-work and preexisting commercial and industrial operators. This subject was treated in more detail in the San Francisco Experience sidebar. It is fundamental planning practice to locate concentrations of multiunit housing in places well served by infrastructure and neighborhood services; to not do likewise for most types of live-work is to engage in an irresponsible relaxation.

Work Uses Permitted

The work uses permitted in a live-work space or a live-work building vary widely and depend on a number of factors. Typically, a work use that by itself (in a purely commercial space) would be permitted in a given zone is likely to be appropriate in a live-work space. Work uses are treated in detail in Table A-1 in Appendix A. The exception would be work uses typically compatible with a home environment, such as home office and many arts, crafts, and artisan-type uses that can occur anywhere, even in the most restricted settings. Uses that are classified under the building code as "hazardous" — including welding and a wood shop with more than three fixed appliances—may be permitted in a live-work project but, under the building code, would usually need to be separated from the living portion of the space.

Numerous cities have decided to remove certain kinds of work uses from consideration for live-work or to specify that there be a separation, as in live-near or live-nearby. Among these are: heavy industry and manufacturing facilities (e.g., slaughterhouses and steel mills); auto body shops and the like; bars and restaurants; and institutional buildings such as schools, hospitals, police stations, and planning departments. Assembly occupancies, while they may be allowed in live-work buildings, must include an independent exit discharge and be separated from the live-work units by a fire-rated wall or floor/ceiling.

Duany Plater-Zyberk & Company (DPZ) in Miami is a preeminent New Urbanist firm and designer of Seaside, Florida, as well as scores of other New Urbanist communities. Andrés Duany of DPZ is the coauthor of *SmartCode*, a pioneering form-based code, which contains a simple way to parse work uses according to intensity. They are: Restricted, Limited, and Open, and their location corresponds roughly with residential, commercial, and industrial zones but is also tempered by proximity type, transect location, and locally calibrated character. Based in part on that terminology, a list of Restricted, Limited, and Open work uses is included in Appendix A.

Employees and Walk-In Trade

Employees and walk-in trade are both planning and building code issues. Under most planning codes, if walk-in trade is present, the live-work is no longer a home occupation and therefore cannot be in a residence per se (see Table A-4, Walk-in Trade and Employees by Location and Proj-

ect Type). However, some home occupation regulations do allow a smaller number of employees, and most permit client visits by appointment. By and large, live-work should be configured to accommodate employees and walk-in trade, but there are situations—in addition to home occupation—where this is neither appropriate nor necessary. An artists' studio in a live-work building may never see visitors other than friends and the occasional open studio or gallery visit. In flexhouses, the assumption is that there may be retail on the ground floor at some point, so a level-in entrance and an accessible water closet are a minimum on the ground floor.

The presence of employees and walk-in trade does have an effect on factors governed by other development standards, most notably parking, which is discussed below.

In general, if the work area is too large, a large number of employees are present, or walk-in trade is expected, a live-near proximity type is preferable. In *Work/Live in Vancouver*, the author proposed that a separation be required when the work area exceeds 2,500 square feet. Paragraph 419 of the 2009 IBC requires a separation when the entire unit exceeds 3,000 square feet. See Table A-2 in Appendix A, which lists minimum and maximum sizes by work-use intensity and proximity type.

New Construction versus Renovation

Purpose-built artists' live-work was first constructed in the United States in 1986. New flexhouses—an ancient type—were first built in 1982 in Seaside, Florida. Before that, new live-work did not exist as a named building type. All live-work projects prior to that time were made in renovated buildings, mostly warehouses, factories, and a few schools, armories, and the like. As previously discussed, in an effort to help artists and to reuse abandoned buildings, numerous cities passed ordinances in the 1980s permitting live-work conversion of existing buildings under relaxed planning and building regulations. Such regulations have had mixed results. As measured against the standard of number of affordable units for artists created under such regulations, the record is fair to dismal. Many of the most viable live-work artists' coops were built prior to the adoption of the codes. Some have legalized, some have not, and even fewer have both legalized and stayed affordable.

Yet, were one to measure the success of new-construction live-work from the standpoint of demands being met, housing units created, and development activity generated, both San Francisco and Vancouver would come down resoundingly on the positive side. Using live-work regulations to create what is essentially a housing product, thousands of lifestyle lofts, or—as referred to in Vancouver, "lawyer lofts"—were created in response to huge demand. Most were condominiums, selling at times for staggering sums.

Where there have been problems, displacements, and protests over new construction lofts, the primary issue has been location. Deciding where lifestyle lofts belong in a city (such as Oakland's Jack London Square; see Figure 6-31) and planning to provide for an orderly transition from an industrial district to a mixed-use housing district is a way to revitalize a downtown without sacrificing a city's commercial/industrial vitality.

Formerly industrial land that is rezoned to permit housing will rise steeply in price, to the point where the only viable development on it will be housing, and industry will be forced out. Any planner who contemplates allowing other uses in industrial areas must be aware of this fact and the history that has borne it out in cities like San Francisco.

New construction is also generally more expensive than renovation of an existing building. However, this is not always the case, depending on how close an existing structure is to the desired end product. When planning for live-work and weighing new versus renovation, one must assess each building. New construction, with its advantage of being more predictable, is sometimes a better option if permitted in the jurisdiction. The next questions, plus other local considerations, are factors to consider when evaluating an existing building for renovation:

- If the building is in an earthquake-prone area, does it look like an expensive retrofit?

Figure 6-32 Column spacing is an important consideration in an existing warehouse being considered for live-work. In this example, in Oakland, California, the spacing is at least eighteen feet.

- Is the building such a massive volume that it will be difficult to get natural light into much of its interior?

- Is the column bay spacing too close (say 15 feet or less; see Figure 6-32)?

- Are the ceiling heights fifteen feet or higher (see Figure 6-33), thereby allowing the addition of mezzanines?

- Are there too many property line walls that will not permit the addition of windows?

- Is the building too close to a freeway or other source of objectionable noise or odor?

- Is there any evidence of toxic materials in or around the building?

Figure 6-31 Brickhouse Lofts, a well-designed adaptive reuse of an older building as lifestyle lofts in the Jack London Square warehouse district, Oakland, California. Beyond is a second, purpose-built modernist loft building by David Baker & Associates, who also designed the Clocktower Lofts (see case study in Chapter Three).

Figure 6-33 An existing warehouse building with bay heights sufficient for mezzanines, which have in fact been constructed.

- Does it face onto two streets or a street and an alley, thereby making exiting easier and windows more plentiful?

- Is it adjacent to transit and other urban amenities, or does it look like they will be coming along soon?

- Are significant elements of the building's systems—structural, mechanical, electrical, windows, and waterproofing—sufficiently well hidden that there might be unpleasant surprises during construction?

- Are other buildings around being renovated for live-work or already occupied as such? If so, neither land nor a building in that location is likely to be a bargain.

Separation of Functions

Some planning regulations such as those in Alameda and Oakland, California, seek to enforce the work aspect of work/live by requiring that they be live-near or live-nearby proximity types. One project has been constructed in Alameda, California (see Figure 6-34) that meets this requirement in the form of a townhouse-style artists' live-work unit whose work area is on the ground floor. Oakland's work/live regulations incorporate a similar requirement. However, significant numbers of new work/live units have not been built anywhere. In New Urbanist town centers, the typical configuration is a flexhouse with work on the ground floor, a centuries-old model that works well today.

The flexibility provided by separate entrances to living and working portions is considered essential by many New Urbanist market experts (see Chapter Four: Market). Separation of functions is treated more fully in the Chapter Three: Design, and Chapter Seven: Building Codes, mostly under proximity types.

Maximum and Minimum Unit Size

Live-work unit sizes are often set by local planning regulations and—less often—building and housing codes. Minimum sizes are a combination of the smallest space in which one might live plus a reasonable work space size. To distinguish live-work from straight residential, some cites have set sizes larger than typical apartment minimums, and San Francisco, for example, requires ceiling heights to be a minimum of fourteen feet. Oakland uses 660 square feet for the minimum live-work unit size (see Figure 6-35), with the live portion not to exceed one-third of the area, or 220-square feet (see Table 7-5, Master Live-work Building Code Matrix). Maximum sizes are rarely set, although many live-work building codes require a second means of egress from an individual unit over a certain size, say 2,000 square feet or an occupant load of ten. The IBC has set a maximum of 3,000 square feet for a unit in which there is no fire separation between the living and working portions (IBC Section 419).

Figure 6-34 Rhythmix Cultural Works (2007), a community arts center and a live-near work/live project, was built under a very strict live-work planning code in Alameda, California. Its implementation has resulted in only this project, which itself was challenged at every turn of the entitlement process. 2004. Designed by Thomas Dolan Architecture.

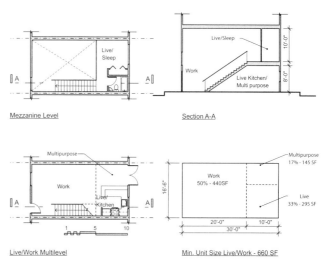

Figure 6-35 The minimum size for live-work units in conversions of existing buildings in Oakland, California, is 660-square feet; this set of drawings shows dimensions and typical space distribution in such a unit.

Proportion of Live-to-Work Area

Many jurisdictions' live-work ordinances regulate the proportion of space devoted to living and working functions, starting with home occupation in a few places and more frequently in work/live and live/work. Because twentieth-century live-work began primarily as renovations of existing buildings, and regulators initially wanted to intervene as little as possible, conversion of a building to live-work essentially allows it to remain a commercial building. To justify this in the world of segregated use zoning and separated occupancy building codes, proportions that keep the live portion below 50 percent have typically been imposed to reinforce the preeminent role of the work, or commercial activity. That having been said, jurisdictions throughout North America have diverged greatly in their regulation of live-to-work proportions.

Some cities, such as Oakland, California, have required that a maximum of 33 percent of a live-work unit be devoted to residential activity. However, of the remaining 67 percent devoted to work 25 percent of that can be "multipurpose," meaning that it can be used for both living and working.

All of the above is primarily directed at lofts, or live-with units, where no walls or floor-ceilings dictate separate uses in separate areas. Experience has shown that, while well intentioned, drawing lines on a floor plan between the living and working portions of a unit has little effect on the eventual uses of that unit's different portions. As noted, hanging one's regulatory hat on use proportions is typically an enforcement nightmare. Live-with space is by definition flexible, and its uses and proportions will shift over time, both short term and long term. When it comes to regulating live-work, it is sufficient:

- To designate a unit as live-work
- To determine what work activities are permitted
- To determine whether employees and walk-in trade are permitted
- To provide minimum residential facilities
- To dispense with attempting to regulate percentage of live and work areas

The reader is directed to the model planning code provisions in Appendix A.

Open Space

Many forward-looking downtown plans substitute payments into an open space fund in lieu of meeting individual open space requirements in individual buildings. That money is then used to provide well-designed, well-maintained parks that serve entire neighborhoods. In the case of live-work, the omission of open space requirements (or fees) in renovations of existing warehouses, or new construction such as San Francisco in the 1990s, has not resulted in such benefits. Clearly it is impractical to provide on-grade open space for an existing building that covers its entire site. However, as stated, live-work is not immune from the basic principles of city planning and design, which means that when individuals are living in a place, they benefit from the provision of open space, either onsite or nearby.

When open space is provided within a project, how it is configured is very important. As discussed, interactive open space within a project is an important way of addressing the isolation of live-work. Design review standards should be developed requiring that:

- The open space in a larger multiunit live-work project be located along the "entry path" between the place where one enters a project and the entrance to one's unit;
- The open space be proportioned to encourage casual interaction between residents as they come and go about their day-to-day lives.

Such open space is difficult to regulate, but the "Courtyards Which Live" pattern in *A Pattern Language*[1] begins to address this need. Provision of well-designed interactive open space can transform what might have otherwise been simply a collection of units into a true place that is far more than the sum of the number of units. For an example of interactive open space, see the South Prescott Village case study in Chapter Three: Design

Parking and Traffic

Live-work, as Zero-Commute Housing, presents different needs for parking and different impact on traffic from single-use buildings and use types. Its mixed-use nature and multiplicity of work types presents complex demands for parking. Both on-street and off-street parking can serve live-work, each in its own way.

In its ideal form, Zero-Commute Housing should not require its occupants to own a car at all; however, most households possess at least one vehicle for out-of-town travel or special purposes, or perhaps their live-work units are in a place that is not sufficiently walkable. Additionally, some businesses need a vehicle to conduct aspects of their business outside the work space or to transport materials and goods. Eliminating the commute for at least one member of a couple in a live-work space usually means both decreased car ownership and a diminished need for either on-street or off-street parking. Needing one less car also results in tremendous cost savings, sometimes referred to as the "one less car land use subsidy," discussed later in this chapter.

Live-work provides an ideal application for car-sharing. Programs like ZipCar® and City Car Share are ideal for live-workers, many of whom have chosen to rely less on the constant presence of a car in their lives. Ready availability of a shared car or truck will encourage even more people to forgo vehicle ownership; therefore, requiring car sharing, particularly in larger live-work projects with large garages, is an excellent idea. Even in smaller townhouse live-work projects, having a dedicated car-sharing space at the curb can be effective. In a live-work neighborhood as defined in this book, trips to meet daily needs can also be accomplished via transit service if available, on foot, or by bicycle if adequate facilities are present such as lanes, routes, and bike parking.

Tip
Always provide at least one car-sharing space in any multi-unit live-work project, either in the parking garage or at the curb in front.

While few empirical studies have been completed on the parking needs of live-work, anecdotal evidence points to reduced demand (see Table 6-5 for proposed parking standards). Most urban live-work projects built today are occupied by single people, couples, empty nesters, and—infrequently—children. The parking needs and traffic—expressed as vehicle miles traveled (VMT)—generated by live-work are lower than those of single-use housing, because the diurnal commute (250 days a year times two, or 500 trips per car) is eliminated for at least one occupant.

Those who work at home almost always have the good sense to drive when there isn't traffic—to schedule meetings and appointments and run errands midmorning to midafternoon, or in the evening. Therefore, a live-work project's impact on traffic, especially as expressed in peak-hour demand and intersection level of service (LOS)—both congestion-driven factors—is minimal. Since traffic impacts are typically measured by how a project affects street and intersection capacity when aggregated with other peak-hour demand sources, the fact that live-work does not add to peak-hour travel means its impact on the need for increased street capacity is minimal compared to a purely residential or commercial project used by commuting occupants. Furthermore, locating live-work that includes retail or services available on a walk-in basis in a compact live-work neighborhood will ac-

tually reduce traffic and generate little in the way of added parking demand, because many neighboring residents will walk to these services.

Most cites have settled on requiring between one and one-and-a-half spaces per live-work unit, or requiring parking in proportion to work area (e.g., one space for every 400 to 800 square feet of aggregate work area of a project). This latter approach has in some cases resulted in many vacant spaces, especially if imposed on a project in which employees and walk-in trade are not generally present, such as Ocean View Lofts in Berkeley, California, where a fourteen-unit project with relatively small units was required to provide twenty-two spaces. The author has visited this project on scores of occasions at all hours of the day and all times of the week, and there are always empty spaces. See the Ocean View Lofts case study in Chapter Five: Community.

Many cities have strived from the inception of their experience with regulating live-work to permit the renovation of existing buildings without off-street parking as an incentive to develop buildings that might otherwise sit vacant. Nevertheless, in many cases, developers of such projects will elect to provide secure parking. Many artists' rental warehouse conversions are not located near transit or city services, and many are in unsafe districts. Rental tenure can be an indication that affordability is an issue for the occupant and that he or she is less likely to own a car—if it is in an area reasonably well served by transit. Unfortunately, many artists' studio projects are not well-served by transit, as their locations are often at a pre–SoHo Cycle stage.

When employees are permitted, or walk-in trade à la retail are part of a live-work project, additional parking may need to be provided (on-street or off-street) for nonresident users of the spaces. When building a project for unknown buyers or tenants, even if one assumes that nonresident uses will be permitted, it is difficult to know how many occupants will actually require extra parking. A study of time-shared parking is desirable in any live-work or mixed use project. Table 6-5 addresses these and other questions with recommendations. The Urban Land Institute's *Shared Parking* handbook is also a great resource.

In San Francisco in the late 1990s, new loft buildings were typically developed with one parking space per unit. Such buildings were usually occupied by a single person or a couple in each unit. However, a few were bought and occupied as offices for high-tech start-ups. Therefore, a ten-unit building with average unit sizes of 1,200 square feet might accommodate as few as ten residents or as many as fifty employees in its 12,000 square feet of net rentable area. Granted, this

Table 6-5 Recommended Parking Standards by Unit or Project Type

Unit Type	Parking Requirement	Comments
Home occupation	No additional parking beyond that required in a residence	Assumes client visits by appointment only with no employees*
Live-work per IBC Sec. 419, (i.e., live-with unit below 3,000 sf)	Minimum one space per unit, maximum two off-street spaces per unit; encourage time-shared parking or common off-site parking facilities	IBC Section 419 allows up to five nonresident employees; work space must be on lowest level; maximum discourages car commutes
Live-with unit above 3,000 sf	See flexhouse parking requirements	Not permitted under IBC Sec. 419 as live-with; must be live-near or live-nearby.
Stage One flexhouse with small retail (NTE 500 sf) or by-appointment client visits	Maximum two spaces per unit. One for resident, one for business, or time-shared.	Best located in a compact, mixed-use neighborhood
Stage Two flexhouse with employees and walk-in trade in ground-floor retail, housing above	One off-street space/unit serving the upstairs (maximum two) + one on-street space per 750 sf of work space, which can also be located offsite at developer's and jurisdiction's option	Best located in a compact, mixed-use neighborhood
Multiunit live-work project, courtyard version or not (single main entrance to building, not townhouses); new construction or renovation, condominium ownership OK	Maximum 1.25 spaces per unit; on-street parking to handle excess over that**	Best located: • In a compact mixed use neighborhood; or • Within one-quarter mile of transit
Warehouse renovation	Zero to one space per unit***	Rental only; employees permitted; retain any existing parking
Mixed use (often podium) project, e.g., mix of housing and retail, or housing and flexhouse liners	Open-access parking for retail at local zoning standards; one secured space per residential or live-work unit.	Study time-shared parking options
Live-work renovation	No new spaces required***	

*If employees and/or walk-in trade are permitted, default to "Live-Work per Section 419 requirements" (i.e., one parking spaces/unit or local residential requirement, whichever is greater).

**Unless the density of the project exceeds forty units per acre and a study of parking demand shows otherwise.

***Unless (1) there is not adequate on-grade space for secure parking outside or inside of the building, (2) parking spaces presently exist, in which case they should be retained or replaced, or (3) the availability of on-street parking is very limited and security is an overriding issue.

is an extreme example of the flexibility of live-work; based on the live-work entitlements, there was no way to anticipate the office use, and yet the examples of which this author is aware have not had parking problems. San Francisco is well served by public transit, and many such projects are located in industrial areas with plenty of on-street parking.

What, therefore, should be the development standards for a building like a flexhouse, whose form is regulated but whose uses can change over time without further entitlement? A typical flexhouse will start out as a vertically demised townhouse live-work unit (Stage One—see Figure 2-28), and its parking needs will be met by a one- or two-car rear-loaded garage, or by structured or surface parking nearby. As the neighborhood matures, such buildings are designed to respond by flexing to accommodate retail or other businesses on the ground floor (Stage Two). Employees and customers are introduced, some of whom will drive to that location.

Upstairs, there will continue to be smaller live-work or residential units (or possibly office or other commercial uses). In a well-designed town center or well-chosen infill location, the additional need for parking will be accommodated:

• In the building's garages, possibly based on a time-shared parking scheme
• On the street
• In aggregated parking garages or surface parking

If there is ample on-street parking in the daytime, depending on the nature of the streets surrounding a live-work project, it can supplement a live-work project's off-street parking. Conversely, some pioneering live-work renovations may exist in neighborhoods where on-street parking is not so readily available in the daytime but is easily available at night because the workers in surrounding businesses have gone home.

Such was the case in Tribeca in the 1970s, where free and easily available on-street parking was legal between 6:00 pm and 8:00 a.m., but not so in the daytime, requiring car-owning live-workers to store their vehicles elsewhere, such as the numerous disused piers that had been converted to garages at that time—another unintended consequence of the adoption of shipping containers.

According to transportation planner Wade Walker, "Parking in proximity can be expected to happen within the five-minute/quarter-mile walk radius and utilize supply in that area. In great urban environments where the walk is interesting or at least streetscaped well, that radius can be extended. Many cities are now accommodating this parameter in their development ordinances."[2]

In most multi-unit live-work projects, unless the units are quite large or configured as live-near or live-nearby, the number of employees will not be large, if there are any at all. In the case of live-with units, a live-worker tends to move on to a dedicated work space when the business he or she is incubating begins to require employees, rather than have employees continually in his or her live-with unit. The same is true of walk-in trade, a rarity in live-with units. The transition from a live-with space—where employees and walk-in trade can be an inconvenience if not an annoyance—to a live-near situation or a stand-alone commercial space is an important marker along the incubator cycle, which is discussed in Chapter Three: Design.

Most jurisdictions' home occupation regulations allow client visits by appointment without any added parking requirements. This is logical because most client visits are during daytime hours, some neighboring residents are likely to be gone, and therefore on-street parking is likely to be readily available. Even if local home occupation regulations permit one or two employees, parking is typically not a problem.

Loading

Loading is an issue that is typically restricted to larger, multi-unit live-work projects or ones in which the uses are relatively specialized and there are requirements for moving large objects, such as sculptures, or large amounts of small objects, such as from a mail order operation. Some townhouse live-works have dock-high rear exits that facilitate truck loading, as in Mt. Laurel, Alabama, shown in Figure 6-36.

Local zoning regulations often require loading docks when the total area of a commercial building is over a certain size. This can be a workable guideline; however, despite the disclaimer regarding the efficacy of regulating live versus work portions, the area used to calculate whether loading is

required should be only the aggregate work portion of the building. Additionally, the range of activities that will go on in the building, determined in part by the width of the unit entrances and corridors, the presence of a freight elevator, and the floor loading capacity of the building (which might be quite high in a former warehouse), should be taken into consideration. If most of the characteristics listed in the prior sentence are present in the building, it is likely that it will need a loading dock where a truck might park for some time.

Noise and Odor Generation

Most cities include performance standards in their planning regulations that limit noise and odor generation as well as vibration and glare. One needs to consider both the noise and odors generated by the live-work project and also those generated by commercial or industrial operations nearby. Significant conflict and complaints can result when new live-work residents are not informed that the place where they are locating does not resemble a residential neighborhood. Disclosures, covenants, lease terms and possibly nuisance easements are important ways of heading off imported NIMBYism before it becomes too great a problem. Odor is less easy to quantify and the perception of it tends to be subjective, but there is no doubt that odor will lead to complaints.

Certain types of live-work, most notably work/live in renovated buildings, are more likely to be generators of noise (e.g., loud music, power tools, or motorcycles). Chapter Seven: Building Codes, addresses sound attenuation between

Figure 6-36 Dock-high loading at the back of flexhouse live-work units in Mt. Laurel, Alabama. Unlike The Waters (see case study in Chapter Three), this rear entrance and its loading dock serves only the ground-floor work space. All residential and retail entrances are on the street.

units and also a proposed standard for dealing with higher ambient noise levels.

Tip
Specify maximum decibel levels permitted to be generated by a unit in the building rules and regulations. Also specify quiet hours, and require that, in cases of excessive noise, additional structural sound attenuation techniques be deployed and that the noise level must be brought into a permissible range, or the unit must be vacated.

Design Review

Many cities have exempted renovation of existing buildings for live-work from design review, under the assumption that they are encouraging the reuse of a building that otherwise may sit vacant indefinitely and that use of the building under minimal regulation is preferable to vacancy and blight. Additions to buildings and new-construction live-work are typically subject to local design review standards, although the question would be: residential or commercial standards? Clearly, residential standards would apply to home occupation. Work/live might fall under commercial standards, if any exist in the jurisdiction.

When design review is imposed on live-work projects, it is important to be aware of its special needs and requirements, such as interactive open space, loading, parking, and the potential need for large access openings into units and into the building. An understanding of the unique qualities of live-work and its role in shaping or responding to the public and semipublic realm must be well understood. For example, in flexhouses, it is typically not appropriate to configure a building such that the only way to access the upstairs portions of units is via an entrance from the rear of the building (although this was done with success at Habersham—see case study in Chapter Four: Market). Front entrances and facades that activate the street are important elements of a flexhouse or townhouse live-work project. Liner units in larger projects—whose purpose is to both mask parking structures and activate the street—must be designed to effectively accomplish these tasks.

Inclusionary Zoning

A common planning code relaxation for live-work has been to eliminate requirements for a percentage of units in a project to be offered at below-market rents or sales prices, which—when imposed—is called inclusionary zoning. Under such regulations, common in many larger cities, de-velopers are required to subsidize such units out of their presumed profits.

As discussed in the "Affordability" section later in this chapter, if one accepts the premise that affordable housing exists to accomplish a social good, then omitting inclusionary zoning as an exception to make it more possible to renovate a building or build new live-work is a tenuous proposition at best. Affordable units are intended to serve lower-income, underserved populations: It worth noting that many artists fit that description very well. Nevertheless, true live-work located in a neighborhood served by transit, shops, and city services within walking distance can lead to significant savings in one's total cost of living before inclusionary zoning is factored in; such a "land use subsidy" is arguably a substitute for inclusionary zoning.

Tip
Develop a formula specifically targeted for live-work that takes into account the savings realized by not commuting and owning one less car or no car at all, and apply this Zero-Commute living formula to offset—entirely or partially—any preexisting inclusionary zoning requirements

Codes and Permitting Processes

Because live-work flies in the face of both single-use zoning and single-occupancy building codes, it is extremely important that a city's planning and building regulations regarding this hybrid land use and building type be very well coordinated. It is an everyday occurrence for an applicant to request permission to build a house or apartment building. For city staff operating under Euclidean zoning, it's all in the regulations: Put the house in a residential zone, put the apartment building in a multifamily residential zone; the house is R-3 occupancy, the apartment building is R-2 occupancy. For live-work, such neat categories do not exist. As a result, many cities have attempted, with varying degrees of success, to reinvent the wheel by enacting live-work planning and building codes that bear little resemblance to any enacted elsewhere. As noted in the sidebar by Dan Parolek, form-based codes are an effective way to regulate live-work.

One of the primary purposes of this book is to create common definitions and to put forward coordinated, model live-work planning and building codes that can be used wherever live-work is planned, designed, and built. Fortunately, the latest model code, the 2009 IBC contains Section 419, Live/work units. Planning codes tend to be more locally calibrated and will therefore always deviate somewhat from, say, the suggestions for a model live-work planning code in Appendix A.

Because live-work defies easy categorization, it is often beneficial for a city to avail itself of live-work experts when formulating live-work policy and regulations, as each city's needs will vary. When the regulations—well coordinated between planning and building departments—are enacted, experience has shown that it is wise to appoint a live-work czar—either staff or a consultant, perhaps on a project-by-project basis—to review incoming projects before they are submitted, to make comments that assist the applicant, and to shepherd the application through all of the approvals needed, including zoning review, staff reports, entitlement hearings, fire department review, building permit submittal, and plan check. The appointment of such a czar for the transitional time after a city adopts or updates its live-work regulations enables these projects to get approved and built more smoothly. In the process of doing his or her job, the czar can train staff so they are prepared to take over this role eventually.

Social Issues and Planning Reponses

The effects of live-work development on existing districts and the roles live-work plays in new development are often profound. When live-work is introduced into a district that was formerly commercial or industrial use only, complex forces come into play that usually result in the area's transformation into an entirely new place. When executed well, live-work introduced into new town centers and as infill redevelopment can have an extremely beneficial role in its role in activating the public realm immediately upon completion.

The job of planners and policy makers in cities is to steer development in ways that are best for a city. Many planners in established cities are not as comfortable with live-work because it often springs up before regulations are in place, putting the planners in reactive, catch-up mode. That having been said, the SoHo Cycle—how it arises and what its benefits and drawbacks are—has been studied and understood for at least twenty years. Most cities can't wait to have an arts district/loft neighborhood spring up in vacant warehouses, soon to accommodate the well-heeled creative class and revitalize the downtown. There are signs that can point to the likelihood of such a place arising in a city, and there are steps that a city planner can take to encourage such an evolution if it is desired and to avoid some of the pitfalls.

Therefore, a challenge for planners in existing built-out cities is to be in touch with what areas are being colonized by illegal residents, to recognize the irresistible forces that are creating a draw to that place in spite of its lack of services, to accept the fact that it is happening, and to respond by making one of two choices:

1. After consideration, affirm that the SoHo Cycle should be allowed to proceed. Begin to think about the services and infrastructure required to support this new neighborhood, about the stages of its likely evolution, and about who benefits and who does not.

2. Alternatively, determine that the existing district should be restricted to users who do not threaten its commercial/industrial nature, which means that live-work should be limited to rentals in renovations of existing buildings, possibly only for artists and other similarly situated individuals.

Many cities opt for the former option; however, it is a decision not to be taken lightly, as it means the demise of what may be the only place where industry can exist in a city. One should never attempt the SoHo Cycle option in an isolated commercial/industrial district that does not have the possibility of providing transit, retail, and other city services and infrastructure.

Warehouse Conversions and the SoHo Cycle

All vacant buildings that were originally designed for commercial or industrial use, or civic buildings such as schools, churches, hangars, or other large or small structures, are candidates for conversion to live-work; examples of all of these types have experienced such repurposing, which has often helped to transform entire districts into neighborhoods.

The most important planning issues surrounding live-work in existing commercial and industrial areas are the effects that the new residents have on the preexisting businesses, rather than the reverse. As mentioned, struggling artists renting and living and working—possibly illegally—in industrial districts are generally happy to be there, not make waves, and certainly not complain about the preexisting, well-established commercial and industrial activities of their neighbors.

However, one needs to look at the same location ten or twenty years later to observe the effects of the SoHo Cycle. Following on the heels of the artists, cafés and galleries opened up, nonartists moved in, city officials began to take notice, live-work buildings were legalized under new regulations, rents went up, most artists were priced out, and developers began to offer lofts as condominiums. Middle-class

The New Urban Workplace

By Rod Stevens

Rod Stevens is a business development consultant specializing in urban ventures. His White Paper on the New Urban Workplace can be found on his Web site www.spinakerstrategies.com.

Call it the revenge of the city: Today an increasing number of the United States' fastest-growing and most admired companies are relocating to or expanding in the center city, rather than in the suburban business parks, where they would likely have gone thirty years ago. These "center city" companies include Amazon, Starbucks, Adidas, AT&T, United Airlines, Quicken, American Eagle Outfitters, Pixar, and Lucasfilm.

Why are they coming back? In a word, *talent*. A new generation of younger workers—raised on *Seinfeld* reruns and seeking more choice and community connection—wants to live in more urban places. The companies that want to hire them are following them there. Even outside the center city, in places like the San Francisco Peninsula, office rents and occupancy patterns are dictated by how long it takes to commute there from the city.

Many of the best-educated workers choose the city where they want to live first and the place where they work second, not because they are necessarily attracted to a given place, but because they want to settle themselves in cosmopolitan places where they can stay connected to their career networks. Many are foreign-born students who have elected to stay in this country. The center city better meets their eclectic needs and tastes.

Like many trends, the corporate return to the city started in the mid-1970s with individual pioneers. In San Francisco, for example, independent professionals started informally converting old warehouses on the piers along the Bay, in South Park, and near China Basin into places to both live and work, sometimes bicycling to clients' offices in the high-rises of the Financial District. Later, companies like Landor Associates and Macromedia followed them into these areas.

The new generation of workers, dubbed "millennials" because they have come of age since the year 2000, are changing not only where we work but how.

This generation, perhaps more accustomed to collaboration than baby boomers, needs a greater variety of meeting spaces to reflect the new style of work. Many mix their work and personal lives, coming and going at odd hours. Focusing, learning, collaborating, socializing—all of these are elements of the modern workday, and together the workplace and the center city around it are becoming a chassis for this activity.

What lies ahead? For office space, less quantity and more quality. Companies like HP and Microsoft are finding that many of their cubicles sit empty much of the day, and they are racing to reduce their leasing costs even while they make the remaining space more productive and centrally located. Some companies, eager to sign the most sought-after talent, are creating "hoteling" centers in dense urban places where workers can join one another in posh conference rooms and enjoy state-of-the-art video link-ups to coworkers in other parts of the world. "Walk-to-coffee" locations with an interesting character are winning out over the sterile financial districts developed in the 1970s and 1980s. The first ring suburbs are catching on that their main streets can help them compete for talent if they are centrally located, with good rail transit and walkable, quality neighborhoods nearby.

Like the economy, much of the energy and focus in the urban development world during the last ten years was focused on the "consumption" side, on housing and retail uses. As individual cities compete with one another for jobs and investment, more and more are looking critically at how they can attract and retain talent. The winners will be those who can offer a setting for work that is truly urban and connected.

Tip

Many communities cling to old stereotypes about who is living in their midst. This can hold back planning to meet the needs of newer households, especially for live/work spaces and the "business infrastructure" of modern freelancers (i.e., gathering places and healthy main streets). For less than $100, a "lifestyles" report from Esri or Claritas will profile the kinds of households living there now, including typical occupations, education levels, and leisure patterns.

folk began to buy units, and services grew up around them to make a real urban neighborhood. In the process, industry was usually priced out or forced out.

The positive benefits of the SoHo Cycle are tangible and, arguably, legion. Some say that live-work conversion is one of the most viable forms of urban housing and that it leads to significant neighborhood revitalization. New neighborhoods are created where abandoned buildings once sat vacant. Historic buildings and sometimes entire historic districts are saved through adaptive reuse of these sturdy and still-serviceable old buildings. Nightlife, restaurants, tourism, ballparks, and prosperity abound. Those who don't work in their units (and many don't) can walk or take a short bus ride to work. For every downtown unit that is created, another acre (or so) of farmland is saved from suburban sprawl. For every building that is saved rather than demolished and replaced, huge amounts of energy, materials, and landfill space are saved, giving voice to the simple truth of reuse: that it is the greenest, most sustainable use of an existing urban property possible, made even more so if the building is mixed use, the streets are walkable, the live-workers truly don't commute, or, if they do, transit is nearby.

Between World War II and the present, the predominant direction of migration in the United States has been from cities to suburbs. Urban centers have suffered massive disinvestment while suburban sprawl has been subsidized by numerous federal programs and projects. Nevertheless, it is arguable that artists' live-work began the most important countertrend to suburban flight ever. With the notable exception of New York City, the only population that typically doesn't live in urban lofts are families with children—they are rarely seen in our urban areas, certainly in part due to the sad state of our urban public schools.

When the SoHo Cycle occurs in the right locations, great new neighborhoods are created, albeit on the backs of the artists who pioneered them and were pushed out. History has shown that if there is momentum for a neighborhood to change—the models are there for all to see—there is often not much one can do to stop it.

Rental versus Ownership

A loft district in its early stages of colonization is a paradise for artists and small entrepreneurs: lots of cheap space, great light, freight elevators, wide straight stairs, and nobody around to bother you. Once a district evolves from a predominantly rental environment to one where lofts are being sold as condominiums, major change is generally a fait accompli.

Allowing some affordable artists' rental space to remain can be a way to retain some of the original feel of the neighborhood as it was pioneered. Such "artists' protection" is ultimately a question of money rather than planning or building regulations.

Renting housing and owning a home are each appropriate at different times in a person's life and depending on their situation. Particularly during one's student years and for some indeterminate time thereafter, the slightly transient, perhaps less secure nature of renting is perceived as a good thing. Sooner or later—often when kids, or marriage, or some financial success come along—thoughts turn to owning one's place of residence, or perhaps one's live-work space. Pride of ownership is tangible. The control over one's destiny that ownership confers is empowering and satisfying. Knowing that one is free to renovate or otherwise alter one's space and that there is no landlord who can throw one out are important, basic freedoms, albeit tarnished by recent economic turmoil.

Until the 1990s, almost all live-work situations were rental, often governed by commercial leases. Once much of live-work came to resemble housing, condominiums arose as a popular form of live-work ownership. In many cities, former rental buildings were converted to condominiums. New purpose-built lifestyle loft buildings became wildly popular in cities like San Francisco and Vancouver as a form of trendy entry-level housing in the mid-1990s and into the first decade of the new millennium.

A number of phenomena accompany the transition of a district from a primarily rental live-work to primarily ownership lifestyle lofts:

- Owners have a different attitude from renters toward their neighborhood, being concerned with stability, safety, and property values. Their reference point, while usually misguided, is a single-use residential zone.

- Owners, particularly those who paid high prices for their units and especially those who don't work in their spaces, tend to treat their units like apartments and vocally agitate to make their neighborhood more resemble the residential enclave where they may have lived in the past, or where they expected to be living, having paid so much. Such actions can wreak havoc on long-standing neighboring commercial operations.

- Tenants, however, who are, not necessarily there for the long haul or as personally invested, are often forgiving of nearby conditions. Artists aren't about to complain about neighboring industrial or commercial uses. Their leases often say they aren't permitted to live there, they live in fear of city officials, and they have nowhere else to go should they be evicted—always a threat—that offers anything like the amenities suited to artistic production or freewheeling entrepreneurship that their building provides—unless they want to move on to the "next" artists' district.

Ideally, opportunities for both rental and ownership live-work should be made available. Following on these points, live-work condominiums are best located in neighborhoods closer to amenities and farther away from major commercial /industrial activity. Conversely, districts whose continuing commercial and industrial character are important are best served by minimally finished rental live-work aimed at artists and other similarly situated individuals.

Imported NIMBYism and Its Impact on Commercial and Industrial Districts

As discussed, in existing commercial/industrial districts where live-work—often a primarily residential "product"—is well considered and planned as a component of an intentional transformation of a neighborhood, the result can be urban revitalization at its best. When, however, cities permit ill-advised relaxations of planning and building codes that result in residential loft condominiums' being built or converted in existing, viable commercial and industrial zones—whether they are called live-work or artists' live-work, as in the case of San Francisco, or not—problems can and most likely will occur.

Imported NIMBYism (first discussed in Chapter Two: Definitions) has resulted in the eventual forcing out of countless businesses in scores of cities. This pattern has driven dramatic changes and birthed new neighborhoods in port cities and railheads all over the world while disrupting sometimes viable commercial/industrial districts (see Figure 6-37).

As a result of imported NIMBYism, many of the businesses necessary to the operation of a city—and the jobs they provide—are shunted to different, sometimes distant locations or forced out of business altogether. For those that stay, expansion is nearly impossible because buying the lot next door—now valued as residential land—is likely to have become too expensive or is already occupied by lifestyle lofts. Imported NIMBYism in San Francisco during the loft boom of the late 1990s was a particularly egregious example, and it was the most significant factor leading to a live-work moratorium in that city (see the San Francisco Experience sidebar earlier in this chapter).

Figure 6-37 A new loft building in Vancouver, immediately adjacent to a commercial operation in an industrial area; this is potentially a prescription for imported NIMBYism.
Photo Credit: Robert McGilvray

Residential Reversion

Residential reversion is a term used to describe the tendency for live/work and work/live spaces—particularly in historically commercial or industrial areas—to be used less and less for work purposes and over time to become primarily residences. Some say this trend is inevitable, and that so-called live-work spaces are never intended as anything more than apartments with mezzanines. Efforts have been made in many cities to head off this phenomenon, because it can be incompatible with existing businesses in a district and can elevate prices for the live-work spaces themselves and for surrounding real estate, thereby pricing out both the original live-work pioneers and existing industrial landowners who may seek to expand their businesses.

There are two approaches a regulator can take in response to the threat of residential reversion, depending on the desired outcome:

1. Accept that it is likely to happen, and plan for transition to a mixed-use neighborhood by either providing standard urban infrastructure and city services or allowing live-work to be a generator of market demand for such services in a way that can be steered by the city, if necessary.

2. Institute measures to prevent residential reversion, which can be draconian and can test the limits of a planning department's regulatory reach. This author was hired by the City of Vancouver, B., in 1997 to consult on ways to regulate work/live (as all live-work is typically called there),

resulting in a report called *Work/Live in Vancouver* (see sidebar of that title).

One can view the type of regulation cited in the "Work/Live in Vancouver" as a fruitless effort to prevent a city from naturally evolving. Artists and other urban pioneers will eventually be forced out by residential reversion, and existing businesses and low-income residents will be forced out by imported NIMBYism. But perhaps the most important lesson learned is that adopting codes to allow live-work typically do not help these arguably aggrieved parties. A legal path for live-work primarily eases the way for market-rate developers, who are naturally responding to a demand for this building type. If the citizens of a city decide that long-term affordable live-work—for artists' and/or others—is desirable because it enriches the cultural and economic life of that city, then the solution has more to do with money than with codes, and it must be addressed head-on.

Disclosures, Covenants, Lease Clauses, and Nuisance Easements

Nuisance easements and disclosures are an idea that was floated in Vancouver and other jurisdictions where conflicts between new live-work residents and existing operators of commercial and industrial operations are anticipated. The idea is to require buyers or tenants in live-work buildings to record an easement that acknowledges the rights of neighboring users—both within their building or project and in the surrounding neighborhood—to continue their legal business activities without harassment from the new neighbors. This author has conferred with several lawyers who question the efficacy of nuisance easements in the United Staes, which have been employed to date only in the vicinity of airports to require that homeowners sign away their rights to complain about noise, vibration, and the like.

However, it is possible for covenants to exist in a condominium, or lease terms in a rental structure, that state:

- Owners or tenants waive the right to complain about the legal work activities of their neighbors in the building and about the legal activities of those in the immediate vicinity
- In ownership situations, any decision regarding the existence and nature of work activity in the building must be unanimous and have the consent of the applicable jurisdiction's planning authorities

Providing disclosures to new residents of live-work are a minimum measure that should always be taken. In Richmond and Oakland, California, and elsewhere, disclosure of neighboring industrial uses in the form of language in leases and condominium documents is required.

Gentrification

Gentrification is normally a pejorative term employed to deride a phenomenon whose primary negative effect is displacement of low-income residents by more well-heeled residents. It sometimes occurs directly, through evictions, eminent domain, and the like. Displacement can also occur indirectly—when neighborhoods change, rents and property values change too. When they go up, people are often forced to move elsewhere. Some would call this gentrification; others would simply call it neighborhood improvement. The line is not always a clear one, especially in the case of live-work.

The live-work form of gentrification is unique because often buildings (or sometimes vacant land) that were previously unoccupied by residents of any kind are converted (or newly built). Therefore, its impacts are as much about the change in actual land use in a neighborhood as they are about displacement of one resident for another. Another common phenomenon is that of illegal—and usually more affordable—live-work projects that coexist easily with surrounding industrial users. When newer, more expensive projects—rental or condominium—are developed in a neighborhood already occupied by illegal projects, the tendency is for the more affordable live-work buildings to become less so in response to surrounding price increases and pressures to legalize such buildings, a process that often raises rents significantly. This is a variation on the SoHo Cycle, in which artists and others pioneer neighborhoods and then are forced to move when their rents become too high.

Neighborhood Amenities

Live-work in existing commercial districts and buildings has often been portrayed as an urban pioneering experience, pursued by artists and others on the margins of society. While such is true of a some live-workers, the typical live-work resident today is online 24/7, needs an daily espresso fix and organic produce, and wants a safe walk to both (see Figure 6-38).

When one lives and works in the same place, one spends a tremendous amount of time there and begins to truly care about that place, which includes the neighborhood around it. Live-work is part of a new wave of reinhabitation of the United States' city centers not only by young and mostly single workers but also by those who grew up in the suburbs, maybe went to college in the city, maybe raised kids in the suburbs but now want to be where the action is. And though they may drive an SUV, they don't want to get into it every time they need a quart of milk or a latte. They are attracted to pedestrian-oriented downtowns and neighborhoods, and many are voting with their feet as they forsake the suburbs, as is discussed in Chapter Four: Market, and the sidebar "The New Urban Workplace," in this chapter.

Almost all forms of live-work have something fundamental and obvious in common with residential development: people live in them. Live-work residents' needs are not so very different from those of any person living in a residence. The most significant difference is that almost all live-work exists in either former industrial or commercial buildings in established urban districts, or in greenfield town centers and infill development. As such, live-work is decidedly urban. Its residents want the environment in which they live and work to be of high-quality design and to function well as a community. Any developer of live-work who ignores these simple truths does so at his or her economic peril.

Neighborhood Revitalization

Conversion of former industrial and commercial buildings to live-work use—or new construction of live-work on land in such districts—brings in new people who add life and vitality to what were often deserted places. With them come the need for services, from art supplies to cappuccinos, from dry cleaners to pediatricians. City governments have entire departments devoted to encouraging neighborhood revitalization; live-work often can accomplish this aim—or at the very least serve as the catalyst—without governmental intervention.

Neighborhood revitalization can mean higher real estate values and improved services and quality of retail. It can also mean increased opportunities for business owners and jobs

Figure 6-38 Neighborhood revitalization via live-work: a mixed-use live-work, retail, and entertainment complex in Claremont, California, located in an area that appears to have been bereft of any such services prior to its construction: a brave move by the developer and a place that was thriving when the author visited in 2007.

for their employees. In terms of employment and economic development, it is arguable that in a given 10,000-square foot industrial building that might have employed ten people, the ten live-work spaces that could go in it might employ more people than that, and any one of them might incubate a much larger business.

The Role of Artists in a City

The presence of artists in a city (see Figure 6-43) adds great vitality to its cultural life and makes all of our lives more interesting. Studies have shown that the arts' contribution to a city's economy is often in the range of 10 percent.

In the face of many societal trends, the tenure of low- and moderate-income artists in inexpensive live-work spaces is often limited without intervention of nonprofit developers or other agencies of subsidy. Illegal live-work is a great form of affordable housing that accommodates artists and others

Urban Live-Work Revitalization Stories

Two examples of locations in the United States that have experienced great success in the realm of real estate and "urban lifestyle" transformations are SoMa (South of Market) in San Francisco (see Figure 6-39) and TriBeCa (Triangle below Canal Street, hereafter Tribeca) in New York City (see Figure 6-40). Initially both became popular as artists' districts. While there are many similarities between them, their differences illustrate some of the pitfalls of

Figure 6-39 Newly built San Francisco lofts next to heavy industry, a problematic adjacency that contributed to a live-work moratorium being declared in 1999.

Figure 6-40 An artfully renovated loft building in Duane Park, the former center of the butter, eggs, and cheese district and now a charming part of Tribeca in lower Manhattan.

assuming that the SoHo Cycle is a smooth path to urban revitalization.

Table 6-6 is a compares of the state of the two districts and the times when their explosion of development occurred, as well as how they evolved.

What does this comparison teach us about sizing up a district for colonization by artists and other similarly situated individuals and possibly a subsequent transition from arts district to mixed-use urban neighborhood?

First of all, artists are notoriously independent, so a developer or planner deciding that they will colonize a neighborhood is a nonstarter. What happens after a district is "discovered" is sometimes possible to regulate and manage. The comparison between Tribeca and SoMa contains many useful lessons, in addition to those discussed in the sidebar "The San Francisco Experience." Lessons include:

1. Loft districts are not exempt from basic community planning principles.

    If a district is to have a chance of becoming a neighborhood, it must be near transit, contain building stock that can accommodate ground-floor mixed uses, and ideally be in a place with a fine-grained, connected street grid. SoMa, particularly its far-flung reaches, provided none of this, and many of the new loft buildings did little to activate the street, as seen in Figure 6-41.

    Tribeca, in contrast has in the past thirty-five years gone from mostly vacant ground floors to a place where the street-level lights have come on, literally. Retail and fine dining is alive and well there in its original buildings, and evidence of children is everywhere in Tribeca today.

2. Preexisting industrial or commercial uses that are viable today can be a recipe for disaster in the face of well-heeled live-work buyers.

    While the goal of a great live-work neighborhood is a lively mix of uses, a concrete batch plant, a slaughterhouse, or a zinc-plating plant is not typically part of that desired mix. Two different outcomes can occur as a

Figure 6-41 New lofts typically were built with virtually no connection to the street and therefore did not anticipate the possibility of a more convivial street life. SoMa, San Francisco.

result of locating live-work in active industrial neighborhoods:

1. The neighborhood remains the province of artists—themselves working people who usually don't have a problem with industrial neighbors

Figure 6-42 A restaurant in Tribeca whose sign was painted by the children of the local public school.

Table 6-6 Comparison of Live-Work and Revitalization in Tribeca (New York City) and SoMa (San Francisco)

Qualities	Tribeca	SoMa
General character	A compact district comprising largely built-out, multistory loft buildings, many historic.	A relatively sprawling commercial/industrial district with many vacant lots.
Transit access	Manhattan narrows in Tribeca and the subway lines converge; mass transit is never more than a five-minute walk away.	Not well served by transit.
Initial time frame	Mostly occupied by artists in the 1970s, many of whom were fleeing the gentrifying SoHo; New York City was struggling at that time, being bailed out by state and federal government and struggling to maintain basic services.	Colonized by artists from the 1950s into the 1990s. San Francisco was a more affordable city prior to the dot-com boom.
Nature of new development after initial artists' colonization	Existing buildings were renovated and occupied by increasingly well-heeled residents. Vacant ground floors became shops and restaurants, even schools.	Live-work boom was largely new construction, poorly planned and regulated, and widely dispersed. It was a response to a housing crunch brought on by the dot-com boom and the rise of the "creative class."
Place in the history of live-work	Initially a first-generation live-work conversion of a district made redundant by the adoption of shipping containers. Classic gentrification but not as much displacement because many buildings were still vacant as the transition took place, therefore, more of an organic transition.	As new construction, SoMa exemplified the second generation of live-work enabled by the Internet and small-office automation.
Current occupants	The new occupants of Tribeca are some of the most affluent in New York. Some have children, as evidenced by the many schools, pediatricians, dentists, and toy stores in the neighborhood. All necessary neighborhood services are present by this time (2011). Even Duane Park, center of the butter, eggs, and cheese district forty years ago, is now renovated as an urban jewel.	Later occupants are mostly single people, couples, and empty nesters, car-dependent and not well served by local retail, transit, parks, or other urban amenities.
Plight of original live-work residents	Virtually all artists are gone except very successful ones or those who have somehow held on in rent-controlled situations.	Some displacement of low-income residential units; artists mostly displaced from existing buildings.
Status as a vital urban neighborhood	Today Tribeca is a thriving urban neighborhood in all senses of the word. It is walkable, mixed use, safe, and enjoyable to be in at all times of the day. As a transformation from an artists' district to an affluent neighborhood, it is a success; it could be termed a "climax" community.	While some services have come, and a major light rail line now goes through a portion, the live-work in SoMa is still a dispersed collection of projects interspersed with what commercial and industrial uses remain—and there are many. Coexistence between lofts and industry continues to be uneasy at best. SoMa will no doubt continue to change significantly in the coming decades.
Compatibility with preexisting neighbors	Since Tribeca was largely vacant due to containerization and other economic conditions of the 1970s, the transition from mainly artists to upscale "arty" types was not accompanied by imported NIMBYism. Most artists were displaced and have moved on to Brooklyn, Long Island City, and beyond.	The new residents of SoMa often complained about preexisting industrial and commercial activities—businesses that were there first, of course. This imported NIMBYism caused the displacement and flight of many San Francisco employers that provide needed goods and services.
Regulatory response and planning assessment	Tribeca exists and thrives as a viable and desirable neighborhood in which to live, work, and play. It is home to many celebrities and Michelin-rated restaurants (see Figure 6-42) and has been compared to Greenwich, Connecticut. Planners are not complaining.	A moratorium on live-work was declared in San Francisco in 1999. Planners consider the live-work boom to have been a planning failure. Many of the developers, long gone, do not agree.
Quality of the transformed urban environment	Only a few new live-work buildings have been constructed in Tribeca, as it was already largely built out. Those that have been built were subject to design review and fit in well. It is evident that efforts have been made to preserve the historic character of Tribeca; its affluence has clearly aided this effort.	Some renovations were sensitively done, and a new building type—the new construction live-work complex—was essentially created. Most were less than contextual and often stand today as anomalies in the urban environment, maverick buildings.
Overall result	Before its transformation, Tribeca had going for it a stock of historic buildings, an established grid, and great transit access. While spontaneous at first and affordable at that time, the transformation of Tribeca into a thriving, sustainable neighborhood has been a success for all but those who came before, who popularized it, and who were displaced. Such is urban economics, especially in New York City.	The overall impression of much of SoMa is that individual buildings were constructed that did meet a need for relatively affordable residential units within San Francisco. However, most exhibited very little awareness of what it takes to build a new neighborhood. It is arguable that some of the more isolated live-work buildings of San Francisco may become the tenements of the future.

(Continued)

who enjoy living on the margins of mainstream society. Gentrification of loft districts can be a real problem; most artists are not equipped to pay condominium prices. True work/live projects, where the live portion is clearly accessory to the work component, are difficult to maintain as long-term affordable. The market pressures are simply too compelling for most owners.

Arts groups all over the country agitated for legislation to allow artists to live in their spaces legally, which meant that laws were enacted that required live-work buildings to meet these newly written planning and building codes. With few exceptions, the enactment of such regulations worked to the disadvantage of the artists, hastened change in their neighborhoods, and eventually resulted in their being priced out and forced to move.

So what happened in the long run? Who were the winners and who were the losers? Did the city get better? The answers to these questions touch on complex issues and reveal some unintended consequences.

Creating a path to legalization that does not lead to displacement of the artists it was intended to assist is very difficult. It generally involves

- Additional relaxations of building codes
- Some sort of subsidy
- A process to determine who is eligible for such relaxations and subsidies

Continuing Role of Artists and Others in the Evolution of Live-Work

Desperate building owners were happy to look the other way as artists and others living voluntarily on the social, legal, and economic fringe paid a dime a square foot or less for such space, made their own improvements, and—as an aggregation of individuals—created some of the first artists' districts in places like SoHo, Tribeca, SoMa, and LoDo. What these named districts all have in common is:

- The fact that artists spontaneously occupied underutilized commercial buildings.
- The artists' occupation of the buildings as live-work was generally illegal (i.e., not officially sanctioned by building or planning departments).
- The first successful reinhabitations of many downtown urban districts, the aggregation of occupied buildings in previously nonresidential districts often led to the birth of a neighborhood.
- Real estate values in such new neighborhoods soared at a time when urban flight was still the norm.
- The original artists who occupied the derelict buildings, often absent any city services such as garbage collection, neighborhood-serving retail, parks or—in many cases—

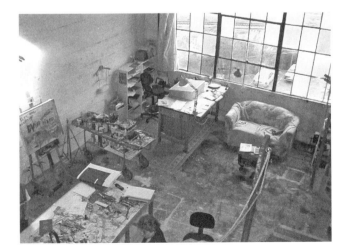

Figure 6-43 An artists' live-work space in a renovated industrial building.

public transit, lived and worked happily in their lofts until the realities of urban economics overtook them, and they were forced to move out of the very districts they had transformed into neighborhoods.

• What accompanied the displacement of artists was the creation of real urban neighborhoods, occupied by many folks from other walks of life—professionals, telecommuters, entrepreneurs, regular nine-to-fivers

• "Post-artist" live-work accommodates middle- and upper-class singles, couples, more recently empty nesters, and even families who benefit from the pioneering that the artists accomplished. These neighborhoods have retained at least a veneer of "artiness."

• Those who chose to evolve with the neighborhood, or even profit from its evolution, were well rewarded. Essentially the only way to do this is by owning property and watching it appreciate as the neighborhood becomes desirable—which it will do even in times of stagnating values. Changes in form of ownership from rental to coop or condominium were an important value-add, conferring liquidity to lofts that were previously transferred via long leases often accompanied by a fixture fee to pay for improvements made, sometimes called key money.

Some have suggested an arts transfer tax on the sale of all real estate in a loft district, whose proceeds would be invested in the creation of long-term affordable space for bona fide artists. The only way to ensure long-term affordable space for artists—or for anyone—is to provide either opportunities for ownership or open-ended leases that provide protection from eviction (see Figure 6-44).

Following are three examples of ways to achieve affordable live-work for artists, only one of which guarantees long-term stability:

1. A group of artists secures a building at very low rent or (less common) a low purchase price. They develop it on a quasi-legal basis, build up a constituency and goodwill, and then ask for and secure forgiveness from city officials for code transgressions—many of which are corrected over time. In general, projects that have followed this path, such as Project Artaud in San Francisco, California, The Emeryville Artists' Coop in Emeryville, California, and to a lesser degree Westbeth in New York City, make the transition from rental to ownership, thereby providing greater long-term security along with significant, sometimes crippling maintenance responsibilities.

Figure 6-44 A newly built artist's studio-cum-storefront in a New Urbanist greenfield development in Brea, California.

2. A nonprofit developer—such as Artspace Projects, based in Minneapolis, Minnesota—sets out to create an affordable live-work project for artists. It works within the system, securing government and grant funding and all planning and building code approvals, building according to union and prevailing wage standards as is true in all affordable housing, taking a hefty fee for its work, and creating an officially affordable artists, live-work project operating under long-term subsidy.

3. A maverick developer—usually an artist or former artist—buys a building for very little money, designs it to be efficient and affordable to build out, and improves it using inexpensive labor, often provided by fellow artists.. Legal status for the live-work arrives at different times in each project, often instigated by landlord-tenant disputes. Such projects remain affordable for as long as the owner wishes them to remain so. Unless the owner sells to the tenants as a group, these projects have no enforceable affordability safeguards other than an uneasy stand-off between tenants in inexpensive space and a landlord's fear of being turned in by a disgruntled tenant.

How do these three scenarios work differently? The first is initially less expensive, generally more community-based, more risky, and likely includes beneficent leaders with some access to capital. The author is aware of a project presently in operation that was built out in a rented building entirely without building permits. The mayor and city manager have been there; the planning director has been there. All have commended the project and have expressed a hope that more will occur. The directors' attitude is that when someone asks where the permits are, they will use the goodwill they have generated to ask for and largely receive forgiveness, which will likely be granted.

The second scenario for creating long-term affordable space for artists is more expensive initially but can and has been done with government funding by reputable nonprofit developers. These developers have successfully addressed several questions, including whether one can use affordable housing funds for a specific occupation (i.e., artists). Court cases have held that non-artists are not a protected group, and as long as one does not discriminate on other bases such as race, age, disability, and so on, it is apparently legal to use affordable housing funds to build artists' live-work.

Another question that comes up is that live-work is not entirely residential space, and can therefore be subject to financing constraints—for example the lender could find it difficult to sell a mixed-use building if the project failed mid construction. Affordable housing funds typically stipulate that the proportion of the project that is non residential—measured either by individual units' percentage of commercial area or the aggregate amount in project—be very low or zero. For this reason, such projects often have multiple sources of funding. For example, economic development or redevelopment funds can sometimes be used to fill the work space gap.

The third scenario, that of the maverick artist developer, is—in the author's experience—a common one. Artists with an entrepreneurial bent are often the first to locate buildings well suited to live-work and buy them at a low price. The scenario just described is one with an unpredictable ending: The tenants may buy the building from the landlord, the landlord may hold the building and keep rents low, or he or she may raise rents as the district changes. Affordability is a relative term, and this third scenario often evolves into a project that is part of the transformation of its location from an artists' district to a mixed-use urban neighborhood. Nevertheless, a market for minimally finished renovated live-work rentals does exist and is an important niche worth filling in most cities.

Legalization of Illegal or Quasi-Legal Live-Work

The most common catalyst for live-work legalizations—the process of bringing illegal live-work into compliance with planning, building, and fire codes—is a landlord-tenant dispute resulting in the tenant's calling the city to report the landlord. While many cities are relatively lenient about illegal live-work, once a complaint is filed, they usually have no choice but to initiate a code compliance action.

Most live-work legalizations cause some harm or inconvenience to all parties involved. The author has participated in many such actions, generally as consultant to the building owner, and has observed some ways in which the process can be pursued in a manner that preserves, to the greatest extent possible:

- The affordability of the live-work units
- The integrity of the community of tenants
- The intent of the building code
- The rights of the landlord to pass on the costs of the improvements in an even-handed way

Ideally, a building that is being legalized, regardless of the event that initiated the action, will go through the process

---

Tribeca and Uptown: A Tale of Two Cities, Three Thousand Miles and Forty Years Apart

The author lived in Tribeca in lower Manhattan in the mid-1970s (see Figure 6-45). He estimates that one thousand people, mostly artists, lived below Canal Street (that's fifteen hundred acres, or twice the size of Central Park). Most Tribeca loft dwellers at the time—some were refugees from the already gentrifying SoHo—worked by day in their spaces and socialized by night in the few bars and restaurants to be found there. Delphi, a Greek

Restaurant at Reade Street and West Broadway (recently closed and up for rent) was one of those places, and one was almost guaranteed to run into someone one knew at dinner there. So there was a community of sorts in that pioneering loft district, where rents hovered around $0.10–$0.20 per square foot, and 3,000- to 5,000-square-foot lofts occupied by one person were not uncommon. Everything was rented, and when one moved on,

Figure 6-45 Tribeca (Triangle Below Canal Street) in the 1970s: Mostly boarded-up storefronts and some artists' lofts above. Before the days of cell phones, and in the absence of doorbells, one needed to carry pebbles in one's pocket to throw at the destination loft's windows. They key would be thrown down wadded up in a sock. One knew how to work a freight elevator (keep your hands in!) and learned to accurately size up a space's square footage at a glance.

one sold one's "fixtures" to the next lessee for a few thousand dollars.

Tribeca has of course long since gentrified (see Figure 6-46) and become an outrageously expensive and highly desirable place to live (see Figure 6-47), not least due to its proximity to Wall Street, where many Tribeca residents work. As noted, the SoHo Cycle tends to create a diaspora of former residents and is the antithesis of a stable community. For many, that is fine. Tribeca, however, is now a relatively stable community, in what one might call a climax state, to borrow a term from the science of ecology.

Contrasting the example of Tribeca is the ongoing colonization of a previously mixed-use neighborhood that has experienced significant

Figure 6-46 The corner of Chambers Street and West Broadway today, which is the lower vertex of the triangle in Tribeca; just about any service or product one might need is now available in the neighborhood, unlike thirty-five years ago.

disinvestment and—not linked to any technological advance such as shipping containers—is now home to many vacant or underutilized buildings and properties. Fast forward forty years from 1970s Tribeca to 2010: Oakland, California's Uptown, home of a burgeoning and entirely spontaneous, homegrown art scene. Uptown is a typical down-on-your-luck area, complete with Greyhound Bus Terminal, a lively extralegal street scene, a city-funded redevelopment project at its lower end, and a significant (and uncounted) number of former

Figure 6-47 The lights literally came on in Tribeca as it transformed from a district to a neighborhood; in that respect it resembles neighborhoods all over Manhattan yet retains most of its historic architectural character.

(Continued)

warehouses, storefronts, and other commercial buildings illegally occupied by young, risk-oblivious artists.

There is a burgeoning club scene in Uptown, a former locus of many of Oakland's car dealers and ancillary services such as body shops, and it has become famous for the Art Murmur (see Figure 6-48), a unique monthly happening that is part coordinated gallery opening, part street fair, and a consistently great party. Until it is co-opted by too many folks driving in from the suburbs (possibly by the time this book is published), Uptown's Art Murmur is a bona fide expression of a place newly colonized without real gentrification or gentrification's calling card, displacement of low-income residents. As with all illegal live-work, a cat-and-mouse game with the building and fire departments is ongoing, and unless an enlightened amnesty and legalization program is adopted, many of the spaces will be vacated or legalized at such an expense that the average Uptown resident won't be able to afford them. By that time the Uptown art scene will likely have moved on to a grittier location (if that's possible; San Francisco has essentially run out of them).

At the moment, Oakland's building department—which also supports its planning department with building permit fees—is hungry for code compliance cases to cure its severe shortfall in building permit applications, which does not bode well for the quasi-legal scene in Uptown.

What the two examples have in common are elements of live-work's unique status as an outlaw reuse of old buildings that initially caught planners off guard. While there have certainly been live-work urban design success stories across the country, the ad hoc nature of live-work and how it can find its way into the most unexpected places has

Figure 6-48 Rock Paper Scissors, a gallery and sewing collective located at the corner that is the epicenter of the Art Murmur every first Friday in Oakland, California's entirely spontaneous Uptown arts district.

meant that numerous cities have found themselves illegally housing thousands of residents with no place to park, no place to shop for dinner, no garbage pickup, no nearby schools or parks, and a car-dependent sort of pioneer existence. While this example is extreme, it is not atypical of the artists' vanguard role in the SoHo Cycle. The challenge for planners, then, is to be in touch with which areas are being colonized by illegal residents, to recognize the irresistible forces that are creating a draw to that place in spite of its lack of services, and to respond.

What can be done to preserve, protect, and create long-term affordable live-work for artists and other similarly situated individuals?

1. Designate certain areas of a city off-limits for condominium live-work but appropriate for rental or limited-equity coop ownership. The most likely candidate for such a designation would be industrial areas where amenities are few and the likelihood of conflict between upscale buyers and established local businesses is great.

2. Create incentives for developers to include artists in their projects, through such means as density bonuses, parking requirement relaxations, and other building code relaxations. If these measures fail to achieve the desired result, consider the imposition of artists' inclusionary zoning, which targets not only income but also a specific occupation: artists. Also consider an arts transfer tax on the sale of real estate in targeted arts districts, to go into a fund to provide long-term affordable artists' live-work.

3. Encourage nonprofit developers to view low- and moderate-income artists as an underserved group deserving of their support through the development of affordable live-work projects.

4. Create an amnesty program to encourage legalization of illegal live-work, with clear guidelines as outlined in the "Legalization" section that follows.

5. Create programs that encourage tenants in existing legal or illegal live-work buildings to organize as a group and purchase their building from the owner, sometimes in combination with a legalization of the building in cooperation with city officials.

under a previously adopted live-work building code and planning regulations (if they exist). Nevertheless, in the case of verifiable artists' live-work, there are rational arguments for further relaxations or liberal interpretations of code—particularly building codes—when a legalization is pursued properly, meaning that all parties win. In Oakland, California, a building code variance is called an Administrative Modification Request (AMR). To receive an AMR, one must make the case that the alternate means being proposed meets the intent of the building code—in this case the live-work building code. The author's experience is that in live-work legalizations—in which the owner seeks forgiveness rather than permission—the most expedient permitting of the building is similar to an Omnibus AMR. One can argue that this process involves asking for forgiveness for prior illegal acts; to some extent that is true, but judicious, selective relaxation of some requirements can make the process work for everyone.

The last thing that building or other city officials want to spend time on is a landlord-tenant dispute. In an ideal legalization, meetings are held between the owner, the architect, and the tenants as often as is necessary to keep the tenants

informed regarding the legalization, including their right to resume tenancy in their unit at a rent that fairly compensates the landlord for his or her incurred expenses. Tenants, as part of this ideal arrangement, must agree not to take further complaints to the building department and must agree to either move within the project or to other accommodations to allow the work—which can be significant—to proceed.

The landlord must agree not to use the legalization process to engage in retaliatory or wholesale evictions; what the landlord gets in return is tenants agreeing not to harass him or her or the city during the process and fair, if not preferential, treatment from the city when it comes to interpretation of codes.

Most large cities have their share of large illegal live-work buildings that have been occupied for a long time and consequently are home to strong communities of tenants. Experience has shown that considering the element of time is essential in live-work legalization. Rather than vacate a building wholesale, thereby devastating the existing community of tenants, a more measured approach is to allow 10 to 15 percent of the units to go vacant by attrition, to legalize these vacant units first, and to treat them as temporary accommodations for existing tenants while other units are legalized, including their own. At the end of the process, it is far more likely that a high percentage of the original tenants will remain. The author is aware of at least one legalization that has stretched out over fifteen years; such a long view has enabled the community of predominantly artists to remain as intact as possible.

One other path to legalization involves the tenants of a building pooling their resources and cooperating with the landlord in the legalization process, at the end of which they purchase the building at a price set prior to the commencement of work. In this case the tenants benefit from the landlord's access to financing, the landlord gets a guaranteed buyer at a set price, and the tenants end up owning their units. Such a scenario could be made even more possible through financial subsidy, which is beyond the scope of this section.

Forms of Ownership

A word about forms of ownership: While having a live-work unit with affordable rent is a great thing, the only way to ensure one's future housing expense is some form of ownership. The most common forms are:

1. Fee-simple ownership. The simplest and most common, in which an individual or some entity owns a property outright, with or without a mortgage. Examples would be an entire building, a single-family house, or a piece of land.

2. Condominium. This is what is called a common interest subdivision, in which fee simple ownership of one's individual unit is combined with shared ownership of the common areas, such as elevators, corridors, courtyards, roof, and building shell, the land on which the project sits, and so on. Each owner has a separate mortgage. Condominiums can be bought and sold more or less like houses, and they usually don't have any restrictions on sale price.

3. Limited-equity co-ops are the most common form of ownership organized around long-term affordability. The building is owned by the cooperative, and individuals own shares that entitle them to occupy a particular unit. The limited-equity provision works like this: When one sells, one can only receive one's down payment plus a small amount of appreciation on one's equity (i.e., down payment) based on the consumer price index or some other index, plus the cost of any improvements one has made

---

CASE STUDY: DUTCH BOY STUDIOS

Type of Live-Work: Work/Live legalization

Proximity Type: Live-with

Location: Oakland, California: San Leandro Street Industrial District

Architect: Thomas Dolan Architecture (renovation/legalization)

Developer: Francis Collins

Located on East Oakland's famed Studio Row, the Dutch Boy Paint factory produced the paint that graced the bottoms of America's warships during World War II (see Figure 6-49). Sometimes called the mother of all live-work conversions (at least in the Bay Area), the sprawling complex was bought by a young art school graduate who created a thriving community of artists, some of whom have been there since 1979. Issues of lead contamination on the property were raised over the years, and the owner's leases specifically forbade children to live at Dutch Boy. Unfortunately, in 1996 a child did live there briefly, was tested for lead, and allegedly showed high levels. Within a short time, an informal task force

of city, county, state, and federal officials showed up, forty-seven strong.

It was at about this time that Thomas Dolan Architecture (TDA) became involved in the code compliance issues involved in legalizing Dutch Boy, which had been converted with virtually no

Figure 6-49 Dutch Boy Studios before legalization work got under way, 1996. Designed by Thomas Dolan Architecture.

Figure 6-50 Significant seismic work was required in some of the buildings, whose unconventional construction (e.g., three-inch-thick stucco at some exterior walls, tested at 4,000 psf) was a challenge to engineers and inspectors alike. Designed by Thomas Dolan Architecture.

Figure 6-51 The huge volumes in some of the spaces at Dutch Boy Studios were some of the most spectacular live-work spaces the author has ever seen—or likely ever will; unfortunately, most are too large to be affordable to artists. 1996–2011. Designed by Thomas Dolan Architecture.

permits. As lead remediation proceeded on a parallel track, TDA began to sort out how to legalize fifty-three existing units. Few egregious code violations existed, and by 1996, Oakland had in place an excellent live-work building code (written in part by Thomas Dolan). Nevertheless, seismic work was needed in some buildings (see Figure 6-50), sprinklers were needed in others, and the owner attempted to retain as many members of this unique community of artists as possible by moving them around from unit to unit as they were completed.

Planning permits for the existing fifty-three units were obtained, and some work began in 2000. At about this time the owner realized (see Figure 6-51) that he needed a larger number of smaller units to meet the price point most artists are willing to commit to. The use permit was modified to allow eighty-three units within the same building volumes. At of this writing (2011), a little more than half (see Figure 6-52) of the eighty-three units are completely legalized, fifteen years after TDA first became involved in the project. Nevertheless, the project's legalization has been considered a success (see Figure 6-53) by most parties involved.

Figure 6-52 A legal unit ready for occupancy at Dutch Boy Studios, Oakland, California, with a very basic kitchen, simple Sheet rocked mezzanine parapet walls, and a raw concrete floor, ready for the new tenant to add his own identity to the space. 1996–2011. Designed by Thomas Dolan Architecture.

(Continued)

Figure 6-53 The same building as shown in Figure 6-49, complete and legalized. Dutch Boy Studios, Oakland, California. 1996-2011. Designed by Thomas Dolan Architecture.

Lessons Learned

1. Illegal live-work has its place in cities, and likely always will. Some have said it is a valuable form of affordable accommodation for artists, artisans, and similarly situated individuals. Dutch Boy has existed as a viable community—the mother of all live-work projects—in Oakland for thirty-two years.

2. Life-safety issues eventually must be addressed, and doing so with flexibility and sensitivity is the best way to accomplish this process, which can take many years. The lessons learned from Dutch Boy and other projects whose legalization the author has managed are summarized in "The Legalization Process," which is Module 5 in the Model Live-Work Building Code System in Appendix B.

that were preapproved by the co-op board. This form of ownership was created specifically for those who want to stay in their space indefinitely: think "long-term affordable." Its one downside is that without the appreciation of one's home, what is for many their only nest egg is absent. If at some point one chooses to leave a limited-equity coop and reenter the conventional housing market, a brutal awakening likely awaits in the form of housing prices that are out of reach.

There are variations on these forms of ownership, including stock cooperatives (popular in New York City) and "equity cap condominiums," an attempt to create longer-term affordability in condominium projects.

It is possible for a group or partnership to purchase a property on a fee-simple basis and then convert the property to condominiums or limited-equity coops. To do so means taking on the role of developer and assuming some of the risks. A developer is much like a producer in the world of motion pictures. He or she puts the deal together and manages the overall process, including financing, securing all necessary permits, design and construction, subdivision processes, and so on. However risky, the end result of being your own developer can be a building bought wholesale, subdivided without a developer profit, and in the end, individual ownership of far more affordable units. Such "self-development" is not for the faint of heart and requires the help of professionals who do it all the time: an architect and a paid project manager, a surveyor or civil engineer, attorneys, builders, a good title

officer who knows subdivisions, and if possible a member of the group who has some experience with the process, or—alternatively—one member of the group who has the time to be the group's lightning rod and possibly meeting facilitator and recorder.

Tip

Create a revolving loan program, perhaps funded by an arts transfer tax, to provide technical assistance and seed money for groups of artists desiring to buy and develop buildings for their own use as long-term affordable live-work.

Industrial Protection Zones

Numerous cities, including San Francisco, Berkeley, and Oakland, California, have adopted measures to protect their existing industrial base. Each has taken a different approach, and each has had to deal with forces that bear some similarity to the SoHo Cycle as they made efforts to protect industry that is threatened by offshoring, automation, and the transition to a postindustrial United States, all the while allowing some forms of live-work.

San Francisco

San Francisco, which is treated in a more complete case study (see sidebar, "The San Francisco Experience"), was experiencing such a demand for live-work during the dot-com boom of the late 1990s that 3,500 units were built, mostly new construction and mostly in existing industrial areas. Due to neighborhood complaints of gentrification and the displacement of

Do-It-Yourself Development 101, A Possible Scenario

Ten artists, each with $25,000 in savings available for studio purchase/improvement, are sitting around having a beer in a pub one night. An idea occurs to them: "We're all artists, we all rent, our rent keeps going up, a few of us have been evicted recently, and we know the only way to really control your space is to own it. Why don't we get together and buy a building and fix it up ourselves?"

Table 6-7 is a step-by-step guide to the typical tasks that this hypothetical group must perform.

Table 6-7 Shared Building Purchase and Development

Task

1. Form group, designate individual as lightning rod, total up available cash and skills
2. Identify space needs: Measure spaces where group members have lived and worked
3. Decide on search location(s)
4. Get prequalified with a loan broker. Determine price range and project size/cost limits
5. Hire a real estate agent (or don't)
6. Interview architects
7. Hire architect
8. Find and visit properties; take architect to one(s) you like
9. Make a purchase offer (or purchase option proposal)
10. Offer accepted! Open escrow.
11. Begin due diligence/feasibility study process
12. Inspections: contractor, structural engineer, termite, roof, etc.
13. Phase I toxics study
14. Sketch design with architect
15. Presubmisssion conference with Planning Department
16. Preliminary building plan check
17. Cost estimate by contractor
18. Create what-if spreadsheets, called *pro formas*
19. Secure financing for property purchase
20. Get financing commitment for construction
21. Get financing commitment for permanent, or "take out," financing
22. Begin working with architect to refine design and create construction documents
23. Form a relationship with a general contractor. Interview several
24. "Value engineer" the project during design refinements
25. Design team (led by architect) completes construction documents, submit for building permit
26. Issue bid sets
27. Negotiate construction contract
28. Revise drawings for value engineering and permit purposes
29. Sign construction contract
30. Pull building permit
31. Close on construction loan
32. Close on property purchase
33. **Begin construction**
34. Begin subdivision process: hire engineer to do tentative map
35. Hire a lawyer to create subdivision documents: bylaws and Codes, Covenants & Restrictions. (CC&Rs)
36. Finalize form of ownership with your group, attorney
37. File subdivision with city
38. Tentative map approved
39. File with state department of real estate
40. Receive DRE approval of "Subdivision Public Report"
41. Complete construction
42. Get Certificate of Occupancy
43. Close on take-out financing or individual mortgages
44. Move in and celebrate

low-income residents and commercial operations, a live-work moratorium was declared citywide in 1999 by the city's board of supervisors. Soon afterward, in 2001, the city established Industrial Protection Zones designed to prevent further displacement of the industrial and commercial operations that are essential to the operation of a city and the employment of its residents.

Berkeley

Berkeley is a city where strong opinions are held on all issues public and political. The western part of the city, known as West Berkeley, has been home to various industries for many years, some of which are upwind of nearby residents and do produce some noxious emissions. There are factions in Berkeley that would like industry to leave. However, the West Berkeley Plan was adopted in 1993, and it envisioned most of this three-mile-long stretch as home to all kinds of industrial employment centers. At the same time, with the exception of transitional buffer zones called Special Industrial, live-work was prohibited. While a few companies opened new operations, notably Bayer, West Berkeley languished for many years due to the West Berkeley Plan's restrictive zoning requirements. Meanwhile its neighbor to the south, Emeryville, has thrived by adopting a far more un-restricted, albeit mainly commercial, laissez-faire model.

An organization called WEBAIC (West Berkeley Artisans and Industrial Companies) has existed for a number of years and is active in fighting the city's efforts to introduce larger research and development and mixed use projects into West Berkeley. At a recent hearing, WEBAIC representatives pointed out that 33 percent of Berkeley residents do not have a college degree, that their members employ seven thousand people, and that such large site development should be stopped. Others claim that such a position is a form of NIMBYism (homegrown, not imported), and that WEBAIC's position obstructs Berkeley's advance into the twenty-first century and capitalization on the vast intellectual resources of the nearby University of California and its graduates.

Oakland

Oakland is a city where industry has been an important part of its identity for a long time. While it has suffered from the problems of industrial decline as much as any American city, its industrial land owners have been strong advocates for protection of their turf (i.e., the manufacturing zones). Oakland's live-work planning regulations were adopted early (1980), are very simple, and have remained largely unchanged until recently. In short, what they state is that live-work is permitted only in buildings "originally designed and constructed for commercial or industrial use" and in zones that allow residential uses. In zones that do not permit residential use—essentially the manufacturing zones—a conditional use permit is required.

The effect of these regulations has been that while there have been numerous renovations of existing buildings for live-work in industrial areas, most have been relatively low-budget rental projects that do not lead to conflicts with their industrial neighbors. In order to head off such problems, language has been added in code bulletins requiring work/live leases and condominium documents to explicitly state that there are legitimate surrounding businesses that have the right to remain there.

The measures in Oakland worked well for about twenty-five years and are still on the books. The city has more recently adopted mixed-use zones, such as Housing and Business Mix (HBX), which allow commercial uses, residential, and live/work and work/live use types as new construction under very specific, fully separated live-near configuration requirements. In a classic case of regulation falling behind economic cycles, the specificity of the work/live unit types has never been tested in real projects as none has been built recently.

Meanwhile, the industrial lands of Oakland have continued to be a battleground over what is a very small portion of the city's land area. A new-mixed use zone called Commercial-Industrial Mix (CIX) was created, and—in a victory for industrial owners—it forbids new construction work/live in CIX unless it is within three hundred feet of a residential zone—thereby relegating it to buffer status. It also forbids renovation of existing buildings for work/live unless there are "existing artists or artisans" living in the building (presumably illegally) or the building is within three hundred feet of a residential zone. This is a back-door means of legalizing units, a subject that is treated above.

While industrial land owners are the first to stand up for their right to exist and not be pushed out by imported NIMBYs, they have also been observed to act in ways akin to farmers in exurban areas who love their farms, but at the same time wish to have the right to sell the farm to a subdivider, retire comfortably, and put their kids through college. In a specific Oakland example, a multiacre site in a manufacturing zone was sold to a national homebuilder for a vast sum of money. The builder pushed through a general plan amendment and proceeded to build scores of houses on a prime piece of industrial land, close to but not immediately adjacent to a very few city services.

These three examples of Bay Area cities describe controversy amid transition in ways that don't precisely match the SoHo Cycle model. The first sign of change is often the presence of live-work, usually extralegal. As was true of all real estate transactions and development initiatives during the last decade, the boom had its effect on live-work. Housing—and anything that looked or smelled like it—was front and center, easy to finance and sell, and therefore a source of tremendous pressure on land everywhere, whether it was greenfields or brownfields, in the form of urban infill or re-use of existing buildings. Only time will tell what emerges for live-work after the current recession, although it is this author's opinion that the proximity and affordability inherent in live-work will be seen as a great advantage by many.

Affordability

Inclusionary zoning, as described earlier under "Development Standards," is a term used to describe requirements imposed by some cities that a certain percentage of units in multiunit housing projects be set aside as long-term affordable housing, usually for low- and moderate-income people as locally defined. Fifty percent of area median income (AMI) is considered low income, 80 percent is considered moderate income, and units that are affordable to those who make 120 percent of AMI are considered workforce housing. Live-work has long been held to be exempt from such requirements as well as residential rent control due to its commercial characterization.

Table 6-8 Live-Work Affordability Strategies without Subsidies

Zero Commute = one less car

No separate work space = multiple uses of one unit

Rental income possibilities in a live-near or live-nearby proximity type

Food production in community gardens

Mutual support of a community of shared values: child care, security, socializing

Reuse of an existing building: greener, cheaper

Congregate examples: unlikely to gentrify

To the extent that certain forms of live-work evolve more in the direction of housing types, this exemption may need to be reexamined. Experience has shown that affordability is an issue that can be addressed only in part by planning and zoning regulations, or by government subsidies.

Many people are attracted to live-work as a way to save money by combining the two most important functions in their lives into one location. Additionally, not commuting results in other significant savings of time and money. It is estimated that the average automobile costs over $9,000 per year to own, maintain, fuel, and insure (source: American Automobile Association). If a couple can do without one car, they are saving roughly $750 per month. Thus, inherently live-work makes one's overall living expenses far more affordable without any government subsidies. This is sometimes called "affordable living" as distinct from affordable housing (see Table 6-8), and involves examining one's total living expenses, including transportation expenses. True live-work, especially when located in a live-work neighborhood, will be accompanied by significantly decreased transportation expenses. Low income families can spend as much as 40 percent of their income on transportation, and roughly 40 percent of their income on transportation and housing combined, so any reduction in the need for automobile transportation can mean real savings freed up for other pressing needs.

As live-work has moved into the mainstream and become an accepted real estate "product" in the form of lifestyle lofts, home offices, and the like, prices for such units increased, and the likelihood of finding an affordable live-work space has generally decreased. However, affordability is a relative term. Many San Francisco lofts have been occupied by people who work in Silicon Valley, for whom $750,000 for a spacious lifestyle loft is a bargain compared to a $1,250,000 bungalow in Mountain View (home of Google), where the real estate market is still strong.

Compact, Pedestrian-Oriented Communities

As is made abundantly clear throughout this book, live-work is by its very nature a mixed-use building type and land use. As such, it enables both the possibility of far less reliance on the automobile by its residents and the relief that diminished traffic impact brings to its neighbors. Compact pedestrian-oriented mixed-use communities, such as those designed and built by New Urbanists (see Figure C-39 in the color folio), are a natural setting for live-work projects, and in fact many live-works have been included in some of the best-known New Urbanist communities, including Celebration, Seaside, Rosemary Beach, Serenbe, Habersham, Kentlands, Livermore, and Hercules (in California). In fact, one could say that when one includes all three proximity types (live-with, live-near, and live-nearby), virtually all housing in New Urbanist communities, save for some detached single-family residences, qualifies as live-work.

When it comes to social issues and planning solutions, new live-work in New Urbanist town centers is relatively straightforward and noncontroversial. While the constraints of building codes and single-use zoning have been discussed in this chapter, the archetypal live-works of New Urbanist communities are typically built in a flexhouse configuration (see Figure 6-54) that allow uses to evolve over time along with the communities they occupy.

Figure 6-54 Flexhouse live-works at Kentlands, Maryland. 1993. Designed by Duany Plater-Zyberk & Company, Town Planners and Architects. New Urbanist developers like to include live-works in their downtowns early in the life cycle of their projects, because the options for street activation are great and the units sell well.

Flexhouses embody two American ideals: owning one's own home and being one's own boss. Their inclusion in both new town centers and in infill locations well served by urban infrastructure tends to be a force for activating that location, a fact that is disputed by few. Therefore, taking the effort to code for live-work, using the model code suggestions and tables found in Appendix A, is recommended.

CHAPTER 7

Live-Work Building Code Issues

Regulating This Strange Animal Called Live-Work

Live-work building codes, where adopted, are some of the newest provisions in modern building codes, having been enacted in the larger cities of North America as a result of the first wave of artists' lofts in the mid- to late twentieth century. Early live-work codes were often a makeshift effort to accommodate a phenomenon that was already happening: the occupation by artists and others of former industrial buildings for residence and work combined in one unit. For most of the denizens of such spaces, the imposition of a legal distinction between "living" and "working" was illogical and unwarranted. Conversely, to a building official, a code that allows living and working to occur in the same "common atmosphere" flies in the face of a safety tenet of all model codes, which is that "occupancies" must be separated from each other with fire-rated assemblies (walls or floor/ceilings), according to the hazard that the work use might present to that unit's residents.

For many building officials looking at live-work, the questions have been "How do I combine B (business) and R (residential) occupancies?" and "Do I use one set of requirements in the work space and one for the living portion?" The result has generally been a hybrid occupancy type, which has recently found its way into an important

model code. In 2009, the International Building Code (IBC) caught up with this enigma and included Section 419, "Live/Work Units," which will be discussed in this chapter and in Appendix B.

Until very recently, the standard live-work loft configuration familiar to most, live-with, was either illegal or the result of extensive negotiations among citizens, developers, or architects and the local building department. The regulations adopted might have been a code bulletin, an adopted live-work building code ordinance, or simply a helpful interpretation on the part of the building official. California, for example, enacted a law in 1980 that specifically empowered local jurisdictions to relax building regulations to make it possible for commercial and industrial buildings to be converted to "joint living and work quarters." Even the terminology varies from city to city. An important function of this book is to introduce a standard set of terms into common parlance, thus allowing a developer in Memphis to converse with an architect in Oakland. As noted, this task was made easier in 2009 as a result of the addition of Section 419 (see Figure 7-1), "Live/Work Units." (Unfortunately, International Codes Council, the author of the code, links *live* and *work* with a slash [/], contrary to the convention established in this book of using a hyphen.)

This chapter consists primarily of detailed, pragmatic discussions of numerous building code issues and how they

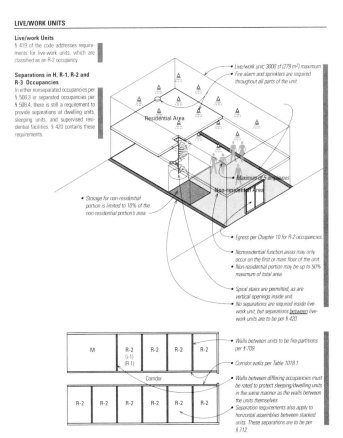

Figure 7-1 Section 419 of the 2009 International Building Code, "Live/Work Units," the first use of the term in a model building code; as a modified R-2 occupancy, live-with units are permitted up to 3,000 square feet and must be sprinklered, only have work use on the lowest floor, and allow up to five nonresident employees.
Source: Francis D.K. Ching and Stephen R. Winkel, *Building Codes Illustrated.* Hoboken, NJ: John Wiley & Sons, 2011, p. 44.

specifically apply to live-work, summarized at the end of the chapter by an annotated chart.

Disclaimer: The information contained in this chapter and throughout the book should not be construed as professional advice that can be applied verbatim, especially in the case of live-work at this point in history. Each project presents unique sets of problems and challenges that are best met with the assistance of architects and other professionals who have had experience in the field of live-work. Nevertheless, the author hopes that this distillation of his twenty-five years of experience with live-work codes will prove useful.

Right out of the gate, live-work is suspect in the eyes of building officials as a hybrid composed of two occupancies: residential and commercial. The more intense, hazardous, or heavy the work uses are, the more uncomfortable they become with the proximity inherent in live-work of almost all kinds. That said, home occupation is typically not a problem building code-wise because the entire unit or house is considered a residential occupancy. However, welding,

woodworking making use of floor-mounted tools, and glassblowing are all considered hazardous occupancies and typically would be permitted only as work-live in a live-nearby or live-near proximity arrangement (i.e., the work space located in a separate building from the residence or separated by a three-hour fire-rated assembly). Between these two extremes resides the majority of live-work types, such as the urban loft and New Urbanist flexhouse.

The results of a building code analysis are the shape, height, area, and other important attributes of the building one intends to build. A code analysis, such as the one described, should be performed early in the design process. There are of course, many other elements in the design of a code-compliant building, including structural design. One needs to keep the rain out, to make the building energy efficient, and to make it a place where the occupants are comfortable in all ways. Many such issues are addressed in this chapter and others within this book.

Tip
Most building departments are willing to review designs at an early stage, a valuable service that can save money now and headaches down the road (i.e., during actual plan check when drawings are far more developed). Availing oneself of such early reviews is highly recommended.

Overall Building Life Safety

What follows is organized to address three sets of code topics:

1. Overall building life safety (i.e., issues that typically apply to a live-work building that is comprised of multiple units)
2. Codes that apply within live-work units
3. Code issues parsed by project type

Occupancy and Occupant Load Factor

Model codes make assumptions about the number of people who might reasonably occupy a building. Occupant load factor expresses the number of square feet that each person might typically occupy. As noted in the Building Code Primer (p.169) the calculation of occupant load is essential to determining exiting and other important life safety considerations within a building. Paradoxically, with one notable exception (assembly occupancy), occupant load is not about how many people are actually permitted to occupy a building but about how many people its exiting and other systems can accommodate. Similar to the example in the primer, live/work—

Building Code Primer

Model building codes, which are usually amended locally, set forth a method of designing buildings and ensuring that they are code compliant. A brief summary of the process of taking a design through a building code check follows. Further study of the applicable code in your area, which will likely contain local and possibly state amendments to the model code on which they are based, will flesh out the details of this primer. At this time, jurisdictions within all fifty states and the District of Columbia have adopted the International Building Code.[1]

First, one needs to determine the *occupancy*, or use, of the building. A building can have multiple occupancies, which must be separated from one another by a fire-rated assembly called an "occupancy separation," according to a table in the code. Most codes specify that residential and commercial occupancies require an occupancy separation rated at one hour, meaning a wall or floor/ceiling between them that would take one hour to burn through in the event of a fire (see Table 7-1).

Table 7-1 2009 IBC Table 508.4. Required Separation of Occupancies

OCCUPANCY	A^d,E		I-4, R-2.1		I-2, I-2.1		I-3		R-1, R-2, R-3, R-3.1, R-4		F-2, S-2^b, U		B, F-1^g, M, S-1		L		H-1		H-2		H-3, H-4, H-5	
	S	NS	S	NS	S	NS	S	NS	S	NS	S	NS	S	NS	S	NS	S	NS	S	NS	S	NS
A^d,E	N	N	2	2	2	NP	2	NP	1	2	N	1	1	2	2	NP	NP	NP	3	4	2	3^a
I-4, R-2.1	—	—	1^e	NP	2	NP	2	NP	1	NP	2	2	2^f	2	2	NP	NP	NP	4	NP	4	NP
I-2, I-2.1	—	—	—	—	N	NP	2	NP	2	NP	2	NP	2^f	NP	2	NP	NP	NP	4	NP	4	NP
I-3	—	—	—	—	—	—	N	NP	2	NP	2	2	2	2	2	NP	NP	NP	4	NP	4	NP
R-1, R-2, R-3, R-3.1, R-4									N	N	1^c	2^c	1	2	4	NP	NP	NP	3	NP	2	NP
F-2, S-2^b, U	—	—	—	—	—	—	—	—	N	N	1	2	1	NP	NP	NP	3	4	2	3^a		
B, F-1^g, M, S-1	—	—	—	—	—	—	—	—	—	—	N	N	1	NP	NP	NP	2	3	1	2^a		
L													1	NP	NP	NP	2	NP	1	NP		
H-1	—	—	—	—	—	—	—	—	—	—	—	—	N	NP	NP	NP	NP	NP				
H-2	—	—	—	—	—	—	—	—	—	—	—	—	—	—	N	NP	1	NP				
H-3, H-4, H-5	—	—	—	—	—	—	—	—	—	—	—	—	—	—	—	—	1^e,f	NP				

Source: International Codes Council, *2009 International Building Code.*

However, live-work is often treated as a single *occupancy* under specific code provisions: either IBC Paragraph 419 or local variations. Once the occupancy of the building is determined, one needs to calculate the floor area of each occupancy, to which the building code assigns an *occupant load factor*, which is tabulated to determine the building's total occupant load, a number that affects exiting and other life safety factors. Multifamily residential, for example, has an occupant load factor of two hundred; if, for example, the total area is nine thousand square feet, then the occupant load is forty-five.

One then proceeds to calculate the allowable height (in feet or meters), number of stories, and basic allowable area of the building. There is typically a table in the code that lists occupancies, construction types, height, and allowable area. (See Table 7-2.)

One then scans across to find the basic allowable area depending on the *construction type*, which is normally expressed as a Roman numeral from I to V. Type I is all concrete and noncombustible construction, and Type V is anything allowed under the building code, which usually means wood frame. Most construction types are expressed as either one-hour (A) or nonrated (B), denoting whether they must be built entirely of fire-rated construction or not. Again using the example of multifamily residential (live-work comes later), the maximum

(Continued)

Table 7-2 2009 IBC Table 503, Allowable Building Heights and Areas

GROUP		TYPE I A	TYPE I B	TYPE II A	TYPE II B	TYPE III A	TYPE III B	TYPE IV HT	TYPE V A	TYPE V B
HEIGHT (feet)		UL	160	65	55	65	55	65	50	40
		STORIES(S) AREA(A)								
A-1	S	UL	5	3	2	3	2	3	2	1
	A	UL	UL	15,500	8,500	14,000	8,500	15,000	11,5000	5,500
A-2	S	UL	11	3	2	3	2	3	2	1
	A	UL	UL	15,500	9,500	14,000	9,500	15,000	11,5000	6,000
A-3	S	UL	11	3	2	3	2	3	2	1
	A	UL	UL	15,500	9,500	14,000	9,500	15,000	11,5000	6,000
A-4	S	UL	11	3	2	3	2	3	2	1
	A	UL	UL	15,500	9,500	14,000	9,500	15,000	11,5000	6,000
A-5	S	UL	UL	UL	UL	UL	UL	UL	UL	UL
	A	UL	UL	UL	UL	UL	UL	UL	UL	UL
B	S	UL	11	5	3	5	3	5	3	2
	A	UL	UL	37,500	23,000	28,500	19,000	36,000	18,000	9,000
E	S	UL	5	3	2	3	2	3	1	1
	A	UL	UL	26,000	14,500	23,500	14,500	25,500	18,500	9,500
F-1	S	UL	11	4	2	3	2	4	2	1
	A	UL	UL	25,000	15,500	19,000	12,000	33,500	14,000	8,500
F-2	S	UL	11	5	3	4	3	5	3	2
	A	UL	UL	37,500	23,000	28,500	18,000	50,500	21,000	13,000
H-1	S	1	1	1	1	1	1	1	1	NP
	A	21,000	16,500	11,000	7,000	9,500	7,000	10,500	7,500	NP
H-2[d]	S	20	3	2	1	2	1	2	1	1
	A	21,000	16,500	11,000	7,000	9,500	7,000	10,500	7,500	3,000
H-3[d]	S	20	6	4	2	4	2	4	2	1
	A	UL	60,000	26,500	14,000	17,500	13,000	25,500	10,000	5,000
H-4	S	20	7	5	3	5	3	5	3	2
	A	UL	UL	37,500	17,500	28,500	17,500	36,000	18,000	6,500
H-5	S	4	4	3	3	3	3	3	3	2
	A	UL	UL	37,500	23,000	28,500	19,000	36,000	18,000	9,000
I-2/ I-2.1[f]	S	UL	4	2	1	1	NP	1	1	NP
	A	UL	UL	15,000	11,000	12,000	NP	12,000	9,500	NP
I-3[e]	S	UL	2	NP	NP	NP	NP	NP	NP	NP
	A	UL	15,100	NP	NP	NP	NP	NP	NP	NP
I-4	S	UL	5	3	2	3	2	3	1	1
	A	UL	60,500	26,500	13,000	23,500	13,000	25,500	18,500	9,000
L	S	20	6	5	3	5	3	5	3	2
	A	UL	60,000	37,500	17,500	28,500	17,500	36,000	18,000	6,500
M	S	UL	11	4	2	4	2	4	3	1
	A	UL	UL	21,500	12,500	18,500	12,500	20,500	14,000	9,000
R-1	S	UL	11	4	4	4	4	4	3	2
	A	UL	UL	24,000	16,000	24,000	16,000	20,500	12,000	7,000
R-2	S	UL	11	4	4	4	4	4	3	2
	A	UL	UL	24,000	16,000	24,000	16,000	20,500	12,000	7,000

Table 7-2 Continued

R-2.1	S	UL	6^h	3^g	NP	3^g	NP	NP	3^g	NP
	A	UL	55,000	19,000	NP	19,000	NP	NP	10,500	NP
R-3/R-3.1	S	UL	11	4	4	4	4	4	3	3
	A	UL	UL	UL	UL	UL	UL	UL	UL	UL
R-4	S	UL	11^h	4^g	4^i	4^g	4^i	4^i	3^g	2^i
	A	UL	UL	24,000	16,000	24,000	16,000	20,500	12,000	7,000
S-1	S	UL	11	4	2	3	2	4	3	1
	A	UL	48,000	26,000	17,500	26,000	17,500	25,500	14,000	9,000
S-2^{b,c}	S	UL	11	5	3	4	3	5	4	2
	A	UL	79,000	39,000	26,000	39,000	26,000	38,500	21,000	13,500
U^c	S	UL	5	4	2	3	2	4	2	1
	A	UL	35,500	19,000	8,500	14,000	8,500	18,000	9,000	5,500

Source: International Codes Council, *2009 International Building Code.*

For SI: 1 foot = 304.8 mm, 1 square foot = 0.0929 m^2.
A = building area per story, S = stories above grade plane, UL = Unlimited, NP = Not permitted.
a. See the following sections for general exceptions to Table 503:
    1.   Section 504.2, Allowable building height and story increase due to automatic sprinkler system installation.
    2.   Section 506.2, Allowable building area increase due to street frontage.
    3.   Section 506.3, Allowable building area increase due to automatic sprinkler system installation.
    4.   Section 507, Unlimited area buildings.
b. For open parking structures, see Section 406.3.
c. For private garages, see Section 406.1.
d. See Section 415.5 for limitations.
e. [SFM] See Section 408.1.1 for specific exceptions for one-story Type IIA, Type IIIA or Type VA construction.
f. *Restraint shall not be permitted in any building except in Group I-3 occupancies for such use (see Section 408.1.2).*
g. *Nonambulatory persons shall be limited to the first two stories.*
h. *Nonambulatory persons shall be limited to the first five stories.*
i. *Nonambulatory elderly clients are not permitted in buildings of these types of construction. See Sections 425.3. and 425.3.4.*

basic allowable area of a Type V-A one-hour-rated building is 10,500-square feet, and the maximum height is 50 feet and three stories.

There are exceptions to the table that prove quite useful. A multistory building can automatically double its *allowable area*; providing an automatic sprinkler system likewise allows a further doubling of the allowable area. If one finds that the building is still over its allowable area, an *area-separation* wall can be inserted. Such a wall must extend from the foundation to the roof without horizontal jogs, and it renders each side a separate building for most purposes, including allowable area. Height in feet (or meters) is normally not a malleable number; however, an additional story can be added when sprinklering a building under certain circumstances, as long as it remains within the measured height of the building in feet (or meters).

Once the occupancy, occupant load, construction type, and allowable area, height, and number of stories are determined, then one must look at the building's location on the property. If a building is too close to an interior lot line (not a street front), its walls may need to be of a certain construction type or fire rating and, more important, openings

(i.e., windows) may not be permitted. Under the 2009 IBC, a set of formulas and tables determines the allowable area of openings and the distance they must be from a property line shared with another private property.

Each occupancy has particular requirements that are spelled out in the IBC. Residential occupancies, for example, require all bedrooms to have an *emergency escape and rescue opening* that is large enough for a firefighter with an oxygen pack to enter and rescue a resident. Live-work exceptions to this rule are covered later in this chapter.

Exiting requirements are one of the most important life safety features of any building code, and compliance with them is essential to a properly designed building. In general, with the exception of a single-family house or townhouse, two means of egress must be provided out of all buildings. In multifamily housing, an occupant load of over ten on a second story means that two means of egress are required off that floor (i.e., two independent stairs, each of which must maintain its fire-rated status all the way out to the street). In the case of exit paths serving occupant loads over fifty, all required exit doors must swing in the direction of travel.

designated R-2 in IBC paragraph 419—is usually assigned an occupant load factor of two hundred 200, which means that a live-work building with six thousand square feet would have an occupant load of thirty (6,000/200 = 30). In situations where there is a large work space and a relatively small residential portion, usually a work-live unit, it is reasonable when writing live-work code to set the occupant load factor higher, to three hundred. In such case, the same six-thousand-square-foot have an occupant load of twenty (6,000/300 = 20).

As noted in the primer, model codes generally require two *means of egress* when there are more than ten occupants on a floor above- or below-ground level. Assuming that the occupant load factors are two hundred for live-work and three hundred for work-live or fee-simple townhouses, any live-work building that contains more than two units whose upper floors or basement are over two thousand square feet—including corridors and other common space in addition to units—will require two ways off that floor and out to a public way. Likewise for a work/live building (if its occupant load factor is set at three hundred), a second floor or a basement with three thousand square feet or more will require two means of egress.

Progressing to individual units, this means that a two-thousand-square-foot live-work unit would require two exits out of that individual unit (see Figure 7-2).

In many typical live-work building layouts, especially warehouse conversions, achieving two doors out of a unit—which must be at least one-half of the longest diagonal of the

unit apart (one-third in sprinklered buildings)—can be difficult. However, most live-work units on one floor are less than two thousand square feet. Work/live units tend to be larger. The proposed higher occupant load factor of three hundred assumes that roughly the same number of people or fewer will be living and working in a work-live unit, even though it might be larger due to its more spacious work portion, but that the hazard to the occupants is less per square foot than in a more compact live/work unit. Therefore, a work/live unit with an area under three thousand square feet would be permitted to have only one exit from the unit itself. As will be discussed later, both live/work and work/live units are limited in the amounts of hazardous materials and processes they can contain.

Live-work buildings that include clear separations between living and working portions of either an individual unit or between working and living activities in an entire building are considered mixed-occupancy buildings. Different occupancies typically must be separated from each other by fire-rated assemblies, according to a table found in the code (see Table 7-1). An example, treated under "Separation within a Unit," (p. 184) would be a live-work townhouse that has a fire-rated floor/ceiling between the downstairs retail space and the upstairs residence. Another example requiring an occupancy separation might be a common work space that allows individual units to be smaller, even residential-only.

Some artists and craftspeople, for example, do work such as metal sculpture, which employs welding; woodworking, which uses fixed appliances (saws, drill presses, planers); or fire arts. These work activities would all fall under "hazardous occupancy." The typical separation between hazardous occupancy and residence is a three-hour-rated assembly, which would constitute a fully grouted *CMU* (concrete block) wall or a concrete floor/ceiling. However, at least one city—Oakland, California—permits limited activities and storage of materials, both classified as hazardous occupancy, to occur within a live-with unit (i.e., in the same "common atmosphere" as the residence). This code relaxation is covered in more detail below.

Assembly occupancy is defined as a place where people assemble for dining, entertainment, meetings, or worship where fifty or more people are permitted. One often sees signs in restaurants or other smaller places of assembly stating "maximum room occupancy forty-nine people." This is because assembly, a very heavily regulated occupancy, only begins at fifty occupants. The occupant load factor found in the IBC for the most common forms of assembly without

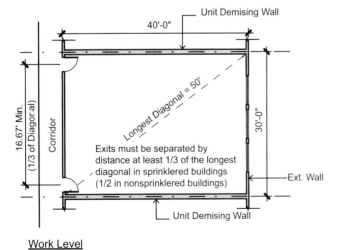

Work Level

Figure 7-2 Two independent means of egress are required out of a unit over two thousand square feet, and they must be separated by a distance equal to or exceeding one-third of the longest diagonal of the unit.

fixed seating is fifteen. That number times fifty results in 750 square feet being the largest gathering area that can occur before assembly kicks in (750/15 = 50), with strict exiting, signage, and other requirements. As with hazardous occupancy, but this time due to the hazard *to* the occupants in an assembly occupancy rather than the hazard posed *by* the work activity, it means that no live-work code of which this author is aware permits activities classified as assembly occupancy to occur within a live-with unit (i.e., in the same common atmosphere as the residence). Model codes typically require a one-hour occupancy separation between residential and assembly occupancies, and the same is true in most live-work codes.

Construction Type, Height, and Allowable Area

The building code establishes basic fire and life safety by limiting the size of buildings that are permitted to be constructed of any material. The larger and taller the building, the more stringent are the construction type requirements, fire protection requirements, exiting requirements, and other life safety requirements. Live-work project types have typically—but not always—fallen into five categories:

1. New construction live-with townhouses

2. New construction flexhouses

3. Home occupation (i.e., live-work in a residence)

4. New two- to five-story urban infill buildings (sometimes high-rise)

5. Warehouse renovations for live-work, often in brick, concrete, or heavy timber structures

The first of these five categories poses very little in the way of problems. In fact, a designer of live-work townhouses or flexhouses may never need to consult the code to ascertain allowable construction type, height, and area. However, townhouse or multilevel live-work where the living and work portions are not separated is treated specifically in section 419 of the IBC. A townhouse is typically considered a separate building under the code, particularly if it is:

- Mapped as a separate fee-simple property

- Built with separated, rather than party, walls with airspace in between

- Built with masonry or concrete party walls with a high fire rating (four hours is typical)

In such cases, the residential portion of the model codes (e.g., International Residential Code [IRC], if adopted locally) would apply as in a single-family house, with all-important new live-work provisions as applicable. The IRC does include live-work as an exception to paragraph 101.2., which is a general description of one- and two-family dwellings, stating:

> **Exception:** Live/work units complying with the requirements of Section 419 of the International Building Code shall be permitted to be built as one- and two-family dwellings or townhouses. Fire suppression required by Section 419.5 of the International Building Code when constructed under the International Residential Code for One- and Two-family Dwellings shall conform to Section 903.3.1.3 of the International Building Code.[3]

Higher-density urban infill live-work requires careful attention to construction type, height, and allowable area. A typical project of this kind might consist of a concrete parking garage, whose roof forms a "podium" on which wood frame or other construction types are built. Important code-determined maximum allowable heights to keep in mind (under the 2009 IBC) are:

- For Type V wood-frame construction, four stories over the podium (when sprinklered) and a total maximum height from grade of sixty feet (see Figure 7-3)

- For Type III wood-frame construction, five stories of wood frame and a total height from grade of sixty-five feet

- For concrete or steel and concrete construction, just under seventy-five feet is an important maximum height because, above that, a building is considered a high rise, triggering expensive life safety measures

Allowable area typically comes up as an issue in specific instances in live-work, not unlike in housing. When the allowable area of a building exceeds that allowed by the code, even with the permissible increases for multiple stories, sprinklers, and location on property, one can elect to insert an *area-separation wall* into the building. Such a wall must extend from foundation to roof without horizontal jogs, often requires a parapet at the roof, and must be rated at two or four hours depending on the situation. An area-separation wall creates two separate buildings, each of which on its own can be calculated for allowable area. Thus a project can be brought into compliance with allowable area requirements through the use of area-separation walls.

A useful code exception for area-separation walls occurs when a residential or live-work occupancy is built over a

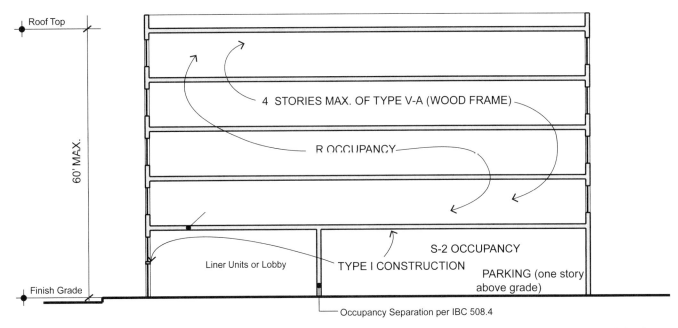

Roof Top

60' MAX.

4 STORIES MAX. OF TYPE V-A (WOOD FRAME)

R OCCUPANCY

Liner Units or Lobby

S-2 OCCUPANCY

TYPE I CONSTRUCTION

PARKING (one story above grade)

Finish Grade

Occupancy Separation per IBC 508.4

Figure 7-3 An illustration of the IBC provision (509.4) that allows four stories of wood frame over podium to an allowable height of sixty feet from grade.

ground-floor or basement concrete parking garage that is Type I construction (i.e., noncombustible, usually concrete construction). In that case, the horizontal podium atop the parking can act as an area separation as long as the Type I construction garage includes only a lobby, retail, mechanical rooms, and other occupancies listed in IBC section 509.4. This exception to the building code requirement that area-separation walls extend upward without horizontal jogs is often useful for two reasons:

1. It allows the construction above the podium to be considered a separate building, and, for the purpose of allowable stories, the podium is considered to be grade level. In Type V-A (wood frame) construction under the IBC, four stories would be permitted *above a podium* to a height of sixty feet *above actual grade.*

2. The smaller area of the above-podium portion is often easier to make comply with allowable area. Even if an area-separation wall is needed to achieve the allowable area, it can begin at the top of the podium.

Podium projects typically have significant frontage along one or more streets. Good urban design practice suggests that no part of a parking garage actually front on a street except its entrance, because blank fronts make for empty, unsafe streets that are often devoid of life. The need engendered by this situation offers great opportunities for live-work in the

form of live-with or flexhouse liners (i.e., street-activating spaces that can be immediately occupied upon completion of the building, and may evolve into retail use when the neighborhood is ready for it).

Renovation of former warehouses and similar industrial or commercial buildings into live-work brings many building code issues into play, largely because most jurisdictions consider such a conversion to be a *change of occupancy* or *change of use.* As a result, developing a live-work building in a former warehouse requires—unless local code relaxations rule otherwise—treating the building as if it were new and therefore required to comply with today's codes. The building might have been built when allowable areas for its former occupancy were less stringent, or the building might have been constructed before building codes were adopted, which was usually about 1923 (although it is said Benjamin Franklin originated the idea for building codes in 1735). In the case of any existing warehouse, it is important to perform an initial assessment that includes an analysis of area, height, and allowable area as well as construction type. Again, area-separation walls can play an important role in the process of complying with allowable area limits. However, one must keep in mind that each separate building created by an area separation must have one independent means of egress. Its second exit route is permitted to pass out through the area separation and allow an occupant to proceed to safety along a rated corridor and exit discharge.

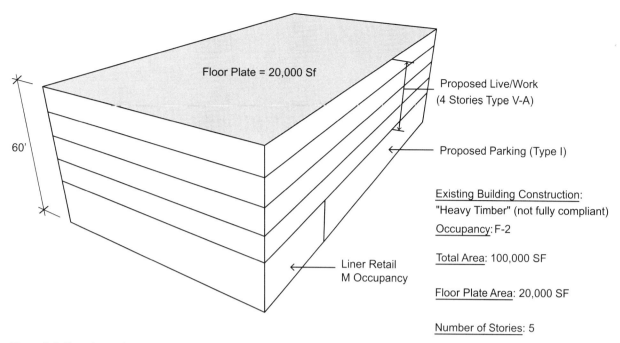

Floor Plate = 20,000 Sf

60'

Proposed Live/Work
(4 Stories Type V-A)

Proposed Parking (Type I)

Existing Building Construction:
"Heavy Timber" (not fully compliant)
Occupancy: F-2

Total Area: 100,000 SF

Floor Plate Area: 20,000 SF

Number of Stories: 5

Liner Retail
M Occupancy

Figure 7-4 If you know the code well, it can be your friend: height, number of stories, and allowable area example, depicting four stories of wood frame live-work over liner units and parking.

Height, Number of Stories, and Allowable Area Example

As an example, use an existing sixty-foot-tall, five-story building of 100,000 square feet, say twenty thousand square feet per floor, presently constructed of heavy timber framing and floors, concrete stairwells, and brick exterior walls in Oakland. This is known as heavy timber, or Type IV construction. However, its construction does not meet today's definition of Type IV because the heavy timber definitions have become more stringent over the years. Indoor parking is proposed in a portion of the building set back from the street to allow for liner flexhouse units. The building was formerly used for light industry, an occupancy called F-2. The conversion will create seventy-five work/live units, change to F-7 work-live occupancy (as designated in Oakland, California; IBC section 419 would also work), and contain parking for fifty cars, which is S-2 occupancy.

Looking at Table 503 in the 2009 IBC (see Table 7-2), one sees that an F-2 occupancy, the most similar to F-7 in Type IV construction, allows 21,000 square feet in a single-story building of three stories with a maximum height of sixty-five feet. Under allowable area increases, one can double the square footage for a multistory building and double it again for sprinklers to equal 84,000 square feet. This is not enough without an area-separation wall, which would be one way to deal with an over-area building. Sprinklers allow one to add a single story, bringing it from three to four. However, the building is five stories, one too many.

There is a saying among architects that if you don't know the code, it can be your worst enemy, but if you do know it well, the code can be your best friend. In this case, a variation on the horizontal area separation comes to the rescue (see Figure 7-4).

A conversion to live-work is almost always a change of occupancy, and, as noted, this building does not fully comply with today's heavy timber Type IV requirements. (See Figure 7-5 for a building similar to this example.) However, the building would comply with Type V construction requirements, which are less stringent. If the ground floor contains parking for fifty cars, using the generally accepted space planning figure of 350 square feet per car, that equals 17,500 square feet of S-3 construction. The remaining 2,500 square feet of the building's ground floor can be used for lobby, utilities, circulation, and liner units. (If that's not enough, the Parklift® system[3] [see Figure 7-6] can be employed to save parking area and can also make room for more liner units.)

To achieve this code tour de force, one must make the ground-floor Type I construction (concrete, masonry, and noncombustible framing [i.e., steel studs]). And the second floor must become a podium, which means

Figure 7-5 California Cotton Mills Studios, a building similar to that depicted in the example in Figure 7-4. See case study in Chapter Three. Designed by Thomas Dolan Architecture, 2005.

pouring a minimum of eight inches of concrete to make it a three-hour floor/ceiling assembly. Assuming the project budget can take this expense, the four stores of Type V-A construction above the podium would comply as long as the building's overall height does not exceed sixty feet.

Wall Rating and Openings in Walls near Property Lines

The Great Chicago Fire of 1871 casts a long shadow over the code-writing profession, as do the Triangle Shirtwaist Factory Fire of 1911 and the more recent inferno at a rock

Figure 7-6: The Parklift system allows compression of the parking "kernel" in a building, often resulting in enough space saved to include liner units that enliven the street and hide the parking.

Figure 7-7 Had the industrial windows in this picture been in a portion of the building that was subject to a change of occupancy, they would have been required to be replaced with protected assemblies or removed altogether. This portion remained commercial and was therefore was not subject to change-of-occupancy code upgrades, thereby escaping that regulatory fate. Union Street Studios, 2000. Designed by Thomas Dolan Architecture.

concert in Warwick, Rhode Island. Each disaster pointed up an important principle, and the lessons of any one of them might be applied to live-work. One of the greatest life safety dangers in urban settings is fire spreading from building to building. Codes try to prevent this by requiring that walls must be of fire-resistive construction when they are either on or too close to property lines shared with others (called an interior lot line). Additionally, openings—usually windows— are either prohibited or required to be protected fire-resistive assemblies when they are too close to an interior lot line. An example is in Figure 7-7, where protection was avoided because that part of the building remained commercial and therefore did not undergo a change of occupancy.

Prior to the adoption of the IBC, most model codes determined exterior wall and opening protection using a table that cross-referenced occupancy, construction type, and distance to property line. The application of these code provisions has the effect of creating setbacks from property lines for many building types, including residential and live-work. Under the IBC, multi-unit live-work in Type V-A construction (most is R-2 occupancy, according to paragraph 419) is required to conform to a formula to arrive at the number of allowable openings and their distance from an interior lot line. While one must perform the actual calculations, typically any wall closer than three feet to the line is required to be one-hour rated and have no openings, and any wall farther than five feet or the property line is permitted to have 25 percent of each floor's wall area in unprotected openings (IBC 705.8).

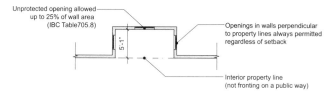

Figure 7-8 Insets in interior lot line walls are often used to accommodate openings slightly more than five feet from the line and because a wall perpendicular to a property line can also contain openings.

This code provision bases its measurements perpendicular to the face of the building; however, a wall perpendicular to a property line is permitted to contain openings. This is why one so often sees insets (see Figure 7-8) near property lines in urban buildings. These exist to allow for openings on both walls perpendicular to the line and to provide the legal distance that allows openings.

Exits/Means of Egress

The manner in which one exits a building, both in normal times and in an emergency, and whether one can both enter and exit in a wheelchair, are some of the most critical elements of the building code. Live-work poses specific exiting issues. For example, sometimes one needs to pass through the work space in order to exit the live portion. Depending on the work activity, such an exit discharge may or may not be suitable. In the design of a typical flexhouse, the downstairs work portion has direct access to the street, and the resi-

dence is entered via a door and stairway that does not pass through the ground floor work space.

Most building codes view live-work as equivalent to residential for purposes of exiting, factoring in occupant load and unit types. For example, a live-with unit that is on a single story (with or without a mezzanine) would require only one exit out of the unit itself as long as the occupant load is less than ten. Therefore, in live-work—assuming its occupant load factor is two hundred—any unit under two thousand square feet would need one exit, and any unit two thousand square feet or greater would require two exits.

As noted in the primer, all stories with an occupant load of ten or more that are not at grade (e.g., second stories and above or basement) require two fire-rated means of egress off that floor and continuing all the way out to a public way.

When two exits are provided, from a unit, a floor, or a building, it stands to reason that if the exits are right next to each other, the added safety that the second exit provides—meaning that if one is blocked, a person can go to the other—is not effective. Imagine a fire in a building adjacent to one of the exits. If the other exit is very close, it might also be blocked. Therefore, the IBC requires that the two means of egress must be separated by at least half (one-third in a sprinklered building) of the longest diagonal measurement of the unit, floor, or building. This separation must also be continued all the way to where the exit path discharges onto a public way.

The separation is normally measured in a straight line. However, as shown in Figure 7-9, if the separation is

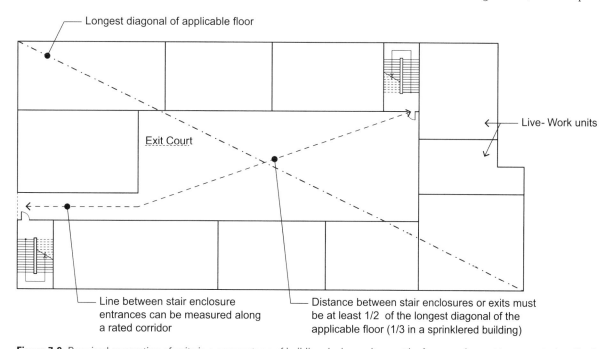

Figure 7-9 Required separation of exits is a cornerstone of building design; exits must be far enough apart to prevent a localized fire or other disaster from being likely to render both exits unusable.

connected by a fire-rated corridor, the measurement can be made along that corridor.

Returning to the specifics of live-work, there are several typical exiting arrangements:

1. Flexhouse live-work, in which the ground floor is work space and a separate entrance is provided at grade for it. The upstairs live portion discharges through a staircase that passes alongside the work space and is separated from it by a rated wall and a rated door. This is essentially mixed occupancy under the building code and can be treated as such (see Figure 2-27, flexhouse drawing).

2. As noted, a live-with unit whose work space is either very large or anticipates use of toxic materials or hazardous processes-meaning that it is work/live–should provide a separate exit from the unit that serves the live portion. Such an arrangement also begs the question: Should such large (in area) or dangerous work uses be allowed in live-with, or should there always be a separation in such a situation (i.e., live-near or live-nearby)?

3. Many types of work activities carried on in live-work units are not hazardous and are compatible with residential activity—this we defined earlier as live/work or home occupation. In such cases, exiting would be governed solely by residential requirements. Live-with is deemed R-2 occupancy under IBC paragraph 419, which is discussed in Appendix B.

Other exiting issues frequently arise in live-work projects:

- All bedrooms or sleeping spaces require an opening that allows a firefighter with an oxygen pack to enter and rescue a resident. Such openings are not technically exits; they provide *emergency escape and rescue* and are treated elsewhere in this chapter.

- When exit stairs proceed down through a building and out to a street, they are called "stair enclosures." Stair enclosures must maintain their fire rated integrity all the way down and out of the building. Openings into them are generally limited to those off exit corridors, and entrances into them from "rooms not normally occupied," such as closets and mechanical rooms, are strictly forbidden. Live-work units, even if they contain separated work space (live-near, not live-nearby, and not mixed occupancy), are generally not considered "rooms not normally occupied." However, this statement is subject to local interpretation. Rooms "not normally occupied" must be separated from a stair enclosure by a fire-rated

vestibule, which is essentially two doors and a small intervening space.

Sprinklers

Modern building codes, and in particular the IBC, rely on an *automatic fire extinguishing system*, generally called sprinklers, to provide a high degree of protection in the event of fire. Such requirements extend to almost all live-work buildings constructed today, including—as of 2011—single-family residences. Many cities also mandate that one must sprinkler any building above a maximum size. In Oakland, California, that number is 3,600 square feet.

Regarding renovation of an existing building for live-work, because it is normally considered a change of occupancy whether it is granted other code relaxations or not, live-work would almost always require sprinklers. Referring to the maximum just cited, in the case of a change of occupancy that does not exceed 3,600 square feet, variables such as fire flow to hydrants will determine whether sprinklers are required. Another provision in Oakland—based on the discretion of the fire marshal—is to exempt residential additions below five hundred square feet that do not change occupancy, such as an addition to a house. This exemption could possibly apply to a home occupation or to a separate living or work portion of a live-nearby situation.

There are three basic types of sprinkler systems:

1. NFPA-13, the most common form of sprinklers in commercial buildings. All piping is metal, a dedicated water meter must be employed (an expensive proposition), and typically a telephone line is set up to call the fire department whenever a head is triggered by heat or fire. NFPA-13 is typically accompanied by a central fire alarm system that alerts all residents in the case of a sprinkler head actuation.

2. NFPA-13R is employed in smaller residential projects. Its requirements for sprinkler head density and locations are less stringent, and much of the piping can be plastic as long as it is concealed, saving large amounts of money. A 13-R system might or might not be set up to initiate an automatic call to the fire department, and—depending on the number of units in a project—it might have a central alarm system.

3. NFPA-13D is employed in single-family residential projects, which are mandatory in new houses as of January 1, 2011. These systems utilize the domestic water supply,

thereby reducing installation costs, and use the domestic water plumbing fixtures to purge the sprinkler pipe, maintaining a drinkable water supply. NFPA-13D requires sprinklers to be installed only in living areas. The standard does not require sprinklers in smaller bathrooms, closets, pantries, garages, or carports; attached open structures; attics; or other concealed nonliving spaces.

Under certain circumstances, the provision of an automatic sprinkler system may permit a building constructed of non-rated material (e.g., exposed wood framing) to be considered a one-hour-rated building. Such a *sprinkler substitution* can be useful because rated buildings are allowed to be larger than nonrated construction, and it also can be a useful rule when a building's size as designed requires one-hour-rated construction. As noted above, under the IBC, the allowable area of a sprinklered building can be doubled over its base allowable area. And an extra story can be built due to sprinklering as long as its height in feet does not exceed that allowed under Table 503 (shown in Table 7-2) or its exceptions (see Figure 7-4).

In live-work, sprinklers are a way to address the building code's assertion that a live-with unit is a *mixed occupancy* that requires a rated separation between living and working spaces. Paragraph 419 in the 2009 IBC addresses this issue head on by requiring sprinklers in all live-with units (i.e., without a fire-rated separation). The one-hour substitution (whether or not it is officially called that) provided by sprinklers can—when accepted by a local building official or included in a local code—obviate the need for an unnecessary separation in live-work renovation. As noted, sprinklers are now required in all new residential construction.

To sprinkler or not is a crucial question to resolve as early as possible when considering a live-work project, especially in a jurisdiction whose building department is encountering live-work for the first time. Often planning and zoning officials will happily sign off on live-work projects only to have the building or fire department invoke occupancy separation and other requirements that make moving ahead with the project difficult.

Tip

One should always assume sprinklers will be required, unless and until advised otherwise by both building and fire officials (in writing).

Sprinklers are a very effective way of putting out fires before they rage out of control. However, installing them is expensive, and some people would argue that such a

requirement merely shifts the burden for firefighting from the fire department to the individual property owner or developer. Small live-work renovations might work without them; larger projects benefit from sprinklers and are almost always required to provide them. Sprinklers provide greater safety and peace of mind, an important benefit. Generally, fire insurance premiums are less for sprinklered buildings, and, given the variety of activities that might be pursued over the life of a live-work building, they do provide an extra measure of peace of mind while proactively anticipating hazards posed by unknown future work activities.

Fire Alarms and Smoke Detectors

Fire alarms and smoke detectors, which are a decentralized form of fire alarm, are further means to ensure that live-work occupants are alerted so they can exit a building in case of fire, smoke, or sprinkler actuation. Section 419 of the 2009 IBC includes a provision requiring that sprinklers and a fire alarm system must be installed when required by other sections of the code (IBC 907.2.9.1, "Manual Fire Alarm Systems").

According to the IBC, multiunit residential and live-work buildings over sixteen units or buildings over two stories typically are required to be equipped with an automatic, centralized fire alarm system that is triggered by:

- The actuation of any individual sprinkler head
- The triggering of any smoke alarm (meaning smoke alarms that are connected with each other so that if one goes off, they all do)
- The pulling of an individual fire alarm box (Think: "In case of fire, break glass.")

In some cases, such as live-work buildings that contain fewer than sixteen units, manual pull boxes that set off a fire alarm in the building are an affordable option, combined with sprinklers. Some but not all pull boxes are set up to automatically notify the local fire department.

Building codes require that in residential units and single-family residences, smoke detectors must to be located in or near all bedrooms and along exit routes. Individual smoke detectors are required to be hardwired to a residence's electrical system in a manner that prevents them from being shut off. In minor building retrofits, they may be battery-powered.

In the case of a building equipped with non-interconnected smoke detectors and pull boxes, the assumption is that when a smoke detector goes off, a resident activates the pull box to sound the general alarm. If the alarm does not automatically call the fire department, someone needs to do that. Combine this scenario with a fire starting in a unit whose occupant is not present, and one can see why interconnected smoke detectors and a pull box that calls the fire department should be considered a prudent minimum arrangement, especially in multiunit live-work projects that might include storage of flammable materials.

Tip

Even if not required by code, in all multiunit live-work projects, install a pull station fire alarm(s) that automatically call the fire department.

Provisions in both building and fire codes specify that, in a multiunit building, any smoke detector that is actuated must be audible to all residents who would be affected by the fire. It is up to the local fire marshal to decide whether to require that all smoke detectors be *interconnected*, but the unpredictable work uses of live-work argues in favor of such a measure.

One other strategy that can reduce the spread of fire in case it occurs is to compartmentalize units beyond that required by code. A one-hour fire-rated assembly—walls or floor/ceilings—is required to separate all units from each other and to separate units from corridors or exit paths. Increasing this protection to two hours, meaning an extra layer of five-eighths-inch Type 'x' gypsum board on each side of the demising and corridor wall is a relatively low-cost solution. (And it improves sound attenuation between units.) The result is a unit that typically can burn for two hours before it breaches its confines and spreads elsewhere in the building. While not fail-safe, this strategy can increase safety significantly. However, a two-hour-rated floor/ceiling assembly in a wood-frame building is not as easily accomplished; adding an extra layer of Sheetrock to a unit ceiling can provide some added protection. A typical two-hour fire-rated floor/ceiling would be constructed of structural concrete or a complex assembly beyond the scope of this book. Townhouse buildings—meaning structures whose units do not share a floor/ceiling—are the best candidates for compartmentalization provided by two-hour-rated walls.

Hazardous Occupancy

The hazards posed by certain work activities and the storage and use of hazardous or flammable materials within a unit are common issues in live-work units. While office and other white-collar uses of live-work units are not a problem in this regard, work activities that are classified under the building code as hazardous occupancy are generally not permitted in a live-with unit (i.e., sharing the same common atmosphere with the residential portion).

Hazardous activities that fall under H occupancy and might occur in a live-work setting include:

- Welding or the use of cutting torches
- The use of open flame in a work activity
- The use of three or more woodworking power tools that are fixed to the floor (e.g., table saw, shaper, planer, lathe)
- Storage of flammable or hazardous materials

In work/live spaces (Open work-use intensity), greater levels of hazardous materials and activities are sometimes permitted under controlled circumstances. According to Oakland's live-work building code—as in all jurisdictions where the IBC has been adopted—hazardous occupancies must be separated from live-work occupancies by an occupancy separation (i.e., a fire wall or floor/ceiling). However, in Oakland's live-work building code there are exceptions that allow limited amounts of hazardous materials and processes:

- Open flame may be used for artwork, craftwork, or similar activities provided the quantity of compressed gas or flammable liquid stored within an individual work-live occupancy complies with the limits listed in Table 7-3. The table sets forth the maximum amounts of material that can be present either in the unit or within a "control area," which is a fire-rated room specifically built to store flammable and toxic materials in limited amounts.

- Open flame and welding may be permitted within an individual work-live unit if the open flame and welding occur in a unit separated from the remainder of the building or other work-live units in the building pursuant to IBC Table 508.4, which sets out occupancy separation requirements for the appropriate Group H occupancy.

In other words, unless one uses or stores very small quantities of hazardous or flammable materials, the activities must be separated from any other live-with unit or the remainder of the building by a three-hour fire-rated wall or floor/ceiling. When it comes to separating the hazardous work occupancy from the residential portion of a unit, which is not required but highly recommended, a three-hour separation would be required. This means a concrete or concrete block wall, a wood frame, or a steel stud wall

Table 7-3. Criteria for Defining Limits on Use, Storage, and Quantities of Hazardous Materials Permitted in Individual Live-With Proximity Type Live-Work Units.*

Work-Use Intensity	Live/Work (renovation or new)	Work/Live (renovation or new)
(a) Flammable liquids		
Class I-A	Prohibited	10 gallons per control area*
Class I-B or C	1 gallon per unit	15 gallons per control area*
Class II	5 gallons per unit	30 gallons per control area*
Combined (all classes)	5 gallons per unit	N/A
Combined (I-A, B, and C)	Prohibited	10 gallons per control area
(b) Compressed gas		
Flammable	2 1-quart containers per unit	An amount equal to or greater than what is shown to the left but is also permitted in a B or F-2 occupancy
Corrosives	1 gallon per unit	An amount equal to or greater than what is shown to the left but is also permitted in a B or F-2 occupancy
Others	Prohibited	An amount equal to what is permitted in a B or F-2 occupancy
(c) Corrosives and toxics	10 gallons per unit, includes quantities from (a) and (b) above	An amount equal to or greater than what is shown to the left but is also permitted in a B or F-2 occupancy
(d) Additional quantities of (a), (b), and (c) permitted in approved control areas*	Permitted	An amount equal to or greater than what is shown to the left but is permitted in a B or F-2 occupancy
(e) Woodworking		
Fewer than three appliances with dust collectors	Permitted	Permitted
More than three appliances with dust collectors	Prohibited	Prohibited
(f) Others	Prohibited	An amount equal to or greater than what is shown to the left but is permitted in a B or F-2 occupancy per control area**

Source: Oakland Live-Work Building Code Table 349B-A, 2010.

* All quantities of hazardous materials in live-work units are subject to review by the local fire marshal. This table serves as a general guideline.

** A control area is a fire-rated storage compartment for hazardous or flammable materials.

with three layers of five-eighths-inch Type 'x' Sheetrock on both sides, or a minimum eight-inch-thick concrete floor/ceiling.

Tip

If any use of open flame is anticipated within a unit, either make that unit a live-near proximity type and/or provide a common work space—indoors (noncombustible construction) or outdoors—where such work can be pursued. Fire arts have no place within a live-with space.

For practical purposes, open flame and welding should either be done outdoors or, if indoors, on a noncombustible floor in a noncombustible space. Ideally there should be a separation between the living and working portions of a work/live unit where welding and open flame occur, but the Oakland exceptions exist to allow artists and others who cannot afford such a separation to do their work within the same common atmosphere.

Lateral Forces, Seismic Standards, and Change of Occupancy

While a building must stand up on a quiet day, and most of the forces that act on it are the result of gravity—its own weight plus the weight of people and things in it—earthquakes, high winds, hurricanes and tornadoes, and even tsunamis can exert forces from various angles in ways that would tend to collapse or tear apart a building that was not designed to withstand such forces. Any new building constructed today must meet lateral resistance standards to remain standing in a catastrophic event to the point where loss of life is unlikely. All parts of the United States and most areas governed by model codes are assigned an earthquake zone designation. Much of the "ring of fire" that girds the Pacific Ocean is in a high-risk zone. Large earthquakes, such as those that have occurred in China, Chile, New Zealand, and off the coast of Japan in the last few years (see Figure 7-10) are relatively common.

Figure 7-10 Earthquake damage can cause injuries, loss of life, and huge dislocation and disruption where they occur. Experience has shown that in places where rigorous seismic codes have been enacted, earthquake damage is significantly lessened in buildings that were built or retrofitted to those standards.

Typical examples of lateral-resistance features in buildings include shear walls—sometimes augmented by hold-down hardware, depending on the aspect ratio of the shear walls—heavy foundation elements called grade beams with a dense array of of reinforcing steel in them, floor and roof diaphragms, and hardware to prevent roofs blowing off, such as hurricane ties. All new buildings must meet lateral load-resisting requirements based on their location.

Illegal live-work is usually not truly unsafe, although it often has significant code issues. The exception to this statement is in buildings that have little or no lateral bracing or shear wall systems and are therefore extremely vulnerable to a large earthquake. Live-work in renovated older warehouses in a city like San Francisco or Oakland, particularly if it is constructed of unreinforced masonry or—still worse—hollow clay tile, could be the scene of major injuries or loss of life as a result of a significant seismic event.

The impetus for early live-work building codes, initially pushed by artists and arts groups but quickly seized on by developers, was the reuse of long-vacant industrial buildings coming out of the rust belt era when Germany and Japan were leaving American industry in the dust (or rust). In a rush to allow artists and others to live in these buildings made redundant by economic and technological changes, the two most expensive items in a live-work renovation—sprinklers and seismic retrofit—were perhaps not considered as seriously as they might have been. Fortunately, no catastrophic fires or earthquakes have hit notable live-work projects—yet.

Tip
In earthquake and hurricane country, if lateral resistance requirements are not imposed by local codes, provide a prudent level of protection to live-work users, keeping in mind that they will be sleeping there.

In 1980, the state of California passed SB 812, which was specifically written to provide artists with "joint living and working quarters in buildings originally designed and constructed for commercial or industrial use." The law went on to specifically mandate that local jurisdictions may relax provisions of their local building code to facilitate such conversions. It did not specify how codes were to be relaxed or to what extent they could be relaxed. The general nature of SB 812 is partly responsible for the fact that each city in California has chosen to reinvent the wheel when it comes to live-work codes. The same is true in virtually every jurisdiction that has done so throughout North America. The publication of this book is intended to encourage and facilitate more standardized codes for live-work.

The conversion of a warehouse to live-work is normally considered a change of occupancy. As noted, such a designation means that the entire building must be brought up to current building codes, including life safety, lateral force, and other standards. The case of live-work presents a quandary for building officials, as discussed earlier. Because live-work is a hybrid of residential and commercial occupancies, in many cases within a building that does not contain occupancy separations, the question arises: Is a conversion of a commercial or industrial building to live-work truly a change of occupancy?

A basic provision in building codes states that if only a small portion of a building changes its occupancy, the entire building is not subject to change of occupancy provisions—to require such would be onerous and counterintuitive. In Oakland, the live-work code prescribes that live-work units' live portions must not exceed 33 percent, thereby preserving their designation as buildings that continue to be primarily commercial. Following this line of reasoning, if a very small portion of the building is really being changed to something else (i.e., the residential portions of each unit), the majority of the building remains commercial. Oakland's live-work building code incorporates this concept, stating that if not more than 10 percent of the area of the building or of any individual story is devoted to the aggregate residential portions of live-work units, then—for seismic purposes only—a change of occupancy has not occurred.

However, under this 10 percent rule:

- The designer must certify that the building "has not been declared an unsafe structure."

- If the building is an unreinforced masonry structure or contains a *soft story*, it is subject to the city's underlying requirements for all such structures.

Oakland has also taken a sensible approach to live-work conversions that do not meet the 10 percent exception, consistent with SB 812's mandate to relax code. In such cases, a live-work conversion is considered a change of occupancy in all respects, except that the seismic retrofit requirements are relaxed to 75 percent of what would be required in a new building.

Floor Loads

Many types of work activities occur in live-work, and such work uses will likely change over time. Yet residence is likely to be a constant in the unit. Determining the appropriate floor-loading standards in live-work is therefore a matter of making an educated guess as to the likely range of work activities that will go on. Until now, most live-work conversions have occurred in buildings that were originally designed for heavier types of work activities than go on once they are converted to live-work. Former warehouses, printing companies, factories, and cold storage buildings are generally overbuilt for the vertical floor loading they will encounter as live-work. Paragraph 419 in the 2009 IBC specifies that floor loading shall be designed based on the *function* within the space.

An important factor that determines whether a building will encounter the movement of large and heavy objects in and out is the building's provision of a loading dock, freight elevator, or grade-level units. It stands to reason that if one can drive a forklift into a unit, it is quite possible that exactly that will happen at some point. Therefore, well-thought-out live-work codes require that new buildings and conversions with level-in access and slab-on-grade floors be required to meet higher floor-loading standards.

Forty pounds per square foot is the typical floor-loading requirement in residential construction, where one expects little work activity to go on. The floor loading is typically fifty pounds per square foot in a live-with space where work activity might go on anywhere. In new townhouse live-work, the downstairs portion has a concrete slab floor that is relatively easy to rate at seventy-five pounds per square foot; upstairs, assuming there is no freight elevator, residential floor load-

ing would typically apply. Any floor accessed by an existing freight elevator is likely to already have the capacity for heavy floor loads.

Codes That Apply within Live-Work Units

Fire Separation within a Unit

Every plan checker and building official is trained to see occupancy separations as a primary means of achieving basic life safety. The perception that live-work is a mixed occupancy has historically been the greatest building code challenge faced by designers and regulators alike. In the author's experience, the best way to resolve this issue is to create one or more new occupancy designations. Fortunately, some model codes have recently added live-work to existing occupancy classifications, imposing specific life safety conditions. The 2009 IBC, the prevailing model code, included live-work units (Section 419) as a form of R-2 occupancy (see Figure 7-1). Many building officials are not aware of these newly adopted provisions. Section 419 is discussed in detail in Appendix B.

Live-with proximity types—lofts—are one of the most common forms of live-work, especially in renovations of existing commercial buildings. The fundamental principle that drives the appeal of such loft units is the flexibility of use that a large open space allows. While live-with units are clearly places where both residential and work activities are likely to take place, and which must be permitted in order for such spaces to be viable for their intended use, the matter of occupancy separation must be addressed. Fortunately, this issue has been addressed with success in many jurisdictions. Alas, each has written slightly different regulations regarding this and other live-work building code issues, but the general logic is as follows.

A live-with unit contains both working and living spaces within what building officials label a *common atmosphere*. As noted, most building inspectors unfamiliar with live-work simply turn to the table of occupancy separations and find that commercial and residential must be separated, period. Thus commences an educational process often best begun by talking about the kinds of work one might do in a normal residential situation (i.e., home occupation, which most will agree does not require a separation).

One can approach this issue from two directions:

1. *Reduce the hazard level of the work activity and therefore the life safety danger posed to the live portion.* Require that

work activities be those compatible with and normally found in a residential setting, such as home office, white-collar kinds of consultations by appointment only, and art and artisan uses without any use of open flame or toxic materials. These types of requirements usually begin with zoning regulations but also become criteria for a hybrid building code occupancy or a code bulletin. There are many precedents in existence. As noted, the 2009 editions of the International Building Code and the International Residential Code each contain a provision defining and permitting live-with proximity type live-work, specifically addressing the issue of separation. However, IBC 419 does not specify work use other than to prohibit activities classified as *hazardous occupancy.*

2. *Provide a substitution for the one-hour separation.* In a building where sprinklers are not otherwise required, provide them. They will often be accepted as a satisfactory substitute. Or, as an alternate or addition to sprinklers in a multiunit building, compartmentalize units by increasing demising walls to a two-hour assembly. Doing so will add protection by further limiting potential spread of fire from unit to unit. To really ice the cake, add a centralized alarm system tied to interconnected smoke detectors and actuation of the sprinkler heads (if it's not already required).

Both of these approaches assume a desire for a live-work unit contained within one common atmosphere (i.e., a live-with that will allow activities; read occupancies) that go beyond simply living in the space. There are other kinds of live-work units in which living and working portions are separated by either a wall or floor (i.e., live-near). In such cases, if it is feasible to provide a one-hour separation between living and working portions, the result is a mixed occupancy—an arrangement that any building official will understand.

Separation between Units and between Units and a Corridor

Under residential portions of the building code, all units in a multiunit building must be separated from each other and from a rated corridor by a minimum one-hour fire-rated assembly, be it a wall or a floor/ceiling. In live-work, this is particularly important, because work activities can abut adjacent living spaces and thus pose a potential hazard. Unlike pure residential occupancy, the uses that may occur over the life of a live-work unit will no doubt vary and are difficult to predict or enforce. For this reason, the one-hour requirement must be seen as a minimum. As noted, while a

two-hour floor/ceiling is often not easy to construct, adding a layer of Sheetrock on either side of a one-hour wall to make it two-hour rated is a relatively painless task; and it brings other benefits, such as improved sound attenuation.

Doors into a one-hour-rated corridor are normally rated at twenty minutes. If one is providing a two-hour corridor wall, the code-compliant way to maintain that rating is to provide a ninety-minute door.

Emergency Escape and Rescue

According to the very important code provision regarding emergency escape and rescue, all bedrooms must be provided with an opening of a minimum size, width, height, and maximum distance from the floor in order to enable fire personnel wearing full-sized oxygen tanks to enter and rescue occupants. Live-work poses several unique problems that require a flexible approach to emergency escape and rescue.

Many live-work units, particularly in renovated warehouses and commercial loft buildings, consist of a double-loaded corridor surrounded by a core of utility uses: kitchen below and bathroom and sleeping area on a mezzanine above (see Figures 2-24 and 7-11).

Toward the exterior of the building is often a double-height work space, and beyond that is a bank of industrial sash windows. Very often these are the only windows in the unit, other than skylights if the unit is on the highest story. Thus, there is no emergency escape and rescue opening in the bedroom, but often one can easily see from the mezzanine sleeping area to the windows and vice versa. Therefore, the emergency escape and rescue opening is in the same *common atmosphere* as the sleeping area, but not in it. This is by far the most common version of emergency escape and rescue in renovation live-work, and it is almost universally accepted, as described next.

Most jurisdictions have taken the logical route and ruled that as long as there is "visual access" between the sleeping area and the escape window, it need not be in the bedroom. In the case of a mezzanine in the common configuration just described, the mezzanine parapet wall should not be over the code minimum of forty-two inches so the rescuer can see where there might be a person needing help (see Figure 3-18, emergency escape and rescue drawing). While this approach is both innovative and pragmatic, it is also true that precedents exist in the model codes for similar common atmosphere situations, such as A-frames, vacation houses, and so on.

Figure 7-11 The core of a double-loaded corridor building contains the kitchen and bathroom, the mezzanine sleeping area, and all of the plumbing and concentrated floor loads. California Cotton Mills Studios, 2005. Designed by Thomas Dolan Architecture.

A thornier question arises when a building being renovated for live-work has such large floor plates that not all units can be located on exterior walls. Perhaps they derive natural light and ventilation from air shafts, skylights, or landlocked courtyards. In the latter case, a solution similar to that just described may work, but what about the truly landlocked unit? Oakland has taken the position that there can be alternate means of escape and rescue using available exit paths, the most likely being the corridors and stairs that are already required.

As noted, stair enclosures occupy a rarefied status as relates to their protections and their inviolate nature: As a rule, openings are not permitted into stair enclosures except from corridors, and certainly not from "rooms not normally occupied." Extending that kind of protection from the entrance to the building all the way to the door of a landlocked unit provides a significantly enhanced level of safety for an escaping resident or an entering firefighter in the case of a fire. Under this "stair enclosure" alternative means of escape and rescue, if the stair enclosures of the building are one-hour rated, then the corridors leading from the landlocked unit must be

one-hour rated, and doors from all units entering between the landlocked unit and the two actual stair enclosures must be one-hour rated. Likewise if the stair enclosures in the building are required to be two-hour rated, then the corridors must be two-hour rated and the doors ninety-minute rated.

There are rare cases where a unit is at the top floor of a building and the corridors are long and therefore expensive to rate (including all the doors). This is particularly true in cities like Oakland, where many early live-work projects were built in low, sprawling industrial complexes. In such cases, the route across a roof to an area of refuge where a ladder can be raised to effect a rescue is the best approach. In such case, a proper ladder must be provided to an *escape skylight* of the dimensions that meet emergency escape and rescue requirements. The route across the roof must be clearly marked, and the floor loading and fire resistance of the roof must meet certain requirements similar to those found in corridors or exterior exit balconies. While seemingly remote, the author has encountered several situations where roof escape was the best solution.

Mezzanines and Sleeping Lofts

With the exception of a living-above-the-store scenario or a SoHo style loft, the majority of live-work units contain usable floor area that is above the main level. Under most model codes, a mezzanine is defined as a room or space whose floor area is not more than one-third of the area of the room below into which it opens. Mezzanines are also governed by specific provisions regarding the clear height above and below them that supersede the normal requirements for a story, which might have a sloping ceiling.

In addition to their usefulness in existing buildings that often have high-ceilinged spaces that cry out for a sleeping loft or—as some in the early days of live-work called it—mattress storage (see Figure 7-12), mezzanines are just that. They are not stories. In calculations of allowable height, area, or number of stories, mezzanines do not count as stories. A one-hour-rated, sprinklered, wood-frame multiunit building cannot exceed four stories—but every story could have mezzanines that add nearly 33 percent to the area of that wood-framed building (unless allowable area is exceeded: the floor area of mezzanines does count towards a building's total area). Virtually all of the live-work projects the author has designed over the last twenty-five years, and most others of which he is aware, make use of the code advantages afforded by mezzanines and—more important—the design flexibility they enable (see Figure 7-13).

Figure 7-12 In an attempt to dodge inspectors when living was not legal—as was true of many early loft conversions—tenants half-jokingly referred to their sleeping lofts as "mattress storage."

Figure 7-13 A mezzanine in a multistory building, in this case at the top floor (see skylights). California Cotton Mills Studios, Oakland, California. 2005. Designed by Thomas Dolan Architecture.

Most early artists' lofts were hand-built without benefit of codes, inspectors, or any live-work permissions except early measures like New York's requirements that any loft building post a sign that stated "AIR 3 5," signifying to the fire department and others that there are *Artists in Residence* on the third and fifth floors. People built sleeping lofts so short one had to crawl in off a ladder onto a space barely large enough for a mattress. Others built decent-size mezzanines but without the code-required seven feet clear above and below, because their space simply didn't have fifteen-foot ceilings. People ducked, taped pillows to beams, or otherwise made do, just as they wore sweaters and down jackets in unheated lofts.

When the author and the code officials in the city of Oakland began to work on a building code that would accommodate live-work, they tried to find ways that the types of lofts and mezzanines found in homemade (read: illegal) live-work spaces could reasonably be allowed. There is a basic principle in writing variations on the building code—best

known for its application to disabled-access provisions—called *equivalent facilitation*. This means that if the intent of the code is met through providing some mitigating means or methods, then that deviation from the letter of the code can be granted.

Thus armed, Oakland defined three kinds of mezzanines in live-work renovations, using the basic principle that the more cramped the space, the smaller should be its floor area. They are defined as follows:

1. *Built-in sleeping bunk*, which can be accessed via ladder, can have a ceiling height of three feet if flat or, if the ceiling slopes, any portion whose ceiling is three feet or higher counts toward its maximum allowable area, which is sixty square feet (see Figure 7-14). For reference, a basic full bathroom and a queen-sized bed are both about thirty-five square feet (five feet by seven feet). At least half of the perimeter of such a shelf-like space must be open to below, but it can borrow its light and air from the larger space into which it opens. The assumption is that not much goes on in such a space other than sleeping and other semiprone activities, and access is almost always by ladder (see Figure 7-15).

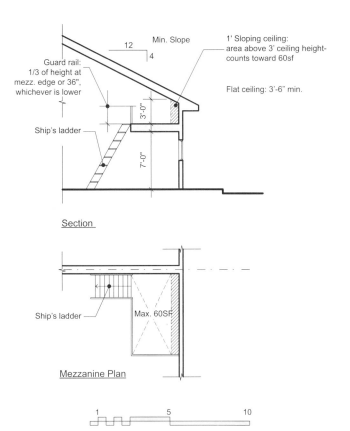

Min. Slope

12
4

Guard rail:
1/3 of height at
mezz. edge or 36",
whichever is lower

1' Sloping ceiling:
area above 3' ceiling height-
counts toward 60sf

Flat ceiling: 3'-6" min.

Ship's ladder

3'-0"

7'-0"

Section

Ship's ladder

Max. 60SF

Mezzanine Plan

1   5   10

Figure 7-14 Built-in sleeping bunk drawing: A space made to be accessed by ladder and not intended to accommodate standing up.

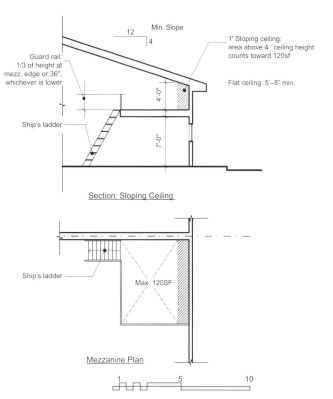

Min. Slope

12
4

Guard rail:
1/3 of height at
mezz. edge or 36",
whichever is lower

1' Sloping ceiling:
area above 4' ceiling height
counts toward 120sf

Flat ceiling: 5'-8" min.

Ship's ladder

4'-0"

7'-0"

Section: Sloping Ceiling

Ship's ladder

Max. 120SF

Mezzanine Plan

1   5   10

Figure 7-16 Sleeping mezzanine drawing: A space made to be accessed by ladder and intended to sometimes accommodate standing up.

2. *Sleeping mezzanine*, which can be accessed via ladder or stairs, can have a ceiling height of five feet eight inches if flat or, if the ceiling slopes, any portion whose ceiling is four feet or higher counts toward its maximum allowable area, which is 120 square feet (see Figure 7-16). Again, at least half of the perimeter of a sleeping mez-

Figure 7-15 This ladder to a built-in sleeping bunk allows one to slip between members of the truss that also supports the bunk. Boise Cascade Studios, Oakland.

zanine must be open to below, but it can borrow its light and air from the larger space into which it opens. The assumption is that most anything one can do while sitting or lying down can occur in a sleeping mezzanine (see Figure 7-17).

3. *Normal mezzanines* in live-work are not quite that. Often they are located in older industrial buildings with sloping trussed roofs; in fact, mezzanines are often located between such trusses. For this reason, the prohibition on sloping ceilings and an absolute clear seven feet above and below were replaced in Oakland's Live-Work Building Code by the provision under most model residential codes that allows sloping ceilings on any story in a residence (see Figure 7-18). Any area in such a mezzanine whose sloping ceiling is above five feet in height counts toward the maximum 33 percent of the room into which it opens (see Figure 7-19). This third type of mezzanine must be accessed by stairs, although alternating stairs (invented by Thomas Jefferson) are permitted, and spiral stairs are permitted as the sole means of egress from any mezzanine not over 250 square feet (IBC Sec. 1009.9) in live-work.

Figure 7-17 A sleeping mezzanine (in background) that is accessed by a short ladder from a "normal" mezzanine. California Cotton Mills Studios, 2005. Designed by Thomas Dolan Architecture.
Photo Credit: Francis Rush (developer and owner).

The Oakland live-work code also permits mezzanines to be up to 50 percent of the area of the applicable unit, provided that:

1. It is part of a renovation of an existing building.

2. It is in a sprinklered building.

3. To designate said oversized mezzanines as stories would adversely affect the building's allowable number of stories.

4. In units containing a mezzanine over 33 percent of its gross floor area, an extra layer of Sheetrock is applied to the inside of all of the unit's demising walls, corridor walls, and ceiling (if there is live-work construction above).

5. The corridors serving any unit containing a mezzanine over 33 percent of its gross floor area are constructed to the same standard as the stair enclosures of the building, including door ratings.

6. The aggregate area of all mezzanines on any floor of the building does not exceed one-third of the gross floor area of that floor.

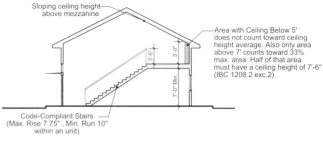

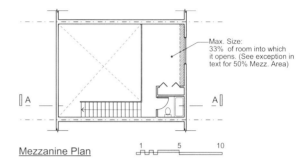

Figure 7-18 A "normal" mezzanine in live-work renovations is not quite that, because it permits sloping ceilings as would be allowed in a residential story.

The basic tradeoff here is that for the privilege of building oversized mezzanines (as opposed to their being considered stories), the primary strategy to ensure that they are safe is to increase the fire rating of demising walls and corridor walls and doors and to make the corridor meet the standards of a stair enclosure, which are significant changes. This strategy is known as compartmentalization, or rendering an

Figure 7-19 A mezzanine looking down into the larger room into which it opens. Stairs are to the left and exposed trusses that established the project's unit bays are to the right, Willow Court, Oakland, California 2007. Designed by Thomas Dolan Architecture.

individual unit or space more fire resistive so that it will contain a burning fire for a longer time.

Habitability Issues: Minimum Residential Facilities

Residential facilities are most often a code issue in renovation of existing buildings for live-work. The basics include these:

- Heat (except in subtropical or tropical locations), often using natural gas
- Kitchen facilities
- Bathing and sanitary facilities (bathrooms)
- Other minimum facilities that meet typical housing codes

Natural Gas Appliances in Live-Work

Being a space in which living, cooking, sleeping, and working all occur in one common atmosphere, live-work does require some rethinking of housing standards. For example, cooking with a gas range just under a mezzanine where sleeping occurs is considered a problem by some jurisdictions, including San Francisco, where for that reason only electric ranges are permitted in live-work. Other jurisdictions have taken a more pragmatic approach, assuming that the small amount of combustion in a gas range is permissible when it is served by a range hood ducted to the outdoors. The exception to these approaches is a new building of unusually tight construction, which means modern windows and skylights, house wrap, significant weather stripping, and other measures at and around openings. In such a case, electric ranges or gas ranges equipped with electronic ignition and — in both cases — a ducted-range hood, are essential.

Most natural gas–powered furnaces, whether they are wall mounted or central, derive their *combustion air* (the air the fire needs to burn) from the room or closet in which they are installed. Under most model codes, bedrooms and bathrooms are not permitted to contain gas-fired appliances that derive their combustion air from that space. The typical solution is either electric heat, which is not an energy-efficient choice, or a direct vent gas wall furnace that derives its combustion air from outside the wall on which it is mounted. This is frequently the author's preferred route.

Heat

Under most housing codes, heat must be provided in a residence. It is typically described as, for example, a minimum of 68 degrees three feet off the floor when it is 32 degrees outside. Most building codes do not require heat in generic commercial spaces, although office buildings are, of course, typically heated and cooled. Many live-work regulations, especially in more temperate climates, do not require heat in the work portions of units. However, if it is a live-with space, it is essentially impossible to condition part of the space without doing so throughout. A sensible approach taken in an earlier version of Oakland's code was to specify that required space heating output is calculated at 35 Btu per square foot in the live portion and 15 Btu per square foot in the work portion. In a live-with space, the two would be added to provide a total required output. In a separated living portion, heat would only be required there at 35 Btu per square foot, and heat would not be required in the work portion.

There are situations, as in industrial buildings, where ceiling heights are very high and insulation so impractical that a radiant heat solution is the only workable one. Radiant heaters are aimed at the person or activity that requires heat. When they are on, they provide heat; when they're off, there is little or no residual heat. Oakland has permitted the use of radiant heaters (see Figure 7-20) under an *AMR, or building code equivalent facilitation variance*.

Kitchen

There is a saying in zoning circles that "A kitchen is a unit, and a stove is a kitchen." To be able to live in a live-work space, at a minimum one must be able to cook, to wash, and to store perishable food. This translates to an electric or

Figure 7-20 A ceiling-hung radiant heater is a good design solution when a space is so large that heating its entirety would be impractical. Such a heater only heats people and objects at which it is aimed, and does so quite well.

gas range, a kitchen sink, and a refrigerator. Some jurisdictions require a minimum length of usable countertop, typically four feet. Building codes require that kitchens must be equipped with two twenty-ampere small appliance electrical circuits, and that all receptacles at countertop height be *GFCI protected*. As noted above, a gas range should be below a properly vented range hood or through-wall fan. Other appliances, such as a dishwasher, garbage disposal, and trash compactor, are optional.

Bathroom

Live-work units in renovated industrial or commercial buildings, as well as ground-up purpose-built live-work, will typically have at least one bathroom within the unit. This consists of a lavatory (sink) with hot and cold water, a toilet, and a shower or a bathtub. Under housing codes, bathrooms typically cannot contain gas heaters, and all electrical outlets in them must be GFCI protected. Any bathroom that does not have an exterior window with a clear open area of 1.5 square feet must be equipped with a fifty-cubic-feet-per-minute vented exhaust fan.

Other Facilities

Depending on the nature of the live-work unit, there might be need for a laundry-style sink (see Figure 7-21) for cleanup of working materials, such as paint or clay; special electrical power or a special gas connection for kilns or furnaces; multiple network connections for Internet use and communication; and other elements that are discussed in Chapter Three: Design.

Figure 7-22 Natural light admitted into the work space of a live-near unit and "borrowed" by the living portion, from which this photograph was taken. Henry Street Studios, Oakland, California, 1987. Designed by Thomas Dolan Architecture.

Natural Light

Artists, the true pioneers of live-work, typically need natural light. In fact, we all do (see Figure 7-22), and codes require a certain amount of natural light and ventilation in any habitable space (see Table 7-5). Windows are also required for emergency escape and rescue from any bedroom, and they must lead to a public way. However, structural engineers take windows out to gain shear walls; energy consultants take them out to increase a building's energy efficiency. And some areas have sufficient ambient exterior noise to require sound-rated windows, which work only when they are closed (and therefore not available for ventilation).

Under residential building codes and housing codes, natural light is required in all habitable rooms in a residence. This means all rooms within a residence except

Figure 7-21 A fiberglass laundry sink is useful for cleanup purposes in live-work designed for artists or artisans.

Table 7-5: Live-Work Building Code Master Matrix

#	Issue	Work/Live (Open Work Use Intensity)	Live/Work (Limited Work Use Intensity)	Home Occupation (Restricted Work Use Intensity)	Comments
1	Minimum Unit Size	660 sf live-with, 750 sf live/near.	440 sf live-with, 660 sf live-near.	Per residential building code and housing code standards.	Often governed by planning code; calibrate locally.
2	Maximum Unit Size	live-with: 3,000 sf. live-near: none	live-with: 3,000 sf. live-near: none	None.	Per IBC/IRC Section 419.
3	Construction Type, Height, Allowable Area	Per F-2 (light industrial) or B (office) occupancy.	Per residential occupancy.	Per residential occupancy.	
4	Property Line Wall Rating and Openings	Per residential or easement or agreement from abutting owner. Exception: work areas in live-near must meet underlying work-occupancy requirements.	Same as work/live.	Per residential occupancy.	IBC formulas for "separation distance" apply.
5	Separation between Units and with Corridor	2-hour separation between units and between units and corridor. 20-minute doors into corridor okay.	One hour.	One hour.	
6	Separation between Live and Work Portions	Over 1,500 sf of work area, separation required. Below that, same as live/work, except sprinklers always required.	(1) Substitute for lack of separation with sprinklers in all but the smallest projects; and (2) In all projects, reduce hazard of work activity by limiting permitted use. Inspect if necessary.	Per residential requirements (i.e., no separation required). No welding or heavy woodworking; no major noise or odor-generating work.	
7	Sprinklers	Always required in new buildings and renovations over 4 units. Full NFPA-13 if units are live-with and more than 3,000 square feet.	Always required in new buildings and renovations over 4 units, usually NFPA 13-R. Full NFPA-13 if units are live-with, more than two units and more than 3,000 square feet.	Per residential requirements, usually NFPA-13 D. Renovations and additions that do not add more than 500 square feet may be exempt depending on local fire marshal.	Under IBC, all new residential buildings required to be sprinklered as of January 2011.
8	Fire Alarms	Manual pull station that calls fire department in 4 or fewer units; full fire alarm system required over 4 units.	Manual pull station in 4 to 16 units; full fire alarm system required over 16 units or two stories.	Full fire alarm system required over 16 units or two stories.	Fire alarm requirements can be subject to the discretion of the local fire marshal.
9	Smoke Detectors	In all residential portions per residential code, interconnected.	In all residential portions per residential code, interconnected.	In all residential portions per residential code, interconnected if > 2 units.	Interconnected smoke detector requirements can be subject to the discretion of the local fire marshal.
10	Occupant Load Factor	300 if unit is 2,001 sf or larger and live-with; otherwise 200 sf in the live portion and per function in the work portion.	200	Per residential requirements: 300 under 3 units, 200 for 3 and over.	Some jurisdictions may not accept occupant load factor of 300 in work-live.

(Continued)

Table 7-5: Live-Work Building Code Master Matrix *(Continued)*

#	Issue	Work/Live (Open Work Use Intensity)	Live/Work (Limited Work Use Intensity)	Home Occupation (Restricted Work Use Intensity)	Comments
11	Exits/Egresses	Two means required out of an individual unit over 3,000 sf. If two exits are present in unit, at least one exit shall not pass through the work space. Two means required from any floor above the first with 3,000 or more square feet sharing a common corridor or exit balcony	Two means required out of an individual unit over 2,000 sf. Two means required from any floor above the first with 2,000 or more square feet sharing a common corridor or exit balcony.	In projects over two units, two means required out of an individual unit over 2,000 sf. Two means required from any floor above the first with 2,000 or more square feet sharing a common corridor or exit balcony.	In all cases, 10 occupants (area divided by occupant load) triggers two means of egress extending (and not converging) all the way to a public way. Some jurisdictions may not accept occupant load factor of 300 in work/live.
12	Bedroom Emergency Escape and Rescue (EER)	Required, but may be across space from residential portion as long as there is visual access between sleeping area and complying escape opening. Live-near units must have independent EER not passing through the work space, regardless of size.	Required, but may be across work space from residential portion as long as there is visual access between sleeping area and complying escape opening.	Per residential requirements (which do permit an escape opening in the larger space into which a mezzanine is open, if the mezzanine is visible from that opening).	In renovations only, landlocked units may use corridors if constructed equivalent to a required stair enclosure in that building; EER across roofs is permitted with conditions.
13	Mezzanines and Sleeping Lofts	Mezzanines, sleeping mezzanines, and built-in sleeping bunks permitted in renovation; "normal" mezzanines permitted in new construction.	Same as work-live.	Per residential code.	Oakland has invented three types of mezzanines (see chapter text above).
14	Floor Loads	75 lbs. per sf at grade; 60 lbs. psf above first floor; 40 lbs. psf in residential mezzanines.	50 lbs. psf in work area and main floor; 40 lbs. psf in residential mezzanines.	Per residential (IBC=40 lbs. psf).	Floor load in office is 125 lbs. psf, 80 lbs. psf in corridors.
15	Seismic Standards	Per F-2 occupancy for new; 75% of current base shear for renovation.	Per R occupancy for new; 75% of current base shear for renovation.	Per R occupancy.	Reduced standards in renovation, none if 10% rule applies. For new; 75% of current base shear for renovation. (Both are Oakland code.)
16	Residential Amenities	Bathing facilities, hot water, water closet (can double as utility sink), kitchen with two small appliance circuits, GFCIs over counters, 60 amp range, 220-volt outlet, one gas line for range, kitchen sink, heat per housing standards in live portion.	Same as work/live.	Per residential building code and housing code standards.	
17	Ventilation	Per F occupancy standards in work portion (2.5% of floor area as operable openings); R occupancy standards in live portion (5% of floor area as operable openings). "Borrowed" air may be employed for live portion. Mezzanines >25 feet from any windows or skylights shall be counted double in calculating ventilation per floor area. Supplementary mechanical ventilation required in work portions to double normal required number of air changes.	Per B occupancy standards in work portion (2.5% of floor area as operable openings); R occupancy standards in live portion (5% of floor area as operable openings). "Borrowed" air may be employed for live portion. Mezzanines >25 feet from any windows or skylights shall be counted double in calculating ventilation per floor area. Supplementary mechanical ventilation encouraged in work portions.	Per residential standards (i.e., 5% the area of all habitable rooms shall be served by operable openings). Area used for work shall be considered habitable space for purposes of this provision.	

#	Issue	Work/Live (Open Work Use Intensity)	Live/Work (Limited Work Use Intensity)	Home Occupation (Restricted Work Use Intensity)	Comments
18	Natural Light	Per residential (i.e., 10% of floor area in windows or skylights). "Borrowed light" is okay in sleeping mezzanines with a minimum 25% of perimeter open in direction of natural light. Mezzanines >25 feet from any windows or skylights shall be counted double in calculating natural light requirement per floor area. Work space may substitute 50% of required natural light from artificial sources.	Per residential (i.e., 10% of floor area in windows or skylights). "Borrowed light" is okay in sleeping mezzanines with a minimum 25% of perimeter open in direction of natural light. Mezzanines >25 feet from any windows or skylights shall be counted double in calculating natural light requirement per floor area. Work space may substitute 50% of required natural light from artificial sources.	Per residential standards (i.e., 10% the area of all habitable rooms shall be lit by windows or skylights providing natural light). Area used for work shall be considered habitable space for purposes of this provision.	
19	Work Area Amenities	200 amps, 220 volts service to each unit, with minimum of one 50-amp capacity outlet in finished space (outlet not required in shell space: occupant to add per individual needs). Separated work space, when present, to have a dedicated utility sink.	100 amps, 220 volts service to each unit, with minimum of one 30-amp capacity outlet in finished space (outlet not required in shell space: occupant to add per individual needs).	Per residential model code standards.	See chapter text.
20	Storage and Use of Hazardous Materials	Per F-2 occupancy and Table 7-3. Otherwise provide an occupancy separation between H occupancy and work/live per code.	Per B occupancy and Table 7-3.	Per R occupancy (essentially none).	Table 7-3 is specific to Oakland, not adopted nationally.
21	Hazardous Occupancy	Not permitted in live-with. Separation per building code mixed occupancy.	Not permitted. Separation per building code mixed occupancy.	Not permitted.	
22	Accessibility	Any presence of walk-in trade or employees = commercial, triggering full ADA: level in, strike side door clearances, accessible parking, WCs, etc. Common M/W WCs in a location accessible to all units are okay. Living portion accessible if residential code so requires.	Same as work-live, only walk-in trade and employees less likely.	Per residential requirements. Single-level units in multiunit projects at ground floor or elevator-accessed levels may need to be adaptable. Most home occupation would not accommodate walk-in trade.	Elevator Exception: IBC 1103B.1, Exception 2.1 Multistoried office buildings (other than the professional offices of a health care provider) ... less than 3,000 square feet per story 9 (this is a footnote, same as #8)
23	Noise and Sound Transmission	Minimums: STC 50/IIC 50; CNEL 45.	Minimums: STC 50/IIC 50; CNEL 45.	STC 50/IIC 50; CNEL 45.	See text for explanation.
24	Heat and Energy Conservation	All residential portions: 35 Btu psf of heat; work portions: 15 Btu psf of heat. Radiant space heaters permissible in voluminous work areas. All new construction shall comply with local energy conservation standards, including insulation, glazing, shading, etc.	Same as work/live.	Per residential code and energy standards.	Upon application to building official and demonstration that meeting normal heat and energy conservations is infeasible.

(Continued)

Table 7-5: Live-Work Building Code Master Matrix *(Continued)*

#	Issue	Work/Live (Open Work Use Intensity)	Live/Work (Limited Work Use Intensity)	Home Occupation (Restricted Work Use Intensity)	Comments
25	Accessory Buildings: *Living, working or both shall be permitted within this building type, which shall be considered accessory to the main residence on the property. Maximum number of employees: three. No walk-in trade or must meet Section 419 (sprinklers, etc.) and ADA accessibility standards.*	F-2 Occupancy if exceeds requirements of exception to right.	B Occupancy if exceeds requirements of exception to right.	R Occupancy.	*Exception: Flexible work space/granny flat in an accessory building shall be considered R occupancy if its footprint does not exceed 2x lot width squared. Number of stories per planning regulations.*
26	New Construction versus Renovation	See separate matrix for renovation in Appendix B.	See separate matrix for renovation in Appendix B.	Residential standards apply equally to either renovation or new construction in home occupation.	
27	Shell Construction	Entire building shell must be completed, including all life safety systems including sprinkler and fire alarms infrastructure; utility service entrances and distribution to all floors, common bathrooms, and corridors to applicable ADA standards.	Same as work-live.	N/A.	In work-live and live-work, minimum facilities need to be completed up to a stubbed-out stage, which means they are ready for utilities or appliances (hot water heater, gas range, space heater or furnace, etc.) and fixtures (kitchen sink and cabinets, bathroom fixtures, etc.). Normally units cannot be occupied by residents until all fixtures and appliances are installed and certificate of occupancy is issued.

bathrooms, hallways, and closets. Most residential codes require that natural light be provided in the form of windows, skylights, or glazed doors in an amount that is at least 8 percent of the area of the room. Some live-work codes have allowed relaxation of these standards, particu-

larly in work portions of renovated spaces. However, if a sleeping mezzanine or built-in sleeping bunk is more than twenty-five feet from any source of natural light, Oakland's code states that its area must be counted twice toward the calculation of required natural light openings. This is a somewhat imperfect way of ensuring that more light will find its way to the loft.

Conditions do exist where there is little or no natural light available to a unit, such as in a landlocked unit that is not on a top floor. Provisions in Oakland's code allow for artificial (electric) light to be substituted for natural light in renovations, along with mechanical ventilation, which is discussed next.

In a live-near or live-nearby space, the purely residential portion of the unit must comply with residential standards for the provision of natural light.

Natural Ventilation

Under residential building codes and housing codes, natural ventilation is required in all habitable rooms in a residence. This means all rooms within a residence except hallways and closets. As noted, bathrooms, while not officially habitable rooms, have their own ventilation requirements. Most residential codes require that natural ventilation be provided in the form of windows, skylights, or glazed doors in an amount that is at least 4 percent of the area of the room. Some live-work codes have allowed relaxation of these standards, particularly in work portions of spaces.

Sometimes it is impossible to provide the required 4 percent natural ventilation. In Oakland's live-work code, that number can be reduced in renovations to 2.5 percent of the floor area of the unit but not smaller than 2.5 square feet, as long as sufficient mechanical ventilation to compensate for this lower amount of natural ventilation is provided. Normally this would mean ventilation equipment capable of continuously providing 0.35 air changes per hour in the room(s) in question, except bathrooms, whose requirements were noted earlier.

It is particularly important to provide natural ventilation for the sleeping area of a live-work space. Therefore, this provision states that if the sleeping space is over twenty-five feet from its required source of natural ventilation, its area should be counted twice in calculating the total required natural ventilation.

Tip
The work activities in live-work spaces often require extra ventilation. Therefore, it is wise to err on the high side of ventilation calculations by installing an extra exhaust fan in the work space.

Noise and Sound Transmission

Due to their hybrid nature, live-work spaces embody contradictions to the "normal" way of looking at performance standards in building codes. In multiunit live-work projects located in single buildings, the issue of sound is often a contentious one. Sound is typically measured in decibels (db) and regulated in three ways:

1. Sound transmitted through the air, typically through walls

2. Sound transmitted as a result of impact, such as walking, typically through floor/ceiling assemblies

3. The ambient sound in a location and how it affects the project being designed

Regulations are mostly aimed at modulating an existing or expected source of noise by creating wall or floor/ceiling assemblies that reduce the number of decibels perceived (heard) on the opposite side of the assembly from the noise source.

Referring to California's state building code (matched roughly by the IBC with respect to sound attenuation requirements), all walls between residential units and between the units and corridors serving them must meet—as a minimum—a *Sound Transmission Class* (STC) rating of 50. This means that if there are seventy decibels of sound being generated on one side of the wall, an STC 50 wall will have the effect of reducing that level to twenty decibels.

Similarly, all floor/ceiling assemblies above residential and live-work units must meet not only STC 50 but also— again as a minimum—an *Impact Insulation Class* (IIC) rating of 50. This means that if there are seventy decibels of sound being generated as a result of people walking on a floor above, an IIC 50 floor/ceiling will have the effect of reducing that level to twenty decibels. Impact-generated sound is sometimes called "the high heels effect." It should be noted that an eight-inch, solid concrete floor/ceiling assembly does not meet IIC 50. In fact, the tapping of a high heel on the floor will telegraph right through and be clearly audible below.

Community noise is an "averaged" sound exposure level (not a maximum level) because of the fluctuation of sound over a twenty-four-hour period. The two major descriptors are the Community Noise Equivalent Level (CNEL) and the Day-Night Average Sound Level (Ldn or DNL). Community noise must be modulated by the new residential or live-work building or renovation (if so coded) to a level of forty-five decibels. For example, if community noise around a proposed building is tested at seventy-five decibels, then an exterior wall assembly of STC 30 would be required. Exterior wall ratings usually hinge on the STC rating of the windows.

A normal double-glazed aluminum window achieves an STC of about 28 to 33, so that could suffice in this example. (Check manufacturer's tested STC rating.) If there are unusual sources of noise, such as freight trains regularly passing by or immediate proximity to a freeway, specialized windows with STC ratings in the high 30s or even low 40s may be necessary. They can be expensive, a factor to consider when looking at a site in a noisy location. California Cotton Mills Studios, described in a case study in Chapter Three: Design, required over $1 million in window upgrades and replacements due to its location adjacent to a major freeway.

It is worth repeating that the required assemblies are minimums, and, particularly when the eventual uses are not fully known, it is prudent to design to a higher level of sound attenuation if feasible. Most tenant complaints and homeowners' lawsuits arise from problems with either sound or water.

Tip

Design and construct all floor/ceilings and walls separating live-work units to a minimum standard of STC 55 and IIC 55.

Another way to regulate sound is to require that noise sources within units not exceed a certain decibel level. This is more difficult to enforce, largely because it is difficult to predict what use will occur in a unit and when that use will change, as it inevitably does. Sources of sound in work-live units are sometimes more intense than those in typical residences. Certain work uses, such as amplified music production (rock bands, etc.) or mechanical devices like grinders or shop tools could easily generate in excess of sixty decibels (possibly up to one hundred decibels). Sixty decibels is approximately the level of two people talking about three feet apart. The worst-case scenario, and therefore that which requires the most extensive sound attenuation measures, is a work space in one unit directly adjacent to the sleeping area of another. In such cases—and they may come up after the conversion is complete, based on the unit occupant's activities—there are two choices under Oakland's live-work code:

1. Add an additional STC 50 to the walls and an additional IIC 50 to the floor/ceiling that separates the higher noise source from any other units' residential portions. This might be accomplished by creating a second demising wall a few inches from the one that could normally be required and which itself is rated at 50 STC. The result would possibly be an STC somewhere around 55 to 60.

2. Hire an acoustical engineer to show that the assemblies being proposed will result in an acceptable noise level in occupied spaces outside the noise source in question. Although this may seem like an expensive way to go, an acoustical engineer is probably needed anyway to determine that the noise source in excess of sixty decibels exists. Rather than adding entirely new 50 STC/IIC assemblies (the default method), the acoustical engineer may recommend a far more economical alternative.

The project will be likely to already have been tested for ambient "community noise," in which case an acoustical engineer is involved in and familiar with your project. Additionally, it is prudent to have your acoustical engineer make construction site visits to verify the proper construction of sound-attenuating assemblies and proper installation of sound-attenuating devices.

Energy Conservation

Most areas in the industrialized world now have codified energy conservation standards for building design. Those that do not will soon. Under Governor Jerry Brown, California adopted in 1978, and has repeatedly updated, its energy standards known as Title 24 (which is actually the entire state building code). As a result, buildings constructed and renovated in California consume roughly one-half the amount of energy as those in the rest of the country.

Live-work has the enviable characteristic of being Zero-Commute Housing, meaning that automobile use by many live-work residents and therefore gasoline consumption and greenhouse gas emissions are typically less than for an automobile commuter. For that reason alone, live-work is a green building type that contributes significantly to improved environmental quality.

New construction of any building, be it live-work or another type, typically needs to meet local energy-conservation regulations, which are determined by building envelope, efficiency of heating and cooling systems, orientation and glazing, and other factors, such as thermal mass, daylighting, and specialized lighting and switching.

The conversion of a large (or small) commercial or industrial building to live-work can present energy conservation challenges that—when weighed against the presumed savings inherent in starting with an existing building—may temper a buyer's enthusiasm. When live-work codes aimed at enabling the relatively affordable conversion of such large, vacant buildings were considered, regulators were faced with a reality that argued against strict compliance with energy standards applying as if the buildings were new. An existing multistory brick warehouse with leaky single-glazed industrial sash windows, high ceilings, and no wall or roof insulation presents a daunting task to retrofit to today's energy standards. In some cases it is neither feasible nor possible. Therefore, code relaxations for conversion to live-work have often been adopted, sometimes requiring no heat and therefore no insulation as an alternative to the prescriptive standards noted in the "Heat" section above. In California, the envelope of a building certified as historic is exempt from state energy conservation standards. However, any new installation of HVAC and the like must meet current standards.

Tip
While local energy efficiency codes may not be stringent, anticipate higher energy costs in the future by providing more than code minimums for insulation, glazing, and appliance efficiencies.

Accessibility

Ever since the adoption of the Americans with Disabilities Act (ADA) in 1990, accessibility has been a part of virtually every kind of renovation or new building, with the possible exception of single-family residences. More recently, the concept of *visitability* has advanced the view that all residences should be fully accessible. Commercial buildings are required to be fully accessible. Therefore, the hybrid nature of live-work presents code conundrums.

Most live-work codes have treated large live-work conversions or single-building multiunit new construction as they would an apartment building. So if the building is elevator-accessed, all units should be "adaptable," meaning that they could easily be made fully accessible; all common hallways and corridors must be fully accessible and level-in. Units on the ground floor of even a non-elevator-accessed building must contain at a minimum an accessible half bath. Multilevel units are typically exempt, except that any level within such units that is either elevator-accessed or is at ground-floor level must contain an accessible half bath, and any other facilities on that floor—such as the kitchen—must be adaptable. Many codes require that a certain percentage of units be fully accessible, and if they are publicly funded, the requirements are slightly different and are subject to Fair Housing Laws as well.

In townhouse and flexhouse live-works and other new live-work buildings, the logical trigger for most jurisdictions

is walk-in trade and employees. Either of these usage attributes renders a building—or perhaps only its ground-floor work space—truly "public accommodation" and therefore subject to full accessibility standards. Many live-work spaces however, are occupied by people who rarely ever have client visits—maybe only by appointment, with no walk-in trade and no employees. Some jurisdictions have held that even client visits trigger accessibility; others have not. In Oakland, the live-work code allows a building's owner to record a *Notice of Limitation* stating that no walk-in trade or employees are to be permitted and that the building's leases and covenants so state.

A question arises regarding true flexhouses that are intended to be preapproved for all living, housing over retail, or office over retail. Accessibility codes would seem to suggest that an upstairs needs to be available to people in wheelchairs, thereby necessitating an elevator. As of this writing, the 2009 IBC contains this exception:

> 1103B.1, Exception 2:
>
> The following types of privately funded multistory buildings do not require a ramp or elevator above the first floor:
>
> 2.1 Multistoried office buildings (other than the professional offices of a health care provider) … less than 3,000 square feet per story.[4]

Accessibility in live-work renovations is often the subject of "hardship appeals," a form of building code variance applying specifically to accessibility issues.

Tip
As has been done in some larger, older live-work buildings, provide common accessible bathrooms on every elevator-accessed floor (water closets only or with roll-in showers) and nonaccessible bathrooms within the units, thereby saving space while arguably meeting the intent of code. Verify with your local building official.

Note: The ADA is federal civil rights legislation. Its provisions, other federal laws such as the Fair Housing Act, and those of local jurisdictions can be extremely complex and subject to frequent changes and updates. This book does not profess to comprehensively depict or interpret current disability law.

Administrative Modification Requests (AMRs)

Live-work conversions often include administrative modification requests (AMRs) to accommodate existing conditions.

AMRs are essentially building code variances, but their names vary by jurisdiction. To apply for an AMR, the applicant—usually an architect—must understand the intent of the code provisions from which that AMR is deviating. A mitigation is proposed that is a tradeoff that allows the overall solution to meet the intent of the code and preserve its life safety intent. In cases of legalization of existing live-work, there are often multiple AMRs, sometimes negotiated as an *omnibus AMR*, that addresses the whole building and proposes alternate means to meet the code's life safety intent.

Tip

In live-work renovations, assemble all of the code deviations and equivalencies you propose and present them to your building department at one time. This will make negotiations faster and more comprehensive, and it should involve--at a minimum—both building and fire departments.

An example of an AMR that the author recently received was a four-story building that was originally constructed as a modified form of heavy timber, or Type IV construction, which is normally rated as one-hour construction. Additionally, the applicant wanted to provide mezzanines constructed of heavy timber construction that did not precisely match the current code's description of heavy timber: His proposed mezzanine floor decking would be two-inch by six-inch tongue and groove instead of three inches thick. The building was already required to be sprinklered due to its height, number of stories, and area. An AMR was granted to allow the mezzanine construction, keeping in mind the overall construction of the building, by providing additional quick-response sprinkler heads under the mezzanines and compartmentalizing the units by providing an extra layer of Sheetrock on the inside walls of the unit. (See Figure 3-26, exposed mezzanine structure.)

Shell Construction

The uses of live-work units and buildings can vary tremendously, both upon completion and throughout the life of the building. Flexibility is key, and the do-it-myself spirit on the part of live-work residents will continue for the life of the building. Some developers have chosen to build what is called shell construction, in which the building's exterior shell, sound and fire-rated demising walls and floor/ceilings, and exiting and life safety systems are complete, but utilities may be only stubbed out, interior walls may be fire-taped

only, and floors may be bare plywood or concrete. This enables a buyer or tenant to finish out the unit to his or her liking, adding cabinets, fixtures, paint, floor finishes, and other elements.

As was noted in Chapter Three: Design, shell construction as a strategy interacts with a jurisdiction's issuance of a certificate of occupancy (C of O), essentially permission to occupy the building and the units. Once shell construction of an overall building has been completed, the building department may issue a *temporary certificate of occupancy* (TCO) that is prerequisite to shell units' completion. At that point, a tenant or buyer can proceed with his or her improvements to the individual unit. An actual C of O or, at a minimum- an inspector's signoff as "OK to occupy," is required before the occupant can move in, which means that the minimum habitability requirements that had not been satisfied by the shell construction need to have been completed.

Understanding this sequence is particularly important for a buyer of a shell space. Most mortgage lenders won't fund a mortgage unless the unit is able to be occupied, so the work that a buyer of a shell construction unit performs would need to be done before he or she technically owns that unit. A loan approval contingent on the work being completed would seem the most logical way to approach this sequencing issue. A sale typically cannot close escrow unless all facilities are actually completed and a C of O is issued, which can sometimes be done unit by unit. Depending on local laws, showing and leasing/writing sales contracts may be permitted to occur prior to the issuance of a C of O but after completion of shell construction. In some localities, *owner-builder permits* may be issued to unit tenants/purchasers with a building owner's permission.

Tip

Particularly during soft real estate markets, build shell space live-work, preserving your capital and giving tenants or buyers the opportunity to provide their own finishes and apply sweat equity to improve their units as they choose.

Building Code Issues by Project Type

Townhouse

Townhouse or multilevel live-work units, a form of live-with whereby no separation is provided or required between living and working portions, are the type that is most fully covered under Section 419 of the 2009 IBC and 2009 IRC, included in Appendix B and this chapter, respectively.

Flexhouse

A flexhouse is, as described, a multilevel unit whose ground-floor space is separated by a fire-rated assembly from the upstairs portion, which can be accessed without going through the work space. A flexhouse is a mixed-occupancy building under the building code. Its purported flexibility does present a quandary for building officials, because any part of a flexhouse could at some time be commercial or residential space. This issue is addressed in the Habersham Case Study in Chapter Four.

Home Occupation

Home occupation is a form of live-work that occurs entirely within a residence and has no code provisions that require it to differ from a residence. However, accessory buildings that might flex among work, storage, and residence should be treated as R occupancy, being accessory to a residence (see Table 7-5 and Appendix B). There is no need to build such structures to commercial standards.

New versus Renovation

Many jurisdictions have adopted special building code relaxations to create incentives for the renovation of existing buildings. While many have been discussed in this chapter, it is helpful to see them in one place. Therefore, Table B-2 in Appendix B lists those relaxations that have been adopted in Oakland.

Master Building Code Matrix

Table 7-5 summarizes the codes discussed in this chapter, with provisions tabulated by use type and corresponding work use intensity.

Further information on live-work building codes can be found on Oakland's *Live-Work in Plain English* Web site, created by the author in 1998 and recently updated to reflect the IBC. It can be found at www.live-work.com/plainenglish-ws.

CHAPTER 8

Epilogue

We have seen in this book that live-work is a way of accommodating those who, *by the manner in which they live*, question the need to separate "life" from "work." Truly mixed-ocupancy buildings that are designed for living and working suit those *who assume a separation between residence and work*. Such people are well served by flexhouse live-works, which constitute a valuable reemergence of an ancient form that is well suited to a mixed-use neighborhood.

This book has explored many examples of successful live-work and a few spectacular failures. The live-work courtyard community was an important innovation that is worth replicating with local variations. Live-work and its occupants function best in an environment that provides opportunities for interaction, either through location on a great street or through the incorporation of semipublic interactive space. This unique and important need must be recognized and met in all live-work.

Likewise, we have seen that renovation and repurposing of buildings for live-work is a valuable component of the way cities grow and change. Policies and regulations should encourage such pioneering while minimizing life safety hazards, use-based conflicts, and exploitation of the pioneers by speculators. The fact remains that when live-work transforms older districts into neighborhoods, on balance it is almost always an improvement. Live-work plays a crucial role in the incubator cycle. The author envisions a sponsored live-work incubator as a possible form of development in the future, possibly combined with a coworking facility.

It has become clear to the author over the years that both Euclidean zoning and separated occupancies under the building code (until recently, thanks to International Building Code Section 419) are often unsuitable tools with which to regulate live-work. Form-based codes are indeed appropriate for live-work, as was stated eloquently in Chapter Six in "Placemaking with Live-Work and Form-Based Codes" by Dan Parolek. As Parolek writes, "The concept of live-work embodies the same objectives as a form-based code at a building and neighborhood scale; it reinforces and enables the organic evolution of places over time and therefore is a critical component of reinforcing, revitalizing, and creating walkable urban places." In all live-work, but particularly in the case of the flexhouse, we have seen that there are ways to fine-tune the degree of separation between residence and work space via the proximity types used in this book. The ability of flexhouses to "learn" and change over time allows them to remain viable in "neighborhoods that learn" as well.

It is the author's sincere hope that the use of a common lexicon to describe live-work, as put forth in this book, will foster greater understanding among practitioners, regulators, and users. Regulating live-work, while tricky, should become easier as a result of some of this book's suggested approaches.

Nevertheless, its complexity demands conscious, ongoing coordination between the silos of specialization downtown (i.e., planning and building departments) and usually the assistance of live-work consultants. The appendices that follow constitute a valuable tool for creating live-work regulations at the planning entitlement level and as part of the building code.

Looking toward the future of live-work, living where one works in some form is likely to become the norm, at least to the extent that all residences are likely to accommodate some form of work activity. Increasingly, one will be able to live where one works in just about any location on the rural-to-urban transect (although it is usually a very urban type), as long as the type and form are appropriate and the work-use intensity is compatible with its surroundings.

In terms of meeting the near-term demands of our aging society, live-work's flexibility makes it a logical building type to be used in lifelong neighborhoods and NORCS (naturally recurring retirement communities), a realization that may come just in time for the baby boomers. Live-work in a walkable community is therefore an obvious choice for someone who doesn't drive, who doesn't want to drive, or who won't be able to make that long automobile commute when gasoline hits $10.00 per gallon.

Millennials– those who have come of age since the year 2000–are poised to form households and are largely disinclined to follow their parents into the suburbs or commit to home ownership. As is noted in Chapter Four: Market, urban live-work rentals in walkable neighborhoods are a natural choice for this group. In the sidebar "The New Urban Workplace" by Rod Stevens in Chapter Six: Planning, there are important observations regarding workplace phenomena occurring today: the return of large employers to urban centers and the shift away from housing towards job as the primary driver of our economy, presaging a possible shift in the focus of some live-work development, which has often been seen as simply a housing type.

As this book discusses, live-work is both a new way and an old way to carry on one's life. For some it is an attitude, for others it is a single building type, and for others it is a continuation of an age-old pattern. For many it is and has been a path to stronger and more convivial communities and an integration of life's previously dispersed functions. Live-work buildings and proximity as an organizing principle of design and planning have been integral to the vision of the New Urbanists, as they have been to this author (since before he knew he was a New Urbanist).

The ultimate beneficiaries of an improved understanding of live-work are those who will enjoy a greater variety of ways both to live and to work and who will be enabled to do so in close proximity. Zero-Commute Living, like the paperless office, is an ideal that many seek and few attain. Even getting part of the way there will make our world a better place and our earth a cooler planet. As the United States appears to be lurching toward a less affluent, less dominant position in the world economy, the elimination of waste inherent in live-work and its provision of opportunities to create community will become increasingly appropriate.

APPENDIX A

Toward a Model Live-Work Planning Code

Unlike building codes, planning regulations tend to be highly calibrated to suit local conditions. Nevertheless, there are regulatory steps that have been proven to work for live-work and some that have not, both of which are described in detail in Chapter Six: Planning.

The goal of a planning code is to encourage and regulate to achieve an intended physical form and character while accommodating appropriate and compatible uses.

Use of Appendix A Tables

This appendix encapsulates—in the form of tables and text—effective ways to encourage and regulate live-work. The tables that follow are intended as a departure point for officials who will then need to calibrate them to suit local conditions. Excel versions of all appendix tables are available at www.live-workplanninganddesign.com.

Work Uses Permitted

Table A-1 lists all of the work uses that are permitted in live-work units and designates what proximity types are permitted to accommodate those uses, what the work-use intensity of each use is, and suggests locations where such work uses would be permitted. Within this table, work-use intensity—restricted, limited or open—is also correlated with zone location and proximity type and will inevitably need to be locally calibrated.

In the highlighted example, a neighborhood grocery store (under "Retail" in the table), live-near and live-nearby are permitted proximity types, meaning there is some separation between the store and the residence, which would typically be above the store. Its work-use intensity is limited, leading to a limitation on its size as shown in Table A-2, and it is permitted to be located in commercial and mixed use zones.

Work Use Intensities and Allowable Unit Areas

Table A-2 establishes the type of work-use intensity permitted in each use type—that is, Restricted, Limited or Open—and further describes the work area minimums and maximum areas for each use type combined with proximity type.

Artisan live-work, for example, looking again at Table A-1, is permitted in all use types; treated as a live/work use type, if it were a live-near unit its work area would be limited to 1,500 square feet based on the potential impact on the residence. This maximum area is a likely candidate for local calibration.

Table A-1   List of Work Uses Permitted in Live-Work

Allowable Proximity Type			Work Use	Work-Use Intensity << low…INTENSITY…high >>			Zones Where Work Use Permitted (This will depend on local regulations: calibrate)				
Live-with	Live-near	Live-nearby	Work Use/Category	Restricted	Limited	Open	Residential	Commercial	Mixed Use	Industrial	Comments
			Cultural/Recreational:								
		x	Arcade			x		x	x		
x	x	x	Artist and artisan studio	x	x	x	x	x	x	x	Hazardous uses according to building code exceptions (see Chapter Seven)
	x	x	Billiard hall		x			x	x		
	x	x	Bowling alley		x			x	x		
	x	x	Club		x			x	x		
	x	x	Community center or neighborhood house		x		x	x	x		Provide separation from A occupancy per building code
	x	x	Fitness center		x			x	x		
		x	Hall (dance, lecture, exhibition)		x			x	x		Provide separation from A occupancy per building code
	x	x	Library		x		x	x	x		
	x	x	Museum or archives		x		x	x	x		
		x	Theatre (motion picture, opera house, proper)			x		x	x		Provide separation from A occupancy per building code
			Institutional:								
	x	x	Post office		x		x	x	x		Larger work in live-near or live-nearby space by conditional use permit (CUP)
x	x	x	Child day care facility	x			x	x	x		Maximum six children in live-with; larger by CUP
	x	x	Church		x		x	x	x		Provide separation from A occupancy per building code
		x	Detoxification center			x		x	x		Larger work in live-near or live-nearby space by CUP
		x	School—Elementary or secondary		x		x	x	x		Provide separation from A or E occupancy; larger by CUP
		x	School—University or college		x		x	x	x		Provide separation from A or E occupancy per building code
	x	x	Social service center		x			x	x		
			Manufacturing:								
	x	x	Bakery products manufacturing			x		x	x	x	
	x	x	Brewing or distilling			x		x	x	x	
x	x	x	Clothing manufacturing	x				x	x	x	
x	x	x	Custom manufacturing*	x	x	x	x	x	x	x	
	x	x	Dairy products manufacturing			x		x		x	
	x	x	Electrical products or appliances manufacturing			x		x		x	
		x	Food or beverage products manufacturing		x			x	x	x	

Allowable Proximity Type			Work Use	Work-Use Intensity << low...INTENSITY...high >>			Zones Where Work Use Permitted (This will depend on local regulations: calibrate)				
Live-with	Live-near	Live-nearby	Work Use/Category	Restricted	Limited	Open	Residential	Commercial	Mixed-Use	Industrial	Comments
	X	X	Metal products manufacturing			X		X		X	
	X	X	Miscellaneous products manufacturing			X		X	X	X	
	X	X	Non-metallic mineral products manufacturing			X		X		X	
	X	X	Paper products manufacturing			X		X		X	
	X	X	Plastic products Manufacturing			X		X		X	
	X	X	Printing or publishing		X			X	X	X	
	X	X	Shoes or boots manufacturing			X		X		X	
	X	X	Textiles or knit goods manufacturing		X			X	X	X	
	X	X	Tobacco products manufacturing			X		X		X	
	X	X	Wood products manufacturing			X		X	X	X	
			Office:								
	X	X	Financial institution		X		X	X	X		
X	X	X	General office	X			X	X	X		
X	X	X	Health care office	X			X	X	X		
	X	X	Health enhancement center		X		X	X	X		
X	X	X	Professional services (architect, lawyer, therapist, etc.)				X	X	X		
X	X	X	Real estate office					X	X		
			Parking Use:								
		X	Parking garage		X			X	X	X	Larger work space in live-near or live-nearby space by CUP
			Retail:								
	X	X	Adult retail store		X			X	X		Provide separation from M or B occupancy per building code
	X	X	Furniture or appliance store		X			X	X	X	Provide separation from M or B occupancy per building code
	X	X	Neighborhood grocery store		X			X	X		Provide separation from M or B occupancy per building code
	X	X	Liquor store		X			X	X		Provide separation from M or B occupancy per building code
		X	Vehicle dealer			X		X	X	X	Provide separation from M or B occupancy per building code

Allowable Proximity Type			Work Use	Work-Use Intensity			Zones Where Work Use Permitted (This will depend on local regulations: calibrate)				
				<< low…INTENSITY…high >>							
Live-with	Live-near	Live-nearby	Work Use/Category	Restricted	Limited	Open	Residential	Commercial	Mixed Use	Industrial	Comments
			Service:								
	x	x	Animal clinic		x			x	x	x	Larger work space in live-near or live-nearby space by CUP
		x	Auction hall		x			x	x		Provide separation from A occupancy per building code
x	x	x	Barber shop or Beauty Salon	x			x	x	x		Larger work space in live-near or live-nearby space by CUP
x	x	x	Body-rub parlor	x				x	x		Larger work space in live-near or live-nearby space by CUP
		x	Cabaret			x		x	x		Provide separation from A occupancy per building code
x	x	x	Catering establishment		x		x	x	x	x	Larger work space in live-near or live-nearby space by CUP
	x	x	Hotel		x		x	x	x		Larger work space in live-near or live-nearby space by CUP
	x	x	Laboratory			x		x	x	x	Larger work space in live-near or live-nearby space by CUP
	x	x	Laundromat or dry cleaning establishment		x			x	x		Larger work space in live-near or live-nearby space by CUP
	x	x	Motor vehicle repair shop			x		x	x	x	
	x	x	Neighborhood bar		x		x	x	x		Provide separation from A occupancy per building code
	x	x	Photofinishing or photography laboratory			x		x	x	x	
x	x	x	Photofinishing or photography studio	x			x	x	x	x	
x	x	x	Print shop		x		x	x	x	x	
	x	x	Production studio		x			x	x	x	
	x	x	Auto repair shop		x		x	x	x	x	
	x	x	Restaurant		x			x	x		Provide separation from A occupancy per building code
	x	x	School—Arts or self-improvement		x		x	x	x		
	x	x	School—Business		x			x	x		Provide separation from A or E occupancy per building code
	x	x	School—Vocational or trade		x			x	x	x	Provide separation from A or E occupancy per building code
		x	Sign painting shop			x		x	x	x	

Allowable Proximity Type			Work Use	Work-Use Intensity << low…INTENSITY…high >>			Zones Where Work Use Permitted (This will depend on local regulations: calibrate)				
Live-with	Live-near	Live-nearby	Work Use/Category	Restricted	Limited	Open	Residential	Commercial	Mixed Use	Industrial	Comments
		x	Courier depot			x		x	x	x	Larger work space in live-near or live-nearby space by CUP
			Utility and Communication:								
x	x	x	Radio communication station			x	x	x	x	x	Larger work space in live-near or live-nearby space by CUP
			Wholesale:								
	x	x	Junk shop		x		x	x	x		
		x	Lumber and building materials establishment			x		x		x	
	x	x	Wholesaling			x		x		x	

*Custom manufacturing activities include the small-scale production of artisan and/or custom products. This activity typically includes the production of finished parts or products by hand, involving the use of hand tools and small-scale equipment within enclosed buildings. Custom manufacturing industrial activities do not produce noise, vibration, air pollution, fire hazard, or noxious emissions that will disturb or endanger neighboring properties. Custom manufacturing includes but is not limited to the production of:

Cameras and photographic equipment
Custom sign-making
Custom clothing
Custom furniture building and refinishing
Professional, scientific, measuring, and controlling instruments
Musical instruments
Medical, dental, optical, and orthopedic instruments and appliances, and similar items
Handicraft, art objects, and jewelry Beverages (including alcoholic) and food (excluding the production of highly pungent, odor-causing items, such as vinegar and yeast) with less than 10,000 square feet of floor area.

Table A-2: Live-Work Unit Types, Work-Use Intensities and Allowable Areas

	Unit Use Type	Work/Live	Live/Work	Home Occupation
	Work-Use Intensity	Restricted, Limited or Open Work Use	Restricted or Limited Work Use	Restricted Work Use Only
	Proximity Type:			
Maximum	**LIVE-WITH**	Minimum work area: 330 sf; Maximum work area 1,500 sf	Minimum work area: 220 sf; Maximum work area 1,500 sf	No minimum work area. Maximum work area 1,500 sf or 10% of unit area, whichever is less.
Minimum	**LIVE-NEAR**	Minimum work area: 375 sf. Maximum work area 3,000 sf.*	Minimum work area: 330 SF Maximum work area 1,500 sf.*	No minimum work area. Maximum work area: 10% of unit area.
Work Area	**LIVE-NEARBY**	No minimum work area. Maximum work area 5,000 sf.*	No minimum work area. Maximum work area 3,000 sf.†	No minimum work area. Maximum accessory building area on one and two unit lots = lot width squared x two stories.

* Larger work areas in live-near and live-nearby are permitted upon the granting of a conditional use permit and are dependent upon underlying zone regulations for work use. Live-with cannot exceed 3,000 square feet, according to the International Building Code (Section 419, see Chapter Seven: Buildng Codes) in live-with and live-near. Provide fire-rated occupancy separations as and if required by building code when unit size exceeds 3,000 square feet.

Table A-3 Live-Work Location and Project Types

Project Type	Home Occupation	IBC Section 419 Live-with	Flexhouse	Housing over Retail	Courtyard Live-work	Loft Renovation: sale	Loft Renovation: rental	New Lofts	New Lofts	Comments (blank cells = not permitted)
Location: Use Zone/Transect Zone										
Single family residential/T3-T4	x								x	
2–4 Family residential/T3-T4	x	x	x	x	x				x	
Multifamily residential/T4-T6	x	x	x	x	x	x	x	x	x	
Mixed use hsg/comm./T4-T6	x	x	x	x	x	x	x	x	x	
Mixed use downtown/T5-T6	x	x	x			x	x	x		
Mixed use comm./ind./T4 or district		x*	x*				x*			
Light commercial/T4-T6		x	x	x	x	x	x	x	x	
Commercial downtown/T5-T6		x	x	x		x	x	x		
Light industrial/district		x*	x*		x*		x*		x*	Require disclosures/nuisance easements
Medium industrial/ district		x*	x*				x*		x*	Require disclosures/nuisance easements
Heavy industrial/ district	n/a	n/a	n/a	n/a	n/a	n/a	x*	n/a	n/a	Require disclosures/nuisance easements

*Artist, artisan or small entrepreneurs, rental only

Live-Work Location and Project Types

Table A-3 is intended to assist an applicant who seeks to develop live-work on a specific property located in a particular zone.

If his property is in a Light Industrial Zone (highlighted in Table A-3), he could build IBC Section 419 live-with, a flexhouse, courtyard live-work, renovate a warehouse for rental but not for-sale units, and provide live-nearby in an accessory building, although the main building would likely need to be a form of live-work permitted in this zone because stand-alone residences usually are not. In all cases in this example, disclosures of existing commercial industrial activity would be required, and the work activity, work-use intensity, and proximity type would need to be checked on Tables A-1 and A-2.

Walk-in Trade and Employees by Location and Project Type

Table A-4 is intended to help an applicant who seeks to develop live-work on a specific property located in a particular zone who wants to know how the work spaces in her project will relate to the outside world.

If her property is in a two- to four-family residential zone and she wants to develop courtyard live-work (see highlighted cell), she will find that employees can be accommodated in her project but that walk-in trade is not permitted.

Live-Work Planning Topics, Objectives, and Suggested Regulations

What follows is a distillation of the planning issues raised in the book with proposed regulations intended to address each issue.

New Urbanist Town Centers and Revitalized Urban Neighborhoods

Objectives:

1. Encourage compact, mixed use, pedestrian-oriented neighborhoods with flexhouses, live-with units and housing over retail; make it possible for upstairs and downstairs uses to be separate and different yet internally connected.

2. Allow flexhouses on walkable streets to be buildings that learn; preapprove them for a variety of uses before they are built (e.g., all live-work, housing over retail, or office over retail).

Table A–4: Walk-in Trade and Employees by Location and Project Type

EMPL = Employees permitted WIT = Walk-in trade permitted	Project Type	Home Occupation	IBC Section 419 Live-with†	Flexhouse	Housing over Retail	Courtyard Live-work	Loft Renovation: sale	Loft Renovation: rental	New Lofts	Live-nearby: accessory bldg.	Comments (blank cells = not permitted)
Location: Zone											
Single family residential		x	WIT*							x	WIT
		EMPL*	EMPL*							EMPL*	EMPL
2–4 family residential		x	x	x	x	x				x	
		EMPL	EMPL	EMPL	EMPL	EMPL*				EMPL*	
Multi-family residential		x	WIT	WIT	WIT	x	x	x	x	WIT *	
		EMPL	EMPL	EMPL	EMPL					EMPL	
Mixed use housing/comm.			WIT	WIT	WIT	WIT*	x	x	x	WIT *	
		EMPL	EMPL	EMPL	EMPL	EMPL	EMPL	EMPL	EMPL	EMPL	
Mixed use downtown		x	WIT	WIT			x	x	x		
		EMPL	EMPL	EMPL			EMPL	EMPL	EMPL		
Mixed use comm./ind.			WIT	WIT			x†				
			EMPL	EMPL			EMPL				
Light commercial			WIT	WIT	WIT	WIT	WIT	WIT	WIT	WIT	
			EMPL	EMPL	EMPL	EMPL	EMPL	EMPL	EMPL	EMPL	
Commercial downtown			WIT	WIT	WIT		WIT	WIT	WIT		
			EMPL	EMPL	EMPL		EMPL	EMPL	EMPL		
Light industrial			WIT	WIT		WIT *	x†			x†	Require disclosures/nuisance easements
			EMPL	EMPL		EMPL	EMPL			EMPL	
Medium industrial			WIT	WIT			x†			x†	Require disclosures/nuisance easements
			EMPL	EMPL			EMPL			EMPL	
Heavy industrial		n/a	n/a	n/a	n/a	n/a	n/a	n/a	n/a	x†	Require disclosures/nuisance easements
										EMPL	

*By administrative conditional use permit

†IBC Section 419 allows live-with units up to 3,000 square feet; see Chapter Seven: Building Code

3. Recognize the role of live-works in greenfield town centers and infill neighborhood revitalization, and provide support and incentives for them to lead the way in bringing such places alive.

Regulations:

1. Flexhouses shall be permitted on main streets in new and revitalized communities, and preapproved for housing over retail, office over retail, or all live-work as live-with (per IBC Section 419) or as live-near (separated).

2. Separate ownership or tenancy of portions of live-work or live-nearby units shall be permitted when constructed with appropriate separations according to the building code.

3. Accessory buildings in residential settings shall be permitted to accommodate live-work and work activities

listed under "Restricted" in Table A-1 and "Limited" in Table A-1 by administrative use permit.

4. In higher-density infill projects where ground-floor retail is the desired use, rental live-work shall be permitted in street-facing ground floor spaces until such time as retail becomes viable in that location (according to a locally calibrated metric).

Gentrification, Artists, and the SoHo Cycle

Objectives:

1. Encourage artists' and artisans' presence in areas not likely to gentrify.

2. Create incentives for artists to secure long-term affordable live-work, either through ownership or secure rental. Encourage artists' efforts at community-building.

3. Be as informed as possible about prior examples of the SoHo cycle, both locally and as described in this book. Understanding the phenomenon allows a regulator to either allow it to proceed or see that it may be causing some unintended damage. In general, the SoHo effect is a spontaneous urban real estate phenomenon, not easily headed off once started. What can have a significant effect is the manner in which a regulator chooses to respond.

Regulations:

1. Newly renovated live-work (not legalization) in districts already substantially colonized by artists and artisans shall be subject to inclusionary zoning for certified artists and/or payment of an arts transfer tax on the sale of all live-work in the district.

2. Disclosures of ongoing commercial/industrial activity shall be included in all residential leases or covenants for live-work located in all preexisting commercial or industrial areas. Eviction of existing low-income residential tenants for purposes of creating live-work shall be prohibited unless accompanied by appropriate compensation of tenant.

3. Funds from an arts transfer tax shall be used to enable artists and artisans to retain long-term affordable space in districts experiencing the SoHo Cycle.

4. Appropriate planning and funding mechanisms shall be enacted to provide the necessary infrastructure, public realm, transit, and city services in any area determined

by planning staff to be experiencing the SoHo Cycle or similar changes.

Use Conflicts and Compatibility

Objectives:

1. Discourage residential reversion and imported NIMBYism in established commercial/industrial areas: Use disclosures, covenants and lease terms to help prevent conflicts.

2. Regulate to minimize imported NIMBYism.

3. Protect existing industry if that is the city's policy.

Regulations:

1. Disclosures of ongoing commercial/industrial activity shall be required in all live-work or residential leases or covenants where such units occur in preexisting commercial or industrial areas.

2. A valid business license unit shall be required for every live-work unit where such units occur in preexisting commercial or industrial areas.

3. Live-work in preexisting industrial areas shall be rental tenancy only and limited to artists, artisans, and similarly situated individuals.

4. Live-work projects in preexisting commercial or industrial areas shall in all cases permit appropriate work activity as permitted in the underlying zone, regardless of subsequent agreements among the owners within the project to the contrary, which agreements shall be unenforceable.

New versus Renovation and Ownership versus Rental

Objective:

1. Distinguish where new construction versus renovation live-work is appropriate, and determine where ownership versus rental are best located.

Regulations:

1. Live-work that is constructed and sold as ownership (i.e., fee simple, condominiums, or other approved ownership structures) shall be permitted in the appropriate form according to Tables A-1, A-2, and A-3, but shall not be permitted in preexisting, viable industrial areas unless it is city policy for the industry to be phased out.

2. Live-work in preexisting, viable industrial areas shall be renovation only, rental tenancy only, and limited to artists, artisans and similarly situated individuals.

Affordability and Revitalization

Objectives:

1. Recognize live-work as perhaps the most important urban revitalization agent in existing American downtowns since the Second World War, and harness the homegrown energy of live-workers while curbing excess speculation at the expense of artists and industry.

2. Understand the inherent affordability of live-work as zero-commute living, and calibrate affordability or inclusionary zoning requirements with this land use subsidy in mind. Perhaps use such requirements only as a tool to preserve the tenancy of artists and artisans.

3. Relax development standards for renovation of warehouses for live-work if such incentives will help desired revitalization efforts. Understand the potential for displacement of existing uses and residents inherent in such a relaxation.

Regulations:

1. Existing buildings originally designed for commercial, industrial, or civic use shall be permitted to be renovated for live-work in the form permitted in Table A-1, in the locations permitted in Table A-3.

2. Relaxed planning and building regulations shall be enacted to encourage renovation of existing buildings for live-work, to include parking and open space. There shall be no density limit for renovation live-work other than the confines of the existing building and minimum unit sizes.

3. Newly renovated live-work (not legalization) in existing districts substantially colonized by artists and artisans shall be subject to inclusionary zoning for certified artists and/or payment of an arts transfer tax on the sale of all live-work in the district.

4. Inclusionary zoning, if required elsewhere in a city, shall be deemed to have been satisfied in live-work that is located within one-quarter mile of a transit stop or neighborhood center, or in such locations deemed by planning staff to provide affordable living when the cost of necessary automobile commuting is included in such calculation.

Spontaneous Live-Work and Legalization

Objectives:

1. Understand that live-work will sometimes—often—arise of its own accord, usually for good reason, as described in the many examples and case studies in this book.

2. Take into account the inevitable existence of illegal live-work in any jurisdiction: Develop a method to fairly and sensitively legalize such projects as they become known.

Regulations:

1. Legalization of existing live-work shall be permitted according to the process described in Appendix B Code Module 5 and its reference to Chapter Seven. Said legalization shall result in the issuance of a certificate of occupancy for legal live-work that conforms to Tables A-1, A-2, and A-3.

2. Legalizations of existing live-work communities shall be granted adequate time to undergo the transition to legal status with minimum displacement of tenants.

Development Standards

Objectives:

1. Downplay live versus work space designation within units: Proximity types take care of this issue and lines on paper do not.

2. Permit any work activity in a live-work space that is allowed in the underlying zone, plus a list of uses compatible with residence that are permitted in any live-work of any kind.

3. Develop simple home occupation regulations.

4. Allow employees and walk-in trade in live-work wherever it is appropriate, which is usually everywhere except in a low-density home occupation setting, where client visits might be by appointment only.

5. Regulate minimum unit sizes to observe housing codes and differentiate live-work from apartments, and maximum sizes that acknowledge the impact of large work areas on units' residents in a live-with proximity type.

Regulations:

1. Live-work units' respective space allocation for living and working shall be primarily governed by proximity type and permitted work use and area according to Tables A-1 and A-2.

2. Live-with units' living portion shall not be less that 220 square feet for up to two residents, and 150 square feet for each additional resident.

3. Live-work units' maximum area shall be governed by Table A-2 and the building code.

4. New construction live-work shall be governed by a maximum density in units per acre equivalent to that for residential units in that zone or in the most similar zone per planning staff.

5. Housing density bonuses—if they are in effect in the applicable jurisdiction—shall apply one-for-one to live-work units.

6. Work activities in a live-work unit shall be as permitted in the underlying zone or Table A-1 as locally calibrated.

7. Walk-in trade and employees shall be permitted in live/work and work/live use types; walk-in trade is prohibited and employees are limited in home occupation. See Table A-4.

8. The following uses are permitted in any live-work unit or home occupation: clerical, office, consultation services, art, craft, and a home workshop. Said uses shall be governed as to area, employees, walk-in trade and materials used and stored according to Tables A-1, A-2, A-3, A-4 and the building code.

9. Home occupation shall be subject to the following requirements (or as locally calibrated):
   a. A home occupation shall occur in a residence, and its activity shall be accessory to the primary function of the residence.
   b. There shall be no specific limit placed on the portion (area in square feet or percentage) of a residence devoted to home occupation; however, IBC Section 419 limits said use to 10 percent of the unit area.
   c. Home occupation is permitted in a building that is accessory to the residence (i.e., on the same property).
   d. Nonresident employees shall not exceed three persons.
   e. There shall be no walk-in trade; client visits by appointment are permitted.
   f. Home occupation shall not require dedicated parking unless it is shown to adversely affect parking or traffic in its neighborhood.
   g. A home occupation shall not generate any noises or odors perceivable beyond the property line of the residence in which it is located.
   h. Minimal signage consistent with context and transect zone.

Design Review Standards that Encourage Interaction

Objective:

1. Design projects that either (a) are located on a great street whose activity they help to activate or (b) provide opportunities for interaction within the project. This should be the primary focus of any design review standards for live-work beyond contextual design and functional considerations.

Regulations:

1. In multiunit live-work projects containing eight or more units and whose Walk Score is less than 85, provide a minimum of 10 percent of the gross floor area of the project devoted to interactive open space.

2. In multiunit live-work projects containing twenty or more units whose Walk Score is less than 90, provide a minimum of 5 percent of the gross floor area of the project devoted to interactive open space

3. In all live-work projects except in single-family or two-to-four family residential zones, the ground floor shall be visually permeable and serve to activate the street. A minimum of 40 percent of the surface area of the ground-floor facade shall be glazed. Utility rooms and other facilities without windows shall be located away from the primary street facade of the building.

4. Vehicular entrances shall not be located on the primary street facade of the building, with the exception of entrances to parking garages in larger multiunit projects.

5. In multiunit live-work or mixed-use buildings, all structured parking shall be shielded from public view from the street or public way by liner units, which shall be retail, unseparated live-work, or flexhouse units.

Parking, Loading, and Traffic

Objective:

1. Enact parking requirements for live-work that acknowledge the unique qualities of zero-commute living.

Regulations:

1. Provide off-street parking according to Table 6- and as locally calibrated.

2. Provide loading facilities in live/work containing twenty units or 30,000 gross square feet, or as locally calibrated.

3. Provide loading facilities in work/live containing ten units or 10,000 gross square feet, or as locally calibrated.

4. For all live-work projects containing twenty or more live-work units, perform a traffic study to determine the reduced traffic impact and parking needs of of zero-commute living versus single-use residential or commercial uses, and taking into account opportunities for shared parking.

5. Provide shared vehicle (e.g., ZipCar®) stations in or adjacent to all live-work projects.

Charts: Type, Location, and so on

Objectives:

1. Understand that there is at least one type of live-work that is appropriate in every part of a city.

Regulations:

1. Create and use a table of work uses permitted in the different proximity types and use types, by location, using Table A-1 as a model.

2. Create and use a table of use types and work-use intensities/allowable work areas in live-work units, using Table A-2 as a model.

3. In order to assist applicants, create and use a table of live/work location/project types, using Table A-3 as a model.

4. In order to assist applicants, create and use a table of walk-in trade and employees by location and project type, using Table A-4 as a model.

5. Refer to Table 5-2 to learn how each live-work project type can create opportunities for community.

6. See Table 6-1, Best Locations for Live-work Types and Permitted Work-Use Intensity.

Administration and Coordination

Objectives:

1. When enacting live-work planning and building regulations, be sure that the two are well coordinated and work well together. Employing the terms used in this book will help the process of communication between planning and building officials—and between them and the people on the other side of the counter.

2. Make use of consultants who are well aware of live-work's unique needs when adopting codes, and set aside funds for a temporary live-work czar as described in Chapter Six.

Regulations:

1. Enactment of live-work planning regulations shall be coordinated closely with the jurisdiction's building and fire departments and their applicable regulations.

2. Live-work regulations of all types shall adhere to the terminology used in this book.

3. Prior to their adoption, proposed live-work regulations shall be reviewed by a qualified architect or planner experienced in live-work regulation.

A Model Live-Work Building Code System

The year 2009 saw a revolutionary occurrence in the world of live-work, which was the adoption of IBC Section 419, Live/work Units (while the IBC uses a slash rather than a dash, we revert to the dash hereafter). While Section 419 covers a specific type of live-work unit, with a little interpretation it can be applicable to most types described in this book, except mixed occupancy, which is already covered under all model codes.

As shown in Figure B-1, a reprint from *Building Codes Illustrated*, International Building Code Section 419 permits live-work units and describes them as R-2 occupancy. In it, the work activity must go on at the main or ground-floor level, it cannot exceed 50 percent of the unit area, the entire unit cannot exceed 3,000 square feet, five nonresident employees are permitted, and *no separation is required between the living and working portions*.

What follows is a line-by-line annotated, plain English interpretation of IBC Section 419, followed by a list of items that it does not cover (which are few) and then instructions for how to apply it to the many types of live-work using the modules included below, which deal with variations such as renovation, live-work for artists, legalization, and shell construction. The goal is for the reader to have at his or her disposal a specific set of modules that can be combined to address any situation in live-work building regulation. After the treatment of the seven code models, there is an all-important table: Use of the Model Live/Work Building Code System (Table B-3), which shows the additive use of the modules depending on the project type.

2009 International Building Code Section 419

We start with annotations to IBC Section 419, working from the actual code text. Interpretation and explanation are in italics. Passages from other parts of the building code are in plain text. This is **Code Module 1**.

Building Code Provisions Not Spelled Out in IBC Section 419

In Table B-1 are items in the Master Building Code Matrix in Chapter Seven that are not spelled out in Section 419 but are not relaxations for renovation live-work only. Their numbers correspond to the Master Building Code matrix, Table 7-5. This is **Code Module 2**.

Live-Work Units

§ 419 of the code addresses requirements for live-work units, which are classified as an R-2 occupancy.

Separations in H, R-1, R-2 and R-3 Occupancies

In either nonseparated occupancies per § 508.3 or separated occupancies per § 508.4, there is still a requirement to provide separations at dwelling units, sleeping units, and supervised residential facilities. § 420 contains these requirements.

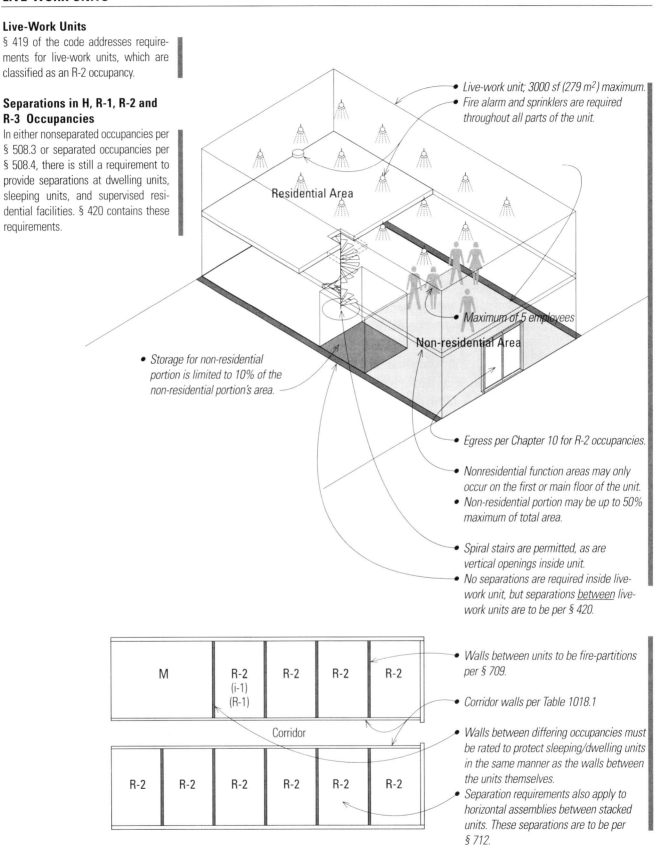

- *Live-work unit; 3000 sf (279 m2) maximum.*
- *Fire alarm and sprinklers are required throughout all parts of the unit.*

Residential Area

- *Maximum of 5 employees*

Non-residential Area

- *Storage for non-residential portion is limited to 10% of the non-residential portion's area.*

- *Egress per Chapter 10 for R-2 occupancies.*

- *Nonresidential function areas may only occur on the first or main floor of the unit.*
- *Non-residential portion may be up to 50% maximum of total area.*

- *Spiral stairs are permitted, as are vertical openings inside unit.*
- *No separations are required inside live-work unit, but separations between live-work units are to be per § 420.*

| M | R-2
(i-1)
(R-1) | R-2 | R-2 | R-2 |

Corridor

| R-2 | R-2 | R-2 | R-2 | R-2 | R-2 |

- *Walls between units to be fire-partitions per § 709.*

- *Corridor walls per Table 1018.1*

- *Walls between differing occupancies must be rated to protect sleeping/dwelling units in the same manner as the walls between the units themselves.*
- *Separation requirements also apply to horizontal assemblies between stacked units. These separations are to be per § 712.*

Figure B-1 Live-work units in Section 419 of the International Building Code, as portrayed in *Building Codes Illustrated*.[1]

SECTION 419

Live-Work Units[2]

419.1 General. A live-work unit is a dwelling unit or sleeping unit in which a significant portion of the space includes a nonresidential use which is operated by the tenant and shall comply with Section 419.

A person living there must be the operator of the nonresidential use; a sleeping unit is "A room or space in which people sleep, which can also include permanent provisions for living, eating and either sanitation or kitchen facilities but not both."[3] The typical plain English term used to apply to a sleeping room is a single-room-occupancy unit (SRO).

Exception: Dwelling units or sleeping units which include an office that is less than 10% of the area of the dwelling unit shall not be classified as a live-work unit.

In such case the unit would be considered a home occupation (i.e., purely residential occupancy). More than 10 percent (up to 50 percent) is "a significant portion," which then must meet all Section 419 requirements. However, since work area delineation in home occupation often variable, this is a difficult provision to enforce. This is an area where planning regulations could overrule this building code provision, at least in a de facto way. As stated earlier in this book, regulating percentage of live versus work area is very difficult and—in most cases—ultimately ineffective.

419.1.1 Limitations. The following shall apply to all live-work areas:

1. The live-work unit is permitted to be a maximum of 3,000 sq ft;

Therefore when the unit gets too large, there should be a separation, regardless of the fact that it is sprinklered.

2. The non-residential area is permitted to be a maximum 50% of the area of each live-work unit;

That is, up to 1,500 square feet of work area in a 3,000 square-foot unit.

3. The non-residential area function shall be limited to the first or main floor only of the live-work unit;

This is important, because some live-work has upstairs work space. Some of the work space could occur in a mezzanine opening onto the main floor, because a mezzanine is not a story but is a portion of the story into which it opens; however, accessibility in a mezzanine could be an issue (see IBC Section1103B.1, Exception 2 in Chapter Seven).

and

4. A maximum of 5 non-residential workers or employees are allowed to occupy the non-residential area at any one time.

That would mean five employees in addition to at least one resident operator of the non-residential use. Above five employees, a separation between the "non-residential area function" and the residence would be required.

419.2 Occupancies. Live-work units shall be classified as an R-2 dwelling. Separation requirements found in [IBC Paragraphs] 420 and 508 shall not apply when the live-work unit is in compliance with section 419. High hazard and storage occupancies shall not be permitted in a live-work unit. The aggregate of storage in the live-work unit shall be limited to 10% of the space dedicated to non-residential activities.

This paragraph captures the essence of Section 419, which is that the need for an occupancy separation between live and work is not required when all conditions of this section are met.

While lower-hazard commercial activities are allowed in a live-work unit, high-hazard occupancies—such as a wood shop with more than three fixed appliance, or a welding operation—are not permitted. This is normal in a residential occupancy, which Section 419 deems live-work to be. Storage needs to be carved out of the work portion, again on the main floor.

419.3 Means of egress. Except as modified by this section, the provisions for R-2 occupancies in Chapter 10 shall apply to the entire live-work unit.

This normally means one exit out of any individual unit that is less than 2,000 square feet in area and two means of egress off of any floor that contains more than 2,000 square feet.

419.3.1 Egress capacity. The egress capacity for each element of the live-work unit shall be based on the occupant load for the function served per Table 1004.1.1.

Typical occupant load factors based on "function" served are: 200 for multifamily residential; 300 for single-family residential; 100 for office; and 15 for a restaurant.

419.3.2 Sliding doors. Where doors in a means of egress are of the horizontal-sliding type, the force to slide the door to its fully open position shall not exceed 50 pounds (220 N) with a perpendicular force against the door of 50 pounds (220 N).

419.3.3 Spiral stairs. Spiral stairs that conform to the requirements of Section 1009.9 shall be permitted.

Spiral stairs can serve as the sole means of egress from a relatively small area, such as a mezzanine no larger than 250 square feet, when located within a live-work unit or residence.

419.3.4 Locks. Egress doors shall be permitted to be locked in accordance Exception 4 of Section 1008.1.8.3.

Dead bolts and security chains are allowed at live-work units' exit doors, but not double-cylinder dead bolts (which are keyed from both sides and can be dangerous in an emergency if the inside key is missing).

419.4 Vertical openings. Floor opening between floor levels of a live-work unit is permitted without enclosure.

A live-with proximity type is permitted.

419.5 Fire protection. The live-work unit shall be provided with a monitored fire alarm system where required by Section 907.2.9, and a fire sprinkler system in accordance with Section 903.2.7.

Under 907.2.9, reproduced here, there are numerous exceptions to the requirement for a monitored sprinkler system (e.g., a sprinklered townhouse, most buildings not over two stories in height, and buildings whose units have direct exits to the outdoors or corridors that enable one to exit in two directions). However, one must always sprinkler in a Section 419 live-work unit.

[F] 907.2.9 Group *R-2 and R-2.1*. Fire alarm systems and smoke alarms shall be installed in Group R-2 and R-2.1 occupancies as required in Sections 907.2.9.1 and 907.2.9.3

[F] 907.2.9.1 Manual fire alarm system. A manual fire alarm system that activates the occupant notification system in accordance with Secction 907.5 shall be installed in Group R-2 occupancies where.

1. Any *dwelling unit* or *sleeping unit* is located three or more *stories* above the lowest *level of exit discharge;*

2. Any *dwelling unit* or *sleeping unit* is located more than one story below the highest l*evel of exit discharge* of *exits* serving the *dwelling unit* or *sleeping unit;* or

3. The building contains more than 16 *dwelling units* or *sleeping units.*

4. *Congregate living facilities or congregate residences with more than 16 occupants.*

Exceptions:

1. A fire alarm system is not required in buildings not more than two *stories* in height where all *dwelling units* or *sleeping units* and contiguous attic and crawl spaces are separated from each other and public or common areas by at least 1-hour *fire partitions* and each *dwelling units* or *sleeping unit* has an *exit* directly to a *public way, exit court,* or *yard.*

2. Manual fire alarm boxes are not required where the building is equipped throught with an automatic *sprinkler system* installed in accordance with Section 903.3.1.1 or 903.3.1.2, and the occupant notification appliances will automatically activate throughout the notification zone upon a sprinkler water flow.

3. A fire alarm system is not required in building that do not have interior *corridors* serving *dwelling units* and are protected by an *approved automatic sprinkler system* installed in accordance with Section 903.3.1.1 or 903.3.1.2, provided that *dwelling units* either have a *means of egress* door opening directly to an exterior *exit access* that leads directly to the *exits* or are served by open-ended *corridors* designed in accordance with Section 1026.6, Exception 4.

[F] 907.2.9.2 Smok alarm. Single- and multiple-station smoke alarms shall be installed in accordance with Section 907.2.11.

[F] 907.2.9.3 Licensed Group R-2.1 occupancies.

Licensed Group R-2.1 occupancies housing more than six nonambulatory, elderly clients shall be provided with an approved manual and automatic fire alarm system.

Exceptions: Buildings housing nonambulatory clients on the first story only and which are protected throughout by the following:

1. An approved and supervised automitic sprinkler system, as specified in Sections 903.3.1.1 or 903.3.1.2, which upon activation will initiate the fire alarm system to notify all occupants.

2. A manual fire alarm system.

3. Smoke alarms required by Section 907.2.11.

419.6 Structural: Floor loading for the areas within a live-work unit shall be designed to conform to Table 1607.1 based on the function within the space.

This means that one must look up "function" in the building code. Residential, for example, is 40 pounds per square foot (psf); some light commercial functions are 50 psf; others are higher.

419.7 Accessibility: Accessibility shall be designed in accordance with Chapter 11.

Accessibility is a large and complicated subject. In simple terms, if one has walk-in trade or employees, at least the non-residential portion should be made accessible to people with disabilities under the Americans with Disabilities Act (ADA). There is some debate as to whether client visits by appointment only are subject to ADA, although most officials rule that they are not.

419.8 Ventilation: The applicable requirements of the *International Mechanical Code* shall apply to each area within the live-work unit for the function within that space.

Residential standards dictate that 4 percent of the floor area of a habitable room must have natural ventilation via doors, windows, or operable skylights. Commercial standards are more complicated and may include mechanical ventilation, although unless the work activity is specialized, meeting residential standards will usually suffice.

Changes to the IRC

The International Residential Code is the single-family companion to the International Building Code, and the next excerpt states that live-work units that comply with IBC 419 are permitted under the IRC.

R101.2 Scope. The provisions of the *International Residential Code for One- and Two-family Dwellings* shall apply to the construction, alteration, movement, enlargement, replacement, repair, equipment, use and occupancy, location, removal and demolition of detached one- and two-family dwellings and townhouses not more than three stories above-grade in height with a separate means of egress and their accessory structures.

Exception: Live-work units complying with the requirements of Section 419 of the *International Building Code* shall be permitted to be built as one- and two-family dwellings or townhouses. Fire suppression required by Section 419. 5 of the *International Building Code* when constructed under the *International Residential Code for One- and Two-family Dwellings* shall conform to Section 903.3.1.3 of the *International Building Code.*

Table B-1: Buildng Code Items Not Specifically Included in Section 419 of the International Building Code (extracted from Table 7-5, Master Building Code Matrix). Items not included in Section 419 are shown in italics.

Numbers from Master Building Code Matrix (Table 7-5)	Issue	Work/Live (Open Work-Use Intensity)	Live/Work (Limited Work-Use Intensity)	Home Occupation (Restricted Work-Use Intensity)	Comments
1	Minimum Unit Size	*660 sf live-with, 750 sf live/near*	*440 sf live-with, 660 sf live-near*	Per residential building code and housing code standards.	*Often governed by planning code; calibrate locally*
5	Separation between Units and with Corridor	*2-hour separation between units and between units and corridor. 20-minute doors into corridor OK.*	One hour	1 hour	
8	Fire Alarms	*Manual pull station that calls fire department in 4 or fewer units; full fire alarm system required over 4 units.*	Manual pull station in 4–16 units; full fire alarm system required over 16 units or two stories	Full fire alarm system required over 16 units or two stories	*Fire alarm requirements can be subject to the discretion of the local fire marshal.*
12	Bedroom Emergency Escape and Rescue (EER)	*Required, but may be across space from residential portion as long as there is visual access between sleeping area and complying escape opening. Live-near units must have independent EER not passing through the work space, regardless of size.*	*Required, but may be across work space from residential portion as long as there is visual access between sleeping area and complying escape opening*	*Per residential requirements (which do permit an escape opening in the larger space into which a mezzanine is open, if the mezzanine is visible from that opening)*	In renovations only, landlocked units may use corridors for emergency escape and rescue if constructed equivalent to a required stair enclosure in that building; EER across roofs is permitted with conditions. See Table 7-4.
20	Storage and Use of Hazardous Materials	*Per F-2 occupancy unless employing a control area and not exceeding maximum allowed under Table 7-3 (Chapter Seven). Otherwise provide an occupancy separation between H occupancy and work/live per code.*	Per B occupancy and Table 7-3.	Per R occupancy (essentially none)	*7-3 (Chapter Seven) is specific to Oakland, not adopted nationally*
25	Accessory Buildings: *Living, working or both shall be permitted within this building type, which shall be considered accessory to the main residence on the property. Maximum number of employees: 3, no walk-in trade or must meet Section 419 (sprinklers, etc.) and ADA accessibility standards.*	F-2 Occupancy if area exceeds requirements of exception to right	B Occupancy if area exceeds requirements of exception to right	Per R Occupancy	*Exception: Flexible work space/granny flat in an accessory building shall be considered R occupancy if its footprint does not exceed 2x lot width squared. Example: A 25-foot lot width squared equals a footprint of 625 square feet. Number of stories per planning regulations.*

Code Provisions that Apply in Live-Work Renovations Only

Many jurisdictions have chosen to relax building codes in renovations of existing buildings. Table B-2 is adapted from Oakland's live-work building code, written in collaboration with the author Most, if not all, of the provisions below are dependent on the building's being sprinklered. The Oakland Code contains more items and much greater detail, which is beyond the scope of this appendix. However, most of the important issues are highlighted in the Table below. This is **Code Module 3**.

The author has adapted the Oakland Building live-work Code into a document that is applicable to renovation live/work and work/live. This detailed code is an important part of Code Module 3. It can be found at www.live-workplanningdesign.com, the Web site for this book.

Artists' Relaxations

Arriving at further building code relaxations for artists, artisans, and similarly situated individuals is not an entirely conflict-free process. Affordability is at the top of the list of the vast majority of artists, which almost always means the renovation of an existing building in the least expensive way possible. The above relaxations in **Code Module 3** are also aimed at achieving cost savings, and their provisions have essentially addressed the "low-hanging fruit."

The role of artists in society and the extent to which they can be (1) defined and (2) certified as such in a manner that

Table B-2 Code Provisions that Apply in Live-Work Renovations Only

Seismic and Lateral Standards	75% of current required base shear value for all renovations; except when 10% rule applies (i.e., when aggregate live portion does not exceed 10% of the area of the original building), no change of occupancy occurs (for lateral purposes only) and therefore no retrofit is required.
Mezzanines	Three special types invented: (1) built-in sleeping bunk (NTE 60 sf); (2) sleeping mezzanine (NTE 120 sf); and (3) "normal" mezzanine (NTE 1/3 of room below). Provision also allows mezzanines to be ½ area of room below with strict conditions. Ladders and approved folding stairs to mezzanine types 1 and 2 are permitted.
Guardrails	36-inch height permitted throughout all unit interiors.
Emergency Escape and Rescue	Opening not required to be within sleeping area; alternate means of emergency escape and rescue adopted for cases of "landlocked" units, allowing escape through corridors or across a roof.
Exiting	Fire escapes are permitted as one of the required exits A second exit may be constructed next to the existing stairway if the arrangement of the stairways meets certain conditions:
	The entries to the stairways are at opposite ends.
	Any hallway or corridor connecting the entries to the stairways is constructed pursuant to Section 1004.3.4.3 of the International Building Code.
	A horizontal exit wall bisects the building and stairways.
	All areas of the floor have access to either stairway.
Accessibility	Units that are not regularly open to the public or have employees can record a "notice of limitation" so stating and thereby avoid compliance with accessibility standards. This provision is definitely subject to local interpretation as well as potential ADA claims. ADA is federal civil rights legislation.
Alternative Materials and Methods	Existing construction permitted when it approaches the levels of fire resistive assembly required (e.g., ½)² Sheetrock instead of type, gypsum board to achieve one-hour rating; existing stair and landing dimensions permitted to remain.
Sound	Consideration of exterior noise sources not required.
Hazmats	Limited hazardous activities and materials permitted within live-with units.
Natural Light	Relaxed requirements with conditions
Natural Light and Ventilation	Relaxed requirements—generally to about ½ of normal residential requirements—with conditions
Heat and Energy Conservation	Relaxed, especially when demonstrably infeasible to bring building into compliance. Prescriptive standards permitted when feasible.
Plumbing	ABS and PVC drain waste and vent permitted within units that themselves are no more than two stories in height. Cast iron required in building shell if building exceeds two stories.

is not subject to rampant abuse is beyond the scope of this appendix. However, assuming that these issues can be resolved, one can look at:

(1) What artists need:
- **Natural light** via windows or skylights
- **Spacious quarters** with high ceilings and few partitions
- Easy **access** to bring large works in and out

(2) What artists do not need or can do without:
- A fancy kitchen or multiple bathrooms
- Excess privacy, as in one-artist-one-unit

(3) What the minimum levels of life safety and habitability are that should not be compromised.

Nobody wants to see artists—or anyone—injured or killed in an earthquake, fire, or similar catastrophe. Building codes' life safety provisions do in fact save lives, either by preventing collapse or by providing a safe way out in the case of a fire, to name two important examples. However, there are provisions in renovation of existing buildings that bear examination.

The first is change of occupancy and its requirements that buildings be brought up to today's code as if they were new. It can be argued that what makes artists different from the rest of us is that they value their work as an expression of themselves, and they tend to view "life" and "work" as all of a piece rather than separate, segmented parts as many of us do. Most buildings targeted for live-work renovations are commercial or industrial occupancy under the building code; the artists who first illegally occupied such buildings did so with little desire to change the nature of the buildings—they simply moved in and improvised living arrangements. Therefore, a set of principles for artists' relaxations could be:

- *Acceptance of its present state*
- *Minimal intervention in the existing building, and*
- *The assumption that the use artists are putting it to is essentially aligned with its earlier uses*

How this translates to relaxed building codes might go as follows:
- Raise the threshold for declaring a building a change of occupancy. For example, allow up to 33 percent of its existing floor area to become residential portions of artists' work/live units before a change of occupancy is triggered. However, employ prudent treatment of seismic and other lateral force hazards, such as un-

reinforced masonry buildings, "soft story" buildings, and manufactured housing.
- Consistent with a prudent exiting regime and reasonable attention to life safety, treat each building as existing on its own merits, keeping in mind that—if its use did not change—no work at all would be required. Perform the necessary life safety upgrades to make it a safe place, with minimal intervention.
- Allow shell construction; allow artists to take out their own permits and perform their own construction with the owner's permission, and create minimal standards for habitability, examples of which might be:
  - Allow artists to take over their spaces in as raw a form as possible, and institute an informal system of monitoring the work they do on their units that bypasses usual permit processes, possibly by permitting an architect to observe and certify the work;
  - Require only a four-foot-minimum kitchen counter with one GFCI-protected countertop receptacle;
  - Consider eliminating the requirement for a vented range hood if there is sufficient exterior ventilation;
  - In areas of moderate climate, consider eliminating requirements for heat in artists' live-work;
  - Allow "borrowed" light and ventilation for interior bedrooms, which must still meet "visual access" requirements for emergency escape and rescue, possibly through interior operable windows and prominent signage at the actual openings;
  - Encourage large, congregate unit forms such as six bedroom/six workspace units with two bathrooms (M/W), one large kitchen, and "hangout" space. The savings in plumbing and fixtures are what really create affordability, as well as the sharing of common facilities.

These suggestions constitute more of a direction than a prescription. Nevertheless, this is **Code Module 4.** Some would say it is best to leave artists alone and let them occupy buildings as they choose, for the simple and important reason that illegal artists' live-work is a great form of affordable incubator space for young artists and other similarly situated individuals.

A middle way—designed to avoid the inevitable clash between the culture of codes, permit process, inspectors and red tags, and the world of those who choose to live outside the mainstream—is to create a live-work "master builder" position, someone on retainer to work with the artists' community building by building to achieve a modicum of life safety at a minimum of cost. Such a person could be an architect, or a contractor, or perhaps a retired inspector. The author has often visited illegal live-work in an effort to help ensure that there are not any egregious violations. The first thing he says when he goes in is: "I'm not the cops! I'm here to help." Such an approach often proves effective, as is described in the section below on legalization.

Legalization Process

The following are steps that an orderly legalization of an illegal live-work will ideally undergo (i.e., a legalization plan involving cooperation between owner, tenants, and city): All must participate in good faith for it to work. This is **Code Module 5.**

1. The jurisdiction is made aware of the illegal situation, either by a tenant or via some accidental revelation (the two most common causes).

2. The owner hires a knowledgeable architect, if one is available (may happen after number three).

3. The city sends out one or more inspectors to go through the building and create a list of required corrections and creates a citation requiring the work to be done, often under threat of emptying the building.

4. The owner and architect sit down with the city and work out a timetable for bringing the building into compliance, which may take anywhere from weeks to years.

5. City-required meetings are held between the owner, the architect, and the tenants.

6. Tenants, assured of their right to return, agree not to take further complaints to the building department or the landlord.

7. The city provides a reasonably relaxed interpretation of the building code, consistent with its obligations to preserve life safety.

8. The architect submits drawings to the city and a permit is issued.

9. The work proceeds; tenants move around within in the building when possible to accommodate the work without being required to move altogether.

10. After a possibly extended period of time, the project is completed and those tenants who so desire are given the opportunity to move back in.

Shell Construction

Where a live-work building shell is proposed to be constructed, allowing improvements within the units to be constructed later under separate permits, roughed-in facilities are provided pursuant to applicable code sufficient to serve the proposed facilities with not less than the minimum residential facilities The shell—sometimes called "core and shell"—is required to be constructed pursuant to applicable code and signed off as complete per code. See Chapter Seven for a more detailed description of shell construction. This is **Code Module 6.**

Mixed Occupancy

Mixed occupancy under the building code is simply the treatment of different portions of a building under different occupancy classifications or uses that are separated from each other by a wall or floor-ceiling assembly that is fire-rated according to IBC Table 508.4. In live-work, a live-near building or flexhouse is typically viewed as a mixed occupancy. The main floor work space would typically be B, or Gneral Commercial Occupancy, and the upstairs—separated from below by a one-hour rated floor-ceiling assembly—would be either R-3 (1–2 units) or R-2 Occupancy (3 or more units). Using mixed occupancy, there are no special live-work building code provisions needed, which generally makes life easier for all concerned. This is **Code Module 7**, which typically—but not always—stands on its own. Housing over retail, referred to as a form of live-nearby in this book, is also mixed occupancy.

Use of the Model Live/Work Building Code System

As noted, the system presented in this appendix constitutes a series of seven modules that are can be combined to address any situation in live-work building regulation. While IBC Section 419 addresses the most common issues in live-work regulation that were—until its adoption—the most problematic, use of the modules in the combinations specified in Table B-3 should result in a well-coordinated set of rules that add clarity to what has often been a reinvent-the-wheel code-writing process.

Table B-3 Use of the Model Live-Work Building Code System

Code Module #	Project Type and Applicable Code Modules	New *live-with*, live-work townhouse or unit in building	Renovation of commercial, industrial, or civic building for live-work	Renovation of vacant commercial, industrial, or civic artists' live-work	Legalization of illegal live-work for artists	Live/work or work/live *live-near*; also *flexhouse*	Home occupation in new or renovated (less common) SFR or multifamily building	New live-nearby and housing over retail	New or renovated live-work shell construction
1	IBC Section 419 Live-work Units	x	x	x	x	x*		x**	x
2	Provisions not in Section 419	x	x	x	x	x*		x**	x
3	Relaxations for Renovations Only		x	x	x				x
4	Additional Relaxations for Artists			x	x				x††
5	Legalizaton of illegal live-work				x				
6	Shell Construction								x
7	Mixed Occupancy					x		x	
	Code(s) Applicable	IBC Sec. 419	IBC Sec. 419 + Relaxations	IBC Sec. 419 + Relaxations + discretionary relaxations for artists	IBC Sec. 419 + Relaxations + Legalization Process + discretionary relaxations for artists	Mixed Occupancy R/B or F-2; or 419 with a separation—which is not required but not prohibited	Residential code only applies	Live=R occupancy or live-work per 419†; Work=B or F-2 occupancy (or others); R occupancy if accessory to a residence and not over twice the lot width squared x 2 (a square, two-story zero lot line building)	Comply with R-2 reqts for shell including all life safety and construction reqts. Unit finish-out per Sec. 419.
	Comments	See annotations to 419 in Code Module 1.		Artists and artisans = an additional set of relaxations	See Table B-2.	Overall shell requirements per which occupancy?	Residential Occupancy: Residential code only applies	Exception: Flexible work space/granny flat in an accessory building shall be considered R occupancy if its footprint does not exceed 2x lot width squared.	Sec. 419 may affect shell design; and applies to unit build-out.

*Alternate: use Sec. 419 if NTE 3,000 sf or 5 employees (must sprinkler)

** Section 419 may also be employed for live-with within an accessory building.

†† If applicable, i.e., renovation for artists and artisans

APPENDIX C

Live-Work Resources

Books

Ahrentzen, Sherry, *Hybrid Housing: A Contemporary Building Type for Multiple Residential and Business Use* (Publications in Architecture and Urban Planning No R92-1). Milwaukee: University of Wisconsin Press, 1992. An early work that explores live-work from numerous directions, with an emphasis on housing.

Alexander, Christopher, Sara Ishikawa, and Murray Silverstein with Max Jacobson, Ingrid Fiksdahl King, and Shlomo Angel, *A Pattern Language*. New York: Oxford University Press, 1977. The most important book this author has read—he makes use of its lessons every day. Its patterns and approach are present throughout his work, including the contents of this book, as they have been for two generations of designers.

Appleton, Jay, *The Experience of Landscape*. London: John Wiley & Sons, 1975. In this book, the English geographer introduces the concept of "prospect and refuge," a very useful term borrowed from ethology, the study of animal behavior.

Brand, Stewart, *How Buildings Learn: What Happens After They're Built*. New York: Penguin Books, 1994. The book that really put into words what later became known as the flexhouse and other live-work types. A must-read for all students of architecture and anyone who builds or regulates those who do so.

Ching, Francis D.K., and Stephen R. Winkel, *Building Codes Illustrated: A Guide to Understanding the 2012 International Building Code*. Hoboken, NJ: John Wiley & Sons, 2011. An excellent resource, beautifully illustrated, that helps to explain the many intricacies of building code. (The author used the 2009 edition while writing this book.)

Dietsch, Deborah K., *Live/Work: Working at Home, Living at Work*. New York: Harry N. Abrams, 2008. A fine "shelter publication" filled with pictures and ideas, with a foreward by Sarah Susanka of Not So Big House fame.

Dolan, Thomas, "The Nuts & Bolts of Project Development," a chapter in ArtHouse California's *Conversion Frontiers: Military Bases and Other Opportunities for Artists*. San Francisco: California Lawyers for the Arts, 1996.

Dolan, Thomas, and Robert Leshgold, *Work/Live in Vancouver*. Vancouver: Central Area Planning, City of Vancouver, British Columbia, 1997. A study of live-work in Vancouver, including specific planning and building regulatory recommendations.

Duany, Andrés, Sandy Sorlien, and William Wright, *SmartCode Version 9.2 and Manual*. Ithaca: New Urban News Publications, 2010. The most well-known form-based code, based on the rural-to-urban transect as originally formulated by Andrés Duany.

Duany, Andrés, and Jeff Speck with Mike Lydon, *The Smart Growth Manual*. New York: McGraw Hill, 2010. The back cover says it best: "From the expanse of the metropolis to the detail of the window box, they address the pressing challenges of urban development with easy-to-follow advice and a broad array of best practices."

Dunham-Jones, Ellen, and June Williamson, *Retrofitting Suburbia: Urban Design Solutions for Redesigning Suburbs*. Hoboken, NJ: John Wiley & Sons, 2008. An excellent resource that addresses perhaps the greatest challenge facing the next generation of urban designers.

Durrett, Charles, and Kathryn McCamant, *Creating Cohousing: Building Sustainable Communities*. Gabriola Island, B.C.: New Society Publishers, 2011. The latest, much-expanded edition by the couple who introduced cohousing into the United States with its original publication in 1988; a valuable resource for anyone interested in building community. Foreword by sustainability guru Bill McKibben.

Florida, Richard, *The Rise of the Creative Class*. New York: Basic Books, 2002. A seminal work about the kinds of people that for whom employers are competing today, who—by the manner in which they live and work—comprise a natural constituency for live-work.

Gehl, Jan, *Life Between Buildings*. Copenhagen: Danish Architectural Press, 1990. A tremendously useful book regarding what really enlivens cities and can render the public realm livable and fully functional. After Christopher Alexander's *A Pattern Language*, the other most influential book on this author's work and ideas.

Gehl, Jan, *Cities for People*. Washington DC: Island Press, 2010. A greatly expanded update of the ideas expounded in *Life Between Buildings* and therefore worth reading in addition to the above.

Gurstein, Penny, *Wired to the World, Chained to the Home: Telework in Daily Life*. Vancouver: University of British Columbia Press, 2001. A detailed examination of at-home contract workers with a focus on the effects of such work on women's lives.

Kartes, Cheryl, *Creating Space: A Guide to Real Estate Development for Artists*. New York: American Council for the Arts, 1993. An excellent resource that addresses where live-work in the twentieth century really started and how to serve those who are often shunted aside (i.e. artists).

Kinsman, Francis. *The Telecommuters*. New York: John Wiley & Sons, 1987. An early, seminal work.

Oldenburg, Ray, *The Great Good Place*. New York: Marlowe and Company, 1989. The book where the term "third place" came into the lexicon, in Oadenburg's words: "Cafes, coffee shops, bookstores, bars, hair salons and other hangouts at the heart of a community." The founder of Starbucks studied this book very closely before starting his chain.

Parolek, Dan, Karen Parolek, and Paul C. Crawford, *Form-Based Codes: A Guide for Planners, Urban Designers, Municipalities and Developers*. Hoboken, NJ: John Wiley & Sons, 2008. A great resource for understanding the type of planning regulations that enable flexhouses and will eventually replace Euclidean zoning (see Form-Based Coding sidebar, Chapter Six, by Dan Parolek).

Smith, Mary, *Shared Parking*. Washington DC: Urban Land Institute, 2005. An important resource for multiunit live-work.

Steuteville, Robert, and Phillip Langdon, *New Urbanism: Best Practices Guide*. Ithaca, NY: New Urban News Publications, 2009. An encyclopedic and useful guide to best practices according to the New Urbanism.

Tachieva, Galina, *Sprawl Repair Manual*. Washington, DC: Island Press, 2010. From a review by Leon Krier: "*The Sprawl Repair Manual* is so far the only complete physical planning manual for handling the impending transformation of suburbia into vital human communities. It is not only hugely instructive but formidably inspirational."

Websites

- www.live-workplanninganddesign.com

  The web site for this book, including additional material and updates.

- www.live-work.com

  The author's website, which introduces many of the concepts detailed in this book as well as the work of his firm, Thomas Dolan Architecture.

- www.live-work.com/plainenglish/

  Live-Work in Plain English, prepared by the author for the City of Oakland, California, based on that city's comprehensive live-work building code.

- www.cnu.org

  Congress for the New Urbanism is the leading organization promoting walkable, mixed-use neighborhood development, sustainable communities and healthier living conditions.

- www.smartgrowthamerica.org

  Smart Growth America is a national organization dedicated to researching, advocating for and leading coalitions to bring smart growth practices to more communities nationwide.

- www.walkscore.com

   Walk Score®, a numerical rating of a location's walkability, increasingly used as a reference by planners, realtors and developers.

- www.transect.org

   Center for Applied Transect Studies, which promotes understanding of the built environment as part of the natural environment, through the planning methodology of the rural-to-urban transect.

- www.formbasedcodes.org

   Form-Based Codes Institute. Form-based codes use physical form, rather than separation of land uses, as their organizing principle. They foster predictable results in the built environment and a high quality public realm. Live-work is often a component of a form-based code.

Endnotes

Chapter 1

1. Robert Cervero, "Suburban Employment Centers: Probing the Influence of Site Features on the Journey-to-Work," vol. 8, no. 2 (1989), *Journal of Planning Education and Research*, pp. 75–85.
2. *Highway Statistics 2003*, Washington, DC: U.S. Department of Transportation, Federal Highway Administration, 2004.
3. Gallup News Service Web site, August 24, 2007, www.gallup.com/poll/28504/workers-average-commute-roundtrip-minutes-typical-day.aspx.
4. Diane Dorney, recounted in conversation with the author, October 2001.
5. Andrés Duany, Address to the Council of the New Urbanism, Santa Fe, NM, October 2001.
6. See www.newurbanism.org.

Chapter 2

1. Author's email exchange with Todd Zimmerman, February 24, 2011.
2. Author's email exchange with Todd Zimmerman, February 23, 2011.
3. www.businessdictionary.com/definition/telecommuting.html
4. A Guide to Telework in the Federal Government. Washington DC: Office of Personnel Management, Jun 23, 2006 (paraphrased).
5. Carsten Foertsch, "The Coworker's Profile," *DeskMag*, January 13, 2011.
6. Global Coworking blog, http://wiki.coworking.info/w/page/16583831/FrontPage, accessed by Thomas Dolan in March 2011.
7. Philip Langdon, "When Coworking Comes to Town," *New Urban News*, January 2011, http://newurbannetwork.com/article/when-coworking-comes-town-13950.
8. Christophe Aguiton and Dominique Cardon, "The Strength of Weak Cooperation," *Communications & Strategies*, No. 65 (first quarter 2007), pp. 57–65.
9. Langdon, "When Coworking Comes to Town."
10. Web site for The Cohousing Association of the United States, http://www.cohousing.org.
11. Jeremy Liu, "Housing for Families, Not Just Households." *Shelterforce: The Journal of Affordable Housing and Community Building*, July 25, 2011, www.shelterforce.org/article/2362/housing_for_families_not_just_households/.
12. Zero-Commute Living is a trademark of Thomas Dolan Architecture.
13. Zero-Commute Housing is a trademark of Thomas Dolan Architecture.
14. Form-Based Codes Institute, definition of a form-based code, www.formbasedcodes.org/definition.html, June 27, 2006
15. John Massengale, "For Those Who Don't Understand the Transect," Veritas et Venustas blog, http://massengale.typepad.com/venustas/2006/02/for_those_who_d.html, February 24, 2006.

Chapter 3

1. Christopher Alexander, Sara Ishikawa, and Murray Silverstein with Max Jacobson, Ingrid Fiksdahl King, and Shlomo Angel, *A Pattern Language*. Oxford University Press, 1977, p. 610.
2. Andrés Duany, speech at Seaside, Florida, June 2002.
3. Coworking Community blog, http://blog.coworking.info/.
4. Alexander et al., *A Pattern Language*.
5. John Protopappis, email exchange with the author, February 2011.
6. Rick Holliday, developer of Clocktower Lofts; email to the author, March 20, 2011.
7. Alexander et al., *A Pattern Language*, pp. 561, 610, and 557.
8. Andrés Duany, "Flexible Use Space: Coming to Terms with the Terminology," Council Report II, 2001, p. 9. *Town Paper*, Kentlands, MD.

Chapter 5

1. Text by Jean France, architectural historian and a member of the original building committee for the First Unitarian Church, Rochester, New York, from the descriptive brochure distributed by the church. Louis Kahn's First Unitarian Church (www.rochesterunitarian.org/Building_desc.html) © 2011 First Unitarian Church.
2. Author's email exchange with Wade Walker, March 24, 2011.

Chapter 6

1. Alexander et al., p. 561.
2. Email exchange between the author and Wade Walker, March 28, 2011.

Chapter 7

1. "International Code Adoptions." International Codes Council. January 12, 2011. www.iccsafe.org/GR/Pages/adoptions.aspx. Retrieved January 19, 2011.
2. International Codes Council, *2009 International Residential Code*, Section 101.2, Exception 1.
3. Parklift is a registered trademark of Klaus Multiparking GmbH.
4. International Codes Council, *2009 International Building Code*, 2009, Section 1103B.1, Exception 2.

Appendix B

1. Francis D.K. Ching and Stephen R. Winkel, *Building Codes Illustrated*. Hoboken, NJ: John Wiley & Sons, 2009. p. 44.
2. International Codes Council, *2009 International Building Code*, Section 419, p. 123.
3. Ibid., p. 53.

Index

Note: page numbers in *italic* refer to figures.

Live-work, 1–28. *See also specific topics*
    artists' role in, 7
    and building codes, 7–8
    cohort housing, 26
    cohousing, 25–26
    common mistakes in, 8
    courtyard live-work, 22–23
    coworking, 25
    defining, 10
    districts, 26
    factors contributing to rise of, 4
    flexhouses, 21–22
    form-based coding, 27
    future of, 201
    high density/podium, 24–25
    history of, 1–2
    home occupation, 11–12
    home office, 20–21
    implications of, xi–xii
    lifestyle lofts (lawyer lofts), 25
    live-near, 17–18
    live-nearby, 18–19
    live-with, 17
    live/work, 12–14
    neighborhoods, 11, 26–27, 100–101
    New Urbanism, 27
    overview of, 5–6
    planning and urban design for, 6–7
    project types, 19–15
    proximity types, 16–19
    resources for, 223–225
    retrofitting suburbia for, 8–9
    selling, 91–92
    Smart Growth, 27
    technology that enables, 2–3
    telecommuting, 25
    telework center, 25
    terminology used for, 6
    townhouse (shophouse), 21
    types of, 4–6. *See also specific types*
    unique aspects of, 99
    urban life complex, 23–24
    Urban-to-Rural Transect, 27–28
    use types, 11–16
    warehouse conversion (district), 19–20
    work/live, 14–16
    work-use intensities in, 28
    Zero-Commute Housing™, 26
    Zero-Commute Living™, 4, 26
Live/work, 12–14
    defined, 11
    planning for, 121
    unit in Oakland, California, *13*
Live-workers:
    artists as, 3, 7
    isolation experienced by, 4
    needs of, 99
Live-work neighborhoods, 11, 26–27, 100–101
Live-work renovation development, 49
Loading standards, 143
Location selection, 118–120
LoDo (Denver, Colorado), 7, 129
Lofts, 3, 3, 7, 85. *See also* Live-with proximity type;
        Warehouse conversions and renovations
    artists', *31*, 36, *36*
    California Cotton Mills Studios, 33
    hard, 52
    infill, 73–74
    lawyer, 24, 25
    lifestyle, 24, *24*, 25, 36, *36*, 52
    mezzanines in, 3, 30. *See also* Mezzanines
    in multiunit buildings, 49
    new-construction, 130–133
    Ocean View Lofts, *17*
    sleeping, 184–189, *186–188*
    soft, 24, 52
    types of, 52
    urban, *13*
    urban loft complexes, 19, 23–24
The Lofts at Habersham (Beaufort, South Carolina):
    case study, 87–90
    flexhouses, 86
Louisville, Kentucky (Norton Commons), 90–91
Lower Arsenal Specific Plan (Benicia, California),
    115

M
MacLeod, Montana (West Boulder Reserve), *125*
Maisonette, 22
Market for live-work, 77–90
    developer/investor market, 85–86
    end-user market, 78–85
    The Lofts at Habersham, 87, 87–90, 88
Marketing communications, 92–93
Marketing live-work, 90–93
Marketing materials, 92

Ocean View Lofts (Berkeley, California), 4, *17*
    case study, 107–109, *108*
    courtyard of, *134*
    level of finishes, 39
    light at, *30*
    and need for interaction, 32
    parking for, 141
Odor generation, 143
Omnibus AMR, 198
Openings in walls near property lines, 176–177
Open space standards, 140
Open work-use intensity, 28
Opticos Design Inc., 113
Ownership:
    forms of, 160, 162
    rentals vs., 147–148

P

Parking:
    accommodations for, 40–42
    development standards for, 140–143
Parklift system, *175, 176*
Parolek, Dan, 113
A Pattern Language (Christopher Alexander), 45
Pearl District (Portland, Oregon), 7
Permitting processes, 144–145
Phoenix Lifts (Oakland, California), *16*
Pinetree Associates, 69
Pinetree Studios (Oakland, California), *12*
    case study, 69–71, *70, 71*
    as community, 107
    design of, *46*
    plan and section, *63*
    variation in live-near units, *47*
Planning for live-work, 6–7, 110–166
    artists' work/live rental renovation, 128–129
    development standards, 136–145
    Dutch Boy Studios, 160–162
    flexhouses, 134–136
    form-based codes, 113–118
    home occupation, 120–121
    James Avenue Live-Work Compound, *122*, 122–123, *123*
    live-nearby proximity type, 127–128
    live-near proximity type, 125–127
    live-with proximity types, 124–125
    live/work, 121
    live-work courtyard communities, 133–134
    location selection, 118–120

    market rate live-work condominium renovation, 129–130
    model live-work planning code, 202–212
    new-construction lofts, 130–133
    social issues in, 145–166
    townhouse live-work, 134
    work/live, 123–124
Podiums, 24–25
    building codes, 173–174, *174*
    described, 19
    design of, 75–76
    for infill development, 51
    The Sierra liner units, 75
Portland, Oregon (Pearl District), 7
Project types, 11, 19–15. *See also specific types*
Prospect and refuge, 46
Providence, Rhode Island, 129
Proximity types, 11, 16–19. *See also specific types*

Q

Quasi-legal live-work, 156–160, 162

R

Relaxed development standards, 136
Renovation:
    artists' work/live rental renovation, 128–129
    building codes, 199
    California Cotton Mills Studios, 56–58
    market rate live-work condominium renovation, 129–130
    new construction vs., 34–35, 137–139
    warehouse, *see* Warehouse conversions and renovations
Rentals:
    artists' work/live rental renovation, 128–129
    ownership vs., 147–148
    sale of units vs., 35–36
Residential components:
    common residential facilities, 43
    of live-work spaces, 37–38
Residential reversion, 15–16, 148
Restricted work-use intensity, 28
Retrofitting suburbia, 8–9
Reurbanization, 85
Revitalization, 3, 150–151
Rhythmix Cultural Works, *139*
Richmond, California, "career homes" in, 22
Rock Paper Scissors, *158*
Rosemary Beach, Florida:
    case study, 72, *72*
    selling properties at, 93